Library of
Davidson College

Meaning, Form, and Use in Context: Linguistic Applications

Deborah Schiffrin
editor

Georgetown University Press, Washington, D.C. 20057

BIBLIOGRAPHIC NOTICE

Since this series has been variously and confusingly cited as: Georgetown University Monographic Series on Languages and Linguistics, Monograph Series on Languages and Linguistics, Reports of the Annual Round Table Meetings on Linguistics and Language Study, etc., beginning with the 1973 volume, the title of the series was changed.

The new title of the series includes the year of a Round Table and omits both the monograph number and the meeting number, thus: Georgetown University Round Table on Languages and Linguistics 1984, with the regular abbreviation GURT '84. Full bibliographic references should show the form:

Kempson, Ruth M. 1984. Pragmatics, anaphora, and logical form. In: Georgetown University Round Table on Languages and Linguistics 1984. Edited by Deborah Schiffrin. Washington, D.C.: Georgetown University Press. 1-10.

Copyright © 1984 by Georgetown University Press
All rights reserved
Printed in the United States of America

Library of Congress Catalog Number: 58-31607
ISBN 0-87840-119-9
ISSN 0196-7207

CONTENTS

Welcoming Remarks
James E. Alatis
   Dean, School of Languages and Linguistics   vii

Introduction
Deborah Schiffrin
   Chair, Georgetown University Round Table on
   Languages and Linguistics 1984   ix

Meaning and Use

Ruth M. Kempson
   Pragmatics, anaphora, and logical form   1

Laurence R. Horn
   Toward a new taxonomy for pragmatic inference:
   Q-based and R-based implicature   11

William Labov
   Intensity   43

Michael L. Geis
   On semantic and pragmatic competence   71

Form and Function

Sandra A. Thompson
   'Subordination' in formal and informal discourse   85

Wallace Chafe
   Speaking, writing, and prescriptivism   95

Gillian Sankoff
   Substrate and universals in the Tok Pisin verb
   phrase   104

Talmy Givón
  The pragmatics of referentiality   120

Jerrold M. Sadock
  Whither radical pragmatics?   139

Meaning and Form

Richard Hudson
  A psychologically and socially plausible theory of
  language structure   150

Richard Bauman
  The making and breaking of context in West Texas
  oral anecdotes   160

Thomas A. Sebeok
  Enter textuality: Echoes from the extraterrestrial   175

Michael Silverstein
  On the pragmatic 'poetry' of prose: Parallelism,
  repetition, and cohesive structure in the time course
  of dyadic conversation   181

Contexts: Institutional and Interpersonal

Thomas Kochman
  The politics of politeness: Social warrants in
  mainstream American public etiquette   200

Don H. Zimmerman
  Talk and its occasion: The case of calling the police   210

Alan Davies
  Idealization in sociolinguistics: The choice of the
  standard dialect   229

Ellen F. Prince
  Language and the law: Reference, stress, and context   240

Howard Giles and Mary Anne Fitzpatrick
  Personal, group, and couple identities: Towards a
  relational context for the study of language
  attitudes and linguistic forms   253

John J. Gumperz
  Communicative competence revisited   278

Susan Gal
   Phonological style in bilingualism: The interaction
   of structure and use   290

The Acquisition of Meaning, Form, and Use

George A. Miller
   Some comments on the subjective lexicon   303

Marilyn Shatz
   A song without music and other stories: How
   cognitive process constraints influence children's
   oral and written narratives   313

Elinor Ochs
   Clarification and culture   325

WELCOMING REMARKS

James E. Alatis
Dean, School of Languages and Linguistics
Georgetown University

Ladies and gentlemen, it gives me great pleasure to welcome you on behalf of Georgetown University and the School of Languages and Linguistics to the Georgetown University Round Table on Languages and Linguistics (GURT '84). The chairman of this year's conference is Dr. Deborah Schiffrin, who has chosen for this, the 35th annual Georgetown University Round Table, the theme: 'Meaning, form, and use in context: Linguistic applications.' The program she has prepared is impressive, and the superb organization of all the conference details is her work and that of her able assistant, Susan M. Hoyle.

Like many of you, I was fortunate enough to attend some of the preconference sessions earlier today. One cannot help but remark that, once again, the preconference sessions present almost as wide and as interesting a range of topics as the conference itself. This is a tribute to the energy and enthusiasm of Deborah Schiffrin and our good colleagues who dedicated so much time and effort to the success of the presessions; to all these colleagues, I would like to offer our heartfelt thanks. I especially want to extend a hearty welcome to the members of the Inter-Agency Round Table of the U.S. Government. I assure them of my intention to continue the tradition of acting as their host at all future Georgetown University Round Tables on Languages and Linguistics, for as long as they wish.

It is a pleasure to see that, as in previous years, some of the best scholars in linguistics and related disciplines have assembled for this year's Round Table, thus ensuring a most exciting and productive conference. One of the few prerogatives reserved to the Dean of the School of Languages and Linguistics is the honor of thanking our speakers for having agreed to come, many from very long distances, to share the results of their research with us. You do Georgetown University a great honor, and render a great service to our colleagues at this Round Table. Thank you for coming.

I do not wish to delay unduly what will surely be a very profitable and productive session. Before concluding, however, I am pleased to note that other segments of society have come to appreciate both language teaching and linguistics. Thanks to the dedicated research and skilled writing of scholars in these fields, the world has begun to realize what vital ingredients language teaching and linguistics are in the creation of the mutual understanding necessary for people to function constructively and beneficially in a multicultural, interdependent society. Surely then, in a world that all too frequently edges toward the brink, I am very pleased to welcome you to a conference that will contribute to the educational goals which we all cherish and the sense of mission which we all have.

INTRODUCTION

The theme of this year's Georgetown University Round Table on Languages and Linguistics is 'Meaning, form, and use in context: Linguistic applications.' Because this is so broad a theme, and one which can be approached from so many different directions, I would like to say a few words about how we will be approaching meaning, form and use of language in context during the next few days at the Round Table.

A continuing task in any academic discipline is carving out a special domain to be a focus of inquiry, and finding a special set of problems for which to seek resolution. Sometimes, it seems that these tasks repeat themselves over and over again, as we attempt to find some area of scholarship (which necessarily gets smaller and smaller) within which to achieve expertise.

During this progressive--and inevitable--narrowing of our interests, our larger, more holistic frameworks may seem to disappear. Our initial assumptions and definitions, concepts and ideas, theories and metatheories, may seem to be overshadowed by specific findings within a very small area of research. But our larger frameworks never really totally lose their salience. Rather, they continue to provide implicit models--because it is within such frameworks that answers are sought and problems are resolved. Even more basically, it is within such frameworks that our questions and our problems actually take shape.

In a way, our disciplinary paradigms are like cultures: just as cultures provide, organize, and sustain our perception of reality, our paradigms provide, organize, and sustain our academic realities. They do so not only by providing the questions that we ask and the problems that we try to resolve, but by helping to form the methods that we bring to bear on those problems. Our disciplinary paradigms also frame the interpretations that we provide for our findings. In addition, our paradigms help define the everyday issues to which we seek to relate and apply our findings. And just as we accept our cultural constructs without question, so too, do we accept our academic constructs.

These comments are all relevant to the Georgetown University Round Table on Languages and Linguistics because meaning, form, and use of language, in context, have all been domains of inquiry for many very different academic disciplines, each providing its own sets of paradigms, models, and constructs: linguistics, anthropology, sociology, psychology, philosophy, to name just a few. Furthermore, within those disciplines, an inevitable division of labor often results in different subareas, each of which focuses on one or another of those domains.

In linguistics, for example, we have the familiar three-part distinction among semantics (for meaning), syntax (for form), and pragmatics (for use). Focus on language in context actually undergoes further subdivision as different levels of contextual frames are pulled apart from one another. For example, we differentiate sociolinguistics, which focuses on social context, from psycholinguistics, which focuses on cognitive and perceptual contexts; ethnolinguistics, which locates language in cultural context, from discourse analysis, which (at least in one very narrow interpretation) focuses on linguistic context.

The more we become partitioned by our particular academic worlds, however, the more our overall academic world view becomes confined to the paradigms, models, and constructs specific to our own relatively narrow fields of interest. In a way, of course, such partitioning is a strength, because it allows us to understand and describe, perhaps even explain, something that has been perplexing. Thus, such partitioning allows us to catch at least a glimmer of insight into some small part of an often confusing world--and this is certainly a strength.

But our academic partitions can also be a weakness, because they can prevent us from looking outside of our own paradigms, our own models, and our own constructs.

It is my hope that the 1984 Georgetown University Round Table on Languages and Linguistics can be one small step toward offsetting this weakness. More specifically, it is my hope that the Round Table will not only help us identify and appreciate the different frameworks through which we understand meaning, form, and use of language in context, but that it will also help us to use the diversity provided by frameworks that are different from our own, to build a more holistic theory of language-- a theory which is based upon a wide empirical base, and which can contribute to the resolution of a wide variety of real-world problems.

In sum, I hope that in listening to--and reacting to--the discussions of the next few days, we will begin to view the diversity of frameworks for analyzing meaning, form, and use of language in context as a strength, and that we will be able to capitalize upon that strength when we eventually return to our own academic world views.

I would like now to thank several people who have contributed to the materialization of this conference (although there are many more such people than I can thank individually). First, I want to thank Dean James E. Alatis for giving me the opportunity to organize this year's Georgetown University Round Table on Languages and Linguistics. I also want to thank my colleagues here at Georgetown for their moral support: Deborah Tannen deserves special mention in this regard. The Georgetown students, both graduate and undergraduate, have been extraordinary in their willingness and eagerness to help in many different capacities. And for this, they have my gratitude. In addition, the program could not have taken shape without the cooperation and enthusiasm of the organizers of special interest sessions, the participants in those sessions, and, of course, the main session speakers. All of these people have my heartfelt thanks.

Finally, I want to thank Susan M. Hoyle for her tremendously able assistance, her never-ending patience, and her infectious cheerfulness in wading through the countless tasks that are a necessary part of organizing a conference.

Deborah Schiffrin

PRAGMATICS, ANAPHORA, AND LOGICAL FORM

Ruth M. Kempson
University of London

This paper is simultaneously an outline of a unitary, pragmatic account of anaphora and a sequence of arguments advocating the pragmatic theory of Sperber and Wilson (forthcoming). First, I present evidence that a unitary account of anaphora is the only correct one. Second, I show that a natural account of anaphora emerges if we assume the Sperber-Wilson approach to pragmatics. Finally, I draw out the consequences of this conclusion for syntactic theory, and for the analysis of discourse.

My argument concerns the parallelism not normally noticed between bound-variable anaphora, as in (1), and discourse anaphora, as in (2).

(1) Every actor$_i$ worries that he$_i$'s ugly.
(2) He$_i$'s ugly.

Despite the widespread assumption that these are discrete phenomena, every pragmatic aspect of discourse anaphora is displayed also by bound-variable anaphora. The parallels are as follows.

(A) The phenomenon of bridging cross-reference. This is where the use of an anaphoric expression is licensed by a preceding noncoreferring expression in virtue of some link between the objects those expressions describe. Thus in (3) and (4) there is no relation of identity between a car and its driver, and yet the introduction of the term car allows us to use a definite NP in virtue of the link between cars and drivers.

(3) John lifted a car. The driver was underneath.
(4) John lifted a car with the driver.

Exactly parallel is (5), except that the expression a car can be interpreted within the scope of the quantifying expression everyone and the term the driver is accordingly interpreted as a variable bound by the expression a car, itself sensitive to the outermost quantifier.

(5) Everyone who was able to lift a car found the driver underneath.

A similar set of examples is given in (6) and (7).

(6) John's house is a mess. The roof needs mending.
(7) Every house needs the roof mended.

That this is not simply a matter of lexical specification of hidden arguments is shown by (8): <u>singer</u> does not have <u>accompanist</u> as a lexically specified argument.

(8) Every accompanist needs the singer to be quiet in the opening bars.

(B) The use of anaphoric expressions can be licensed by extra information made available by the total implicit content of the preceding sentence and not any one constituent. Thus (9) allows the term <u>the insult</u> on the basis of the assumption that calling someone a Conservative is an insult. This has long been recognised as a pragmatic phenomenon. But there are exactly parallel examples with bound-variable anaphora which is not recognised as a pragmatic phenomenon, as in (10).

(9) Jake called Jess a Conservative. The insult made him bristle.
(10) Everyone who called his neighbour a Conservative later apologised for the insult.

(C) One may have to manipulate extra premises and principles of deduction in order to establish an antecedent. Thus in (11), we have to know that Jaguars are cars and two negatives make a positive in order to use the first disjunct in (11) to provide an antecedent for the definite NP <u>the car</u>. And (12) is exactly parallel.

(11) Either my friend hasn't bought a Jaguar, or the car'll be in the garage by now.
(12) Each of my millionaire friends who isn't so anti-British that they haven't bought a Rolls-Royce will soon be fed up with the car's gas consumption.

(D) The givenness associated with pronouns and definite NPs as opposed to the 'newness' of indefinite NPs. This is familiar, but it is not so often pointed out that this concept of picking out something already 'given'/previously established is displayed equally by bound-variable anaphora. Examples (13) and (14) are straightforward cases of definite NP and pronominal anaphora. But (15) and (1) present the same phenomenon for bound-variable anaphora.

(13) John bought a house and discovered later that the house needed damp-proofing.
(14) A man came in. He sat down.

(15) Everyone who bought a house discovered later that the house needed damp-proofing.

In these cases, the definite NP and pronoun are licensed and in some sense given by the preceding quantified expression. The difference is, of course, that with a quantified antecedent, the bound-variable anaphor is in some sense given by each instantiation of the quantified expression.

(E) Similar to this is the property of uniqueness. This problem is widely recognised to be pragmatic, relative to the circumstances in some unanalysed way. Thus in (2), there is only one male assumed to be under consideration, in (3) and (4) only one driver, and in (6) only one roof. This phenomenon, too, is displayed equally by bound-variable anaphora cases such as (1), (5), (7), (8), and (15), though in these cases the value of the interpretation of the pronoun or definite NP is again uniquely determined by each instantiation of the quantifying expression.

In (1), for example, for each instantiation of the subject quantifying expression there is only one possible object picked out by he; for each instantiation of car in (5) there is only one possible object picked out by the driver; and so on. Of course, we analyse these in terms of identity of variables; the pretheoretic phenomenon, however, that the anaphoric expression is on each interpretation uniquely identified as something, is exactly parallel in both referring and bound-variable uses of NPs and pronouns. Thus for all the listable, apparently pragmatic properties of referring, discourse-anaphoric uses of pronouns and definite NPs, there is a direct analogue for bound-variable uses. Yet it is these pragmatic properties which provide the motivation for analysing discourse anaphora as a pragmatic phenomenon. But quantifier binding, which displays the same properties, is universally assumed to be a phenomenon of grammar.

It seems that if we are to give a unitary account of problems of anaphora, we have to assume a pragmatic basis to bound-variable anaphora as well as to discourse anaphora. This is what I am going to propose. However, it does not follow from this conclusion that we are forced into abandoning the formal characterisation of sentence-based grammars for the more informal alternative of discourse grammars, or for the incorporation of pragmatics within the grammar. On the contrary, I argue that an orthodox sentence-based grammar, in conjunction with the principle of relevance, predicts exactly the right results. All that has to be changed is the assumption that the articulation of semantics within the grammar provides the full propositional content/ logical form/truth conditions expressed by a sentence. In its place I propose that we should look at the semantic content of any linguistic expression, simple or complex, as a set of instructions on utterance interpretation. These include a set of instructions on the construction of logical forms, but may also include instructions on other aspects of interpretation. In all cases, these instructions are fleshed out by pragmatic principles to give the full content of the utterance on any occasion of use.

This conception of linguistic semantics, and the unitary analysis of discourse and bound-variable anaphora I am going to propose, are both dependent on the theory of relevance. There are five main claims of the theory that I make direct use of.

1. Utterance interpretation is an inferential, largely deductive exercise which involves the construction by the hearer of a context set of premises which combine with the propositional form of what he hears to yield indirect implications (the implicit content of the utterance--roughly equivalent to implicatures). Thus, contextual information is not in general antecedently given, nor accumulated throughout a discourse: it is the construction of the context that is an essential part of utterance interpretation.

2. The linguistic content of sentences of natural language is underdetermined with respect to propositional content; and the construction of a context set of premises, the decision as to the propositional content expressed by the sentence, and the consequent deduction of contextual implications are driven by a single principle, that of relevance.

3. The speaker has done his best in the circumstances to say something of maximal relevance to the hearer. This principle of relevance is the sole maxim of the theory. It needs some explication. Relevance itself is defined as the nontrivial deduction of contextual implications from a pair comprising a context set of premises, and a proposition expressed. The hearer's task is to select what that pair should be. The principle of relevance is the guarantee that the speaker believes that the form which he uttered makes immediately accessible to the hearer a context set and a proposition from which he can derive contextual implications. Implicit in the concept of maximal relevance is a trade-off between maximum amount of information (contextual implications) for minimal processing cost. (The motivation behind this is the stated aim of Sperber and Wilson to provide a theory of pragmatics which is not yet another module, but a theory of performance in which memory storage, processing costs, inferential properties of the central cognitive mechanism, information presented in a grammar, all come together.)

4. Linguistic specification of elements of language may involve a dual specification: (1) their contribution to propositional content, (2) their contribution to what information is made accessible for purposes of context construction.

5. The only factor that constrains the construction of contexts in addition to any relevant specification of elements of the language and the principle of relevance, is the assumption that certain types of information are immediately accessible, viz. the preceding utterance, the scenario of the utterance itself, and information associated with concepts expressed by the lexical items used (this last stored in a mental lexicon of discrete concepts with both encyclopedic and analytic knowledge entered with such concepts).

It is this concept of accessibility that is central to my analysis of anaphora. What I propose is that the concept of definiteness associated with both pronouns and definite NPs simply is that of guaranteed accessibility. If a speaker uses a pronoun or a definite NP, then he is indicating to the hearer that a representation of an NP type is immediately accessible to him in the sense specified--either from the scenario of the utterance itself, or from the preceding utterance, or from preceding parts of the same utterance, or from concepts expressed by what precedes the anaphor. Thus, in (2) the referent of *he* has to be accessible from the immediate scenario. In (14) it is provided by the previous utterance, in (13) by some previous representation in the same utterance; and in the bridging cross-reference cases of (3) and (4) by a premise, accessible from the conceptual address associated with <u>car</u>, that cars normally have a driver. This analysis is, of course, merely a restatement of earlier characterisations of the concept of definiteness (cf. Jesperson 1942, Chafe 1976). But what is new in this account is the way in which the bridging cross-reference cases and cases where extra premises are required, i.e. (A)-(C), are all immediate consequences of the analysis, given the Sperber and Wilson framework. Since the content of all anaphoric expressions is a guarantee that an antecedent is immediately available, we can predict that where no such antecedent is provided--either by the explicit content of the discourse or indexically-- the anaphor will act as an instruction to the hearer to construct a context premise which will provide that antecedent as the implicit content of the discourse. Consider example (3): on this analysis, the use of an anaphoric expression is by the principle of relevance a guarantee of instant accessibility of some representation of an individual described by the predicate 'driver' about which the speaker is making some assertion. But the immediately accessible environment (in this case, just the preceding utterance) does not provide such a representation. Yet the speaker is using an anaphor as the guarantee of such a representation. He must therefore be using the anaphor as an indication to the hearer that he should construct a context premise such that the appropriate representation is derived as the implicit content of what he hears. This effect is directly predictable from the proposed analysis in terms of accessibility and the principle of relevance, without any further postulation. Cases such as (9) are simply the same. The only difference is that the contextual premise required (triggered by use of the predicate <u>insult</u>) cannot be accessed from any particular constituent of the preceding utterance. It is the whole of <u>Jake called Jess a Conservative</u> that combines with 'To call someone a Conservative is to give them an insult' to provide by deduction the contextual implication 'Jake gave Jess an insult'. And the only way to construe (9) so that the expression <u>the insult</u> fulfils the guarantee of accessibility of its antecedent is to construct such a context set.

I have so far characterised a definite NP as expressing, as its intrinsic content, a guarantee of instant accessibility of its antecedent. But the guarantee of immediate accessibility simply is an intrinsic part of the principle of relevance. It is this that determines the context set of propositions and the propositional content the hearer selects. Thus, all we require of an analysis of anaphora is that an anaphor is some expression whose value is not given by rules of grammar.[1] For all the rest will fall out from the application of the principle of relevance. And this is what my analysis will provide. An anaphor will be represented as a metavariable whose value is not determined by any principle of grammar. Given my assumption of the Sperber-Wilson framework, it follows that it will have to be identified by a relevance-controlled principle of antecedent identification.

What we need now is an account of quantification compatible with this analysis. In order to get this account to extend to sequences relative to the binding of a quantifier, all we need to do is to assume that we can manipulate a name-like entity which can stand arbitrarily for any one of the individuals over which the domain of the quantifier ranges. Arbitrary names, manipulated in natural deduction systems, do just this. And this is what I shall do.

Given, then, that a quantifier introduces an arbitrary name, this name will be accessible in just the same way as a referring expression, and can enter into deductive and context-specifying processes. The only difference is that its availability is restricted to the scope of the quantifier that introduced it, so it is not invariably available like a name. And this is just the distinction we want. In particular, we predict exactly the phenomena listed in (A)-(C) initially:

(A) The phenomenon of bridging cross-reference
(B) The use of anaphoric expressions can be licensed by extra information made available by the total implicit content of the preceding sentence and not any one constituent.
(C) One may have to manipulate extra premises and principles of deduction in order to establish an antecedent.

Yet we also preclude examples such as (16).

(16) *A woman grinned at every man$_i$. He$_i$ smiled back.

This binding is precluded because the pronoun is not within the scope of the quantifier, so the name associated with the quantifier is not accessible as an antecedent for that pronoun. Consider example (17), equivalent in all important respects to (8).

(17) Every singer worries that the accompanist is too loud.

This is a paradigm case where we have to manipulate information about accompanists and singers in order to determine not merely what follows from what the speaker has said, but also what it is that he has said. I assume that the quantified expression <u>every singer</u> introduces an arbitrary name 'a_1', and definite NPs, like pronouns, are characterised by a special variable 'β', where β is some variable whose distinguishing feature is that it is not characterised by the grammar. The expression <u>the accompanist</u> is accordingly characterised as 'accompanist(β)'. The interpretation instructions associated with the lexical items and the individual nodes of the tree provide a mapping up the tree in the manner of Katz's (1972) 'projection' rules, projecting the sentence string onto: singer(a_1) $\rightarrow$ a_1 worries that β is too loud and accompanist (β). Now a_1 is not identical to β, so there is no antecedent for β in this immediate discourse. However, the β-variable is used as a guarantee that there is some such antecedent, even when the intended referent is not indexical. So, in order to identify the antecedent of β from this immediate discourse, the hearer is forced to access what information he knows about the concepts used in the sentence--in this case the information associated with <u>singer</u> that 'Singers have accompanists'. This information, by an orthodox process of logical deduction, enables him to deduce an antecedent for β in the form of: $\exists y$ (accompanist(y) & a_1 has y). With this information, he can therefore construct the total propositional content asserted, to wit: $\forall x\ (singer(x) \rightarrow \exists y\ (accompanist(y)\ \&\ x\ has\ y\ \&\ x\ worries\ that\ y\ is\ too\ loud))$. The significance of this example is twofold. On the one hand, the example demonstrates how the interpretation of some element bound to a quantifier as a variable (in this case, the definite NP <u>the accompanist</u>) may involve interaction between information in the grammar and contingent world knowledge in a way that is precluded by most current accounts of variable-binding. On the other hand, it demonstrates how the process of working out the implicit content of the utterance by the hearer takes place even for subparts of a sentence-string. That is, the process involved in deducing an antecedent for <u>the accompanist</u> is exactly that involved in deducing implicatures of a standard sort; and, as in the case of implicature calculation, is a direct consequence of the principle of relevance.

I am not attempting here to give a formal specification of the interaction between grammar and pragmatics, so this informal sketch is just a promise of a properly formal account (cf. Kempson 1984 for the specification of a formal recursive algorithm projecting linguistic strings onto fully specified logical forms). However, even at this informal level, there is more to say about this concept of accessibility. For I am claiming that all anaphoric dependencies, quantifier-bound and discourse-bound, can be explained in terms of this concept, that there is therefore no configurational difference between the two types except as can be predicted from the nature of the antecedent. How then can it explain the asymmetry between (18) and (19)?

(18) His$_i$ mother likes John$_i$.
(19) *His$_i$ mother likes everyone$_i$.

These represent the so-called 'weak cross-over' facts, a phenomenon that constitutes a by now familiar argument for a distinction between coreference and bound-variable pronominal anaphora and for a configurational restriction associated with the latter which has to be configurationally stipulated (cf. Chomsky 1977, Higginbotham 1980). The analysis proposed here has a straightforward account, if we make one plausible extension to it--that proper names should be analysed like pronouns. So the proper name, <u>John</u>, like a pronoun, is a guarantee of there being some immediately accessible individual named John. In (19) then, given the system of projection rules associated with lexical items and constituent structure, we predict that the quantifier <u>every</u> binds its variable in object position, thereby guaranteeing that any arbitrary name associated with it is not accessible for purposes of identification with the subject, since the subject does not have information about the arbitrary name bound by the quantifier accessible to it. In (18), by contrast, there is an independent guarantee (by the use of the name <u>John</u>) that some individual named John is believed by the speaker to be immediately accessible to the hearer. But if such an individual is immediately and uniquely accessible, then that individual can be accessed directly by the pronoun <u>he</u>. To put it in possibly more familiar terms, <u>he</u> and <u>John</u> may be coreferential but <u>he</u> is not referentially dependent on John; and the account of anaphor-antecedent relations proposed here is exclusively in terms of anaphoric dependency. So within the theory, the relation between he and John is coincidental yet predictable as a possiblity, given the analysis of proper names.

But, you should reply, this assumes a simplistic left-to-right account of both processing and anaphoric dependencies and we know this is not right for two reasons: (1) not all pronouns display a dependency with an antecedent to their left, as witness (20). (2) NPs are not necessarily interpreted left-to-right, as witness the phenomenon of scope variation exemplified by (21).

(20) By his$_i$ bed each child$_i$ kept a teddy bear.
(21) Everyone in this room speaks two languages.

So why can't a hearer 'sit tight' on the interpretation of the pronoun in (19), so to speak, and identify it with the later arbitrary name associated with the quantifier, this being given wide scope over the whole sentence?

The answer is simple, and predictable. Hearers cannot randomly reject a left-right processing mechanism, but only as the linguistic structure of what they hear gives explicit directions to that effect. There are two types of case where this is possible, one obligatory, the other optional.

The obligatory case is represented by (20). Preposed prepositional phrases are modifying expressions which are interpreted as modifications either of VPs or of Ss. In semantic terms, they are functional expressions which operate on VPs or Ss, to give another expression of that same sort. In other words, they are expressions which have to be interpreted as modifications of the constituent they modify. Thus they are only interpreted together with the interpretation of that constituent, and the projection rule associated with them has to specify this. Hence we get the reversed dependency directions in these constructions:

(22) Each child$_i$ kept a teddy bear by his$_i$ bed.
(23) *He$_i$ kept a teddy bear by each child$_i$'s bed.
(24) *By each child$_i$'s bed, he$_i$ kept a teddy bear.
(20) By his$_i$ bed, each child$_i$ kept a teddy bear.

The optional case is the scope vacillation displayed in (21). Orthodox accounts of scope variation characterise it as a phenomenon to which all NPs are subject, with the caveat that in the case of referential NPs it makes no difference because their interpretation is independently fixed. But suppose we say instead that scope variation between NPs is available only to pairs (or triples) of nonreferential expressions. This could either be a stipulation of the rules of interpretation associated with quantifiers, or a direct consequence of the principle of relevance. It is certainly not without pragmatic motivation--nonreferential NPs are the only NPs whose interpretation is not fixed by the guarantee of immediate accessibility. Either way, the predictions made are now correct--(18) and (19) do not contain a pair of quantified expressions. In particular, (19) contains only one. Hence it is not subject to scope variation. Moreover, the pronoun is not contained within a constituent which permits its interpretation to be subsequent to that of the quantified expression. Hence the interpretation is left-right and the pronoun has to be identified independently of that quantified expression. The account of anaphora in terms of accessibility is vindicated.

Despite the informality of this presentation, I hope that I have shown, at least in principle, how with just three assumptions--relevance theory, an uncontroversial mechanism for quantifiers, and a minimum linguistic account of the definiteness intrinsic to pronouns and definite noun phrases--we can predict the bridging cross-reference phenomenon, its interaction with quantifier binding, and the weak cross-over effects, all without stipulations particular to the structures in question. There are two nontheoretical consequences of this analysis which should not be missed. First, there should be no level of logical form within the grammar which characterises the binding of definite anaphors since all definite anaphors are subject to exactly the same pragmatic explanation. Second, the linguistic content of a sentence is neither a full specification of the truth conditions of the proposition it expresses, nor is it exclusively directed towards such specification.

And here, finally, we have the basis for characterising discourse-related phenomena without having to abandon the assumption that a grammar is a sentence-generating mechanism. For the semantic specification of linguistic content within this framework is not a set of rules which predicts actual interpretations but rather is a set of instructions on utterance interpretation, a set which may include instructions on propositional content, indications of accessibility or more specific indications of context-construction, or even indications as to the speaker's attitude to what he says. Each of these instructions is then fleshed out by the principle of relevance to give the full content of the utterance. It is striking that those aspects of semantic specification which were most embarrassing to a straight truth-conditional semantics as part of sentence-based grammar fall out as a direct consequence of the stand taken here, despite the fact that it, too, assumes that grammars are sentence-generating devices. Thus, by way of a coda, I propose that we abandon the Gazdar slogan 'PRAGMATICS = MEANING - TRUTH CONDITIONS' (Gazdar 1979) in favour of a new slogan: SEMANTICS = UTTERANCE INTERPRETATION - THE PRINCIPLE OF RELEVANCE.

Note

1. There is no stipulation of uniqueness as an intrinsic property of definiteness, either. Antecedent identification is made in virtue of the guarantee of the principle of relevance that immediately accessible to the hearer is a representation of an individual about whom he is to understand the speaker as making an assertion. If there were any doubt as to which individual that should be, the hearer would have to put processing effort into deciding which individual it was. But the speaker's utterance in that form is a guarantee that he believes no such processing cost is necessary. Given the principle of relevance then, the speaker must be intending to convey that there is only one such individual.

References

Chafe, Wallace L. 1976. Givenness, contrastiveness, definiteness, subjects, topic, and point of view. In: Subject and topic. Edited by Charles Li. New York: Academic Press. 25-56.
Chomsky, Noam. 1977. Conditions on rules of grammar. Essays in form and interpretation. Amsterdam: North-Holland.
Gazdar, Gerald. 1979. Pragmatics. New York: Academic Press.
Higginbotham, James. 1980. Pronouns and bound variables. Linguistics Inquiry 11.679-708.
Jesperson, Otto. 1942. A modern English grammar. London: Allen and Unwin.
Katz, Jerrold. 1972. Semantic theory. New York: Harper.
Kempson, Ruth M. 1984. Anaphora, the compositionality requirement, and the semantics-pragmatics distinction. North-Eastern Linguistics Society Proceedings, vol. 14.
Sperber, Dan, and Deirdre Wilson. (forthcoming) Relevance: Foundations of pragmatic theory.

TOWARD A NEW TAXONOMY FOR PRAGMATIC INFERENCE: Q-BASED AND R-BASED IMPLICATURE

Laurence R. Horn
Yale University

1. The Principle of Least Effort (and the Principle of Sufficient Effort). Thirty-five years ago, George Kingsley Zipf set out to explain all of natural language (along with almost everything else in the human universe, from dreams, art, and ritual to war, schizophrenia, and the incest taboo) in terms of an overarching Principle of Least Effort. In the linguistic realm, however, Zipf (1949:20ff.) acknowledged two basic and competing forces. The Force of Unification, or Speaker's Economy, is a direct least effort correlate, a drive toward simplification which, operating unchecked, would result in the evolution of exactly one totally unmarked infinitely ambiguous vocable (presumably <u>uhhhh</u>). The antithetical Force of Diversification, or Auditor's Economy, is an anti-ambiguity principle leading toward the establishment of as many different expressions as there are messages to communicate. Given m meanings, the speaker's economy will tend toward 'a vocabulary of one word which will refer to all the m distinct meanings', while the hearer's economy will tend toward 'a vocabulary of m different words with one distinct meaning for each word'. As Zipf (1949:21) (under)states, 'The two opposing economies are in extreme conflict.'

It is in the crucible of this conflict, argue Zipf, Martinet, and allied functionalists, that language change is forged. As Martinet notes (1962:139):

> In order to understand how and why a language changes, the linguist must keep in mind two ever-present and antinomic factors: first, the requirements of communication, the need for the speaker to convey his message, and second, the principle of least effort, which makes him restrict his output of energy, both mental and physical, to the minimum compatible with achieving his ends.

In this paper, I seek to demonstrate that these same two antinomic forces--and the interaction between them--are largely responsible for generating Grice's conversational maxims and the schema for pragmatic inference derived therefrom.

2. The maxims of conversation. In his ground-breaking work on language use and the logic of conversation, Grice (1975) suggests a procedure whereby participants in a conversational context may compute what was meant (by a given speaker's contributing a given utterance at a given point in the interaction) based on what was said (by that speaker, in that utterance, at that point). The governing dictum is the Cooperative Principle: 'Make your conversational contribution such as is required, at the stage at which it occurs, by the accepted purpose or direction of the talk exchange' (1975:45). Within this basic guideline, Grice establishes four specific subprinciples, the general, almost trivial-sounding, and presumably universal maxims of conversation which he takes to govern all rational interchange (Grice 1975:45-46; cf. Levinson 1983:100ff. for discussion).

Quality: Try to make your contribution one that is true.
1. Do not say what you believe to be false.
2. Do not say that for which you lack evidence.

Quantity:
1. Make your contribution as informative as is required (for the current purposes of the exchange).
2. Do not make your contribution more informative than is required.

Relation:
Be relevant.

Manner:
1. Avoid obscurity of expression.
2. Avoid ambiguity.
3. Be brief. (Avoid unnecessary prolixity).
4. Be orderly.

The assumption that speaker and hearer are both observing the Cooperative Principle and its component maxims permits the exploitation of these maxims to generate conversational implicata, conveyed messages which are meant without being said.

The partial reductionist program I envision would retain the Maxim of Quality with its special character noted by Grice: unless Quality (or what Lewis 1969 has called a Convention of Truthfulness) obtains, the entire conversational and implicatural apparatus collapses. But the first Quantity maxim (henceforth Quantity$_1$, or simply Quantity) is essentially Zipf's Auditor's Economy, the need for the speaker to convey his message fully. Most if not all of the remaining Gricean rules respond to the Speaker's Economy, either directly (as consequences of the least effort principle) or indirectly (through the interaction of this principle with its antithesis). Notice in particular that the second quantity principle, as stated, is essentially akin to Relation (what would make a contribution more informative than required, except the inclusion of material not strictly relevant to and needed for the matter at hand?). Note also that Grice in effect builds in Relation when defining Quantity$_1$, and similarly builds in Quantity$_1$ in defining Quantity$_2$. In section 3, I have tentatively boiled down the maxims (leaving aside Quality) to two fundamental principles, echoing the two functional economies of Zipf and Martinet.

3. Minding our Qs and Rs.

(1a) The Q Principle (Hearer-based):
MAKE YOUR CONTRIBUTION SUFFICIENT (cf. Quantity$_1$)
SAY AS MUCH AS YOU CAN (given R)
Lower-bounding principle, inducing upper-bounding implicata

(1b) The R Principle (Speaker-based):
MAKE YOUR CONTRIBUTION NECESSARY (cf. Relation, Quantity$_2$, Manner)
SAY NO MORE THAN YOU MUST (given Q)
Upper-bounding principle, inducing lower-bounding implicata

In the current coy style (cf. Chomsky 1982) which has given us D-structures and S-structures, LF and PF, R-expressions and A-binding (corresponding, more or less, to Deep and Surface structures, Logical and Phonetic form, Referring expressions, and Argument-binding, respectively), I am using Q and R to evoke Quantity (i.e. Quantity$_1$) and Relation while leaving open the extent to which my principles map onto these two maxims.

The hearer-based Q Principle is essentially a sufficiency condition. A lower-bounding law in terms of information structure, it may be (and systematically is) exploited to generate upper-bounding conversational implicata, as described by Grice (1975), Ducrot (1972), Horn (1972, 1973), and Gazdar (1979): a speaker, in saying '...p...', implicates that (for all she knows) '...at most p...'

The primary examples of generalized Q-based implicata arise from scalar predications. If I tell you that some of my friends are Buddhists, I license you to draw the inference that not all my friends are Buddhists. (If I knew they all were, and this knowledge was relevant to your interests, it would have been incumbent on me to obey the Q Principle and say so; the assumption that I am obeying Quantity allows you to infer that I did not know for a fact that the stronger predication --All of my friends are Buddhists--held.) Like all rules of pragmatic inference, Q-based implicature is context-dependent; as a generalized implicatum, the aforementioned inference goes through in unmarked contexts, but it may be cancelled--explicitly (cf. Some, {if not all/and perhaps all,} of my friends...) or implicitly (by establishing the appropriate context, in which all that is relevant, or can be known, is the lower bound).

Examples of Q-based scalar implicature are legion. The following sentences all assert (or entail) a lower bound ('at least __', their 'one-sided' reading as Aristotle dubbed it), and characteristically implicate an upper bound ('at most __'); the conjunction of the assertion and implicatum results in conveying the corresponding 'two-sided' understanding ('exactly __').

(2a) He ate 3 carrots — 1-sided: 'at least 3'
                              2-sided: 'exactly 3'

(2b) You ate some of the cookies — 1-sided: 'some if not all'
                                       2-sided: 'some but not all'

(2c) It's possible she'll win — 1-sided: 'possible if not certain'
                                  2-sided: 'possible but not certain'

(2d) Maggie is patriotic or quixotic — 1-sided = inclusive or
                                      2-sided = exclusive or

(2e) I'm happy — 1-sided: 'happy if not ecstatic'
                     2-sided: 'happy but not ecstatic'

(2f) It's warm — 1-sided: 'at least warm'
                     2-sided: 'warm but not hot'

(cf. Horn 1972, 1973, to appear b for additional details)

This analysis, foreshadowed a century ago by DeMorgan (1847:100) and Mill (1867:501), allows us to preserve semantic parsimony by taking the infinitely many weak scalar predicates to be logically unambiguous while pragmatically ambivalent (cf. Hamilton 1860 and Kempson 1980 for alternative accounts in which the sentences of (2) are treated as logically ambiguous; these accounts are reviewed and rebutted in Horn 1973, to appear b).

    If the Q-Principle corresponds to Quantity$_1$, the countervailing R-Principle collects not only Relation, but Quantity$_2$ and possibly all the manner maxims (although I shall not go through the arguments for that claim here). The R-Principle, mirroring the effect of the Q-Principle just discussed, is an upper-bounding principle which may be (and standardly is) exploited to generate lower-bounding implicata. A speaker who says '...p...' may license the Q-inference that he meant '...at most p...'; a speaker who says '..p...' may license the R-inference that he meant '...more than p...' The locus classicus here is the indirect speech act (Heringer 1972; Gordon and Lakoff 1975; Searle 1975): if I ask you whether you can pass me the salt, in a context where your abilities to do so are not in doubt, I license you to infer that I am doing something more that asking you whether you can pass the salt--I am in fact asking you to do it. (If I know for a fact that you can pass me the salt, the yes-no question is pointless; the assumption that I am obeying the Relation maxim allows you to infer that I mean something more than what I say.)

    Grice notes that a speaker may 'quietly and unostentatiously violate a maxim' as well as exploit it to generate an implicature. Clark and Haviland (1977:2) have suggested that intentional covert maxim violations result in lies, while unintentional violations are simply misleading. In fact, what is crucial is just which sort of maxim or pragmatic principle is violated: intentional quality violations result in lies (another reason for the special status of quality; cf. Coleman and Kay 1981 for additional factors in defining lie), intentional violations of the Q-based sufficiency principle result in a speaker's misleading the addressee, and intentional violations of the R-based least effort principle are often simply unhelpful or perverse. A courtroom witness must swear to tell the whole truth and nothing but the truth, i.e. to obey quantity and quality, while violations of relevance lead only to a possible lawyer's objection or judge's scolding.

4. Q-based vs. R-based inference: Some early skirmishes. Like the antinomic economies from which they derive, the Q-based and R-based principles just outlined often directly collide. A speaker obeying only Q would tend to say everything she knows on the off-chance that it might prove informative, while a speaker obeying only R would probably, to be on the safe side, not open her mouth. In fact, many of the maxim clashes Grice and others have discussed do involve Quantity$_1$ vs. Relation. In delineating the operation of quantity to generate upper-bounding scalar implicatures in my thesis (Horn 1972: Chapters 1 and 2), I was bothered by the contrast between (3a), where Quantity is in force, and (3b), where the principle of relevance is apparently responsible for the implicatum (as Karttunen 1970 suggests).

(3a)   It is possible that John solved the problem ⟶
      (For all S knows) John didn't solve the problem   (Q)
(3b)   John was able to solve the problem ⟶
      John solved the problem   (R)

An application of quantity in the latter case would generate the opposite implicatum, viz. that John didn't solve the problem. Similarly, in (4a) quantity leads to an upper bound on the information communicated, while in (4b) an R-based inference renders the indefinite more informative than its logical form suggests (both examples from Grice 1975:56; cf. Harnish 1976).

(4a)   X is meeting a woman this evening ⟶
      The woman in question is not X's wife, sister, or
      close platonic friend   (Q)
(4b)   I broke a finger yesterday ⟶
      The finger is mine   (R)

5. Politeness rules, pragmatic competence, and maxim clashes. A parallel to these clashes emerges from work by Robin Lakoff on the maxims of politeness outlined in (5), and by Brown and Levinson in their reformulation of Lakoff's maxims in terms of face wants and needs:

(5) Rules of politeness (Lakoff 1973, Brown and Levinson 1979)

	Lakoff:	Brown and Levinson:
Rule 1.	Deference: 'Don't impose', 'Keep aloof'	Negative politeness, polite formality
Rule 2.	Give options (special case of Rule 1, or derived as theorem from Rules 1 and 3?)	Respect 'negative face', i.e. freedom from imposition and freedom of action.
Rule 3.	Be friendly (Camaraderie)	Positive politeness, polite friendliness
		Respect 'positive face', i.e. positive consistent self-image and approval/ appreciation by others.

Crucially for us, the Deference or Aloofness maxim, Rule 1, is an upper-bounding R-based constraint on one's actions, while Friendliness, Rule 3, is a lower-bounding Q-based imperative.

Lakoff has noted several instances in which Rule 1 Politeness seems to clash with Rule 3, e.g. belching after a meal, which may signal appreciation (via Rule 3) or may simply be taken as offensive (by Rule 1). More systematically, when we look at languages like those in the Romance, Germanic, Slavic, and Indic families of Indo-European, in which two different forms for the second person singular coexist but are associated with different presuppositions or conventional implicata (cf. Levinson 1983:128-29), we find that the use of a (familiar) T form rather than the more formal V form for the addressee may convey polite friendliness by Rule 3 or presumptuousness by Rule 1 (depending on the context and the interlocutors' assumptions and beliefs). Similarly, the use of a V form for the addressee may be polite by Rule 1, or aloof and unfriendly by Rule 3.

A particularly devastating kind of maxim clash which has been analyzed in similar terms is the communication mixup example from work by Tannen.

(6) Conversational breakdowns and marital breakups (Tannen 1975, 1979)
First exchange:
Wife: Bob's having a party. You wanna go?
Husband: OK.
Second exchange (later):
Wife: Are you sure you want to go?
Husband: OK. Let's not go. I'm tired anyway.
Post-mortem:
Wife: We didn't go to the party because you didn't want to.
Husband: I wanted to. You didn't want to.

On Tannen's gloss of this canonical interchange, one partner (the wife) is operating on a direct strategy utilizing Rule 3 politeness: if one had meant more, s/he would (and should) have said it. Her partner (or opponent), on the other hand, is employing an indirect, hint-seeking strategy which emanates from Rule 1 politeness: avoid saying too much when you can get it across by hints. As Tannen observes, each strategy may link up with a different pragmatic competence, the difference involving not the set of operative rules but the relative strength of opposing rules within that set.

Notice that Tannen's account of the clash instantiated in (6) superimposes directly onto an alternative gloss utilizing Grice's Quantity and Relation maxims (or Quantity$_1$ and Quantity$_2$), respectively. Crucially, in either version we have to deal with Q-based vs. R-based inference patterns.

A closely related example of maxim clash is cited by Keenan (1976). As she reports and interprets the facts, the Malagasy-speaking culture of Madagascar is a speech community in which the Cooperative Principle, and in particular the maxim of Quantity, is not observed. Informativeness is apparently absent as a working principle in conversation, and the participants in a talk-exchange tend not to draw what we have been calling Q-based inferences in situations where such inferences would be drawn in Western communities.

> [Interlocutors] regularly provide less information than is required by their conversational partner, even though they have access to the necessary information. If A asks B, 'Where is your mother?' and B responds, 'She is either in the house or at the market', B's utterance is not usually taken to imply that B is unable to provide more specific information needed by the hearer. The implicature is not made, because the expectation that speakers will satisfy informational needs is not a basic norm. (Keenan 1976:70)

In fact, however, as Keenan makes clear in her discussion, Quantity and Q-based inference do play a significant role in some conversational contexts. Where they do not, it is because Quantity is overridden by a countervailing R-based principle, in particular the imperative of avoiding *tsiny* (the responsibility, guilt, or other unpleasant consequences incurred by uttering claims which turn out to be false and/or offensive to other members of the society living or dead). Sex of speaker, and significance and accessibility of the information contributed, are other variables influencing the relative weights of Q-based and R-based principles and inference patterns in the Malagasy community. (Cf. Prince 1982 for a related critique of Keenan's conclusions.)

Both Tannen's and Keenan's cases involve situations in which different speakers practice different utilizations of essentially the same tools; pragmatic competence often differs across cultures--and across speakers within the same culture--in accordance with the assignment of relative weightings to different maxims or principles, and consequently with the inference patterns associated with the exploitation of those maxims.

6. Quantity vs. informativeness. The most detailed and careful discussion in the literature of Q vs. R clashes in English is due to Atlas and Levinson (1981) (cf. Levinson 1983: section 3.2 for related discussion). Atlas and Levinson begin by summarizing the evidence for the inference from Quantity for the scalar cases. Examples (after Horn 1972 and Gazdar 1979) include the implicata in (7a); the general principle for the Q-based cases is given in (7b).

(7)   The inference from Quantity: What is communicated is more informative, more definite than what is said.

(7a)   some ⟵⟶ not all
       may ⟵⟶ may not
       3 ⟶ no more than 3
       p or q ⟶ not both p and q
       a believes that p ⟶ a does not know that p
       (cf. discussion of example (3).)

(7b)   'Given that there is available an expression of roughly equal length that is logically stronger and/or more informative, the failure to employ the stronger expression conveys that the speaker is not in a position to employ it.' (Atlas and Levinson 1981:38)

But, Atlas and Levinson point out, there is a substantial class of (somewhat disparate) cases for which Quantity gives exactly the wrong results. For these cases, including those in (8a), they invoke a Principle of Informativeness, (8b).

(8) The inference from Informativeness: What is communicated is more precise than (is a subcase of) what is said.

(8a) if p then q ⟶ if -p then -q (Geis and Zwicky's 1971 'invited inference' of conditional perfection)

p and q ⟶ p preceded q (cf. Grice 1975, Schmerling 1975 on 'asymmetric' conjunction)
⟱
p caused q

a and b VP'd ⟶ a and b VP'd together
a ate the cake ⟶ a ate the whole cake ⎫
a ate the apples ⟶ a ate all the apples ⎭ (cf. Harnish 1976)

Do you know the time? ⟶ If you know the time, tell me what it is. (Indirect speech acts, cf. Cole and Morgan 1975)

I don't think that p ⟶ (I think that) not-p (Neg-raising, cf. Horn 1978b)

I have a new car and the windows don't close ⟶ ...the windows of my new car.... (Bridging inferences, cf. Clark and Haviland 1976)

(8b) The Principle of Informativeness: 'Read as much into an utterance as is consistent with what you know about the world' (Levinson 1983:146-47)

Atlas and Levinson (1981:42) formulate their informativeness-based inference as an 'inference to the best interpretation'.

(8c) 'If a predicate Q is semantically nonspecific with respect to predicates P_i, $1 \leq i \leq n$, but for some j, $1 \leq j \leq n$, P_j is stereotypical of Qs, then in saying ⌜Qt⌝ a speaker will convey ⌜P_jt⌝.'

The key notion here is the restriction of a more general predicate to a stereotypical instance. Two examples of this inference to a salient subset or exemplar cited by Atlas and Levinson are those in (8d).

(8d) The secretary smiled. ⟶ The female secretary smiled.
John had a drink. ⟶ John had an alcoholic drink.

The class of indefinite descriptions provides a major source of clashes between Quantity-based inference (cf. (9a)) and Informativeness-based inference (cf. (9b)).

(9) Quantity vs. informativeness (Atlas and Levinson 1981:49ff.; cf. Harnish 1976)

(9a) Quantity in force:
I slept on a boat yesterday⟶
The boat was not mine.
I slept in a car yesterday⟶
The car was not mine.
Mort and David took a shower⟶
They took separate showers

(9b) Informativeness in force:
I lost a book yesterday⟶
The book was mine.
I broke a finger yesterday⟶
The finger was mine
Mort and David bought a piano⟶
They bought a piano together

A number of factors are involved in determining which principle takes precedence when the two are at odds; notice, for example, that the speaker in (9a) could have chosen the more precise genitive form (I slept on my boat, in my car) but did not do so, while the use of the genitive in (9b) (my book, my finger) might suggest wrongly that I have but one book or one finger. Atlas and Levinson cite two additional factors which are relevant to the weighting of Quantity vs. Informativeness: if an entailment-based 'Horn scale' (cf. Horn 1972) can be constructed on which the predicates in question can be readily ranked, Quantity is more likely to win out; if the application of Quantity tends to contradict our assumed 'Conventions of Noncontroversiality', Informativeness takes precedence.

Within the framework being explored here, Atlas and Levinson's inference from Quantity corresponds directly to our Q Principle. There is an equally strong parallel between Atlas and Levinson's inference from Informativeness and our R Principle; my only objection to their formulation concerns their terminology. First of all, Informativeness suggests the Q Principle to me more strongly than, as intended, the R Principle (note the language of Grice's Quantity$_1$ maxim, which Keenan 1976 indeed glosses 'Be informative'). Furthermore, Ducrot (1972), who independently proposes a 'Loi d'exhaustivité' to do the work of Grice's maxim of Quantity, also invokes a 'Loi d'informativité' of a rather different nature from Atlas and Levinson's Principle of Informativeness (cf. Ducrot 1972:132-34).[1] Thus, I feel justified in taking Atlas and Levinson's so-called Informativeness as an instance of the R Principle.

7. Negation as implicatum-canceller: Q-based vs. R-based inferences. An opposition as fundamental as that between the Q Principle and the R Principle would be expected to have major linguistic consequences, and indeed this expectation is not disappointed. We begin by considering the effect of negation on conversational implicata. What we find is that Q-based implicata can be readily cancelled by a negation which does not affect what is said (through what I have elsewhere termed 'metalinguistic' negation: cf. Horn to appear a), but R-based implicata cannot be cancelled by negation at all.

This is illustrated in what follows. First, some instances of negated scalar implicata are given in (10a-f). That negation is being used in a marked way to deny the Q-implicated upper bound in these examples can best be seen by considering the well-formed affirmative counterparts of these sentences in (10a'-f') (cf. (2); also Horn to appear b, and references there).

(10a) He didn't eat 3 carrots--he ate 4 of them.
(10b) You didn't eat some of the cookies--you ate all of them.
(10c) It isn't possible she'll win--it's certain she will.
(10d) She isn't patriotic or quixotic--she's both.
(10e) I'm not happy--I'm ecstatic.
(10f) It isn't warm--it's downright hot.

(10a') He ate 3 carrots--in fact, he ate 4.
(10b') You ate some of the cookies--indeed, you ate all of them.
(10c') Not only is it possible she'll win--it's certain she will.
(10d') She's patriotic or quixotic--in fact, she's both.
(10e') I'm happy--indeed, I'm ecstatic.
(10f') It's warm--in fact, it's downright hot.

But now consider R-based implicata. To say that someone was able to solve the problem may R-implicate that she in fact solved it (Karttunen 1970). Similarly, to assert that someone was clever enough to do something generally implicates that he did it. As we have seen, my confiding to you that I broke a finger would normally be taken to refer to a finger of mine (given Atlas and Levinson's Conventions of Noncontroversiality) unless I knew you knew that I was an enforcer for the mob. And, as Wittgenstein and others have pointed out, an assertion of the form 'I believe that S' would normally be taken as an indirect assertion of S rather than merely a statement about my beliefs; this indirect speech act, too, works by R-inference. Yet none of these implicata can be cancelled by negation.

(11a) She wasn't able to solve the problem.
 (≠ She was able to solve it, but didn't)
(11b) He wasn't clever enough to figure out the answer.
 (≠ He was clever enough to do it, but he didn't)
(11c) I didn't break a finger yesterday.
 (≠ I broke a finger, but it wasn't one of mine)
(11d) I don't believe the Yankees will win the pennant.
 (≠ I believe they'll win the pennant, but I'm not [weakly] asserting that they will)

Why should this difference in cancellability exist? The answer lies in the logic of Q-based and R-based inference. Let S represent a given (stronger) proposition, and W the weaker proposition which it unilaterally entails and from which the relevant implicata are to be drawn. In the case of Q-based implicata, the assertion of 'W' Q-implicates -S. Where W is a scalar predicate truth-conditionally defined by its lower bound, the ordinary negation of W negates that lower bound, i.e. as 'less than W', and is hence incompatible with S; the assertion that he did not eat three carrots would be taken to amount to the assertion that he ate less than three (and hence not four, five, or more). But 'not W' uttered in a context where S is affirmed (as in (10a-f)) self-destructs on the unmarked 'less than W' understanding and must therefore be sent back through, in effect--whence the marked, metalinguistic quality of this variety of negation.

In the case of R-based implicata, the assertion of 'W' R-implicates not -S but S: the proposition that she solved the problem unilaterally entails the proposition that she was able to solve it (S entails W), but the assertion that she was able to solve it may implicate that she in fact solved it ('W' R-implicates S). Once again, 'not W' signifies 'less than W' and hence licenses the inference of -S (via modus tollens from the original S ⊩ W entailment). But crucially, there are no circumstances under which the implicatum S is cancelled and 'not W' cannot be interpreted consistently, as an ordinary descriptive negation. The negation in (11a-d) thus never gets sent back through to be interpreted metalinguistically, as an implicatum-canceller. Schematically, the situation we have is that in (12).

(12) Q-based implicata:
S entails W
'W' Q-implicates -S
normally, 'not W' = 'less than W', incompatible with S
'not W', asserted where S is given, reinterpreted as metalinguistic negation

R-based implicata:
S entails W
'W' R-implicates S
normally, 'not W' = 'less than W'
'not W' ⊩ -S (modus tollens)
'not W' never gets reinterpreted, since it's always compatible with -S (the denial of W's implicatum)

Now, R-based implicata can be cancelled without negation, simply by assigning the contradiction contour (cf. Liberman and Sag 1974) and stressing the implicatum-inducing element.

(13) She was able to solve the problem (but she didn't solve it).
I believe the Yankees will win the pennant (but I'm not saying they will).
I broke a finger today (but not one of mine).

Notice that we tend to get the opposite, Q-based implicatum in these contexts; the contour which cancels the R-based inference sets up a strong expectation for the kind of continuations exemplified above.

When we appear to get cancellation of an R-based implicatum by negation, the implicatum in question has, in fact, become conventionalized as part of literal meaning (cf. Grice 1975:58 and Morgan 1978 on the gradual conventionalization of conversational implicata). Thus, for example, predicate expressions which denote various personal relationships may take on a narrowed symmetric sense (cf. X and Y are {married/friends/lovers/in love}) but need not (cf. X and Y are spouses). When the symmetric sense of these predicates is intended, negation may leave the more general sense unaffected.

(14) They aren't {married/friends/in love}. (i.e. with or to each other)

To confirm the claim that only conventionalized R-based implicata can be cancelled by negation, we need only reconsider the pair of examples from Atlas and Levinson (1981) cited in (8d). Both speakers' intuition and lexicographers' practice suggest that the implicatum associated with <u>drink</u> ('alcoholic drink') has become fossilized into conventional meaning, while the implicatum associated with <u>secretary</u> ('female secretary') has not. Thus, in the terms of Horn (to appear b), <u>drink</u> represents an autohyponymous lexical item while <u>secretary</u> does not. In this light, negation behaves precisely as predicted.

(15a) My secretary didn't smile--I have a male secretary.
(15b) John didn't have a drink--that was a Shirley Temple.

A male secretary is still a secretary (although not one of the salient variety), but a nonalcoholic beverage may or may not count as a drink.

8. The division of pragmatic labor. While the Q Principle and the R Principle are diametrically opposed forces in inference strategies and language change, it is perhaps in the resolution of the conflict between them that they play their major role in both 'langue' and 'parole'. The most general pattern for this resolution, the synthesis of the two antitheses, is summarized in (16) and derived more explicitly in (17a-f).

(16) The use of a marked (relatively complex and/or prolix) expression when a corresponding unmarked (simpler, less 'effortful') alternate expression is available tends to be interpreted as conveying a marked message (one which the unmarked alternative would not or could not have conveyed).

(17a) The speaker used marked expression E' containing 'extra' material (or otherwise less basic in form or distribution) when a corresponding unmarked expression E, essentially coextensive with it, was available.

(17b) Either (i) the 'extra' material was irrelevant and unnecessary, or (ii) it was necessary (i.e. E could not have been appropriately used).

(17c) (17b(i)) is in conflict with the R Principle and is thus (ceteris paribus) to be rejected.

(17d) Therefore, (17b(ii)), from (17b), (17c) by modus tollendo ponens.

(17e) The unmarked alternative E tends to become associated (by use or--through conventionalization--by meaning) with unmarked situation s, representing stereotype or salient member of extension of E/E'. (R-based inference; cf. Atlas and Levinson, (8b), (8c).)

(17f) The marked alternative E' tends to become associated with the complement of s with respect to the original extension of E/E'. (Q-based inference; cf. (6.12))

The key steps in the argument are those sketched in (17a), (17e), and (17f); they represent a characteristic shift which can be schematized as in (18):

(18)

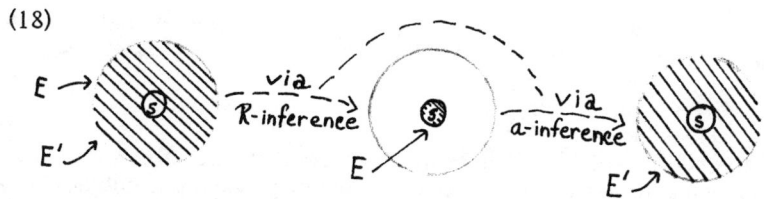

The result is an equilibrium which I shall call the division of pragmatic labor. (The equilibrium is, in fact, somewhat unstable; in particular, either the R-based inference represented in the second diagram or the Q-based inference in the third can become conventionalized, as we shall see later.) The remainder of this essay is devoted to rehearsing a number of instances of this pattern, varying in the details but essentially parallel in terms of the overall dynamics.

9. Avoid Pronoun (and unavoidable pronouns). In considering the near-complementary distribution between his abstract, phonetically unrealized PRO element (which usurps many of the functions of Equi-deletion sites in the earlier Standard Theory) and overt pronominals, Chomsky (1982:65) arrives at a general principle which he calls Avoid Pronoun, 'interpreted as imposing a choice of PRO over an overt pronoun where possible'. To illustrate, he cites the two cases of (19a-b).

(19a) John would much prefer [his going to the movie]
(19b) John would much prefer [his (own) book]

PRO may appear in the frame of (19a) in place of the pronoun (cf. <u>John would much prefer going to the movie</u>), and so <u>his</u> is taken here as non-coreferential with <u>John</u>; in (19b), PRO cannot appear and the overt pronominal <u>his</u> may be (and with <u>own</u> present must be) taken as coreferential with <u>John</u>. As Chomsky notes, the Avoid Pronoun principle

> might be regarded as a subcase of a conversational principle of not saying more than is required, or might be related to a principle of deletion-up-to-recoverability, but there is some reason to believe that it functions as a principle of grammar. (Chomsky 1982:65)

Three important points emerge from this brief passage: the link between Avoid Pronoun and analogous principles applying to deletion, the grounding of the principle(s) in least effort (i.e. our R Principle), and the fossilization or grammaticization of the functional principle into conventional rules and constraints within particular grammars.

The transderivational nature of Avoid Pronoun is clear from Chomsky's discussion of (19a-b) and an analogous contrast in French (Chomsky 1982:146).

(20a) Je veux qu'il vienne. 'I want him to come'
(20b) Il$_i$ veut qu'il$_j$ vienne. 'He$_i$ wants him$_j$ to come' (where i ≠ j)
(20c) *Il$_i$ veut qu'il$_i$ vienne. 'He$_i$ wants him(self)$_i$ to come'

Avoid Pronoun, in ruling out (20c), must refer to the availability of a corresponding derivation, that of (21).

(21) Il veut venir. 'He wants to come'

In (21) the subject of 'come' is realized as an abstract PRO argument of the embedded infinitive rather than an overt pronominal subject of an embedded subjunctive, as in (20a-c).

The applicability of Avoid Pronoun is also partially dependent on ambiguity avoidance, a fact not discussed by Chomsky. Thus, in the English versions of (20a-c) and similar sentences, coreference is ruled out totally only in third person cases (cf. Morgan 1970:387).

(22a) *He$_i$ wants him$_i$ to win. (no coreference possible)
(22b) (?)I$_i$ want me to win. (coreference possible in contrastive contexts)
(22c) (?)You$_i$ want you$_i$ to win.

(Technically, Avoid Pronoun should be activated in (22c), since one can be speaking to different addressees within a single sentence, distinguishing them by pointing or eye gaze. This situation, however, is too marginal to trigger the ambiguity avoidance condition on Avoid Pronoun, and the second person case thus works like the first person case in (22b).)

The literature on reflexives offers further grist for a suitably upgraded Avoid Pronoun mill. As is well known, it is usually (although not always) the case that a nonreflexive pronoun can be interpreted as coreferential with a given antecedent just in case a reflexive (bound by that antecedent) could not have appeared in that position. Many instances of this pattern respond to the Disjoint Reference principle suggested in Postal (1974) and discussed further within the EST (cf. Chomsky 1982). Thus, compare (23a) and (23b).

(23a) He$_i$ likes {himself$_i$/*him$_i$}.
(23b) He$_i$ said that she likes {*himself$_i$/him$_i$}.

Here again, as with the 'Equi' cases, ambiguity avoidance is relevant in the determination of when coreference is possible.

(24a) He's voting for him. (no coreference possible)
(24b) I'm voting for me. (OK contrastively)

In 'pro-drop' languages, PRO may appear in place of overt NPs freely in a wide range of positions, including subject and object; generally, verb agreement and/or pragmatic context permits recoverability of the missing referent. As expected, the scope of the Avoid Pronoun principle is commensurately widened in these languages. In her analysis of one pro-drop language, Turkish, Enç (1982) shows that semantically redundant pronouns (i.e. those whose referent would be recoverable) tend to be interpreted as expressing contrast--including topic-change, which she argues is a subtype of contrast. (Notice that in English, too, the occurrence of an overt nonreflexive pronoun in a frame which permits a referentially equivalent gap or reflexive, e.g. (22b) or (24b), is likewise interpreted contrastively.) Ençc argues that the interpretation of such marked pronouns, whose appearance seems to violate parsimony, is based on a conventionalization of a quantity-based inference--but she is referring here to Grice's Quantity$_2$ which we have previously subsumed under our R Principle (i.e. least effort).

In fact, while Avoid Pronoun, or whatever more general principle ultimately includes it, is basically a least effort correlate (as Chomsky observes), the division of labor we ultimately arrive at (in which abstract pronouns, i.e. PROs, are interpreted one way and real pronouns another) requires reference to both R and Q Principles, in the manner outlined in section 8.

A related instantiation of this division of pragmatic labor makes this clear. Chomsky proposes a 'general discourse principle' for R(eferring)-expressions, i.e. names and descriptions (1982:227).

(25a) 'Avoid repetition of R(eferring)-expressions, except when conditions warrant.'
(25b) 'When conditions warrant, repeat.'

Note that this discourse principle comes in two parts, one (25a) R-based and one (25b) Q-based; furthermore, as with Grice's two submaxims of quantity, each of Chomsky's subprinciples is explicitly bounded in its applicability by the other (as the subordinate clause material indicates).

The choice among referentially equivalent referring expressions for picking out a given individual is also subject to R- and Q-based considerations, as Prince shows in working out her Scale of Assumed Familiarity (1981:245). The matter is rather complex, however, and I shall not pursue it here.

One last example of the division of pragmatic labor emanating from the domain of reference is presented by Levinson (1983:75):

The deictic words <u>yesterday</u>, <u>today</u>, and <u>tomorrow</u> pre-empt the calendric or absolute ways of referring to the relevant days. Thus the following, said on Thursday, can only be referring to next Thursday (or perhaps some more remote Thursday), otherwise the speaker should have said <u>today</u>:
   I'll see you on Thursday.
The same holds if it is said on Wednesday, due to the pre-emptive <u>tomorrow</u>.

10. The division of pragmatic labor and the lexicon. Aronoff has shown (1976:43ff.) that the existence of a simple lexical item can block the formation of an otherwise expected affixally derived form synonymous with it. In particular, the existence of a simple abstract nominal underlying a given -<u>ous</u> adjective blocks or prevents the formation of an -<u>ity</u> nominalization based on that adjective.

(26a) fury   furious   *furiosity
       *cury   curious   curiosity
(26b) fallacy fallacious *fallacity
       *tenacy tenacious   tenacity

Aronoff's blocking phenomenon is the limiting case of a more general pattern independently observed and discussed by McCawley (1978), Kiparsky (1982), and indeed Bréal (1900); a pattern which directly reflects the division of pragmatic labor sketched in section 8 and exemplified in section 9: unmarked forms tend to be used for unmarked situations (via R) and marked forms for marked situations (via Q).

Kiparsky (1982) begins by noting that Aronoff's blocking paradigm is both too strong and too weak. Contrary to Aronoff's predictions, productive derivational processes are sometimes but not always blocked by the existence of a less productive corresponding form: decency and aberrancy block *decentness and *aberrantness, but gloriousness and furiousness survive alongside glory and fury. Blocking may also extend to inflectional processes as well, although again inconsistently: *mans/men, *goed/went, but kneeled/knelt, dreamed/dreamt. Aronoff's formulation of blocking, limited as it is to less than fully productive derivational processes, has nothing to say about these obviously related cases.

Kiparsky suggests a reformulation of Aronoff's blocking as a subcase of the (Pāṇini-Anderson-Kiparsky) Elsewhere Condition ('Special rules block general rules in their shared domain'--specifically, in morphology, irregular forms preclude regular forms). Kiparsky notes that 'blocking can be partial in that the special [less productive] affix occurs in some restricted meaning and the general [more productive] affix picks up the remaining meaning'. (These two components of the blocking process correspond to the second and third diagrams in our representation of the division of pragmatic labor, (18).) He cites as examples of partial blocking refrigerant/refrigerator, informant/informer, contestant/contester; full blocking results when there is no meaning 'left over' for the more productive form to pick up (*borer/bore$_N$, *inhabiter/inhabitant).

To handle these and other cases, Kiparsky formulates a general condition which he calls Avoid Synonymy.

(27) Avoid Synonymy: 'The output of a lexical rule may not be synonymous with an existing lexical item'.

This principle applies to both derivation and inflection, if we assume a level-ordered morphology. Its transderivational nature allows blocking between morphologically unrelated stems: thief blocks *stealer (but cf. base-stealer, with a noncompositional meaning), cutter ≠ knives, scissors, etc.

While there is something right about this principle, it is still too strong, as Kiparsky concedes. For one thing, we need to define a notion of 'corresponding item' relativized to a given speech level or register; words like fridge (underived), icebox (derived by compounding), and refrigerator (derived by affixation) can coexist within a single idiolect despite their referential equivalence. Indeed, the principle is almost self-falsifying: the doublets <u>synonymy</u> and <u>synonymity</u> strike me as perfect synonyms!

Working independently of the Aronoff-Kiparsky line, McCawley (1978) collects a number of examples where the appropriate use of a given expression formed by a relatively productive process (including syntactic formations) is restricted by the existence of a more 'lexicalized' alternative to this expression (i.e. one formed by a relatively nonproductive process). One case in point is originally due to Householder: the collocation <u>pale red</u> is (in the language of Aronoff and Kiparsky) fully or partially blocked by the lexical alternative <u>pink</u>. For some speakers <u>pale red</u> is simply anomalous (or at least nonoccurring); for others, it picks up whatever part of the 'pale' domain of 'red' <u>pink</u> has not preempted. In either case, <u>pale red</u> is limited in a way that <u>pale blue</u> and <u>pale green</u> are not.

In the same way, McCawley observes, the distribution of productive causatives (in English, Japanese, and other languages) is restricted by the existence of a corresponding lexical causative. Lexical causatives (e.g. (28a)) tend to be restricted in their distribution to the stereotypic causative situation: direct, unmediated causation through physical action.

(28a) Black Bart killed the sheriff.
(28b) Black Bart caused the sheriff to die.

This restriction can be viewed as a straightforward R-based conversational implicatum--an inference 'to the best interpretation', in the language of Atlas and Levinson (1981). The use of the relatively marked, morphologically more complex periphrastic causative (e.g. (28b)) will then Q-implicate that the unmarked situation does not obtain. Thus, (28b) suggests that (28a) could not have been used appropriately, possibly because Bart caused the sheriff's gun to backfire by stuffing it with cotton, or arranged for scorpions to be placed in the room of the sheriff (who is known to have a weak heart), etc. Similarly, the use of the unmarked lexical causative in (29a) R-implicates that the action was brought about in an unmarked way (presumably by stepping on the brake pedal), while the choice of the periphrastic (29b) correspondingly Q-implicates that some unusual method was employed (pulling the emergency brake, telekinesis, etc.).

(29a) Lee stopped the car.
(29b) Lee got the car to stop. (Lee made the car stop.)

McCawley's account of the division of labor between lexical and periphrastic causatives, like Chomsky's Avoid Pronoun and Kiparsky's Avoid Synonymy (or indeed, Grice's Avoid Prolixity maxim, which they all seem to reflect), is explicitly transderivational, and thus runs into some of the same problems of overgeneralization. Consider the data in (30a-d), which McCawley borrows from Heringer (1976:207).

(30a) John made the plate move. (indirect)
(30b) John moved the plate. (direct)
(30c) John made the plate fall. (indirect or direct)
(30d) *John felled the plate.

Here, the periphrastic make versions, 'normally used only in a situation involving indirect causation', as in (30a) whose use is restricted (by the existence of (30b)) to situations involving some sort of supernatural power on John's part, may generalize (as in (30c)) to a wider domain of causative situations 'just in those cases where no lexical causative exists to express direct causation' (Heringer 1976:207) (cf. (30d)). But, as Heringer and McCawley fail to notice, there is a simple lexical form corresponding to (30c), (30d), viz.

(30e) John dropped the plate.

If drop does not count as a corresponding form for make...fall because it involves an unrelated stem, then we cannot legitimately invoke (28a) to predict the limited distribution of (28b).

Other problems for the analysis of McCawley (1978) are discussed in Horn (1978a), where it is argued that the general 'least effort' principle employed by McCawley is simply too powerful and, more specifically, that we need to develop a notion of 'corresponding item' which will take into account such variables as morphological relatedness, markedness, speech register, and inherent complexity. For example, lexical causative verbs may indeed be unmarked in English with respect to their periphrastic make or cause counterparts, but this is not the case for lexical causative adjectives. Thus, the distribution of the periphrastic forms in (31a-c) is not constrained by the existence of the corresponding 'simple' forms in (32a-c).

(31a) That sort of behavior really makes me angry.
(31b) I didn't know that teasing your dog would get you so upset.
(31c) Wild horses couldn't make me stay away.

(32a) That sort of behavior really angers me.
(32b) I didn't know that teasing your dog would upset you so (much).
(32c) Wild horses couldn't keep me away.

Similarly, as a variety of linguistic and psycholinguistic evidence demonstrates, incorporated negation remains relatively complex, and so the distribution of (33a-b) is not constrained by the existence of the superficially simpler examples of (34a-b).

(33a) I persuaded Bill not to date many girls.
(33b) It's not likely that your coin will land heads.

(34a) I dissuaded Bill from dating many girls.
(34b) It's unlikely that your coin wil land heads.

In particular, (33a) is neutral with respect to the (conventionalized) R-implicatum associated with the use of (34a), viz. that Bill had previously intended to date many girls, and (33b) is unspecified for the implicatum associated with (34b), i.e. that it is likely your coin will not land heads (the so-called neg-raised interpretation). No Q-implicata are triggered in (31a-c) or (33a-b), and hence the working out of the division of pragmatic labor is not complete. (Cf. Horn 1978a for further examples and related discussion.)

While we must therefore refine and/or reevaluate the transderivational mechanisms invoked by Aronoff, McCawley, and Kiparsky for describing the division of labor between the use (or existence) of a simple lexical form and that of its more complex (lexical or phrasal) counterpart--in particular, by developing the tools to predict just when a given form counts as a counterpart to some other given form--the insight behind their various accounts is real, and it is essentially a single insight: the unmarked form is used for a stereotypical, unmarked situation (via R-implicature) and the marked counterpart for the situations 'left over' (via Q-implicature). This is the division of pragmatic labor outlined in section 8.

11. Division of pragmatic labor: Additional cases. Two more instances of the division of labor are worth mentioning here. First, consider the realm of indirect speech acts (cf. Searle 1975, Gordon and Lakoff 1975, and other articles in Cole and Morgan 1975). We find that modal auxiliaries which can be associated with indirect speech acts (ISAs) tend to become conventionally associated with the ISAs they convey. If (following Searle) we derive the ISA by an exploitation of the maxim of Relation (cf. section 3), we must nevertheless account for the fact that (35a-b) are conventionally used to convey the request in (36), while (35c-e)--which may (very indirectly) convey that request--are not conventionally used to do so.

(35a) Can you (please) close the window?
(35b) Could you (please) close the window?
(35c) Are you able to (?please) close the window?
(35d) Do you have the ability to (*please) close the window?
(35e) It's (**please) cold in here.
(36) (Please) close the window.

Searle observes (1975:76) that 'there can be conventions of usage that are not meaning conventions' by which 'certain forms will tend to become conventionally established as the standard idiomatic forms for indirect speech acts', including the can you/could you forms of (35a-b) for indirect requests. Morgan (1978) takes these usage conventions to represent 'short-circuited conversational implicatures' which, though calculable, are no longer (after short-circuiting) actually calculated in normal conversation. It is this short-circuiting of the R-based implicatum which licenses the preverbal please in (35a-b); cf. (35c-e) where no short-circuiting has taken place. (A parallel account of the neg-raising phenomenon and the triggering of negative polarity items is offered in Horn and Bayer to appear.)

But if the modal auxiliaries, idiomatic and semantically versatile as they are, become associated through a convention of usage or short-circuited implicature with the ISAs they may be used to convey, their periphrastic counterparts tend (predictably) to be interpreted literally. Thus, compare the behavior of the modals in examples (37a), (38a), (39a), and (40a) (where the implicatum to the ISA is short-circuited) with that of their periphrastic equivalents in (37b), (38b), (39b), and (40b) (where the indirect reading is not a conventional use of the expression and may be totally unavailable).

(37a) Can you pass the salt? (request)
(37b) Are you able to pass the salt? (literal question)

(38a) Here, I can help you with that. (offer)
(38b) (?Here,) I am {able/allowed} to help you with that. (not an offer)

(39a) Will you join us? (invitation)
(39b) Are you going to join us? (literal question)

(40a) I will marry you. (promise)
(40b) I am {going to/willing} to marry you. (only very indirect promise)

Noting the tendency for the most colloquial expressions (typically, as we have seen, the modal auxiliaries) to serve as the conventional forms for conveying indirect speech acts, Searle invokes a new neo-Gricean maxim, 'Speak idiomatically unless there is some reason not to'. He observes (in language mutually intelligible with that spoken by Kiparsky 1982 and McCawley 1978),

> In general, if one speaks unidiomatically, hearers assume that there must be a special reason for it, and in consequence,...the normal conversational assumptions on which the possibility of indirect speech acts rests are in large part suspended. (Searle 1975:76-77)

The pattern discerned here by Searle responds not only to our division of pragmatic labor, but also to the set of statistical correlations at the core of Zipf's analysis of the Principle of Least Effort and its linguistic reflexes (Zipf 1949). Zipf's Law of Abbreviation posits an inverse relation between the length of a word and the frequency of its tokens in an arbitrary text. His Principle of Economic Versatility stipulates a direct correlation between a word's frequency and its semantic versatility (i.e. the number of discrete senses or meanings it allows). The Principle of Economic Specialization states that the age of lexical item in the language correlates inversely with its size and directly with its frequency. By these measures, the relative simplicity of (35a), (35b) as against (35c) is directly confirmed: <u>can</u> and <u>could</u> are historically older than their periphrastic counterparts, phonologically simpler and shorter, more frequent in text tokens, and certainly more versatile semantically, as the contrasts in (41a-c) make clear.

(41a) I {can/am able to} stand on my nose.
       This knife {can/?is able to} cut the salami. (cf. ...is capable of cutting it)
       The salami {can be cut/*is able to be cut/is capable of being cut} by this knife.
(41b) Can it really be raining out?/Is it possible that it's raining out?
(41c) Can Billy come out and play?/Is Billy permitted to come out and play?

It is significant that modals, the constituents par excellence of least effort, figure so prominently among those forms conventionalized in English and other languages as conveyors of indirect speech acts, while their more expensive and complex counterparts do not.

Finally, we come to the case of logical double negation. What we find here is that the two negatives of the form not- (not-p) do not cancel out functionally even when they do semantically: they convey a positive which is characteristically weaker than the corresponding simple affirmative. In Jespersen's words,

> The two negatives [in not common, not infrequent] do not exactly cancel one another so that the result is identical with the simple common, frequent; the longer expression is always weaker; 'this is not unknown to me' or 'I am not ignorant of this' means 'I am to some extent aware of it', etc. The psychological reason for this is that the detour through the two mutually destructive negatives weakens the mental energy of the listener and implies...a hesitation which is absent from the blunt, outspoken common or known. (Jespersen 1924:332; cf. Horn 1978c: section 3.1 for discussion)

Rather than appealing, with Jespersen, to the metaphysical (and somewhat Victorian) notion of double negation sapping the listener's mental energy, we can more plausibly ascribe the weakening effect to the same general tendency we have already observed: the use of a marked expression when there is a shorter and less 'effortful' alternative available signals that the speaker felt s/he was not in a position to employ the simpler version felicitously.

With double negation, as with indirect speech acts, we see an especially clear correlation between the stylistic naturalness of a given form, its relative brevity and simplicity, and its use in stereotypic situations (via R-implicature). The corresponding periphrastic forms, stylistically less natural, longer and more complex, are restricted (via Q-implicature) to those situations outside the stereotype, for which the unmarked expression would have been inappropriate.

12. Q-based and R-based processes in language change. Perhaps the clearest lexical correlates of the clash and resolution of the R vs. Q conflict are in the area of diachrony. The most obvious R-based effects in language change are the reflexes in 'langue' of the well-known 'fast speech phenomena' in 'parole': contraction, clipping or truncation, assimilative shifts, and so on. Clipping (truncation) is a direct corollary of the aforementioned Law of Abbreviation: the more frequently a word or expression is used (within a given speech community), the shorter it will tend to become.

Among the contemporary examples of clipping cited by Stern (1931:258) in his standard work on lexical change are pram (from perambulator), specs (< spectacles), rep (<repetition or reprobate); it is striking that the same clipped forms persist even when their conventional value has shifted--specs is now likely to abbreviate specifications, and rep would probably be taken to denote representative (or perhaps reputation, as in the somewhat dated bad rep). More clearly entered in our current lexicon are such conventional truncations as TV (or Brit. telly), phone, bus (<omnibus), and the conventionalized output of an extremely productive process of acronym formation (e.g. US(A), EST (with at least two senses for east-coast syntacticians), UCLA, OSU--'Oregon State University', 'Oklahoma State University', or 'Ohio State University', depending on the shared assumptions of the members of the speech community).

In discussing the development of the truncated forms, Stern (1931:257-58) warns that 'the demands of the speech functions must set a limit to the economic tendency'--i.e. the Q Principle constrains the power of the R Principle. (He also disparages 'the use of pronouns, or of generic words, to save mental effort' as 'especially characteristic of undeveloped minds, unintelligent or immature'. Avoid Pronoun or else!)

A more complex area of language change, involving the interaction of R-based and Q-based processes, is that of lexical shifts. Two traditional categories of lexical change (discussed by Paul 1909 and Bréal 1900, inter alia) worth examining in this light are narrowing (or reduction) of meaning and broadening (or expansion) of meaning.

Narrowing generally involves an R-based shift from a set denotation to a subset (or member) of that set, representing the salient or stereotypical exemplar of the general category. Examples cited in the standard works (cf. Breal 1900, Stern 1931) which fit this definition include Greek alogon (lit. 'speechless one') for 'horse', Latin fēnum (orig. 'produce') for 'hay', and English poison (cognate with potion), liquor (cf. liquid), undertaker (from 'one who undertakes' to 'mortician'), and corn (used for whatever grain is the most important cereal crop of a particular region, e.g. wheat in England, oats in Scotland, maize in Australia or the New World).

In these instances, the shift has become virtually complete (although the original, broader extension may persist in marginal uses). Other cases manifest the intermediate stage of 'autohyponymy'[2] (Horn to appear b), in which the basic, general sense survives in privative opposition with a specific sense derived from it. Autohyponyms which have developed their specific meaning (indicated in parentheses) through R-based narrowing include the following:

(42) color (for 'hue', i.e. the range of colors excluding blacks, whites, and grays): in color, color TV
temperature (for 'fever'): The baby has a temperature
number (for 'integer'): Pick a number from 1 to 10

drink (for 'drink alcohol'): I don't drink. Cf. the second example of (8d)
smell (for 'stink'): Something smells here
Frau (Ger.), femme (Fr.), mujer (Sp.) (for 'wife' as well as 'woman')

Dismissing a contemporary account of this variety of lexical shift in the evolution of homo 'man' from a source akin to humus 'earth', the first century grammarian Quintilian asks rhetorically, 'Are we to believe that homo comes from humus, because man is born of the earth, as if all animals had not the same origin?' (cited by Bréal 1900:114). Yet the derivation is correct, as noted by Bréal, who points out that alogon can likewise designate 'horse' in modern Greek without implying that no other animal lacks the faculty of speech.³ Like those logical fallacies based on real pragmatic inference patterns (e.g. 'denial of the antecedent', 'post hoc ergo propter hoc', and 'secundum quid' (Horn 1973:212-13), all responding to the workings of the R Principle as exemplified in (8a)), the R-based inference from a set to a salient or stereotypical member is as linguistically plausible as it is logically invalid.

In other cases, lexical narrowing is Q-based, typically resulting is autohyponymy. Kempson (1980:15-16) offers a characterization of the general process:

If for some general term, representing a lexical field, there is a gap in the sub-parts of that field, with only one more narrowly specified lexical item, then the gap may be filled by a more specific use of the general term.

Thus, for example, the existence of bitch 'female dog', in the absence of a sex-specific mate, leads the general term dog to develop a hyponymic sense designating the male of the species.

The governing principle for such cases is given as follows (Kempson 1980:15):

If a lexical item L_1 has as its extension a set S_1 which includes the set S_2 which a second lexical item [L_2] has as its extension..., then the lexical item L_1 may be used to denote that subset of S_1 which excludes S_2.

We thus have a partial reconstruction of the division of pragmatic labor, in that the existence of a more informative, marked term (L_2), together with the choice by a (fully informed) speaker to employ a less informative, unmarked term (L_1) (in a context where the additional information would have been relevant), licenses the Q-inference that the speaker was not in a position to employ the more informative term. We can represent this state of affairs schematically as in (43).

(43)   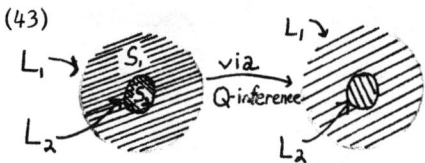   (L_1 may be used to denote S_1-S_2, i.e. the complement of S_1 with respect to S_2)

Thus, we obtain a pragmatic resolution of the semantic asymmetry inherent in the original state diagram. At the same time, L_1 may (and usually does) retain its general application (so as to include S_2) in contexts where there is no contrast at issue with L_2: it is only when the sex of the beast is relevant that bitches do not count as dogs.

Noncanine examples of autohyponymy (i.e. private polysemy) deriving from Q-based narrowing include the following (cf. Kempson 1980, Horn to appear b):

(44) cow (excluding bulls)
      rectangle (excluding squares)
      finger (excluding thumbs)
      gay (excluding lesbians)
      player (excluding pitchers, in baseball)

I have argued elsewhere (Horn to appear b) that these cases are not homogeneous in nature, differing in degree of conventionalization of the relevant Q-based inference, and that (contra Kempson) they do not in any case represent the sole source of autohyponymy, given the examples of R-based narrowing cited earlier and those illustrating R-based broadening to be discussed further on.

The results of R-based and Q-based narrowing may be synchronically indistinguishable. As against the dog/bitch (and lion/lioness) variety, the narrowing of man seems to have preceded the development of its counterpart woman, and thus to represent an R-based rather than Q-based shift, males presumably being reckoned as the salient members of the species. More recent instances of what feminists have appropriately dubbed the masculine usurpation of the generic include mankind, chairman, and poet. Here, it is clearly the prior (R-based) specialization of the general term which created the perceived need for--and conscious innovation of--the corresponding feminine form; it is not the existence of sex-specific womankind, chairwoman, or poetess which led to a (Q-based) restriction on the extension of the general terms.

The specific L_2 term which triggers a Q-based restriction on the meaning or use of the general L_1 term must be sufficiently natural and stylistically unmarked, or (as we have observed in our earlier survey of Q-based restrictions) it will not count as a 'corresponding' item. Thus, Blackburn (1983:495) observes that animal may (or may not) be used so as to exclude humans, and it may likewise be taken in the appropriate context to exclude birds and/or fish, but there is no use of animal which excludes mammals--despite the obvious fact that mammalia constitute just as valid a subgrouping of animals as do birds and fish. Crucially, however, mammal (unlike man, bird, fish) does not correspond to a basic level category in the sense of Rosch (1977) and so cannot trigger the division of pragmatic labor illustrated in (43).

We have seen that narrowing of a lexical item may be either R-based (the spontaneous delimitation of a general term to a sense representing a salient exemplar of the category denoted by that term) or Q-based (the motivated specialization of a general term triggered by the prior existence of a hyponym of that term). The converse process--lexical broadening or expansion--is always R-based: the generalization of a term for a species to cover the encompassing genus, from genus to phylum, from subset to superset. Thus, Latin pecūnia, originally denoting 'property or wealth in cattle' (cf. pecū 'livestock, cattle'), generalizes to signify 'wealth' and eventually 'money', a shift paralleled in the English cognate fee (<OE feoh 'cattle'→'property'). As noted by Bréal (1900) and Ullman (1959), broadening is often accompanied by 'semantic impoverishment' resulting from the attrition of a qualifying context, as in the expansion of (assumed) Late Latin adripare, arripare, 'come to shore' into French arriver 'arrive (tout court)', or the generalization of panarium 'bread basket' into panier 'basket' (Ullman 1959:209).

Broadening tends to apply regularly with place and origin names, as political entities grow and mutate; examples include the expansion of Lat. romanus (or Eng. New Yorker) to designate someone or something from the empire (state) at large, rather than specifically from its major city. An even more productive source of lexical broadening involves trade names which have lost their capital letters and become generics (cf. Mason and Pimm 1982, Horn to appear b), including those in (45).

(45) xerox   jello   good humor
     kleenex   thermos   toll-house cookies
     scotch tape vaseline hoover (Br., 'vacuum cleaner')

As in many of the instances of narrowing discussed earlier, the net result (or at least temporary equilibrium state) here is autohyponymy: the broadened term retains its original specific meaning in at least some contexts. We may even end up with multiple hyponymy, as in the case of the enthogeographic label Yankee, with its three semantically nested extensions cited by McCawley (1981:9-10) and standard lexicographers,[4] 'native or inhabitant of New England; or, more generally, of northern U.S.; or, more generally, of U.S.'

In these examples, broadening results when a specific term representing a salient exemplar (often the salient exemplar) of a wider class generalizes to denote that wider class; lexical expansion thus constitutes a perfect mirror image of R-based narrowing from a set to a salient exemplar of it. Once the new value for the term is entered in the lexicon--alongside or in place of the original specific value--semantic shifts (often culturally triggered) may ensue, obscuring the original set/salient member relation. It was the Romans' use of livestock as the medium of exchange which led to the broadening of pecūnia, a derivative of the term for 'livestock', into a term denoting 'property'--and it was the subsequent abandonment of barter in favor of a monetary system that led to the later loss of the etymological component altogether, to the point where pecūnia simply stood for 'wealth'.[5] So too, in Mayan languages studied by Lounsbury, a word referring to 'serpent' or 'jaguar'--animals with a particular ritual significance--became generalized as the standard term for 'animal', retaining its original specific meaning in compounds. The manufacturers of the items in (45) should therefore find a silver lining in the legal cloud of their copyright loss: their products obviously represent the prototypes or epitomes of their respective kind, even if this results in their brand name coming to stand for that kind.

Broadening and narrowing often operate in tandem within a given language, or in complementary fashion across related languages. Thus, German Tier has broadened from 'wild animal' to include domestic livestock and pets as well as man (especially in compounds like Tierwelt 'animal kingdom'). At the same time, its English cognate has turned autohyponymous (and eventually unambiguous once more) through narrowing. OE dēor, ME deer originally designated beasts in general, especially 'objects of chase' (Stern 1931:416), then became restricted (initially in the lexicon of hunters) to single out the object of chase par excellence, fam. Cervidae. By the early modern period, the general use of deer had been largely supplanted by the Romance loans beast, brute, and animal, although it continued to retain a marginal application to the class of quadrupedal mammals, undifferentiated for species (as in Shakespeare's reference to rats and mice and such small deer). Eventually, only the specialized hyponymic sense survived, spreading from hunters' use into the general speech community.

The adjustment in the extension of deer vis-à-vis animal reflects a general tendency in language insightfully described by Bréal (1900: 27ff.). Bréal's principle, in effect a diachronic precursor of Kiparsky's Avoid Synonymy, is the Law of Differentiation, governing

> the intentional [!], ordered process by which words, apparently synonymous, and once synonyms, have nevertheless taken different meanings, and can no longer be used indiscriminately...either they are differentiated, or else one of the two terms ceases to exist. (Bréal 1900:27-28)

Typically, an older word for a given referent is retained, but limited to a specialized (often humble, 'degraded', or 'trivial') domain. Once again, the marked form is limited to a marked use.

Thus, Bréal informs us, the Swiss patois word for 'room', païlé, is restricted to the meaning 'garret' after standard French chambre is adopted as the unmarked term. The general use of Oscan popina 'kitchen', displaced by its Latin cognate coquina, eventually comes to denote 'tavern'. And now 'the Savoyard uses the names of père and mère for his parents, while he keeps for his cattle the old words pārē and mārē' (Bréal 1900:29).

Among English examples of Bréal's Law of Differentiation we might reckon brethren (whose restricted use is motivated by the adoption of the standard unmarked plural brothers), the deer/animal case already discussed, and the related and notorious hound/dog affair.

Once again, we find broadening and narrowing operating hand-in-hand (or paw-in-paw) until the eventual division of labor is arrived at. OE dogca, referring to a particular breed of dog (it is not entirely clear which one), represented a hyponym of the general term hound, then denoting the entire kind 'dog' (as its German littermate Hund continues to do). Sometime around the fourteenth century, when Chaucer's warning 'It is nought good a slepyng hound to wake' was turning into Heywood's 'It is evyll wakyng of a sleepyng dog', dog and hound were presumably both autohyponyms, with different specific understandings. Eventually, hound was totally displaces by dog in its general application but, in accordance with the Law of Differentiation, continued to retain its specialized use (originally developed via R-based narrowing in the vocabulary of hunters, for whom hounds were the salient representatives of the species, dogs par excellence).

Thus, narrowing and broadening, separately and in conjunction, reflect the centrality of R-based and Q-based shifts in the development of the lexicon. In R-based and Q-based narrowing, in R-based broadening, and in instantiations of Bréal's Law of Differentiation, as in the dynamics of use and meaning described by Chomsky (1982), Aronoff (1976), Kiparsky (1982), McCawley (1978), and Searle (1975), we descry the recurring patterns of our two general pragmatic principles and of the division of labor resulting from their interaction.

13. Varia and concluding remarks. Other apparent reflexes of the R vs. Q dynamic cannot be discussed here in detail, but are worth mentioning as possible topics for further investigation. First, there is the class of rhetorical figures of speech, including synecdoche, metonymy, and litotes, representing the 'parole'-based equivalent of conventionalized narrowing (part for whole) and broadening (whole for part).

Second, there is the privative relation between the meanings (and uses) associated with nominative and ergative case marking for subjects of intransitive verbs in 'fluid' or 'active' systems (cf. Dixon 1979 and especially Holisky 1983). In Bats (a.k.a. Batsbiy and Tsova-Tush), a Caucasian language investigated by Holisky, the facts appear to be as follows:

(46) With intransitive verbs which are typically agentive and intentional (e.g. 'get dressed', 'wash', 'hide', 'run', 'bump into'), NOM(inative) case is semantically marked for nonagentivity and ERG(ative) is unmarked.
(47) With intransitives which are typically nonagentive (e.g. 'die', 'burn', 'become poor', 'forget', 'drown', 'go crazy'), ERG is marked as agentive and NOM is neutral.
(48) With intransitives which allow both agentive and nonagentive interpretations equally freely (e.g. 'fall asleep', 'fall down', 'lose weight', 'be late'), ERG and NOM are equally natural and no markedness relation obtains.

In the first two sets of examples, we are dealing with a privative opposition (Zwicky and Sadock 1975, Horn to appear b), in which 'the marked member conveys its meaning truth-functionally, while the neutral member does so by implicature' (Holisky 1983:5). The existence of the more informative, marked form, together with the speaker's choice of the unmarked, semantically neutral form, allows the addressee to construct a Q-based implicature: the inference from the use of ERG with the verbs of (46) that an agent was involved, and the corresponding inference from the use of NOM with the verbs in (47) that the nonagentive interpretation was intended. Once again, we arrive at a division of pragmatic labor, in which the marked form is used for the marked situation (relativized to the semantics of the verb in question), and the unmarked form for the unmarked situation.

Finally, one more possible locus of the dynamics and resolution of the R/Q conflict is the range of 'switch-reference' constructions (cf. e.g. Finer 1984). As I read the data, there seem to be some languages (including Seri and Washo) in which the presence of a DS (different-subject) marker indicates that an embedded clause has a different subject from the main clause, while the lack of a marker is semantically unspecified for same vs. different referent, but tends to be interpreted as indicating that the subject is the same in contexts where the distinction is relevant and no further disambiguating factors are available. The asymmetry involved here is apparently analogous to that just touched on in Bats case-marking (as well as other examples discussed earlier), and thus similarly reflective of the use of Q-based implicature to complete the division of labor, but further investigation is required to sharpen the account of switch-reference and situate it more clearly within the proposed framework.

We have surveyed (all too cursorily) a wide range of linguistic phenomena, both synchronic and diachronic, both lexical and syntactic, both 'parole'-based and 'langue'-based, from conversation implicature and politeness strategies to the interpretation of pronouns and gaps, from blocking and distributional constraints on lexical items to indirect speech acts, from lexical change to case marking. If I am right, these apparently diverse and unrelated domains are all motivated and governed by the same functional dynamic, the ongoing Zipfo-Gricean dialectic between the Q-based Sufficiency Principle and the R-based Principle of Least Effort.

Notes

1. Ducrot's model of pragmatic inference shares with Grice's the crucial feature of indeterminacy. Given an utterance like (i),

(i) La situation n'est pas excellente. 'The situation isn't excellent'

Ducrot notes (1972:132), an addressee may infer that the speaker intended to convey (ii),

(ii) Elle est franchement mauvaise. 'It's pretty bad'

through the exploitation of the R-based 'Loi d'informativité' (the assumption that the hearer does not already know the information speaker is conveying); since he has not said (ii), however, the speaker can always retreat to the literal meaning of what he has said, i.e. the weaker (i). On the other hand, given the Q-based 'Loi d'exhaustivité' (the principle which demands that the speaker provide the strongest possible information which he possesses and which he believes may interest the hearer; cf. Ducrot 1972:134), someone who utters (i) may, in the appropriate context, implicate that the situation is pretty good. This indeterminacy is perhaps more apparent when the negation applies to a semantically negative predication, as pointed out by Stern (1931:312):

> Not bad, taken literally, leaves a large latitude, from indifferent to excellent, and may mean [sic] either, depending on the intonation used and the circumstances.

2. Following Lyons (1977:9.4), A is called a 'hyponym' of B iff the extension of A is properly included in that of B: Labrador retriever is a hyponym of retriever, retriever of dog, dog of mammal, and so on. But some words are hyponyms of themselves: dog and bitch are (sex-differentiated) co-hyponyms of dog, lion and lioness of lion, etc. In these cases, we can call the unmarked term (dog or lion) an 'autohyponym'. Autohyponymy thus represents privative polysemy or ambiguity within a single lexical item (cf. Zwicky and Sadock 1975 on privative opposition).

3. Bréal (1900:108) suggests that in fact alogon [aloγo] came to stand for the horse simply because 'the rider, speaking of his mount, was accustomed to say "the animal"'; similarly, homines were so-called not merely because of man's preeminent position among the creatures of earth, but because of the intended opposition between the earthbound human race as against 'the inhabitants of the sky Dii or Superii' (Bréal 1900:114).

4. As noted in Horn (to appear b), there is an even more narrowly defined sense of Yankee, the sense in which the Kennedys are disqualified from true Yankee status by their Irish Catholic heritage. On this ultrarestrictive interpretation, a Yankee is someone from New England who approximates to a sufficient degree the prototype WASP of the Pepperidge Farm commercials. (We may need to invoke a Rosch (1977)-style prototype theory in any case to explain why a Vermont farmer or a Maine lobsterman is more of a Yankee than is a Greenwich stockbroker.)

5. The mirror image relation between R-based broadening (from salient subset to superset) and R-based narrowing (from superset to salient subset) is highlighted when we juxtapose the development of pecūnia with the opposite shift exemplified by ktimata in Greek, from the general 'possessions' to the specific 'cattle' (Bréal 1900:109).

References

Aronoff, M. 1976. Word formation in generative grammar. Cambridge, Mass.: MIT Press.
Atlas, J., and S. Levinson. 1981. It-clefts, informativeness, and logical form. In: Cole, ed. (1981:1-61).
Blackburn, W. 1973. Ambiguity and non-specificity: A reply to Jay David Atlas. Linguistics and Philosophy 6.479-98.

Bréal, M. 1900. Semantics. Trans. Mrs. H. Cust. New York: Henry Holt.
Brown, P., and S. Levinson. 1979. Universals in language use: Politeness phenomena. In: Questions and politeness: Strategies in social interaction. Edited by E. Goody. Cambridge: Cambridge University Press. 56-311.
Chomsky, N. 1982. Lectures on government and binding, 2nd ed. Dordrecht: Foris.
Clark, H., and S. Haviland. 1977. Comprehension and the given-new contract. In: Discourse production and comprehension. Edited by R. Freedle. Hillside, N.J.: Erlbaum. 1-40.
Cole, P., ed. 1978. Syntax and semantics 9: Pragmatics. New York: Academic Press.
Cole, P., ed. 1981. Radical pragmatics. New York: Academic Press.
Cole, P., and J. Morgan, eds. 1975. Syntax and semantics 3: Speech acts. New York: Academic Press.
Coleman, L., and P. Kay. 1981. Prototype semantics: The English word lie. Lg. 57.26-44.
DeMorgan, A. 1847. Formal logic. [Reprinted London: Open Court Co., 1926.]
Dixon, R. M. W. 1979. Ergativity. Lg. 55.59-138.
Ducrot, O. 1972. Dire et ne pas dire. Paris: Hermann.
Enç, M. (to appear) Topic switching and pronominal subjects in Turkish. In: Studies in Turkish linguistics. Edited by K. Zimmer.
Finer, D. 1984. The formal grammar of switch reference. University of Massachusetts dissertation.
Gazdar, G. 1979. Pragmatics. New York: Academic Press.
Geis, M., and A. Zwicky. 1971. On invited inferences. Linguistic Inquiry 2.561-65.
Gordon, D., and G. Lakoff. 1975. Conversational postulates. In: Cole and Morgan, eds. (1975:41-58).
Hamilton, Sir W. 1860. Lectures on logic. Edinburgh: Blackwood and Sons.
Harnish, R. M. 1976. Logical form and implicature. In: An integrated theory of linguistic ability. Edited by T. Bever, J. Katz, and D. T. Langendoen. New York: Crowell. 464-79.
Heringer, J. 1972. Some grammatical correlates of felicity conditions. Ohio State University dissertation. Distributed by Indiana University Linguistics Club.
Heringer, J. 1976. Idioms and lexicalization in English. In: Syntax and semantics 6: The grammar of causative constructions. Edited by M. Shibatani. New York: Academic Press. 205-16.
Holisky, D. 1983. The privative nature of agent-marking in Bats (and English). Paper presented at annual meeting of the Linguistic Society of America, Minneapolis.
Horn, L. 1972. On the semantic properties of logical operators in English. University of California at Los Angeles dissertation. Distributed by Indiana University Linguistics Club, 1976.
Horn, L. 1973. Greek Grice: A brief survey of proto-conversational rules in the history of logic. In: Chicago Linguistic Society 9.205-14.

Horn, L. 1978a. Lexical incorporation, implicature, and the least effort hypothesis. In: Papers from the Parasession on the Lexicon. Chicago: Chicago Linguistic Society. 196-209.
Horn, L. 1978b. Remarks on neg-raising. In: Cole, ed. (1981:129-220).
Horn, L. 1978c. Some aspects of negation. In: Universals of human language, vol. 4: Syntax. Stanford, Calif.: Stanford University Press. 127-210.
Horn, L. (to appear a) Metalinguistic negation and pragmatic ambiguity. Lg.
Horn, L. (to appear b) Ambiguity, negation, and the London School of Parsimony. In: Proceedings from New England Linguistic Society 14. Edited by C. Jones and P. Sells.
Horn, L., and S. Bayer. (to appear) Short-circuited implicature: A negative contribution. Linguistics and Philosophy.
Jespersen, O. 1924. The philosophy of grammar. [Reprinted New York: Norton, 1976.]
Karttunen, L. 1970. The logic of English predicate complement constructions. Unpublished MS, University of Texas.
Keenan, E. O. 1976. The universality of conversational postulates. Language in Society 5.67-80.
Kempson, R. 1980. Ambiguity and word meaning. In: Studies in English linguistics. Edited by S. Greenbaum, G. Leech, and J. Svartvik. London: Longmans. 7-16.
Kiparsky, P. 1982. Word-formation and the lexicon. In: Proceedings of the 1982 Mid-America Linguistic Conference, University of Kansas. Edited by F. Ingemann.
Lakoff, R. 1973. The logic of politeness; or, minding your P's and Q's. In: Chicago Linguistic Society 9.292-305.
Levinson, S. 1973. Pragmatics. Cambridge: Cambridge University Press.
Lewis, D. 1969. Convention. Cambridge, Mass.: Harvard University Press.
Liberman, M., and I. Sag. 1974. Prosodic form and discourse function. In: Chicago Linguistic Society 10.416-27.
Lyons, J. 1977. Semantics 1. Cambridge: Cambridge University Press.
McCawley, J. 1978. Conversational implicature and the lexicon. In: Cole, ed. (1978:245-59).
McCawley, J. 1981. Everything that linguists have always wanted to know about logic. Chicago: University of Chicago Press.
Martinet, A. 1962. A functional view of language. Oxford: Clarendon Press.
Mason, J., and D. Pimm. 1982. Generic examples: Seeing the general in the particular. Unpublished MS, The Open University, Milton Keynes, England.
Mills, J. S. 1867. An examination of Sir William Hamilton's philosophy, 3rd ed. London: Longmans.
Morgan, J. 1970. On the criterion of identity for noun phrase deletion. In: Chicago Linguistic Society 6.380-89.
Morgan, J. 1978. Two types of convention in indirect speech acts. In: Cole, ed. (1978:261-80).

Paul, H. 1909. Prinzipien der Sprachgeschichte, 4th ed. Halle: M. Niemeyer.
Postal, P. 1974. On raising. Cambridge, Mass.: MIT Press.
Prince, E. 1981. Toward a taxonomy of given-new information. In: Cole, ed. (1981:223-55).
Prince, E. 1982. Grice and universality: A reappraisal. Unpublished MS, University of Pennsylvania.
Rosch, E. 1977. Human categorization. In: Advances in cross-cultural psychology. Edited by N. Warren. New York: Academic Press. 1-72.
Schmerling, S. 1975. Asymmetric conjuction and rules of conversation. In: Cole and Morgan, eds. (1975:211-31).
Searle, J. 1975. Indirect speech acts. In: Cole and Morgan, eds. (1975:59-82).
Stern, G. 1931. Meaning and change of meaning. Bloomington: Indiana University Press.
Tannen, D. 1975. Communication mix and mixup, or how linguistics can ruin a marriage. San Jose State Occasional Papers in Linguistics.
Tannen, D. 1979. Ethnicity as conversational style. Sociolinguistics Working Paper No. 55, Southwest Educational Development Laboratory, Austin, Texas.
Ullman, S. 1959. The principles of semantics, 2nd ed. Glasgow: Jackson, Son and Co.
Zipf, G. K. 1949. Human behavior and the principle of least effort. Cambridge: Addison-Wesley.
Zwicky, A., and J. Sadock. 1975. Ambiguity tests and how to fail them. In: Syntax and semantics 4. Edited by J. Kimball. New York: Academic Press. 1-36.

INTENSITY

William Labov
University of Pennsylvania

At the heart of social and emotional expression is the linguistic feature of intensity.[1] It is a difficult feature to describe precisely. Intensity by its very nature is not precise: first, because it is a gradient feature, and second, because it is most often dependent on other linguistic structures. Most discussions of intensity involve specialized prosodic contours and a set of adverbs that code intensity directly: really, so, and very in English. But intensity is most often expressed through linguistic forms that are normatively devoted to logical relations and conceptual categories. The use of such forms to signal intensity can lead to changes in the subsystems involved. If grammatical descriptions don't take social and emotional expression into account, and their effect on the underlying system, they will be incomplete and even misleading for language learners.

1. Intensity in adverbs: Cognitive zeroes. Emotion is often expressed through peripheral, gradient systems: by prosody, vocal qualifier, and gesture. Information on emotional states can be conveyed by the central grammatical apparatus, completely verbalized in propositional form, but with lower chances of success. Any imaginable emotional state can be stated as a proposition: 'I am moderately angry with you', or 'I'm entirely committed to this line of action'. But we are all familiar with situations where listeners refuse to accept these words at their face value. On the other hand, De Groot's principle (1949) tells us that whenever the message conveyed by the intonational system is at variance with the information contained by the words, the intonational message will be understood as the one intended. It would follow that the peripheral systems are the primary means of conveying social and emotional information, and the grammatical mechanism is the primary means for conveying referential and cognitive information.[2]

Yet, some elements of the grammatical system are specifically devoted to emotional expression, and the most common of these are adverbs that signal intensity. 'Intensity' is defined here as the emotional expression of social orientation toward the linguistic proposition: the commitment of the self to the proposition. The speaker relates future estimates of his or her honesty, intelligence, and dependability to the truth of the proposition. Intensity operates on a scale centered about the zero, or unmarked expression, with both positive (aggravated or intensified) and negative (mitigated or minimized) poles. A feature notation with [± intensity] is therefore not appropriate. Instead, I will refer to position on an ordinal scale where features marked for intensity raise an expression to a value greater than zero, and those marked for deintensification lower expressions to values less than zero.[3]

Really is one of the most frequent markers of intensity in colloquial conversation, and must figure large in any first approach to intensity in everyday communication. It makes little contribution to cognitive or representational meaning, unless it is directly opposed to the unreal or the insincere.[4] In fact, really can be described as a 'cognitive zero': it would have zero representational content in context-free information processing. Social and emotional meanings are difficult to demonstrate directly, but the presence of cognitive zeroes or cognitive contradictions can give indirect demonstrations of their presence.

To illustrate the use of really and other adverbs of intensity, I will draw from one of the best records we have of intimate colloquial speech, the family conversation of Dolly Ripley.[5] She had just returned to New York City from a visit to her family in North Carolina, helping to mind her nieces and nephews, and she was giving the latest news of the family to her first cousin over the telephone.

(1a) I really worked while I was away!
(1b) He [grandfather] really came out of it good.
(1c) I got nothin' to really stay here for.
(1d) They really had themselves a ball!

Here really acts to intensify the main predication.[6] It can be considered as a part of the mood system, pertaining to the existential status of the predication. It establishes a 'surreal' mood, the converse of irrealis, in designating a state of reality greater than normal.[7]

The adverb sure also occurs in preverbal position; it is in general an alternate of really, as shown in (2).

(2a) Sure it is!
(2b) 'Cause they sure work the hell out of me!

The adverb so is limited to adjectival modification, where it serves as an alternant of sure and really.

(3a) Listen honey, they'll change clothes so fast down here!
(3b) I'm so glad she comes.
(3c) But they were so glad to see me!

Questions are intensified by the insertion of the hell after the WH-word.

(4a) Where the hell you been?
(4b) So what the hell you been doin' for the summer?

The form used to intensify questions can be finely adjusted to the level of mitigation or aggravation desired with a wide range of alternants.[8]

The adverb just has the same privileges of occurrence as really, but has a much wider range of meanings. Just can be a minimizer, as in I didn't yell and scream, I just went like this [gesture]. Here it can be interpreted as 'no more than the following'. When just modifies a strong action or expression or an unusual situation, it can be interpreted in the opposite manner: an intensive meaning 'no less than this'. The examples in (5) are drawn from a narrative of Bobby Andrucci, 23, of Ayr, Scotland.

(5a) I jus' you know whacked 'im.
(5b) He went straight through the glass doors an' I just put it into him! [hit him hard]
(5c) But m' shirt an' all they was just covered with blood.

We encounter in spontaneous speech a wide variety of metaphors that serve as intensifiers: bleeding like a pig, darker than pitch or pitch dark. The metaphor in (6) was repeated many times in a description of a mugging in a conversation among several middle-aged ladies in a park in Carlisle in northern England:

(6) They said she was like a...oooh, they said she was like a battered cucumber when they took her into the infirmary![9]

Closely related to these adverbial intensifiers is the use of the superlative form of attributive adjectives, as in the quotation from Dolly Ripley in example (7).

(7) I told the biggest lie!

This review of adverbs of intensity is not intended as an inventory or a taxonomy. The most common forms of intensification set the basis for the recognition of the feature of intensity when it occurs in more covert settings. Adverbs of intensity play a major role in the resolution of semantic ambiguity in the study of quantifiers to follow.

The most thoroughgoing study of intensification is Thibault's (1977) analysis of Montreal French. She draws on the Montreal corpus to illustrate a wide range of intensifying adverbs, adjectives, interjections, and verbal forms, including the highly developed Quebecois pattern of swearing with forms of religious origin.

2. Intensity and aspect: Cognitive contradictions. The definition and interpretation of aspect is one of the knottiest issues in linguistic description, and there is more disagreement here than in most areas of linguistic inquiry. One reason is that aspect systems are not sets of conjunctively defined concepts. At least some of the distinctions made in the categories of tense are clear and distinct ideas, like past and nonpast; but aspect, by definition, is a 'way of looking' at events. Ways of looking at things are closer to associations than concepts, and there is no clear route to agreement about how such ways of looking at things are to be described.

A second reason for the difficulty is that certain aspect categories tend to acquire the feature of intensity, and eventually the aspect marker is used to signal intensity even when its other associations do not apply. The result is a cognitive contradiction that defeats efforts to find a conjunctive definition for the aspect category. This is particularly true of the perfect aspect that signals the 'completed' state of action.[10] Though most English dialects do not have this aspect category, the particle <u>done</u> serves as a perfect in many Southern dialects, in Caribbean English, and in the Black English Vernacular (BEV). Intensity plays an especially strong role in BEV aspect, which will serve to illustrate how association with intensity affects linguistic behavior and linguistic description.

<u>Done</u> is quite frequent in BEV conversation, formal or informal, and can be illustrated from any half-hour of recorded speech in vernacular contexts. The characteristic, almost stereotypical use of <u>done</u> is shown in example (8) from Baugh (1984).

(8a) I done forgot to turn off the stove.
(8b) Well, we usta get into trouble, and...if Pop'd catch us he say, 'Boy--you done done it now!'

The usual interpretation of <u>done</u> as 'perfect' applies here, and can be rendered by the translation with <u>completely</u>.[11]

(8a') I completely forgot to turn off the stove.
(8b') Boy, you completely did it now!

But many speakers of BEV feel that the intensive meaning is lost here, and that the force of the utterance is best captured as in (8").

(8a") I actually forgot to turn off the stove.
(8b") Boy, you've really done it now!

A further extension of <u>done</u> can be seen in the quotation in (9) from a young woman from North Philadelphia.

(9) But next thing you know...she done stole some o' my mother jewelry. (Jerrie Chisholm, 17, PC193)[12]

Stealing is an action that can be done partially, in the sense of an incomplete attempt, or completely, in the sense of a clean sweep and a getaway unobserved. But the intensive feature is also present, as the intermediary for the sense of 'moral indignation' that is evident here, as in many other uses of <u>done</u>. These meanings--cognitive, emotional, and social--are not inconsistent, and one could argue that the intensive and indignant senses are derived pragmatically from the perfect meaning of <u>done</u>. But the development of cognitive contradictions in the use of <u>done</u> is seen in the quotation in (10), given by Baugh (1979:150), spoken by a woman whose husband was cheating on her.

(10) So he went to where she was...and got the nerve to lie to me...talking 'bout he done went to work.

It is not at all appropriate to apply 'completely' to <u>go to work</u>, since this is a discrete, socially defined action that is not done partially or completely. Nor is it suitable to insert <u>really</u>, since there is no implication that anyone at that time had argued the reverse. The most likely interpretation is that the <u>done</u> agrees with the intensive, morally indignant use of <u>got the nerve to</u>, and is 'lowered' from that higher predicate to the subordinated clause of indirect speech.

(10') ...and done got the nerve to lie to me...talkin' 'bout he went to the office.

Efforts to apply a conjunctive definition to <u>done</u> meet cognitive contradictions in examples like (11), given by the speaker of (8).

(11) No, Miguel he done been to bed with Julia and been to bed with Darlene...and sposta be a good friend o' Henry's.

Henry lives with Darlene, and Miguel's sleeping with Darlene is seen here as a betrayal of Henry. The <u>done</u> cannot be interpreted here as the normal 'completed' sense, since going to bed with someone is again a socially defined act, which is not done partially or completely; or for that matter, even intensively. The only coherent interpretation that remains for this <u>done</u> is 'moral indignation'.

As long as we can locate a plausible interpretation of aspect particles in cognitive terms, oriented to the processing of information, it is not a vital matter to recognize emotional meanings like 'intensive' or social meanings like 'moral indignation'. They play no more important role than any other redundant features that cluster about grammatical structure.[13] It is quite otherwise when no cognitive or referential meaning appears--a cognitive zero--or when the context is inconsistent with the cognitive meanings usually recognized--a cognitive contradiction. We then have no choice but to recognize social and emotional meanings as an integral part of the central grammatical system.

The examples given from BEV indicate that the system of mood has been truncated in most grammatical presentations. Mood is concerned with the speaker's view of the existential status of the proposition: its relation to reality. One pole of this dimension is the negative; the other is usually considered the indicative. Yet the existence of surreal forms like <u>really</u> and the intensive use of <u>done</u>, <u>be</u>, <u>be done</u> in BEV leads us to the view that the unmarked indicative is the midpoint of a scale that extends from the unreal to the surreal.

(12) You didn't do it.
You could have done it.
You must have done it.
You might have done it.
You seem to have done it.
You did it.
You really did it.
You done done it!

Another way of looking at the matter is that a logical representation of reality assigns probabilities of 0, 1, or some value between 0 and 1. But in colloquial conversation, many utterances are assigned probabilities well below 0 or considerably above 1.

3. The intensive use of quantifiers. There is no closed set of markers of intensity. Intensity is signaled by a large and miscellaneous class of devices, ranging from the most peripheral of prosodic variations to the most central categories of the grammar. Labov and Waletzky (1967) listed four kinds of intensifiers that serve as evaluating devices in narrative: verbal and nonverbal gestures; expressive phonology, including sudden changes in length, pitch, duration, and vowel quality; repetition; and the use of quantifiers. The quantifier that drew the most attention in these early analyses of intensification was <u>all</u>.

(13a) and then, when the man ran in the barber shop he was all wounded
(13b) he had cuts all over
(13c) I knocked him all out in the street

In her study of the language used in meetings of a food cooperative, T. Labov (1980:281-83) found that the quantifiers <u>never</u>, <u>ever</u>, <u>always</u>, and <u>all</u> were used in a hyperbolic manner, to indicate degrees of activity that were implausible, and assigned to them the same interpretation as the intensifying adverbs.

For a wide range of colloquial speakers, about half of all the intensive features in colloquial speech are accounted for by the universal quantifiers: <u>any</u>, <u>all</u>, <u>every</u>, and <u>ever</u>. In the 20-minute conversation of Dolly Ripley, there are 20 such examples. Example (14) presents characteristic quotations.

(14a) She ain't had no kind o' nobody to bring her up.
(14b) Just to say you been around and been some place, 'cause you ain't never been no place.
(14c) I didn' bring none of my clothes back...I left 'em all down there. That's right. I left all of 'em down there.

The use of <u>all</u> in (14) is distinct from the adverbial <u>all</u> of (13), which is used to intensify participles and adverbs of place with the meaning of 'completely'. In (14c), <u>all</u> is used as a universal quantifier of continuous quantities with the mass noun <u>clothes</u>. It is the obverse of <u>none</u>: since she left <u>all</u> of her clothes in North Carolina, Dolly Ripley has <u>no</u> clothes in New York.

The interpretation of adverbial <u>all</u> is straightforward: we assign the meaning 'thoroughly'. The translation of adverbial <u>all</u> into a mark of intensity then follows the same route as the perfect: there is a smooth transition between saying that something is completely or thoroughly so, and emphasizing the fact that it is indeed so.

On the other hand, the quantifier <u>all</u> in (14c) and the negative universal quantifiers in (14b) and (14c) involve cognitive contradictions. It is possible in (14a) that a child had no one at all to care for him or her in growing up, though it isn't likely. But it is not possible that the children being addressed in (14b) had never been any place, nor is it possible, looking at Dolly Ripley in New York City, to say that she had left all of her clothes in North Carolina.[14]

This investigation will approach these cognitive contradictions as the result of the interaction of intensity with the semantics of the universal quantifiers. But first it may be helpful to look at the pragmatic framework in which this interaction is embedded.

3.1 Pragmatic approaches. One way of explaining (14b) is to uncover implicit assumptions about what is relevant, or what counts as a member of the set of places that fall within the scope of <u>no</u>: 'You haven't been any place that counts as far as places worth being to are concerned.' We could abbreviate these assumptions by saying that all universal quantifiers are bound in an implicit set of 'things that count' or 'things that are worthy of mention': 'There is no X such that X is a member of places that are worth mentioning and you have been to X.'

To deal with (14c) we would have to interpret 'things that count' as 'clothes that are needed for more than a few days'. The clothes that Dolly Ripley is wearing, and the few that she needs for a short stay in New York City, are perhaps not 'worth counting' in evaluating the statement, <u>I left all my clothes down there.</u> The problem becomes more difficult in dealing with the apparent contradiction of (15), spoken by a working-class woman from eastern Tennessee, whose speech patterns are examined in some detail in section 4.[15]

(15) Seems like everybody's out for theirself. (Louise Adams, 42, Knoxville, Tenn.)

The normal interpretation of <u>everybody</u> does not include the speaker and the addressee. No simple modification of the set of 'things worth mentioning' will handle this situation. Rather than tailor pragmatic rules to each new example, we may have to broaden the framework to something as general as 'For all X, such that X is relevant in this context...'

This pragmatic approach accepts the meaning of universal quantifiers that is conventional for sentence grammar, and tries to show how the apparent illogic of usage is the result of interaction with a larger context. A more direct approach would recognize the role of intensity by stating that in the presence of a feature of intensity, the distinction between <u>all</u> and <u>almost all</u>, between <u>every</u> and <u>most,</u> is neutralized. This might be the result of a pragmatic rule that governs 'pardonable exaggeration'.[16]

(16) A universal quantifier in the presence of a marker of intensity may be interpreted as less than universal...

There are more than a few difficulties facing this proposal. The three dots indicate that there are many more conditions to be stated. We would not want, for example, to include the sentence types of (17).

(17a) I swear to God I'll pay back every cent.
(17b) Every one of my children turned back [to another religion].

More generally, we have to recognize that most universal quantifiers can be interpreted as carrying a feature of intensity without any additional mark. It is well known that negative concord serves to intensify a negation when it is optional (Jespersen 1924:331, Labov 1972:177-78). In BEV, where negative concord within the clause is semicategorical, negatives can be intensified by multiplying the opportunities for negative concord through the introduction of more indeterminate quantifiers any and ever. For all dialects, the introduction of these indeterminates adds intensity, even without negation. Example (14a') reflects an order of intensity 1<2<3.

(14a')
1. She hasn't had anybody to bring her up.
2. She hasn't had any kind of anybody to bring her up.
3. She hasn't had no kind of nobody to bring her up.

The same observation can be made about negative concord to the temporal indeterminate ever in (14b), and the use of ever without negation.

(14b')
1. 'Cause you haven't been any place.
2. 'Cause you haven't ever been any place.
3. 'Cause you haven't never been no place.

Similar interpretations can be made of the difference between My children do what I say and All my children do what I say. But if all universal quantifiers can be interpreted as carrying features of intensity, then (16) amounts to saying that in colloquial speech, the distinction between almost and all cannot be made. This certainly isn't so. Speakers who use universal quantifiers very freely, like Louise Adams, occasionally make it plain that exceptions count. At one point, she said:

(18) Now I think everybody's got a little fear in 'em.

She followed this immediately with a discussion of a possible exception: her son Charles, who had said that he had such a good time in Vietnam that he quit the service when they would not let him go back.

(18 I don't know...Charles said he wasn't scared over there but-- I don't know--I jus' think everybody's got a little bit o' fear in 'em...I got a feeling ol' Charlie boy was scared. You know some people'll talk like they're not--all the time they were.

We must conclude that no global rule accounts for the interpretation of universal quantifiers. Some utterances, like (14b, 14c) are evidently to be interpreted loosely, where all my clothes means 'most of my clothes', and haven't been no place means 'have been to very few places'. Even these glosses are too specific. From this point on, I will use the term 'loose interpretation' to mean a sense of a universal quantifier that focuses only on the whole and makes no division among the members of the class, with no attention to possible exceptions. The term 'strict interpretation' will apply to a sense of universal quantifiers that conforms to logical practice and specifically rules out exceptions. This is the sense needed to understand (18).

The differences between the two interpretations are put into relief by the differences in their entailments. In the strict interpretation of 'I left all my clothes down there' it follows that 'There are not any clothes that I haven't left down there'. But from the loose interpretation, no such conclusion follows.

This distinction does not easily find its way into formal descriptions of the English language. Among the dictionaries, the <u>Oxford English Dictionary</u> and <u>Websters New International Dictionary 2</u> agree that the basic meaning of <u>all</u> is 'the whole of', with a secondary meaning 'any whatever; beyond all doubt'. It is possible to read into the various discussions a sense of loose and strict interpretation, but closer inspection shows that the dictionaries are focusing on distinctions between the quantifiers. It will appear further on in this paper that the universal quantifiers do not differ in their susceptibility to loose or strict interpretations.

The most detailed linguistic analysis of the semantics of universal quantifiers is Sapir's essay on 'Totality' (1930). Sapir focuses on psychological processes that might support distinctions made in formal reflection, and specifically warns (1930:11):

> It is not claimed for a moment that the ordinary English uses of 'the whole', 'all of', 'the whole of', and 'all' necessarily correspond to our exacting distinctions, merely that they tend to do so. In actual practice there is considerable confusion.

Sapir believes that <u>all</u> in generic statements like <u>All men are mortal</u> is merely a class indicator, no different from <u>Men are mortal</u>, and not 'totalizers in the strictly logical sense'. But this suggestion is limited to generics, and does not apply to the concrete statements about past and particular events that are the main materials we have been examining.

To make any progress in locating the intersection of intensity and quantification, we must first examine speech systematically, and locate the conditions that favor the loose interpretation and those that favor the strict interpretation. This reverses the procedure of the first half of the paper. Instead of asking, 'How do people signal intensity?' I will ask, 'How do people interpret universal quantifiers?'

4. The interpretation of universal quantifiers. This section examines 100 universal quantifiers used by Louise Adams, of Knoxville, Tennessee. The focus is on local features of sentence grammar that may influence the listener in the loose or strict interpretation of these quantifiers. There are several special subsets that have acquired conventional meanings, irrespective of the local context. The main classification is concerned with the observations that would have to be made to confirm or disconfirm the statement within the scope of the universal quantifier: primarily the denumerability of these observations, a feature closely involved with other aspects of sentence grammar.

The classification is an ordered series of criteria. Any classification that applies immediately determines the status of a sentence, without regard to cross-classification by other criteria to follow. Following each classification is an example from Louise Adams and an explication of how the meaning of the quantifier would be determined by the ordered series of criteria.

Type A. CONVENTIONAL. Sentences where strict or loose interpretation is given by a fixed convention.

Several special uses of quantifiers have evolved over time which have immediate interpretations as loose or strict, not relative to the immediate context.

[1] Unique. Modifiers of unique objects or events.

(19) Kay Francis was born 'fore I ever left 'em there.

Louise Adams left her in-laws' house to set up housekeeping only once. Ever cannot be a quantifier, strict or loose, but is immediately taken as intensive, like the examples of any prefixed to unique objects.

[2] Approximate. The quantifier is the head of a noun phrase introduced by a conjunction.

Such noun phrases are conventionally interpreted as invoking a set of elements with a rough family resemblance to the prototype in the preceding phrase.

(20a) So I don't work or anything.
(20b) She puts all of it on him, all the cleanes', 'n' everything.

The interpretation is automatically loose.

[3] Adverbial. All functioning as adverb rather than determiner, adjective or noun.

This use is recognized by Websters New International Dictionary 2 with the note: 'all is frequently placed before a word or phrase to add the idea of completely, intensity or thoroughness.' As discussed in section 3, these uses of all are all inevitably the loose interpretation, since they are not focused on discrete elements that can form exceptions. The second all in (20b) is an example, as are the instances in (21).

(21a) And he said, 'When you been like 'at and been all over, you see things', 'n' he said, 'Marriage just ain't for it.'
(21b) Jimmy's been all through it all.
(21c) When he w's a kid, I had to go all the way around the state here gittin' that young 'un.

We must also include the adverbial at all, which is immediately interpreted as [+ intensive].

(21d)   It's not like it used to be at all.

[4]   Limiter. The quantifier is in a sentential context that denies or limits universality.

Such sentences do not make any sense at all if we do not assign them strict interpretation. Speaking of wild game that the men in her family brought home from hunting, Louise Adams said:

(22)   Now me, I don't eat everything come in the house.

The loose interpretation would amount to saying 'It is not true that I eat almost everything that comes into the house', but that might very well be true in this case. This sentence demands a strict interpretation for everything, just as all but one does for all.

[5]   Nonliteral. If the strict interpretation is assumed, the statement is obviously false.

This is the most common of all the conventional uses of quantifiers, exemplified by (14b, 14c) from the speech of Dolly Ripley. It is also quite common in the speech of Louise Adams.

(23a)   She always been like 'at, all through her life.
(23b)   He eats all the time and don't even get fat.
(23c)   Jimmy has give those kids--you ask her--they've got everything!
(23d)   All he wants t'do is wrassle and that's it.
(23e)   There ain't anything he wouldn' do for me, for her or for anybody.
(23f)   She can. She can doctor anything.
(23g)   [They shoot] squirrels, possum...anything they can see!
(23h)   Everything's changed.
(23i)   Seems like everybody's out for theirself! (=(15))

Interpretation is necessarily loose. Section 3 considered some of the possibilities for pragmatic rules that would reinterpret the strict interpretation. This seems especially promising when the listener can construct an unstated context that allows the strict interpretation. For (23d), for example, we can imagine a context 'Whenever you go to play with him...' But in the great majority of nonliteral types, for Louise Adams and others, these reconstructed contexts are hard to find and arbitrary at best.

Type B. UNOBSERVABLE. Sentences where no objective observations can be made to confirm or disconfirm the statement.

Whereas the preceding set of sentences have automatic interpretations, there are a great many sentences where the listener has no means of knowing from the immediate context whether strict or loose interpretation is to be made. From this point on, the questions pertain directly to observations that would confirm or disconfirm the statement within the scope of the quantifier.

[6] Self-defined. The occurrence of the event is determined by the observation, so that any possible observation is a confirmation.

(24a) I could always get in a good argument.
(24b) That would git 'im, oh God, that would git 'im every time.
(24c) In fact, I always said that I had two too many children.

Consider (24c): unless we take the impossible interpretation that Louise Adams repeated the statement endlessly, it can only mean that when there was an occasion for Louise Adams to say that, she said it. Only the speaker would know when the occasion to say it had arisen.

[7] Opinion. The statement is a matter of subjective opinion so that only the person directly involved can decide if it is true or not.

In such cases, the listener can hardly assign an interpretation without the help of further information from the speaker. Usually, we are dealing with the opinion of the speaker, but sometimes, as in (25c), it is someone else.

(25a) That didn' do him no good, and still ain' doin' nobody no good.
(25b) That youngest 'un and that girl o' mine, they don't care anything about wrestlin'.
(25c) I run from anything like that.
[The opinion involved in (25c) is the question of similarity: what is like that? Only the speaker can decide.]
(25d) If I stand and look at anything like 'at, everything jus' turns dark to me, and I pass out.
(25e) Her daddy got a goat one time, I never will forget this.
(25f) Jus' plain ol' cows milk, that's all I like.
(25g) You ain' gon get me on no boat. You ain' gon' get me on no airplane.
(25h) I said [of politicians], 'Well, when one's done one thing dirty, you jus' go t'look at 'em back, they're all dirty. They'll come out dirty. They go in clean, they come out dirty.'
(25i) Now I think everybody's got a little fear in 'em.

In section 3, (25i) was interpreted [as (18)] by Louise Adams herself in the strict sense as she proceeded to consider counterexamples. There is no doubt that the interpretation of universal quantifiers is in the hands of both speaker and listener, and the meaning is often negotiated through social interaction. As outside observers, we must be willing to wait and see what people do make of utterances. But as speakers of the language, we are entitled to search for whatever clues the grammar gives us on the interpretation of such critical matters, before we decide to raise a question or objection. Sentence (25h) expresses a common theme in American political life; a politician addressing Louise Adams would have to decide whether she intended the loose or strict interpretation before knowing what to say next. Sentences of type B offer less opportunity for us to estimate the probability of a strict interpretation than those to follow.

The great majority of Unobservables are in the opinion class, and in the analysis to follow, self-defined are merged with opinions. An overview of all speakers to be considered shows that the self-defined class does properly fall within Type B; in all respects these sentences prove to be prototypical Unobservables, even though the actual statements refer to events that can be observed.

Type C: OBSERVABLES. Sentences where objective observations might be made by listeners or others.

[8] Single. A single observation would confirm the statement.

In spite of the fact that we are dealing with large, inclusive, and often badly defined sets, the deictic configuration sometimes allows the universal to be confirmed in a single observation. This happens when the field is suddenly cleared by an exit (<u>Everybody ran; and I was standing there</u>) or when the field is blank to begin with (compare <u>Nobody came</u> to <u>Nobody left</u>).

(26) They ain't nobody to take him up on it [her husband Charlie's offer to go fishing].

Since Charlie is not going fishing, it is clear that no one has appeared. Sentences like this have the highest probability of a strict interpretation, since they are the most easily confirmed. Because they are relatively rare in the data, they will be merged with the following class of known quantities.

[9] Known. The set to be observed is a known quantity.

The most common examples of such known quantities are the speaker's children, members of a team or a jury. Families as a whole are usually defined more loosely.

(27a) He gets in on time for us all to go to wrestlin' on Friday night, and we go.
(27b) Yeh, they all [the children] went to fishin'.
(27c) Now all my kids go t' water but not me.
(27d) An' every one o' my kids turned back [changed their denominations].

The likelihood of a strict interpretation here is almost as high as in the preceding case.

[10] Denumerable. The quantity of observations to be made is not known, but it could be enumerated.

(28a) I go every Friday night.
(28b) He tries to see Mama goes somewhere every week.
(28c) He'll bite, but he won't marry, marry no girl.
(28d) He had his head sewed up about 4, 5 times; go swimmin', he'll go swimmin', an' he gets his head cut ever' time he goes.

The high frequency of these nondenumerable observables is partly the result of a rhetorical process that introduces universal quantifiers in situations that logically might call for only simple declarative statements. Louise Adams shows this tendency more than most speakers. When I asked her what diapers she used, she responded with (28f), and (28g-28l) followed in quick succession.

(28f) That's all we ever had back 'en.
(28g) You never heard o' Pampers 'til after.
(28h) That's all I ever used.
(28i) That's all I ever did for my kids.
(28j) They never w's bothered with it [diaper rash].
(28k) I always changed 'em.
(28l) I don' remember non o' my kids bein'--what you'd say real sick.

Though (28a-28l) vary in likelihood, they may in general be considered less likely to receive a strict interpretation than those utterances that could be more easily confirmed.

This classification presumes that listeners and speakers are possessed of a sense of fact. Up to this point, there has been no evidence to support this idea. The following has been established for Louise Adams:

1. The variety of interpretations required for universal quantifiers is considerable.
2. There are many sentences where the loose interpretation is required.
3. There are many sentences where the choice between loose and strict interpretation is not easily made.
4. Though sentences vary in the probability of strict interpretation, the only sentences where the strict interpretation is required are those where it is denied.

Section 5 advances indirect evidence that speakers and listeners are alert to the categories that suggest an empirical basis for the choice of strict and loose interpretations.

5. The distribution of intensity. The categorization of quantifiers by the local context has established that in about one-third of our cases, strict quantification would not make sense; in another third, the difference between strict and loose interpretation would be impossible to decide by objective means; and in most of the remaining third, disproof by counterexamples is possible, but positive confirmation is not. It now remains to explore the relevance of these categories to intensity.

Some of the conventional uses of quantifiers are invariant in respect to intensity. The approximants <u>and everything,</u> <u>and all,</u> <u>and anything like that</u> are unstressed and never signal intensity in themselves. Limiting expressions that deny universality also act as deintensifiers: <u>I don't eat everything comes in the house.</u> Certain minimizing expressions use universal quantifiers, as in <u>That's all,</u> normally deintensifying.

On the other hand, adverbial quantifiers like <u>all ruined</u> are uniformly intensive, along with a number of fixed intensifying expressions, e.g. <u>Every time I turn around, all of a sudden.</u>[17] Intensity seems to be heavily concentrated in certain conventional expressions that do not permit strict interpretation, particularly the nonliteral uses. It is true that intensity can be conveyed by universals that are marked for strict interpretation, such as <u>every single one of,</u> and <u>absolutely all of.</u> Yet the use of quantifiers as markers of intensity seems more likely when the loose intepretation is more likely.

Given the loose interpretation, one can ask: why was <u>every</u> used in place of <u>most,</u> <u>all</u> in place of <u>almost all</u>? This choice may be motivated by the fact that <u>every</u> and <u>all</u> can also signal intensity. Given a great likelihood of loose interpretation, a universal quantifier may be assigned the intensive feature even when no other markers of intensity are present.

Since marks of intensity usually cluster, it should be possible to confirm this notion by plotting the frequency of other marks of intensity in combination with universal quantifiers:

prosodic contrast: stress on the quantifier beyond that predictable from phrase and sentence structure; also laughter.
negative concord: the incorporation of negative particles in indeterminates <u>any,</u> <u>ever,</u> <u>either</u> following the first negative of the sentence.[18]
adverbs of intensity: <u>really</u> and other adverbs of intensity with scope including the universal quantifier.[19]
repetition: usually in the form of the repetition of whole clauses in rapid succession.
inversion: shift of placement of the quantifier from its normal position after the first tensed member of the auxiliary: <u>I never will forget this.</u>

Figure 1 shows the distribution of the other marks of intensity that accompany the 100 universal quantifiers of Louise Adams. Slightly more than a third are Unobservables: these show the highest concentration of intensifiers. A little more than a quarter are Observables. The known class is too small to be shown by itself, and it is combined with the denumerable class, so that Observables are divided into only two types. Of these the largest part are nondenumerable, with a low frequency of intensifiers, and even lower are the smaller denumerable group. The conventional uses, with fixed interpretations, show an intermediate range of intensifiers.

The numerical values are given in Table 1, along with the numbers for all other diagrams to follow.

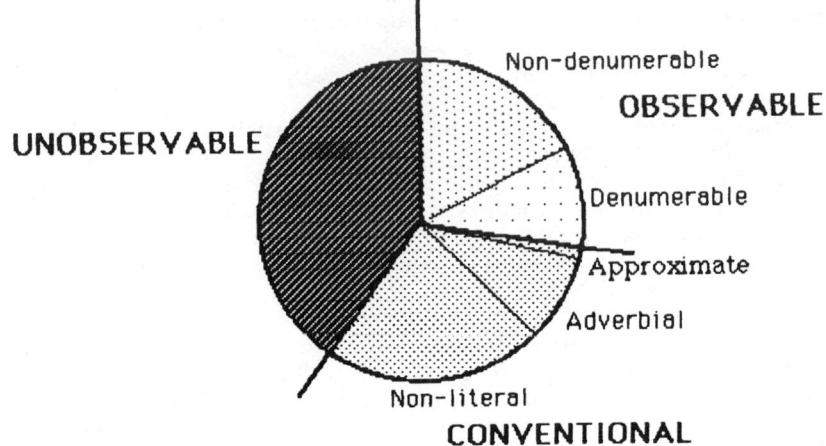

Fig. 1. Per cent markers of intensity accompanying universal quantifiers: Louise Adams, Knoxville, TE [N = 100]

■ 91- ▨ 51-90 ▦ 26-50 ▨ 11-25 ░ 1-10 □ 00

Table 1. Distribution of quantifier classes and accompanying marks of intensity for five English speakers.

	L. Adams	J. Lynch	S. Romano	A. P.	M. Beachy
Conventional:					
Limiter	0/2/1	0/1/3	0/22	0/18/5	0/1
Unique	1/1	0/0	0/0	0/0	0/0
Approximate	1/1	0/20	0/1	0/1	0/0
Adverbial	4/5	5/23	0/16	0/4/1	0/11/5
Nonliteral	8/8/1	7/7	14/19	0/6	0/0
Unobservable:					
Self-defined	3/0	2/0	3/1	0/2/1	0/1
Opinion	25/8/3	11/8	13/30/2	2/8/15	4/3/6
Observable:					
Single	1/0	2/4	0/1	0/4/1	0/1
Known	0/4	0/0	2/5	0/14/1	1/0
Denumerable	1/5/1	0/5	0/5	0/6/2	0/2/1
Nondenumerable	3/13	7/18	11/14	1/3/11	1/2/5
Totals	47/47/6	34/86/3	43/114/2	3/66/37	3/25/11
N:	100	123	159	106	44
% intensified	47	28	27	03	14
% deintensified	06	02	01	35	39

x/y/(/z) = intensified/not intensified (/deintensified).

There is evidently a firm relation between Louise Adams' use of intensifiers and the probability of loose or strict interpretation for the listener. The more likely the strict interpretation of the universal quantifiers, the less likely it is that she will use other intensifiers. It follows that the more likely the strict interpretation, the less likely that the listener will interpret the quantifier as an intensifier itself.

The pattern of Figure 1 is not idiosyncratic to Louise Adams: it is characteristic of almost all of the speakers I have examined so far. Figure 2 shows the corresponding distributions for two older white Philadelphia working-class men. Jim Lynch is a retired stevedore and factory worker from Kensington in North Philadelphia; Stanley Romano is a barber from the central area of South Philadelphia.[20]

Lynch shows a much heavier use of adverbial all than Adams (all over, all the way up, all around); a greater use of approximates like anything else, or anything; and a more limited use of quantifiers in opinions. The Unobservable area is considerably reduced: Lynch does not express a great many opinions with universal quantifiers. Romano, on the other hand, uses roughly the same proportion of Unobservables and nonliteral quantifiers as Louise Adams, but shows a sizeable number of limiting forms: these are mostly the expression that's all.

These differences in the distribution of the quantifiers are relatively superficial differences in personal style and lexical choice. The constant features of the quantifier distributions are: (1) Observables account for only about one-quarter of the data; (2) of these, the greatest part are nondenumerables; and (3) nonliteral uses of quantifiers are quite frequent.

The distribution of intensifiers for Lynch and Romano is basically the same as for Adams. The heaviest use of intensifiers is with Unobservables; next among the Observables are the nondenumerables; and least, the denumerable types. This is the ordering that relates intensity to observability. There is some variation in the amount of intensity associated with the nonliteral forms: with Lynch it is as high as the Unobservables, and there is some fluctuation with the approximates. The only variation in the observability hierarchy is that for Romano: there is no greater use of intensity with Unobservables than with nondenumerables. Within the gross categories of intensity level established here, it appears that:

nonliteral
 = < Unobservable
  = > nondenumerable
   = > denumerable

These speakers appear to have a sense of fact. Their use of universal quantifiers to signal intensity is proportionate to the possibility of the statement being contradicted. Yet the dominant semantic of the universal quantifiers is the loose interpretation, as shown by the free use of nonliteral expressions that would be obviously false if the strict interpretation held; and by the heavy cooccurrence of universal quantifiers with other intensifiers in the majority of uses outlined by Figures 1 and 2.

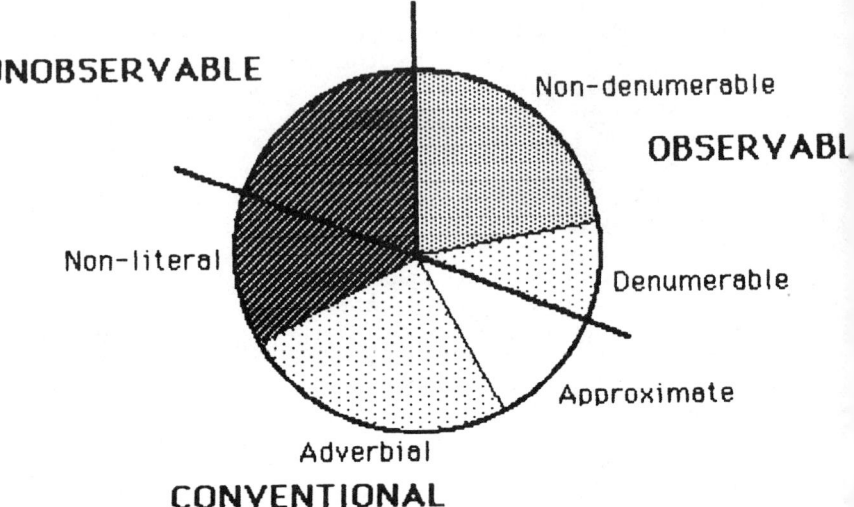

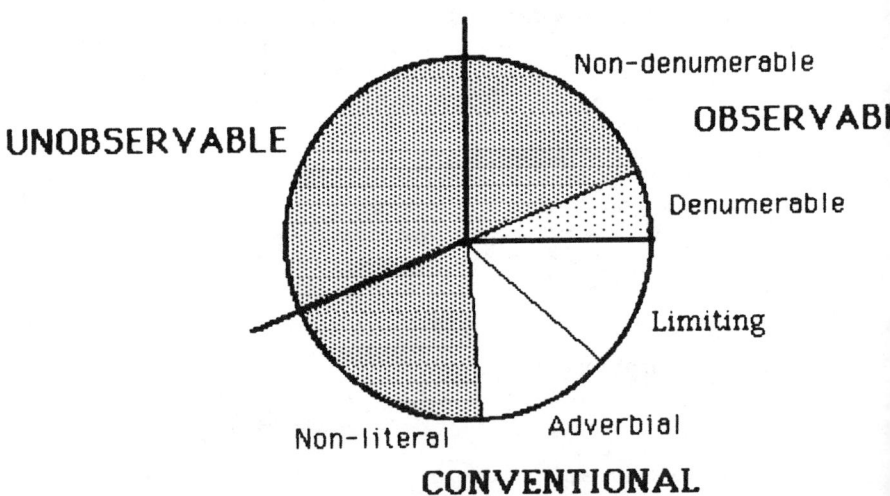

Fig. 2. Per cent markers of intensity accompanying universal quantifiers for two Philadelphia speakers

6. Exceptional speakers. This exploratory analysis of intensity is not intended as a sociolinguistic study of intensification and quantifiers throughout society. But it is evident that the pattern of quantifier use seen here is a part of the colloquial language. It is not confined to vernacular settings, but is used in spontaneous speech in relatively formal situations. The speakers studied here have been recorded in an interview format that sometimes approaches vernacular use (Labov 1984); but much of the speech produced would be classified as 'careful speech' in a thoroughgoing stylistic analysis.

A different pattern prevails in formal writing, where the balance of semantic interpretation tilts strongly toward the strict interpretation, and most of the conventional uses of the quantifiers are missing. There is therefore a strong stylistic constraint on the use of universal quantifiers to signal intensity, and on the loose interpretation. Whether or not there is social stratification remains to be seen. It may be that the pattern of Figures 1 and 2 is typical of all English vernaculars, no matter what the social level of the speaker. But it is not binding on all spontaneous speech. To examine the maximum variation, I turned to an older Philadelphian who is a dominant figure in the upper social stratum of the city.[21] A.P. was 65 years old, head of a family that has influenced Philadelphia social and economic life for many generations. He is a prominent lawyer, has taught law in universities, and has made policy in many of the social clubs that regulate the upper class social life of Philadelphia. His speech is archetypical of the pattern described by Kroch (1980): a conservative but relaxed Philadelphia phonology; a precise syntax with careful attention to logical distinctions but none of the intense concern with grammatical niceties that marks less secure speakers; and a strong tendency to intensify attributions with adverbs and a regressive accent: 'vastly higher', 'a very very small distance', 'a rather small child', 'perfectly satisfactory', 'completely local'.

In an hour of speech, A.P. used 106 universal quantifiers, much less than the rate of Lynch and Romano. The distribution by observability was quite different from the other speakers we have examined. There was about the same proportion of Unobservables (a third), but a greatly reduced proportion of conventional uses (a sixth) and a greatly expanded set of Observables. This expansion is entirely due to an increase in the number of known sets (18%). A.P. was quite conscious of his family connections, and referred to them quite often with universal quantifiers where others might have used simpler expressions: all four of my grandparents, None of the immediate family, my own children have, all three of them... Beyond the family relations, we find such constructions as three people all of whom already had their Ph.Ds.

Among the Conventional uses of the quantifiers, A.P. uses a few approximates and a small number of nonliteral uses (7%). In spite of his precise habits of speech, he occasionally uses nonliteral expressions that can only be heard as the loose interpretation of the quantifier, as shown in (29).

(29a) [Of an early relative] The girl who identified all the witches.

(29b)   They were interrelated as all the people in that county were.
(29c)   [Of the Betsy Ross Bridge] Nobody uses it.

A more profound difference between A.P.'s speech and the others is found in the use of intensifiers. There are only two clear cases in his speech, given in (30).

(30a)   None of the immediate family have any connections up there at all.
(30b)   [Of the use of any word other than nigger in the rhyme 'Eeny meeny miny mo'] Never, never gave it any--never would have occurred to any of us.

The absence of negative concord in A.P.'s speech accounts for a part of this effect. In Louise Adams' speech negative concord accounted for 15 of the 50 marks of intensity that accompanied universal quantifiers. If we subtract these, we are left with 35 intensifiers on her part as against 2 on his. We might also consider the occurrence of multiple indeterminates in A.P.'s speech as marks of intensity, since there is no contrast with negative concord. Multiple indeterminates are found in (30a, 30b) along with repetition, inversion, and the intensifier at all, and in two other cases, given in (31).

(31a)   I never had any trouble with that group.
(31b)   I don't think it ever did me any harm.

All four of these intensifiers are found in the Unobservable class. This confirms the conclusion drawn from A.P.'s use of nonliterals. He has available to him the same mechanism that other speakers use: intensification supporting the loose interpretation. He uses it much less often.

This similarity does not disguise a bigger difference between A.P. and the speakers of Figures 1 and 2: a great development of limiters. The other speakers occasionally weaken or limit the universal quantifiers by several different devices. The main assertion may be mitigated by I guess, I imagine, I think, etc. Louise Adams said:

(32)   I imagine ever' one o' them had t' take their turn there [on the front lines].

In example (33), Lynch modifies the claim that all of his friends were married with pretty near, which I take to mean that most of them were married, not that all were about to be married.

(33)   We were all pretty near married.

As noted, an adverb of intensity can be inserted within the scope of the quantifier. In example (34), Lynch uses an intensifier both without and within, strengthening and weakening the statement.

(34)   I never really got a real beating.

There are not many more examples of limiters in the speech of the first three persons studied. But there are 23 in the interview with A.P., in addition to many limiters that do not accompany universal quantifiers. There are many examples of mitigated assertions, as in (31b). We find a variety of other mitigating devices--adjectives, adverbs, and adverbial phrases--as indicated in example (35).

(35a) All the people from that peninsula have a little bit of that in varying degrees.
(35b) I never knew her entirely well.
(35c) Chestnut Hill Academy's never been a major factor for Harvard.
(35d) Over any period of time, it's pretty substantial.
(35e) We've never been able to reduce it quite to that.

It is not uncommon for the universal quantifier to be directly denied or restricted in a way that demands strict interpretation, as example (36) shows.

(36a) It's not an absolute or anywhere near it.
(36b) Every night or nearly every night.

A.P. often uses an accumulation of limiting devices:

(37a) until I figure nearly virtually until his death.
(37b) I don't think the instruction is necessarily any better.

Examples (31b) and (37b) show both mitigation and intensification. How these patterns combine is a nice problem for semantic calculation: the difficulty is probably no less for the native listener.

The study of intensity must then consider its obverse, the process of deintensification exemplified by these limiting devices. Figure 3 maps the distribution of deintensifying marks used by A.P. against the same classes of universal quantifiers that were used in Figures 1 and 2. The known class, which was combined with denumerables in the other diagrams, is here separated since the numbers are relatively large. The highest concentration of deintensifiers is found in the unobservable and nondenumerable classes of Observables. Fewer deintensifiers are found in the denumerable class, and even fewer in the known class. A.P.'s use of deintensifiers is parallel to the other speakers' use of intensifiers.

This similarity in pattern should not conceal the semantic opposition. The more likely the loose interpretation, the more likely is A.P. to deintensify it. This suggests that his basic definition of the universal quantifiers is the strict interpretation, and he takes care to avoid a loose interpretation by his listeners. In contrast, the other speakers use intensification to reinforce the probability of a loose interpretation as it becomes more probable. They take as target what A.P. takes as pitfall.

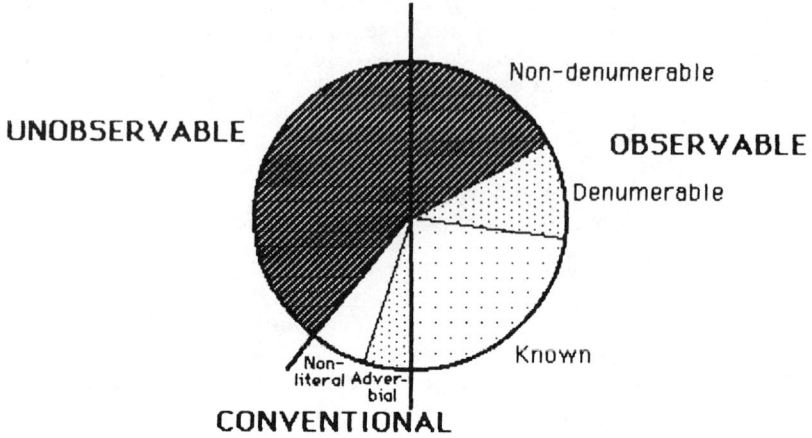

Fig. 3. Per cent markers of de-intensification with universal quantifiers: A.P., 72, Philadelphia [N = 106]

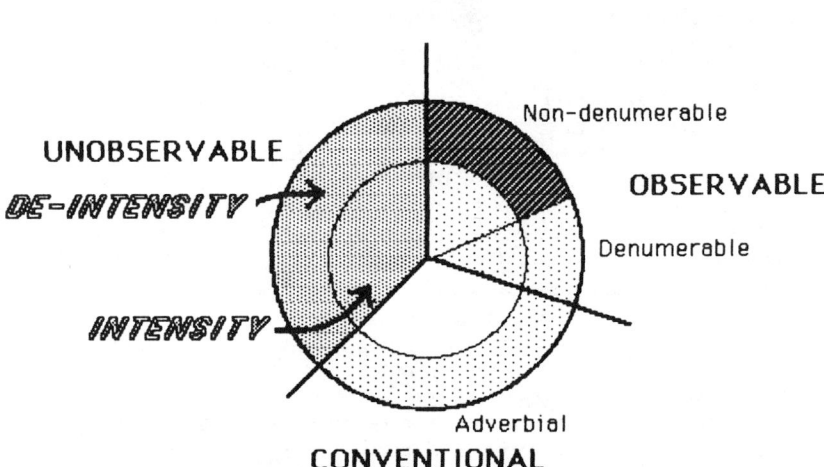

Fig. 4. Per cent markers of intensity and de-intensity with universal quantifiers: Morris Beachy, Iowa [N = 44]

The advanced education and high social status of A.P. might be thought to account for this reversal of semantic process. But this precision of speech and the preference for the strict interpretation is not limited to upper class speakers. For a second exceptional speaker, I turned to an interview with Morris Beachy, 65, from a small town in south central Iowa. Beachy had only a ninth grade education, and he came from a family of small farmers who were members of the Mennonite community which emigrated from Pennsylvania to Indiana and Illinois, and then to Iowa several generations ago. Beachy had followed his father in assuming the duties of bishop of the local Conservative Mennonite church. While he was more open and easygoing than A.P. in his surface manner, he shared with A.P. a long personal history of directing the affairs of others, and setting policies for organizations. He had an even stronger tendency to a judicious and guarded statement of his ideas and policies.

The distribution of Beachy's universal quantifiers was not so very different from the norm established by the first three speakers. He had the usual one-third of Unobservable sentence types, and one-third Observable, with the usual distribution of two-third nondenumerable and one-third denumerable. There was no expansion of the known category as with A.P. The most striking differences emerged in the Conventional area. Beachy did not use a single nonliteral form, and no approximates. All of the conventional forms are adverbial <u>all</u>, with a strong concentration on <u>at all</u>. The other major difference is quantitative: in more than an hour of free conversation, where Beachy spoke almost continuously, he used only 44 universal quantifiers.

The small number of intensifiers showed the usual distribution: mostly in the Unobservables, with fewer in the nondenumerable category, and even fewer in the denumerable category. Figure 4 shows this distribution in the central circle, and in the outer circle, the distribution of deintensifying devices. Beachy is particularly rich in this area. He used a great many nonuniversal quantifiers that are limited by definition, and qualified them even further, as shown in (38).

(38a) We pretty well would agree on basic doctrines, I think.
(38b) I think probably largely so, probably.
(38c) Most of our growth, and we've had some growth...
(38d) We emphasize that quite a little.
(38e) Not nearly as many as one time here.

As example (39) shows, Beachy qualifies most statements carefully, but he also intensifies them, often combining both intensifying and deintensifying devices.

(39a) I think it would be almost very very necessary.
(39b) ...most of our people, and I can speak only for our people, that I know real well...
(39c) I think that people may have that sometimes, I really do.
(39d) I don't suppose that I know a lot of people that really strongly believe that.
(39e) [On whether he knows everyone's church membership] Not quite. But there're not too many in the community that I'm not aware where they go to church at all.

The same combination of intensifiers and deintensifiers is found in statements with universal quantifiers, often with logical double negation.

    (40a)   I guess we've never really regretted...
    (40b)   There's some of that in all the Mennonite groups, really.
    (40c)   I can't say that it doesn't affect doctrine at all.

Some of these sentences include propositions reinforced by intensifiers, but the strengthened proposition is qualified even as it is strengthened. A paradigmatic example is:

    (41)   I'm not sure that's not true with <u>all</u> branches of Mennonites to some degree too.

These deintensifying practices of qualification and restriction suggest a strong orientation toward the strict interpretation of universal quantifiers. This comes to the fore in the exchange in example (42). Beachy made an intensified and unmitigated statement about the church's policy on television, which differentiated it from the most liberal sect.

    (42)   Our three churches, we have no television at all. It's been a church agreement <u>not</u> to have television.

This prompted me to ask if there were any exceptions, assuming the strict interpretation:

    W.L.:   No one has a television set in their homes?
    M.B.:   If they do, it's not known to me. I wouldn't say they are not--absolutely are not. There are not expected to be, but then...

Like A.P., Beachy behaves as if the strict interpretation were the unmarked meaning of the universal quantifiers.

7. Grammatical heterogeneity. The first three speakers examined here showed considerable similarity in their use of quantifiers and intensifiers. The fact that two other speakers showed radical differences should not suggest that the English speech community is evenly divided in this respect. The two exceptional speakers were picked because I expected them to be exceptional. They use a formal English that has many features in common with the written language. It is certainly speech, and there are undoubtedly many other people who talk this way. But these differences in the pattern of intensification and quantification may indicate an imperfect penetration of the vernacular language by patterns that are developed primarily in the written language.
    No mention has been made of the universal quantifier <u>each</u>, which has played a role in many recent linguistic analyses of quantifiers. <u>Each</u> illustrates the heterogeneous character of the grammar in a dramatic way. It is first of all an exception to the pattern of loose and strict interpretation, since it seems to have only the strict interpretation. There is also reason to think that the role of <u>each</u> in the spoken language

is quite limited. There are two occurrrences of <u>each</u> among the 500-odd quantifiers examined here: one is used by A.P., and the other by Morris Beachy.

I won't try to resolve here the problem of writing a realistic grammar of universal quantifiers. But if these exploratory studies of intensity have any significance, that problem must be high on our agenda. It will be hard to solve because the description must deal with the social conflict that is symbolized, and sometimes implemented, by the differential treatment of intensity and quantifiers. It remains to be seen whether we can describe language as it is, and not the way it is expected to be.

Notes

1. This paper is the latest in a series aimed at a description of language that recognizes social and emotional elements in the central components of linguistic structure. These included papers given at the Cognitive Science Society in 1981 ('On restricting the meaning of meaning'); the LSA in 1981 ('A sociolinguistic approach to problems of meaning'); at the University of Colorado ('Defining the meaning of meaning'); at Harvard in 1983 ('How things go together'). This is the first to be published, since I think it is the first that succeeds in building the empirical base that promises cumulative results.

I am indebted to many along the way for constructive and destructive criticism that led me to take down a number of formal models that are all too easy to put up: in particular for brief exchanges with George Lakoff, Charles Fillmore, Guy Carden, David Premack, and Michael Geis. I am grateful to Michael Silverstein for bringing to my attention Sapir's important work on quantifiers. The current version owes much to extended discussions with my colleagues Gillian Sankoff and Tony Kroch. Kroch's contributions are too many to enumerate, including many continued reservations that have made it plain to me that I have not yet got to wherever I am trying to get. Convergence with the work of T. Labov is evident throughout the paper: I am indebted to her for many observations which anticipated my own, and for corrections of many lapses of logic and detail.

2. There is a curious asymmetry of persons involved here. <u>I am angry</u> needs appropriate peripheral signals to be effective. But <u>He is angry</u> is not conveyed better by adding the prosodic signals of intensity, which are not easily transferred to third person objects but continue to refer to the state of the speaker. The same asymmetry applies to social information. A number of linguistic variables operate as claims to specific social identities of the speaker or the addressee, or as signals of accommodation to the addressee. But the social characteristics of the addressee can only be inferred indirectly and with much less certainty from the forms used by the speaker.

3. We will encounter some expressions with both markers of intensification and deintensification. Their position on the scale of intensity is indeterminate, since there is no way of assessing the quantitative value of such marks at present.

4. A pragmatic translation of <u>really</u> is not hard to find. We can say that <u>really</u> informs us that there are others who do not support the proposition that it modifies (that the proposition is a D-event in the

Labov and Fanshel 1977 terminology). The pragmatic periphrasis cannot be entirely satisfactory because it loses the emotional content expressed by intensity, shared by <u>very</u>, <u>actually</u>, <u>basically</u>, and <u>really</u>.

5. The Ripley interview was part of the Lower East Side study of New York City (Labov 1966). Dolly Ripley is a black woman, 46 years old in 1963, whose family was divided between a small town in North Carolina and New York City. In the midst of the interview, the telephone rang. I went into the next room and talked with her nephew, while she talked for 20 minutes with her cousin and her cousin's husband. She was wearing a lavaliere microphone and the Nagra tape recorder was turning in full view, but she unconsciously assumed that the interview situation had been transferred to the conversation in the next room.

6. Note that in (1c) the adverb is lowered to the infinitival complement, but the semantic interpretation normally assumed continues to apply to the matrix clause.

7. The formulation of a surreal grammatical category is difficult to justify on the basis of a semigrammaticalized form like <u>really</u>. In the Black English Vernacular, there are several elements of the grammatical system usually considered aspect markers which appear to have shifted into the mood system with the intensive feature as a major semantic element: <u>be</u>, <u>be done</u>, and (see further on) <u>done</u>.

8. Among the many variants of this intensifier, there are polite substitutions like <u>the heck</u>, and mitigated forms like <u>in heaven's name</u>, <u>in the world</u>. An alternant of <u>the hell</u> is <u>the devil</u>, with euphemistic variants like <u>the deuce</u> and <u>the dickens</u>. A common aggravated form is <u>what the fuck...</u>

9. Recorded by Teresa Labov in June 1971.

10. The term 'perfective' is now generally applied to aspect categories like the English present perfect, which are attached to actions that precede and condition following events of interest. The 'perfect' is used here in the conventional sense of a 'completed' action, viewed as a whole. It may be the prior condition for a present situation of interest, or the result of another event.

11. It is often possible to produce translations with the present perfect of other English dialects, since there is considerable overlap in the appropriateness of the meanings of 'current relevance' and 'completed'. But such translations are only accidental, and not possible in the examples of (9)-(11) to follow.

12. Interviewed by Wendell Harris as part of the NSF project on 'The influence of urban minorities on linguistic change'.

13. As for example, the associations of words tapped by the semantic differential procedure of Osgood, Suci, and Tannenbaum (1957). Though such associations may be reliable and replicable, no one would suggest that dictionaries add for each entry a rating on the dimensions of power, activity, and value.

14. T. Labov found many nonliteral uses of quantifiers in her data, e.g.: 'In other words, the second time you default you're thrown out as a working member, [laughter] and you will never work for the Co-op again...[laughter]' (1980:281). As she observes, the laughter indicates the listeners' recognition that <u>never</u> is an implausible use if taken literally. In this, as in the case of intensifying adverbs, 'it is often difficult to discover any literal contribution to the meaning'.

15. Louise Adams is a 42-year-old white woman, born and raised in Knoxville, Tennessee, of a middle working-class family. Her East Tennessee dialect is quite representative of the Appalachian English described by Wolfram and Christian (1975). She is an extremely voluble speaker, and uses more universal quantifiers than most. The 100 universal quantifiers analyzed in the next section were used in 20 minutes.

16. I owe this term to Guy Carden, together with other insights on the interpretation of quantifiers.

17. There are a large number of other constructions with <u>all</u> that show idiosyncratic properties. When <u>all</u> is the subject head of a relative clause, it can be a mitigating, deintensifying form, as in <u>All(s) I know is...</u>, or intensive in <u>All he wants to do is...</u> Exactly where <u>All I can is...</u> fits is hard to say.

18. It was noted earlier that intensity can be signaled by the implantation of the indeterminers <u>ever</u> and <u>any</u> in the sentence structure without negative concord. However, this is a much weaker signal than the negative concord itself, and it is therefore not counted for those speakers who do use negative concord. I am not sure how its effect should be estimated for speakers who do not.

19. When the adverb of intensity falls inside the scope of the universal quantifier, it has the opposite effect: of limiting the statement made by the quantifier. Compare <u>There really isn't any honor today</u> with <u>There isn't any real honor today.</u> The second intensifier falls within the scope of the quantifier and it can be heard as a modification or limitation of the first. See further on for the effects of such limitation.

20. Both speakers were interviewed by Anne Bower, as part of research on the social origins of sound change in Philadelphia, under a grant from NSF. Both use universal quantifiers quite freely, though not at the level of Louise Adams. While Adams produced the 100 quantifiers in 20 minutes, the 123 items summarized for Lynch, and the 159 for Romano, were used over the course of an hour.

21. Interviewed by Kroch in his study of the upper class of Philadelphia. Data from this series are incorporated in the study of the social origins of sound change (Labov et al. 1982, Labov 1984).

References

Baugh, John. 1979. Linguistic style-shifting in Black English. Unpublished dissertation, University of Pennsylvania.

Baugh, John. 1983. Black street speech: Its history, structure and survival. Austin: University of Texas Press.

De Groot, A. 1949. Structural linguistics and syntactic laws. Word 5.1-12.

Jespersen, Otto. 1924. The philosophy of grammar. London: Allen and Unwin.

Kroch, Anthony. 1980. Dialect and style in the speech of upper class Philadelphia. Paper given at Conference on Social Psychology and Language, Bristol, England.

Labov, Teresa. 1980. The communication of morality: Cooperation and commitment in a food cooperative. Unpublished dissertation, Columbia University.

Labov, William. 1966. The social stratification of English in New York City. Washington, D.C.: Center for Applied Linguistics.
Labov, William. 1972. Language in the inner city. Philadelphia: University of Pennsylvania Press.
Labov, William. 1984. Field methods of the project on linguistic change and variation. In: Language in use. Edited by J. Baugh and J. Sherzer. Englewood Cliffs, N.J.: Prentice-Hall.
Labov, W., A. Bower, E. Dayton, D. Hindle, T. Kroch, M. Lennig, and D. Schiffrin. 1980. The social determinants of sound change in Philadelphia. Philadelphia: U.S. Regional Survey.
Labov, William, and David Fanshel. 1977. Therapeutic discourse. New York: Academic Press.
Labov, WIlliam, and Joshua Waletzky. 1967. Narrative analysis. In: Essays on the verbal and visual arts. Edited by J. Helm. Seattle: University of Washington Press. 12-44.
Osgood, C. E., G. J. Suci, and P. H. Tannenbaum. 1957. The measurement of meaning. Urbana: University of Illinois Press.
Sapir, Edward. 1930. Totality. Language Monographs 6.
Thibault, Johanne. 1977. Les marqueurs d'intensité en français Montréalais. Master's essay, University of Montreal.
Wolfram, W., and D. Christian. 1976. Appalachian speech. Washington, D.C.: Center for Applied Linguistics.

ON SEMANTIC AND PRAGMATIC COMPETENCE

Michael L. Geis
The Ohio State University

0. Introduction. The manufacturer of an antiseptic product once ran a television advertisement saying that it

(1) ...gently penetrates skin injuries to kill germs that can cause infection, helps speed healing (CBS, July 18, 1978, 10:55 a.m.)[1]

This is a rather common kind of claim in contemporary advertising.[2] It is generic in form and seems to make a rather general claim about the efficacy of this product--call it 'P'--but it contains two so-called 'weasel words' (Stevens 1978), <u>can</u> and <u>help,</u> that are said to weaken claims substantially. Stevens (p. 75) claims, for instance, that 'by adding that one little word, <u>help,</u> in front, we can use the strongest language possible afterward', and that claims employing <u>can</u> are (p. 79) 'indicative of an ideal situation.' Even the phrase <u>penetrates skin injuries to kill germs</u> would be considered weak from a literalist perspective, for it would be said to be true even if P only sometimes penetrates skin injuries and only sometimes kills germs. In short, (1) would be considered as true even if P almost never works.

Interestingly, language scholars have taken a rather different view of generic sentences like (1), according to which they make relatively strong claims. Jackendoff (1972:309), for instance, has said that 'semantically, generic sentences resemble sentences with a universal quantifier,' claiming that (2) 'can be paraphrased by' (3).

(2) A rhinoceros eats small snakes.
(3) Every rhinoceros eats small snakes.

In his introductory logic text, Thomason (1970:158) notes that generic sentences are 'very tricky and treacherous,' and then says (p. 170) that a generic sentence like (4) means that '<u>most</u> carrots are good to eat, or

71

that <u>almost all</u> carrots are good to eat' (his emphasis), or that '<u>as a rule</u>, any carrot is good to eat' (his emphasis).

(4)   Carrots are good to eat.

Thus, while Stevens would say that (1) could be true if P almost never kills infection-causing germs, Jackendoff and Thomason would say that (1) cannot be true unless P almost always succeeds in killing infection-causing germs. More recently, Carlson (1979) has provided an explicit, model-theoretic semantic analysis of generics which accords well with the views of Thomason and Jackendoff.

A language must be a peculiar thing indeed to succor such radically different theories of generics. In fact, of course, the problem lies not with English but with differences in theories of sentence meaning. If one takes the position that the truth conditions of sentences must be stated without reference to context (except for indexical expressions, of course), then the literalist view of the meaning of (1) must be correct. In this view, no generic sentence is stronger than the weakest generic sentence, for all must have the same truth conditions. However, this literalist theory of sentence meaning cannot be correct. As Carlson (1979) notes, the truth conditions of pairs like (1) and (5) must be rather different.

(5)   John Jones executes criminals for the state of California.

We might say that (5) would be true even if John Jones has done his job only once or twice, but we would not say that (1) is true if P has killed only one or two infection-causing germs. Thus, the assumption that the truth-conditions of generic sentences can be defined independently of context is clearly wrong.

The narrow truth-conditional approach to a sentence like (1) is wrong in a still deeper way. Sentence (1) is uttered by way of making an offer, an offer to sell a product which is intended by the advertiser to be used by the consumer to satisfy two consumer needs: chemical protection from infection and as speedy a recovery as is possible. Surely, this also is important to an understanding of a sentence like (1).

Most linguists would say, I think, that the truth-conditional meaning of (1), and the fact that it is being used to make an offer, both have a bearing on how (1) is interpreted. The Standard Theory (see Gazdar 1979) is, in fact, that the full meaning of an utterance is a function of the truth conditions of the sentence uttered and such pragmatic considerations as speech act felicity conditions (Austin 1965, Searle 1969), rules of cooperative conversation (Grice 1975), politeness conventions (R. Lakoff 1977), widely accepted factual premises (Boër and Lycan 1976) and context, etc.[3] On this view, the fact that (1) is uttered by way of making an offer is crucial to its interpretation.

Although this Standard Theory of sentence meaning is very widely accepted today, at least in principle, by both pragmaticists and semanticists (see Barwise and Perry 1983), I am reliably informed that it has very little currency in legal circles. Lawyers tend to take the same literalist view of meaning as did Stevens. They, in fact, are surely the source of it. If this Standard Theory of sentence meaning is the correct one, then we should get the story out, for if we do not, the literalist perspective of sentence meaning will continue to dominate in legal contexts, especially in regard to the issue of what advertising claims actually do claim.

In this paper, I propose to do this by arguing that the literalist theory of sentence meaning fails, not just because it makes incorrect predictions about how people will interpret sentences like (1), which it does, but, more fundamentally, because it assumes something false about human linguistic competence, namely, that logically untutored people have some sort of substantive logical capacity. So I have a practical goal, but I have theoretical and methodological aims as well. I argue that truth-conditional semantics is to some degree based on this same false assumption about human linguistic competence, and I then discuss the implications of this fact for an empirically substantive theory of sentence understanding by logically naive speakers.

1. Validity judgments. Logicians, philosophers of language, and linguists would agree with Davidson (1967), I think, that an adequate description of the meaning of sentence (6) should account for the fact that utterance of (6) commits the speaker to the truth of (7a-c).

(6) John buttered the toast with a knife in the bathroom at midnight.
(7a) John did something at midnight.
(7b) John used a knife to butter his toast.
(7c) John was in the bathroom at midnight.

During the heyday of generative semantics, many linguists and some philosophers of language took the line, made most explicit by Harman (1972), that the deep structure or semantic representation of a sentence should be its logical form, that it should be such that it accounts for what inferences are and are not entailed by the sentence.[4] On this view, a correct description of the meaning of (6) should account for the fact that it commits the speaker to the truth of (7a-c). I would heartily agree with this particular claim. However, I would like to question whether or not, in general, speakers of natural languages have the semantic competence presumed by this truth-conditional approach to sentence meaning. I believe and argue that the answer to this is 'no', and that we must to some degree rethink the intellectual foundations of semantics and pragmatics as well as certain of our methodological assumptions in these areas. I also draw out some practical consequences of my views for a theory of truth in advertising and for teaching reasoning in the schools.

Doing truth-conditional semantics presumes the capacity somehow to discriminate valid from invalid inferences. However, making validity judgments is sometimes anything but a trivial intellectual feat. As Partee (1982) has noted in connection with belief-sentences, it is sometimes very difficult for even the most sophisticated speakers to make sound synonymy judgments. And, while most would readily assent to the view that (6) entails (7a-c), do we as readily assent that (8a) and (8b) are synonymous (i.e. entail each other), or that (9a) and (9b) are synonymous, or that (10a) entails (10b)?

(8a)   If you open the refrigerator, it won't explode.
(8b)   If you open the refrigerator, then it won't explode.
(9a)   I will leave if you don't leave.
(9b)   I will leave unless you leave.
(10a) If Boris had gone to the party, Olga would have gone.
(10b) If Olga had not gone to the party, Boris would not have gone.

I hope that we would not assent to these judgments, for they are quite wrong.[5]

It should be clear that judgments of validity are not always quickly and easily made. They often require substantial imagination (to construct an illuminating possible world or situation to test the sentences against) as well as reasoning (to sort out whether the pertinent sentences or propositions are true or are false of these possible worlds or situations). Now, if the validity judgments of semanticians are to serve as the data for descriptions of the semantic competence of ordinary speakers of language, then we must provide some explanation of how ordinary speakers might acquire this semantic competence. The question is: can native speakers of the many languages of the world be assumed to have a substantive, validity-based reasoning capacity (i.e., a mental logic) which they employ in learning and using their languages?[6]

In 1982, Johnson-Laird published a very important paper called 'Thinking is a skill' (Johnson-Laird 1982b). In it he considered the question whether or not we have a mental logic and gave three arguments against saying we do. The first is that people, to a very striking degree, are unable to perform well on certain 'easy' reasoning tasks. Suppose you have four cards put in front of you on the faces of which you see the symbols 'E', 'K', '4', and '7', and you are told to test the following hypothesis by turning over as few cards as possible:

(11)   If a card has a vowel on one side, then it has an even number on the other.

Interestingly, in several experiments involving 128 subjects, only five got the correct answer.[7]

Johnson-Laird's second argument against the 'doctrine of mental logic' is that people are rather imperfect at syllogistic reasoning tasks. Given sentences (12) and (13), some 'highly intelligent' university students were asked to identify what conclusions (from those in (14)) could validly be drawn from these premises.

(12)   All of the beekeepers are artists.
(13)   None of the chemists are beekeepers.

(14a) None of the chemists are artists.
(14b) None of the artists are chemists.
(14c) Some of the chemists are not artists.
(14d) Some of the artists are not chemists.
(14e) None of the above.

None got it right.[8]

More recently, Rips (1983) has reported on an interesting research program in which people's deductive abilities are tested and evaluated with respect to a computer model of propositional reasoning employing a natural deduction system. Rips reports an overall success rate by subjects in making validity determinations of about 50%, with actual success rates ranging from about 17% to 92%. So, given (15), subjects were asked to say whether or not (16) could validly by deduced.[9]

(15) If Mary goes to Boston, then Sue will go to New York.
(16) If Mary goes to Boston and Sandy goes to Chicago, then Sue will go to New York.

In this case, 58% got the correct answer.

Rips appears to assume that we have a perfect mental logic but that we are not very reliable in using it. He assumes that errors result from the failure to retrieve inference rules, the failure to recognize the applicability of a rule, or the failure to apply a rule correctly. Johnson-Laird notes that others (Henle 1962) who believe in the doctrine of mental logic are inclined to account for errors in reasoning by saying that they result from misunderstanding or forgetting premises or bringing in irrelevant or unwarranted information, or the like. One clearly pays a very high empirical price for hypothesizing that we do have a mental logic.

Saying that we have a substantive validity-based reasoning capacity, but that we are very often unable to use it properly, is empirically empty unless an empirically motivated, predictive theory of how it is that we go wrong is provided,[10] for instead of giving us reliable empirical evidence supporting the doctrine of mental logic, it offers a blanket excuse for every past or future failure to demonstrate the existence of this capacity. There is an alternative--that we have a nonlogical system of reasoning (i.e. one without a substantive validity detection capacity), perhaps along the lines of Johnson-Laird (1982a, 1982b), and that we are relatively good at using this. A priori, I believe this more positive approach to reasoning to be superior, for it offers the possibility of a more principled account of reasoning than does the mental logic theory.

Johnson-Laird's third argument against the doctrine of mental logic is that it is very hard to understand how we could have come by it in the natural state. Could it be learned from experience? Given the manifest inability of humans to reason reliably in experimental studies, how can we assume that children will see enough positive examples of valid reasoning from their parents and others to extract this abstract mathematical knowledge from experience? There is, of course, the logical possibility that this wondrous 'gift', a gift we don't seem to be able to use very well, is innate. However, as Johnson-Laird has said (1982b:10), 'positive arguments that the ability to reason is innate are as hard to come by as positive arguments that it arises from divine intervention.'

Johnson-Laird concludes that reasoning is learned and is a skill and that some people do it better than others. This seems to square rather well with the facts. In Geis (1982), I took the line, based in part on earlier work by Wason and Johnson-Laird (1972), that if we do not control the concept of validity as reasoners, then it would be unreasonable to assume that we have control of this concept as language learners and language users. The question arises, for instance, as to how children might come to be able to make the sorts of semantic distinctions that are discovered by linguists through our validity judgments. Some linguists will, of course, claim that we have an innate capacity to make just the sorts of distinctions that are required to develop a full-blown truth-conditional semantic competence in a language. Moreover, some of these linguists might say, to avoid the thrust of Johnson-Laird's arguments, that this validity detection capacity is highly dedicated to language. Fodor's (1983) theory of mental faculties would appear to lend credibility to the thesis that this or that ability could be dedicated specifically to language and thus be unavailable in other mental domains. However, before we say that we have an innate validity detection device highly dedicated to language, which vanishes whenever we test for it, we must first show that we have a validity detection device in the first place. I argue that we have no such device.

The question is: do speakers have a conscious or unconscious, explicit or implicit, capacity to somehow distinguish valid from invalid inferences? Interestingly, as we have noted, even logically sophisticated speakers sometimes have difficulty making validity judgments. What can we say about the capacities of logically untutored speakers? Fox and I (cf. Geis and Fox 1984) have run an experiment on a large number of subjects in which we attempted to determine people's abilities to make validity judgments about pairs of sentences. What we have learned is that significant percentages of people are unable to distinguish valid from invalid inferences when the latter are sustained by speech act felicity conditions and generalized conversational implicatures. Sixty percent of our subjects voted (cf. Geis and Zwicky 1971), for instance, that (17) warrants (18).

(17) I'll give you 5 bucks if you mow the lawn.
(18) I won't give you 5 bucks if you don't mow the lawn.

Of course, they are wrong truth conditionally, but they would not be wrong conversationally (cf. Boër and Lycan 1973) in many of the circumstances in which (17) might be uttered. In a stunning demonstration of the strength of generic claims, we found that 58% of our subjects incorrectly said (19a) entails (19b).

(19a) ABC paint contains water-repelling oils.
(19b) ABC paint doesn't absorb water.

Sixty-four percent of our subjects incorrectly claimed that (20a) entails (20b).

(20a) ABC filters remove bacteria from your drinking water.
(20b) If you use ABC filters, your drinking water should be free of bacteria.

And 82% of our subjects incorrectly said (21a) entails (21b).

(21a) John can solve algebra problems.

(21b) If John is given an algebra problem, he'll probably be able to solve it.

It is clear from this that generic claims are construed as very strong claims and (contra Stevens) <u>can</u> does not weaken claims. Indeed, it seems to be a kind of intensifier.

These results obviously do not show that people have no truth-conditional capacities. What they show is that even in an explicitly truth-conditional task, people have great difficulty distinguishing between entailments and inferences that are warranted by general pragmatic considerations. In naturalistic circumstances (e.g. watching television), they will be all the more likely to draw these sorts of inferences, of course.

The fact that conscious validity judgments are unreliable doesn't prove that we do not have a validity detection device. Much of language comprehension is the result of some sort of automatic unconscious activity. Perhaps our validity detection capacity operates at an unconscious level. Certainly, the recognition of the validity of some inferences--recall (6) and (7)--is virtually automatic. Against the view that we exhibit unconscious control of the validity-invalidity distinction in language comprehension are three facts. First, as Morgan (1978) has ably demonstrated, some nonlogical inferences are also automatic. Morgan would say that recognition that (22) is a request requires no calculation.

(22) Could you take out the garbage?

Second, there is much evidence that people go for the 'gist' of a sentence (cf. Loosen 1981 and references therein) rather than for its literal meaning in comprehension. Third, there is much evidence (cf. Harris, Dubitsky, and Bruno 1983 and references therein) that people don't always distinguish assertions from inferences (including invalid inferences) in comprehension tasks. In an experiment by Brewer (1977), for instance, more people, on being exposed to (23a), recalled the inference (23b) than recalled (23a) itself.

(23a) The safecracker put a match to the fuse.
(23b) The safecracker lit the fuse.

Thus, we may safely conclude that we do not exhibit a conscious or unconscious control of the validity-invalidity distinction in language comprehension.

Might we exhibit an otherwise unconfirmed control of the validity-invalidity distinction in speech production, as opposed to speech perception? I think not. Speech production, viewed truth-conditionally, is extraordinarily simpler than speech comprehension. The advertising copywriter who constructs a sentence like (1) isn't necessarily linguistically cleverer than the consumer who might be fooled by it. The reason the copywriter may seem more clever is that going from facts to sentences is easy. But imagining all of the ways in which this kind of claim might deceive takes real imagination. Thus, I can see no reason to believe that speech production presumes semantically more sophisticated abilities than does speech comprehension.

Finally, let's consider the question of origins. The supposition that we might be able to acquire a full-blown (albeit tacit) notion of validity as an automatic concomitant of language acquisition is very hard to believe. What we learn when we learn language is that we must become inference drawers, that we must draw inferences of all sorts--inferences warranted by what words seem to mean, by felicity conditions, by rules of conversation, by background knowledge, by politeness conventions, by the multifarious aspects of context, and by extraordinarily varied combinations of all of the above. Many of these inferences that we draw in ordinary life are not valid, of course, and no one is there to discriminate those that are valid from those that aren't in any usefully systematic way, either as we learn or as we use our languages. Thus, it is very difficult to see how we could acquire a validity-invalidity distinction as a by-product of acquiring language.

2. **Methodological implications.** There is solid empirical evidence that logically naive people do not control the validity-invalidity distinction consciously, and there is evidence that this distinction does not play a role in ordinary speech comprehension. Theoreticians regularly respond at this point by noting that we linguists often assume the existence of tacit linguistic competences that speakers don't explicitly know about. Speakers may not reliably identify what is and is not a noun phrase, but this does not mean that speakers do not have a tacit knowledge of what is and is not a noun phrase. The problem is that this putative parallel between syntax and semantics is quite specious.

The primary data for syntax come from grammaticality judgments, many of which come from syntacticians themselves rather than from naive informants. This is warranted, at least partially, by the following facts about syntactic judgments:

(24) SYNTAX JUDGMENTS
(24a) Grammaticality judgments are normally automatic in character.
(24b) Grammaticality judgments presume no special skills beyond the capacity to distinguish between two types of automatic judgments--grammaticality judgments and meaningfulness judgments.
(24c) We linguists do not get better at grammaticality judgments to any significant degree over time.
(24d) Our grammaticality judgments are not substantially more reliable than are those of syntactically naive speakers. Indeed, field workers routinely rely on such speakers exclusively for data.

Compare these properties with those of validity judgments.

(25) SEMANTIC JUDGMENTS
(25a) Validity judgments are often not automatic, but, instead, require reasoning--sometimes very sophisticated reasoning.[11]

(25b) Validity judgments presume analytical, essentially logical skills, e.g. the skill to construct model-theoretic counter-examples.
(25c) We obviously get better at making validity judgments with experience.
(25d) We linguists are very much better at making validity judgments than are logically naive speakers.

Now, facts (24a-d) tend to justify empirically our use of our own intuitions in research in syntax, at least to some degree; however, facts (25a-d) render our use of our validity judgments empirically quite suspect in semantic studies. Semanticists who want to say that they are studying the semantic competence of speakers of the languages of the world must come up with some sort of empirical justification for their data collection practices.

In my view, sentence-interpretation is partly automatic (see Fodor 1983) and partly a skill--simply listening or listening with a critical ear--depending on what sort of linguistic activity we are engaged in.[12] And I believe that our mental lexical representations are formed for use in the automatic mode and, thus, consist of truth conditions or meaning postulates that stipulate in a relatively narrow way the 'easy' entailments these words sustain.[13] Thus we will acquire a truth condition (or equivalent meaning postulate) for <u>if</u> saying that 'If P, <u>then</u> Q' is true if P is true and Q is true, and false if P is true and Q is false, but not the more elaborate one according to which 'If P, then Q' is true if and only if P is true and Q is true or P is false.

Interestingly, semanticists have the feeling that when they discover some novel aspect of the truth conditions of some class of sentences they are literally discovering something, something that is already in their heads. I believe that it would be a mistake to take this impression very seriously. I would argue that truth-conditional semantics is a study of the truth-conditional limits of languages, and, thus, that semanticists are not necessarily discovering what is already in their heads, but are discovering what would be in their heads were they fully to develop their semantic competence. An analogy will help make this point clear. If a photographer unknowingly underexposes a piece of negative film and does not compensate by overdeveloping the negative, a thin negative will result, with perhaps only the scene's highlights being easily recognized. This unprintable negative can be enhanced through chromium intensification, a process whereby chromium is deposited on existing grains of silver. The result is sometimes printable. Note that this enhanced image was not there before intensification, but the resulting image was constrained by what was there. In such a way do the semanticists discover--I would say develop (to alter the photographic metaphor slightly)--the truth-conditional limits of their language knowledge.

Some will say that I have gone wrong because I have not made a sentence-utterance distinction. As I've noted, the standard view is that utterance meaning is a function of truth-conditional sentence meaning and contextual pragmatic considerations--as if sentence meaning bears the same kind of relationship to utterance meaning as phonemes do to allophones. I believe that this view is fundamentally mistaken. Gazdar (1979) notes that sometimes truth conditions cannot be defined without reference to pragmatic considerations, that semantics is, in fact, not autonomous of pragmatics. Let us reconsider how this might apply to a sentence like (26), and thus, to (1).

(26) P kills infection-causing germs.

I believe we would say that (26) could happily occur as an assertion in a Food and Drug Administration study of the efficacy of various antiseptics if P proved to kill only five percent of infection-causing germs. But, when a claim like (26) occurs in an advertisement, as in (1), it is being used as supporting argument for an offer to sell P to those consumers who need protection from infection-causing germs. In this case, the pertinent truth condition for (26), and thus (1), is that it is true if and only if it kills a sufficiency of infection-causing germs in conditions of normal use to protect consumers from infection.[14] It must kill enough germs to satisfy the sincerity condition on offers (see Bach and Harnish 1982) that the speaker have a warranted belief that his action, service, or product, etc. will satisfy the hearer need or desire that occasions the offer. In short, the truth-conditions of (26) depend crucially on the speech act it is used to perform--a simple assertion or an assertion used to entice a consumer to accept a commercial offer.

3. Practical implications. In my view, standards of truth in advertising should be based on actual, rather than ideal speaker linguistic abilities and, thus, I would argue that the narrow legalistic truth-conditional theory of sentence meaning must be abandoned by those entrusted to protect the public interest in favor of a holistic, pragmatically based view. I believe also that what I have said forces us to the view that a genuinely empirical theory of language understanding must be based on experimentally sound data gathered from theoretically (including logically) naive speakers. It will not do to use ourselves as informants: we know too much about logic and too little about human behavior. I believe, for these reasons, that pragmatics itself must also be based on naive informant judgments, not ours. Pragmatic judgments are not 'right' or 'wrong' in the sense in which validity judgments are.

What, though, of semantic studies in which data are derived from introspective validity judgments? Clearly, whether or not one sentence entails another is an empirical matter, and semanticists are better than most at making such judgments. I said earlier that truth-conditional semantics is a study of the truth-conditional limits of our language. It is, I believe, the study of the principles of valid reasoning with sentences. It is my impression that much, if not most, serious reasoning is done in connection with sentences, whether these are embedded in advertising, in a political debate, in newspaper reports, in textbooks, or in scholarly papers, etc., and I believe that people's ability to reason could be significantly improved were we to provide students with natural language semantic training, perhaps coupled with grammatical training. People need to be able to reason successfully with generic sentences, with conditional sentences (including counterfactuals), with nominalizations, and so on. Let us not, however, take this kind of truth-conditional semantic analysis of English as an empirically correct theory of what is already in the semantic part of the average speaker's head, or as an empirically correct theory of how utterances should be understood in conversation or in any other naturalistic context, e.g. watching a television advertisement.

Notes

I am indebted to my colleagues Robert Fox, Wayne Cowart, David Dowty, Robert Kraut, Brian Joseph, John Nerbonne, George Schumm, and Arnold Zwicky for their comments on the views presented here.

1. I do not mention the product name, for I don't want what I say about the language of (1) to be taken as a comment on the quality of this product.

2. There are 1984 Listerine advertisements that use very similar language, saying (if my short-term memory can be relied on) that the product 'kills the germs that can cause plaque' and 'kills the germs that can cause bad breath.' Right Guard advertisements of late February 1984 assert (same qualification) that this product 'kills the germs that can cause perspiration odor.' I suspect lawyers tell advertisers to put can in claims like these to render them too weak to be assailed, which is Stevens' (1978) view. This 'theory' of can is very far from the truth. See note 14.

3. Gazdar (1979:2) says 'PRAGMATICS = MEANING - TRUTH CONDITIONS,' but notes in his last chapter that truth-conditions sometimes appear not to be statable without reference to pragmatic conditions and, thus, that semantics may not be autonomous of pragmatics. I argue for this point of view in connection with sentence (1).

4. Though generative semantics is no longer with us, linguists continue to presume that it is sensible to talk about a linguistic level of logical form (see Gueron and May 1984, Bosque and Moreno 1984, or Solan 1984, for example). Just how substantive a logic is presumed in these cases is not wholly clear, to say the least.

5. As Davis (MS) has argued, (8a) is true of normal refrigerators, but (8b) would appear to be true only of refrigerators rigged to explode unless opened. In Geis (1973), I showed (using Lycan's 1984 paraphrases instead of my original ones) that (9a) and (9b) differ, as do (i) and (ii).

(i) I will leave in any situation in which you don't leave.
(ii) I will leave in any situation other than one in which you don't leave.

Lewis (1973:35) argues against the view that (10a) entails (10b), reasoning thus: 'Suppose that Boris wanted to go, but stayed away solely in order to avoid Olga, so the conclusion is false; but Olga would have gone all the more willingly if Boris had been there, so the premise is true.'

6. Janet Dean Fodor (1982) notes that contemporary semantic research presumes the existence of a substantive logical capacity.

7. The correct choices are 'E' and '7,' the latter being the difficult choice.

8. The correct answer is (14d).

9. I have replaced Rips' proposition letters by sentences to illustrate the sort of thing subjects would see. The correct answer is 'yes.'

10. Rips (1983) is trying to come up with such a theory, and I wish him luck.

11. Recall Johnson-Laird's claim that 'thinking is a skill.'

12. I believe that the troublesome sentence (14) provides very nice support for the view that language comprehension is automatic and reflexive, as Fodor (1983) has argued. In Geis and Fox (1984), subjects noted (incorrectly), by a two to one vote, that (i) does not entail (ii).

(i) John won't leave unless Bill doesn't leave.
(ii) If Bill leaves, John won't leave.

Interestingly, in a pretest of 19 subjects, one wrote stay over won't leave, and then decided correctly that (i) does entail (ii). This extraordinarily simple move doesn't seem to be available in automatic sentence processing.

13. See Fodor, Fodor, and Garrett (1975) for a defense of the use of meaning postulates in semantics.

14. The presence of can in claim (1) (contra Stevens) does not weaken this claim. Recall the discussion of (21a). Note further that if can were to signify mere 'possibility', the offer would be an infelicitous (because insincere) offer, for what is required by the consumer is real protection from infection. Since the offer appears to be a sincere offer, can cannot signify mere possibility.

References

Austin, J. L. 1965. How to do things with words. Oxford: Oxford University Press.
Bach, Kent, and Robert M. Harnish. 1982. Linguistic communication and speech acts. Cambridge, Mass.: The MIT Press.
Barwise, Jon, and John Perry. 1983. Situations and attitudes. Cambridge, Mass.: The MIT Press.
Boër, S. E., and W. G. Lycan. 1973. Invited inferences and other unwelcome guests. Papers in Linguistics 6.3-4.
Boër, S. E., and W. G. Lycan. 1976. The myth of semantic presupposition. Mimeograph. Bloomington: Indiana University Linguistics Club.
Bosque, Ignacio, and Juan-Carlos Moreno. 1984. A condition on quantifiers in logical form. Linguistic Inquiry 15.164-67.
Brewer, W. 1977. Memory for the pragmatic implications of sentences. Memory and Cognition 6.673-78.
Carlson, Greg N. 1979. Generics and atemporal when. Linguistics and Philosophy 3.49-98.
Davidson, Donald. 1967. The logical form of action sentences. In: The logic of decision and action. Edited by Nicholas Rescher. Pittsburgh: University of Pittsburgh Press. 81-95.
Davis, Wayne. Weak and strong conditionals. MS.
Fodor, Janet Dean. 1982. The mental representations of quantifiers. In: Processes, beliefs, and questions. Edited by Stanley Peters and Esa Saarinen. Dordrecht: D. Reidel. 129-64.
Fodor, Jerry A. 1983. Modularity of mind: An essay on faculty psychology. Cambridge, Mass.: The MIT Press.

Fodor, J. D., J. A. Fodor, and M. Garrett. 1975. The psychological unreality of semantic representations. Linguistic Inquiry 6.515-31.
Gazdar, Gerald. 1979. Pragmatics: Implicature, presupposition, and logical form. New York: Academic Press.
Geis, Michael L. and Arnold M. Zwicky. 1971. On invited inferences. Linguistic Inquiry 2.561-66.
Geis, Michael L. 1973. If and unless. In: Issues in linguistics: Papers in honor of Henry and Renee Kahane. Edited by B. B. Kachru et al. Urbana: University of Illinois. 231-53.
Geis, Michael L. 1982. The language of television advertising. New York: Academic Press.
Geis, Michael L., and Robert A. Fox. 1984. Mental logic and sentence comprehension. To appear in: Proceedings of the 1984 Chicago Linguistic Society Conference.
Grice, H. P. 1975. Logic and conversation. In: Syntax and semantics, Volume 3: Speech acts. Edited by P. Cole and J. L. Morgan. New York: Academic Press. 41-58.
Gueron, Jacqueline, and Robert May. 1984. Extraposition and logical form. Linguistic Inquiry 15.1-31.
Harman, Gilbert. 1972. Logical form. Foundations of Language 9.36-65.
Harris, R. J., T. M. Dubitsky, and Kristin Joe Bruno. 1983. Studies of misleading advertising. In: Information processing research in advertising. Edited by R. J. Harris. Hillsdale, N. J.: Lawrence Erlbaum Associates. 241-62.
Henle, M. 1962. On the relation between logic and thinking. Psychological Review 69.366-78.
Jackendoff, Ray S. 1972. Semantic interpretation in generative grammar. Cambridge, Mass.: MIT Press.
Johnson-Laird, P. N. 1982a. Formal semantics and psychology. In: Processes, beliefs, and questions. Edited by Stanley Peters and Esa Saarinen. Dordrecht: D. Reidel. 1-68.
Johnson-Laird, P. N. 1982b. Thinking is a skill (Ninth Barlett Memorial Lecture). Quarterly Journal of Experimental Psychology 34A.1-29.
Lakoff, R. 1977. What you can do with words: Politeness, pragmatics and performatives. In: Proceedings of the Texas Conference on Performatives, Presuppositions and Implicatures. Edited by A. Rogers et al. Arlington, Va.: Center for Applied Linguistics. 79-105.
Lewis, David. 1973. Counterfactuals. Cambridge, Mass.: Harvard University Press.
Loosen, F. 1981. Memory for the gist of sentences. Journal of Psycholinguistics 10.17-25.
Lycan, William G. 1984. A syntactically motivated theory of conditionals. Midwest Studies in Philosophy.
Morgan, J. L. 1978. Two types of convention in indirect speech acts. In: Syntax and semantics, Volume 9: Pragmatics. New York: Academic Press.
Partee, Barbara Hall. 1982. Belief-sentences and the limits of semantics. In: Processes, beliefs, and questions. Edited by Stanley Peters and Esa Saarinen. Dordrecht: D. Reidel. 87-106.
Searle, J. R. Speech acts: An essay in the philosophy of language. London: Cambridge University Press.

Solan, Lawrence. 1984. Focus and levels of representation. Linguistic Inquiry 15.174-78.
Stevens, Paul. 1978. Weasel words: God's little helpers. In: Language awareness. Edited by Paul Escholz et al. New York: St. Martin's Press. 74-85.
Rips, Lance J. 1983. Cognitive processes in propositional reasoning. Psychological Review 90.38-71.
Thomason, Richmond H. 1970. Symbolic logic: An introduction. London: Macmillan.

'SUBORDINATION' IN FORMAL AND INFORMAL DISCOURSE

Sandra A. Thompson
University of California, Los Angeles

Important inroads have recently been made into understanding some of the differences among various styles, registers, and modes of communication with respect to the way in which clauses in discourse are combined. Studies on this subject include Tannen (1982a, 1982b), Ochs (1979), Chafe (1982, 1984, to appear), Clancy (1982), Beaman (to appear), and Mithun (1984). My paper is intended as a further contribution to this discussion. I would like to look at some differences between formal and informal discourse in terms of the way people have used the term 'subordination', and to talk about the concept of 'subordination' itself.

My discussion takes as its starting point recent work of Chafe, particularly (1982) and (1984). Chafe (1982) discussed differences between spoken and written languages in terms of a number of parameters, such as fragmentation and integration. By 'integration' he meant 'the packing of more information into an idea unit than the rapid pace of spoken language would normally allow' (p. 39). As measures of 'integration', he used such constructions as nominalizations, participles, complements, relative clauses, attributive adjectives, and conjoined phrases, and he found that formal written language had a larger proportion of all these devices than informal spoken language.

Chafe (1984) has suggested that written and spoken language differ in terms of the percentage of adverbial subordinate clauses they contain. Mithun (1984) has also shown that languages differ in terms of the percentage of 'subordinate' clauses they contain in informal spoken discourse analysis samples, with English topping the list at roughly 34%, while Mohawk and Kathlamet, two indigenous American languages, had only about 6%, and Gungwinggu, an indigenous language of Australia, showed only about 2%.

I think that this work is very important, and that it strongly suggests that both within one language as well as across languages, there is variation in the way in which language users make use of formally marked dependencies among clauses in communication. In what follows, I would like to add to this discussion by comparing formal and informal English discourse with respect to what have been called 'subordinate' clauses. But first, I want to talk about the terms 'subordination' and 'subordinate clause' themselves.

The term 'subordination' is in quotes in my title because I think it is a misleading term. Its use encourages linguists and descriptive grammarians to think that at least some languages have a category of clause types which can be called 'subordinate'. In fact, Haiman and I (Haiman and Thompson 1984) have recently made a plea for abandoning the notion of 'subordination' in grammatical descriptions, at least for the time being, and talking instead about various relationships which pairs of adjacent clauses might have with each other, properties such as whether they share a subject, whether one of them is reduced or not, whether one of them is within the scope of the other, and so on. In this way, we felt, more progress could be made toward understanding how clauses actually combine in discourse than if we simply assume that everybody understands each other when we use the term 'subordinate clause'.

We suggested that experience with the linguistic literature in recent years shows that linguists have typically either taken the term 'subordination' as a primitive requiring no definition, or attempted to establish a set of criteria according to which a 'subordinate clause' can be unmistakably identified. Both of these approaches to 'subordination' have had unfortunate consequences.

If the term is taken as a primitive, then it is usually not made clear just what clauses or clause types within a given language it is intended to cover. At best, it can be assumed that it is meant to include all clauses which are 'nonmain'. But then, we know of no attempt in the literature to define 'main'.

Attempts to establish criteria, however, do not seem to have fared much better. In fact, the traditional criteria for 'subordination'--including dependence, reduction, backgrounding, and preposability, among others--turn out to be at best ex post facto rationalizations of our own (Western educated) 'intuitions', which means that they are all completely circular. Moreover, these criteria are often inconsistent or language specific. The reason for this, I think, is that 'subordinate clause' is not a grammatical category at all. That is, there does not seem to be a single function or even a group of functions that we can think of this 'category' as having been designed, as it were, to serve. So the term 'subordination' seems to be at best a negative term which lumps together all deviations from some 'main clause' norm, which means that it treats as unified a set of facts which we think is not a single phenomenon. For these reasons, we have found it more fruitful to tease it apart into its component parts and try to determine what are the discourse motivations that underlie each of these components. That is, there seem to be a number of properties that are involved in what people have heretofore called 'subordination', and a better understanding of clause-combining phenomena in discourse can be achieved if we consider each of these separately, and give up the idea of a category of 'subordinate clause' entirely.

Chafe (1984) and Mithun (1984) seem to have used the term 'subordinate' for something like 'dependent'; that is, for them, as for many other linguists, a clause which is morphologically marked so that it cannot stand by itself can be considered as 'subordinate'. I think that this subcategory of 'subordinate' needs to be broken down into its component parts too, since there seem to be different types of 'dependency', doing different types of discourse work. My suspicion is that 'dependence' may well need to be defined separately for each language, but, to begin with, we can list a set of properties which may be useful for a given language.

In the remainder of this paper, I would like to describe the research that I have been doing on English in this area and to suggest that it has promise for understanding differences among types of discourse in one language as well as among languages. I emphasize that this is a description of ongoing research, which means that what I say must be taken very much in the spirit of a progress report.

I want to make an important distinction between dependent clause types which represent organizational options available to the language user, and dependent clause types having to do with facts about the grammar of English. This means that I have restricted my study to clauses which do not play a grammatical role in constituency with some noun, some verb, or some preposition. That is, I have not been concerned with relative clauses, complement clauses, or clauses which are the objects of prepositions. An example of each of these is given in (1).

(1) Not included in this study: clauses whose appearance is governed by grammatical principles, that is, clauses which are in constituency with:
(1a) a noun (relative clauses):
Pineapples <u>that don't smell good</u> won't taste good
(1b) a verb (complement clauses):
I don't think <u>that subordination exists</u>
We want <u>to learn Hausa</u>
(1c) a preposition:
I didn't think of <u>checking my shoe size</u>

If we leave aside, then, at least for now, clauses which are in constituency with some noun, verb, or preposition, we are left with essentially those clause types typically called adverbial clauses, participials, and nonrestrictive relatives, as shown in (2).

(2) Clause types which are included in this study:
(2a) adverbial clauses
(2b) participials
(2c) nonrestrictive relatives

That is, unlike the clause types given in (1), which are more or less determined by the grammar of complementation and the pragmatics of reference, the clause types in (2) have everything to do with how one decides to convey and relate propositions. It is the clause types in (2) that concern me here, since these could have conceivably been expressed as nondependent clauses, whereas the clause types in (1) are almost completely determined by the lexical items chosen. Chafe (personal communication) has suggested that the items in (1) also differ from those in (2) in that those in (2) are typically separate 'idea units' or 'intonation units' (or 'punctuation units' in writing), while those in (1) are typically part of the same 'idea unit' or 'intonation unit'.[1]

Now all of the clause types in (2) seem to be formally 'dependent', in the sense that they cannot represent independent utterances on their own, but must occur with some other clause. Pragmatically, of course, almost every utterance we use is dependent, since it requires context for its interpretation, but what grammarians have been concerned about when they use the term 'dependent' has generally been grammatical dependency, not this kind of pragmatic dependency. And grammatical dependency can be broken down into a number of components, as shown in (3).

(3) Indicators of formal dependency[2]
  A. Nonfinite verb form (or no verb)
  B. Nonrestrictive relative pronoun: which, who, where, such as, etc.
  C. Connector for adverbial adjunct:
     Temporal connector: when, as, after, as soon as, etc.
     Conditional connector: if, unless, as long as, etc.
     Causal connector: because, since, as, etc.
     Degree connector: so...that, as many...as, the more...the more, etc.
     Concessive connector: although, except, etc.
     Means connector: by
     Purposive connector: so that
     Manner connector: as if, as

This is perhaps not an exhaustive list, and it is certainly subject to revision, but it is at least representative of the kinds of grammatical properties which have led grammarians to talk about 'dependent' clauses in English. Obviously, the list would be quite different for other languages; indeed, one of the points of Mithun (1984) was that for many languages (perhaps in particular those without long written traditions) such a list might be much shorter, and its devices employed much less frequently.

My data base consisted of three types of short texts, as shown in (4). As is evident, my study contrasts with much earlier work in not being based primarily on narrative discourse data.

(4) Data base
  1. Formal Written
     Excerpts from the writings of Bertrand Russell and the economist Thomas Sowell, UCLA administrative memos, and short articles from the University of California Bulletin and travel literature.
  2. Informal Written
     Letters to the editor, personal letters, and chatty pieces about people in a radio program guide.
  3. Informal Spoken
     Monologues in two-party conversation.

For each of these three groups, out of roughly 300 clauses, I counted how many were formally marked in one of the ways indicated in (3). An example of each follows.

'Subordination' in formal and informal discourse / 89

Example (5) is from the Formal Written data, a short memo from the office of the Chancellor of UCLA. The relevant clauses are numbered (remember that I am ignoring relatives and complements).

(5) Formal Written example (memo from UCLA Chancellor):

ALL UCLA EMPLOYEES:
1. In March 1982 we were informed that the Office of Federal Contract Compliance Programs of the U.S. Department of Labor was initiating a review
2. to determine if the campus, as a recipient of federal funds, is in compliance with federal regulations regarding equal employment opportunity and affirmative action for women, minorities, disabled persons and Vietnam era veterans.
3. The OFCCP has completed its off-site examination of UCLA's Affirmative Action Plan and
4. will begin the on-site phase of its review on Monday, June 28, 1982.
5. As part of that review, OFCCP has asked that all employees who wish to be interviewed or to comment about UCLA's compliance with its obligations contact the OFCCP ofice.
6. Employee organizations,
7. if they wish to be interviewed,
6. may also contact that office.
8. The number to call is (213) 997-3185.
9. The last day for arranging these voluntary interviews is July 9, 1982.
10. Supervisors are encouraged to accommodate changes in work schedules
11. in order to enable individuals to participate in interviews.

There are many interesting things one could say about this text, including the pragmatics of making an offer which the offerer hopes no one will take him up on! But our interest here is in the percentage of clauses which show one of the dependence properties listed in (3). In clause 2, there is one instance of property A, the nonfinite verb <u>to determine</u>, and clause 7 has a conditional marker <u>if</u>, which is C in (3). Finally, clause 11 has another infinitive verb form <u>to enable</u>. So three of a total of 11 clauses are formally marked as being 'dependent' in the sense I have defined.

Example (6) is from the opposite extreme, the Informal Spoken group. It is from a conversation in which a young singer is talking about how it feels to have been a hit in a New York City Opera production of Bernstein's <u>Candide</u>.

(6) Informal Spoken example (young opera singer talking):

1. I got this hysterical phone call from Walker Joyce and John Rice about two weeks into the run of <u>Candide</u>.
2. They left a message on my machine, 'Well, golly, gee, Erie, now that you're a star, could we borrow some money?'
3. I called them back

4. and it was wonderful to talk with them.
5. And Tom Detwiler came to the show.
6. But I think what it did for me was put me on the map as a name that people now recognize.
7. When they see the name,
8. they can think, 'Oh yes, I read about her.'
9. I think it was a wonderful way for me to make a debut.
10. It couldn't have been better, in fact.
11. Though I'm glad that what I do next in New York are two operas: the Fairy Godmother in Massenet's <u>Cendrillon</u> and Mordonna in Handel's <u>Alcina</u>.
12. They aren't as big roles as Cunegonde,
13. but at least it will show the people of New York and the critics that I do other things.

In this sample, two clauses are formally marked for dependency: clause 7 is a temporal clause, C on our list, and clause 11 is a concessive clause, also C on our list.

An illustration of the Informal Written style is taken from a personal letter; example (7) is the body of a letter to me from Cousin Margaret, who explains why she cannot come to visit.

(7) Informal Written example (letter from Cousin Margaret):

1. Your kind invitation to come and enjoy cooler climes is so tempting
2. but I have been waiting to learn the outcome of medical diagnosis
3. and the next 3 months will be spent having the main thumb joints replaced with plastic ones.
4. Thumbs began to be troublesome about 4 months ago
5. and I made an appointment with the best hand surgeon in the Valley
6. to see if my working activities were the problem.
7. Using thumbs is not the problem
8. but heredity is
9. and the end result is no use of thumbs
10. if I don't do something now.
11. I have heard Mother talk about the family arthritis
12. but one never expects to be included.
13. Writing has almost become impossible
14. so we had the typewriter serviced
15. and I may learn to type decently after all these years.

Of these 15 clauses, only two show any markings for dependency: clause 6 is a purpose clause with a nonfinite verb, property A in (3), and 10 is a conditional, property C.³

The totals for the samples I used are given in Table 1; each fraction represents the number of clauses with indicators of formal dependency, out of the total number of clauses.

The Table 1 figures need to be taken with a grain of salt since the total number of clauses at this stage of my research is not very large and since the categorization represented in (3) is still in the process of being refined. But they are suggestive, and they are statistically significant at the .01 level: not only do they suggest that Written Formal English has a higher proportion of clauses of the type I am here calling 'dependent' than either of the 'informal' styles, but the percentage of such clauses is almost exactly the same for Spoken Informal as it is for Written Informal, which confirms the findings of others working on this problem, such as Chafe, Tannen, and Beaman: that in the area of clause combining, the formal/informal distinction, rather than the written/spoken one, may be most relevant.

Table 1.

Written Formal:	Written Informal:	Spoken Informal:
87/302 (29%)	61/306 (21%)	63/306 (21%)

Just as interesting here as the overall numbers, however, may be the way in which they break down. That is, one can also look at how the various components of dependency distribute themselves in the three types of discourse I have been considering. These figures are given in Table 2.

Table 2.

	Written Formal		Written Informal		Spoken Informal	
Nonfinite verb form (A)	19		24		3	
		28 (32%)		36 (59%)		11 (18%)
Nonrestrictive relative pronoun (B)	9		12		8	
Connector for adverbial adjunct (C)	59	(68%)	25	(41%)	52	(82%)
Totals	87	(100%)	61	(100%)	63	(100%)

In Table 2, I have grouped the first two types of dependent clauses, A and B, together and separated them from the adverbial clause types C, so that we may compare the way they are deployed in the three types of discourse I am examining. The most striking thing about Table 2 is that the three types of discourse make radically different use of the three types of dependency.

A comparison of the three columns, for example, shows that fully 82% of the dependent clauses which appear in the Spoken Informal discourse data (rightmost column) are of the adverbial clause type, while the adverbial clauses account for only 41% of the dependencies in the Written Informal discourse (middle column) and only 68% of the dependencies in the Written Formal discourse (lefthand column). Extrapolation from these figures suggests that almost all of the dependencies in Spoken discourse occur in the adverbial clauses, with people giving causal, conditional, and temporal comments on the events they are discussing. In contrast, in the Spoken data, there are very few clauses (only three, in fact) with nonfinite verbs (A in (3)).

The Written Formal discourse column indicates that a larger percentage, 32%, as compared to 18% for the Spoken data, were of one of the types A or B, that is, nonfinite or nonrestrictive. Only 68% were adverbial clauses.

The Written Informal samples (totals shown in middle column), however, were surprising in this respect. First, a large majority of the dependencies, 59%, were of the nonadverbial clause type, that is, one of those shown in A or B. To a certain extent, this could have been due to the subject matter of the texts in this group. Most of the personal letters and chatty pieces contained relatively few occasions for providing reasons, concessions, or, most notably, conditions for the events being discussed. So this could account for the relatively low 41% figure for adverbial clauses in the middle column.

But even more striking is the relatively large number of times that the informal writers (as compared with the informal speakers) took advantage of the option to use nonfinite verb clauses, or clauses with no verb at all (Property A), or nonrestrictive relatives (Property B). As can be seen in Table 2, of the total of 306 clauses in the Written Informal group, 24 were nonfinite (A) and 12 were nonrestrictive (B): 36 of the total 306. An example of property A, a clause with a nonfinite verb form from a letter to the editor, is given in (8).

(8)   Perhaps the hotel is clearing out its rooms <u>to make way for condo conversions.</u>

Example (9), from a personal letter, shows Property B, a nonrestrictive relative clause.

(9)   we were able to start within five minutes after the sound of the gun, <u>which nobody heard.</u>

In contrast, the Spoken Informal column of Table 2 shows only 3 clauses of type A and 8 of type B; that is, 11 of the 306 clauses in the Spoken Informal data were of these two types. An example of each of these is shown in the speech of a man who is explaining that he resembles a number of other people (example (10)). Clause 3 in example (10) shows a nonrestrictive relative clause.

(10)
1. It's probably--easier no:w -for people to think that uh someone looks exactly like me,
2. because, anyone with uh, a beard, of this particular style and cut--
3. which is - partly gray and partly black,

An example of a nonfinite verb form can be found later on in this same monologue, as can be seen in clause 15 of example (11).

(11)
14. There was a <u>long</u> moment,
15. having just come back from::some time:: in funny places like China, an:: hhh! Guam and places like that...

So 36 of the 306 clauses in the Written Informal sample were nonrestrictives or contained nonfinite verbs, while in Spoken Informal, the number of clauses of either of these two types, either with a nonfinite verb, or nonrestrictive relatives, is quite small, only 11. This suggests that in these two clause types the planning involved in writing may make a difference: writers, even those writing somewhat informally, make relatively free use of these particular dependency devices, but speakers hardly ever do.

What do these data tell us then? Table 1 suggests that there is a difference between formal and informal discourse in terms of how users of English employ some of the dependent clause options available to them. That is, the two rightmost columns, those representing somewhat more informal discourse, show a smaller overall percentage of dependent clause types than the leftmost column, which represents formal discourse (around 20% as compared to 30%).

But Table 2 suggests that there is also a difference between speaking and writing in terms of these dependencies. The left and middle columns, representing the written discourse types, contrast with the rightmost column, which represents spoken discourse, in the percentage of nonfinite verb forms and nonrestrictive relative pronouns: the Spoken discourse can be seen to have fewer such forms than the Written. This shows that some of these options are primarily associated with writing, namely, those by which language users create dependent clauses by using nonfinite verb forms and nonrestrictive relatives.

What these data suggest to me is, first of all, confirmation for what previous researchers, such as Tannen, Chafe, Beaman, and others, have found. But they also suggest that my initial suspicion was correct: the notion 'subordinate clause' cannot be assumed. We cannot continue to use the term 'subordination', believing that other linguists will know what we are talking about--partly because linguists do not all mean the same thing by the term, and partly because important facts are missed if we lump various types of 'nonmain' clauses into one group. We have to break down the notion of 'subordination' into its component parts, and try to determine what each of them is doing in different types of discourse.

Notes

I am grateful to Wally Chafe for much helpful discussion of the ideas in this paper.

1. His research also shows that there do not seem to be large differences between written and spoken English, at least with respect to <u>that</u> complements and infinitival complements.

2. This list is adapted from a similar one being used by Chafe in his current research.

3. Tannen (personal communication) makes the interesting observation that this example, as is indeed the case for many of my examples in the Written Informal group, represents not so much an informal genre as an informal notion of formality, a kind of 'folk formality', as she puts it. Evidence for this includes Cousin Margaret's quasi-poetic <u>cooler climes</u>, her use of nominalizations such as <u>using thumbs</u> and <u>medical diagnosis</u>, and her <u>one</u> subject in clause (12). This suggests that my category 'Written Informal' is perhaps somewhat more formal than its position between 'Formal Written' and 'Informal Spoken' would indicate. However, as I show further on, in many ways the two groups which I have characterized as 'Informal' behave alike in contrast to the one which I label 'Formal'.

References

Beaman, Karen. (to appear) Coordination and subordination revisited: Syntactic complexity in spoken and written discourse. In: Tannen (to appear).

Brugman, Claudia, and Monica Macaulay. 1984. Proceedings of the Tenth Annual Meeting of the Berkeley Linguistics Society. Berkeley, Calif.: Berkeley Linguistics Society.

Chafe, Wallace. 1982. Integration and involvement in speaking, writing, and oral literature. In: Tannen (1982b).

Chafe, Wallace. 1984. How people use adverbial clauses. In: Brugman and Macaulay (1984).

Clancy, Patricia. 1982. Written and spoken style in Japanese narratives. In: Tannen (1982b).

Givón, Talmy, ed. 1979. Discourse and syntax. Syntax and semantics, vol. 12. New York: Academic Press.

Haiman, John, and Sandra A. Thompson. 1984. 'Subordination' in universal grammar. In: Brugman and Macaulay (1984).

Mithun, Marianne. 1984. How to avoid subordination. In: Brugman and Macaulay (1984).

Ochs, Elinor. 1979. Planned and unplanned discourse. In: Givón (1979).

Tannen, Deborah. 1982a. The oral/literate continuum in discourse. In: Tannen (1982b).

Tannen, Deborah, ed. 1982b. Spoken and written language. Norwood, N.J.: Ablex.

Tannen, Deborah, ed. (to appear) Coherence in spoken and written discourse. Norwood, N.J.: Ablex.

SPEAKING, WRITING, AND PRESCRIPTIVISM

Wallace Chafe
University of California, Berkeley

For the last several years I have been looking at differences between spoken and written language, trying to establish a little more clearly just what the differences between them are, and trying to identify the reasons for these differences. Here I am going to discuss one of the reasons, one which I have only recently begun to look into in any serious way. I refer to the influence which normative or prescriptive grammar has had on the differentiation between speaking and writing.

To a large extent, prescriptivism itself arose from the fact that written language is visual rather than auditory, and thus has tended to be more permanent than spoken language. The fact that it can be leisurely examined has made it highly subject to reification, to treatment as an object of critical comparison and analysis. People have tended to pay attention to differences between the forms of language used by different writers much more than they have paid attention to the presence of such differences between speakers. The evanescence of speaking allows linguistic differences to slip by unnoticed, whereas the permanence and perusability of written language calls attention to such differences.

When human beings notice differences in the ways they do something, they seem universally to react with a firm conviction that one of the ways is the correct one, and that all the others are at the very least mistaken, but probably also illogical or corrupt. This reaction is as good a candidate as exists anywhere for an automatic human reflex. The permanence and perusability of writing lead inevitably, by this reflex reaction, to the notion that there is one kind of language that is best, and many kinds that should be avoided. If speaking has the freedom and fleetingness of a butterfly, writing pins language to a board. As soon as this happens, it is natural to say 'this is the way a butterfly should be, and other butterflies are monstrosities'.

The ultimate result may be the establishment of an academy whose goal is to establish the right form of language and protect it against corrupting influences. That is what happened in Italy, France, Spain, and

Sweden in the sixteenth, seventeenth, and eighteenth centuries. It did not happen in England, although there was significant sentiment in favor of it. A prescriptive attitude has nevertheless played a noticeable role in shaping the English language. Its influence reached a climax in the nineteenth and early twentieth centuries, particularly as it provided guidance for schoolteachers in need of something to teach (Finegan 1980, Quinn 1980, Baron 1982).

My own interest has been in trying to pin down the ways in which prescriptivism has contributed to the relation between speaking and writing. For one thing, I have been trying to identify some of the specific differences between spoken and written English which are causally attributable to it. At the same time I have been trying to identify the kinds of historical developments and mechanisms which have been at work. Contrary to what I first expected, I have learned that the course of prescriptivism has not always been the same, nor have its results always been of the same kind.

I am going to describe here three courses of development, each quite different from the others. There is no implication that these are the only developments that can occur, but they do illustrate well the range of possibilities.

The chief kind of evidence I have for these developments that is new, and not derived from what others have said, comes from a project (funded by the National Institute of Education, Grant 80-0125) in which Jane Danielewicz and I collected two kinds of spoken language (roughly formal and informal) and two kinds of written language (also roughly formal and informal) from each of 20 individuals, and subjected these samples to an analysis in terms of a number of features hypothesized to have different distributions in at least some kinds of writing as opposed to some kinds of speaking. The four kinds of language are (1) conversational speaking, from dinnertable conversations; (2) academic speaking, from academic lectures; (3) letter writing, from personal letters; and (4) academic writing, from academic papers. I have compared these samples in various ways elsewhere (Chafe 1982, in press, Chafe and Danielewicz in press). Here I am going to discuss only a few examples of differences which appear to be attributable in one way or another to prescriptivism.

There is one kind of development that seems to fit into this picture, but that is not so much a matter of prescriptivism per se as a matter of written language possessing a greater inertia than spoken when subjected to the forces of linguistic change. We might say that speaking, because of its evanescence, is intrinsically more prone to change, whereas writing, because of its permanence and perusability, is slower to accept change. (Like everything I say here, this is an oversimplification, since writing may also foster changes of its own kind.) The result is the course of development which is represented schematically in Figure 1. This figure should be interpreted as two time lines, one representing spoken language and one written language, moving from left to right. The vertical dimension represents the absence or the significant presence of some feature, as indicated on the left. Initially, this feature is absent from both speaking and writing, as shown by the coincidence of the two lines on the left. At some point it emerges in speaking, but remains for a time absent from writing, as shown by the divergence of

Speaking, writing, and prescriptivism / 97

the two lines in the middle. During the middle period, the feature is one which differentiates speaking from writing. Eventually, writing begins to catch up, and eventually, the two lines come back together, with writing as well as speaking making significant use of the innovation.

Figure 1.

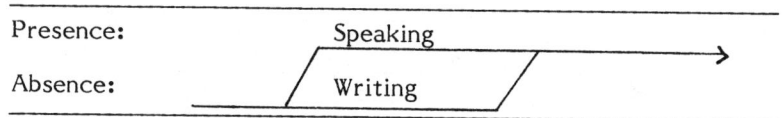

| Presence: | Speaking |
| Absence: | Writing |

A feature which probably fits this pattern is the use of the demonstrative <u>this</u> (or its plural <u>these</u>) as an alternative to the indefinite article. Here are some examples:

...the second thing I heard was this...woman's voice,
...and here's this divider and the...this big wooden thing,
...there's this...nun in the program,
...and he saw these two foreigners,

I do not know exactly when this usage began to be common in spoken English, but it seems to have emerged in fairly recent times. So far as I know, school grammars have not prescribed against it, although I am acquainted with a few older people of a prescriptive turn of mind who are put off by it. Both intuition and the evidence from our study suggest that it has not yet made any significant inroads into careful, edited written English. We found five occurrences of it per thousand words of academic speaking, and no occurrences at all in either academic writing or in letter writing. I do not want to suggest that it never occurs in letters, however, since I recently received a letter in which there were two occurrences in the first sentence. The situation pictured on the right side of Figure 1 is in this case only a prediction: a situation in which the indefinite demonstrative will in the future be used as freely in all styles of written English as it is presently used in conversation. But, except for the inertia of writing and the prescriptive reflexes of people who are likely to become fewer as time goes on, there is nothing to prevent such a development. This is a feature which is neither illogical, productive of ambiguity, nor inelegant, so that it will be difficult to keep it out of writing with arguments along those lines.

Figure 2 shows a very different course of development. It is, I think, the kind of development typically associated with prescriptivism. In Figure 2 there is some feature which is at first equally present in both speaking and writing. It is then found to be undesirable, perhaps because it is at odds with the grammar of Latin; perhaps because it is believed to be illogical, inelegant, or productive of ambiguities; or perhaps because it violates some artificially imposed pattern. Once legislated against, this feature comes to have a reduced frequency in writing, as indicated in the middle portion of Figure 2. Probably it goes on being used naturally in the speech of most people, although attempts to avoid it in speaking may become an index of pedantry. At this middle stage, then, the presence or absence of this feature is diagnostic of written vs.

spoken language. The righthand portion of Figure 2 suggests that, with a relaxation of the influence of prescriptivism, such a feature may sooner or later regain its frequency in writing, with perhaps an eventual return to the original lack of differentiation between speaking and writing in this respect.

Figure 2.

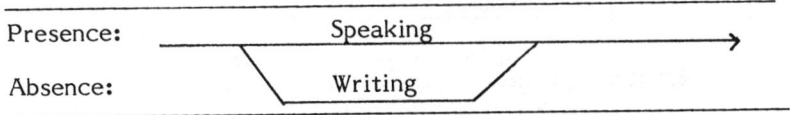

One feature of this kind is evidently the use of shall and will. The story of the prescriptions regarding these two auxiliaries is a long, complicated one, and much of it was told by Charles Fries (1925). Fries not only surveyed the origin of the peculiar rules which came to dictate their use; he also traced their actual occurrences in 86 dramas from the middle of the sixteenth century to the first quarter of the twentieth, looking separately at their use in independent declarative statements, questions, and subordinate clauses. I simplify the story here by focusing on the use of I will as a marker of the future tense in declarative sentences.

As in many such cases, the prescriptions regarding shall and will came to be stated with precision only in the nineteenth century. Even then, different grammarians said somewhat different things. While everyone agreed that I shall was the proper choice for the simple future tense, Brown (1851), for example, said that I will should be used for a 'promise, command, or threat,' whereas Alford (1864) associated I will on etymological grounds with the will of the speaker. It appears that the consistent use of I shall for the future was actually not established until the second half of the nineteenth century. This usage was thereafter carefully adhered to by many who learned to write during the period from approximately 1850 to 1950, including, from the sublime to the ridiculous, Edmund Wilson (e.g. 1971) and me. The evidence is fairly clear that the prescription is quickly running its course at the present time, with the incidences of I shall declining, and those of I will taking over. In our data we found two instances of I shall vs. five of I will in academic writing. In letter writing there was only one instance of I shall vs. seven of I will. I find that I shall has completely disappeared from my own writing. It may not be long before I will has completely vanquished its alternative, so the situation will have become that represented on the right side of Figure 2.

Another feature which has followed the course schematically represented in Figure 2 is the use of prepositions at the ends of relative clauses and question-word questions. The prohibition against this usage is generally supposed to have begun with John Dryden. Citing the following two lines from Ben Jonson:

The Waves, and Dens of beasts cou'd not receive
The bodies that those souls were frighted from.

Dryden found fault with 'the Preposition in the end of the sentence; a common fault with him, and which I have but lately observ'd in my own writings' (1672, quoted from Bolton 1966:60). He then 'went through all his prefaces contriving away the final prepositions that he had been guilty of in his first editions' (Fowler 1965:473). Subsequent prescriptivists were actually less dogmatic in this case than in others. For example, Robert Lowth, who seems to have been about the only eighteenth century grammarian to have paid much attention to final prepositions, said that their use

> is an idiom, which our language is strongly inclined to: it prevails in common conversation, and suits very well with the familiar style in writing: but the placing of the Preposition before the Relative is more graceful, as well as more perspicuous; and agrees much better with the solemn and elevated style (Lowth 1775:164).

Interestingly, Lindley Murray (1795:122) quoted this opinion verbatim, except that he amended it to read 'to which our language is strongly inclined'. Alford (1888:118) was relatively permissive in this regard: 'There is a peculiar use of prepositions, which is allowable in moderation, but must not be too often resorted to. It is the placing them at the end of a sentence as I have just done in the words "resorted to".'

In spite of this fairly relaxed attitude among the best known prescriptivists, our data suggest that final prepositions are even now significantly avoided in more formal kinds of writing. Dryden's prohibition was formulated more clearly and at an earlier date than the prohibition against I will, and it continues to exert a stronger influence. We found 1.2 occurrences of final prepositions per thousand words of conversation, 1.7 occurrences in lectures, 1.1 in letters, but only 0.2 in academic writing.

Figure 3 shows a third course of development, and it is one which contradicts the notion that prescriptivism always increases the distance between writing and speaking. Here there is a situation in which the feature in question has always been absent from or at least has been rare in spoken language. Initially, there is a stage at which the feature has some currency in writing. There then develops a prohibition against it which causes its decline in that medium, with the paradoxical result that writing becomes more, not less, like speaking in this regard. As the prohibition exerts less influence, the feature comes to be written more commonly again, with a paradoxical increase in the differentiation of spoken and written language.

Figure 3.

Presence:	Writing
Absence:	Speaking

I have noticed two features that fit this pattern. Both are well known as usages prescriptivists would like us to avoid. One is the split infinitive, the other the dangling participle. There is some question whether split infinitives fit the lefthand side of Figure 3 or not. In a study of prescriptive grammar in the eighteenth century, Leonard (1929: 95) remarked that

> the most striking circumstances in this array of censured constructions is that no mention whatever of the 'split infinitive' was discoverable, nor was the construction itself observed save once or twice in the authors read. Apparently, it was both a discovery and an aversion of nineteenth century grammarians.

His book includes the following example from George Campbell (written in 1776):

> to vigilantly attend to every illegal practice that were beginning to prevail (Campbell 1963:370).

But, of course, it is quite possible that the construction was used more frequently by writers who were not grammarians, and thus were not surveyed by Leonard.

In any case, in the nineteenth century we find Henry Alford saying with regard to the split infinitive, 'But surely this is a practice entirely unknown to English speakers and writers. It seems to me, that we ever regard the to of the infinitive as inseparable from its verb' (Alford 1888:133). Fowler (1965:579) has an amusing entry in which he says, 'The English-speaking world may be divided into (1) those who neither know nor care what a split infinitive is; (2) those who do not know, but care very much; (3) those who know and condemn; (4) those who know and approve; and (5) those who know and distinguish.' Later, in giving a set of examples of split infinitives, he notes that because they 'are from newspapers of high repute, and high newspaper tradition is strong against splitting, it is perhaps fair to assume that each specimen is a manifesto of independence' (Fowler 1965:581). In our own data we found no split infinitives anywhere at all except in academic writing, where there were three examples in 20,000 words:

> individuals are called upon to verbally display some knowledge or proficiency at recurrent communicative tasks,

> we began to systematically audio and videotape these episodes

> there is more dependence on context to indirectly express these relationships

Two of these examples were from the same writer.

I do not mean to suggest that split infinitives never occur in speaking. They are, however, rare, and usually restricted to cases in which the splitting word is an intensifier like really or actually. The written cases, on the other hand, usually involve a manner adverb, as in the examples I have given. It is thus relevant that in our data, manner adverbs themselves were only half as common in conversation as they were in either academic writing or in letters. Both the use of a manner adverb and the use of such a word to split an infinitive seem to require at least a small amount of planning of the kind that is performed by writers more easily than by speakers.

Split infinitives, then, may have occurred significantly in writing before the nineteenth century (contra Leonard), but more evidence is needed. Only in the nineteenth century did there arise an explicit prohibition against them. Their subsequent avoidance by careful writers has had the effect of making written language more like spoken language from the point of view that both have failed to make much use of them (the situation schematized in the middle of Figure 3). With the current relaxation of prescriptive guilt, split infinitives may be entering careful expository prose more often, though at present individual writers differ in their tolerance of them. We may expect that they will gradually become more common in writing, and if they do, the gap between writing and speaking will paradoxically have been increased.

'Dangling' or 'unattached' participles may also follow the pattern of Figure 3. Again I am unsure of their prevalence before the nineteenth century, though there must have been something there for grammarians to inveigh against. Alford, again, is explicit in this regard:

> One of the commonest of newspaper errors is to use a participial clause instead of one with a verb, leaving the said clause pendent, so that in the reader's mind it necessarily falls into a wrong relation. Thus we had in the Times the other day, in the description of the York congress, assembled under the presidency of the Archbishop: 'His Grace said, &c., and after pronouncing the benediction, the assembly separated' (Alford 1888:191).

Prescriptivists have often been able to point in this way to the fact that dangling participles, if taken literally, will lead to an unintended interpretation. On the other hand, Brown (1851:605) was liberal enough to allow that certain participles 'are frequently used in discourse so independently, that they either relate to nothing, or to the pronoun I or we understood; as, "Granting this to be true, what is to be inferred from it?" ... This may be supposed to mean, "I, granting this to be true, ask what is to be inferred from it?"'

As was the case with split infinitives, views like Alford's reduced the use of dangling participles in writing. And again the paradoxical result was to make written language more like spoken, for dangling participles (or for that matter participles of any kind) may never have been a common feature of spoken language. In our data we found only 3 occurrences of participles of any kind per thousand words of conversation, and no more than 5 in lectures, as opposed to 10 in letters and 19 in academic writing. Although, lacking adequate data on earlier stages of spoken English, we can never be entirely sure, in all probability the incidence of participles in speaking was not significantly higher in centuries past than it is now. The use of clauses built from participles rather than finite verbs represents a strategy foreign to the normal pattern of spoken English, with its preference for the chaining together of relatively independent clauses.

Our materials contained four examples of dangling participles in 20,000 words of academic writing--hardly an impressive number--but there were none at all in any of our other language samples. The four from academic writing were:

Assuming a self-terminating search, the number of decisions should increase with the number of target properties.

Also, objective semantic properties may be used, avoiding the possible displaced rehearsal problem of evaluative ratings.

Based on the research summaries so far, written language contains many more complex syntactic structures than oral language, suggesting that in written language ideas are related or combined in ways not apparent in spoken language.

(The last example contains two.) If these examples can be taken as symptoms of a trend, here too the current relaxation of prescriptive standards has had the effect of widening, not narrowing, the gap between writing and speaking.

To summarize, I have introduced the question of how prescriptivism has affected the relation between spoken and written language. I have described three very different kinds of historical developments, which I summarized schematically in Figures 1, 2, and 3.

The Figure 1 pattern, exemplified by the indefinite demonstrative this, involves an innovation in spoken language whose introduction into writing is resisted by the inertia of that medium, as well as by possible prescriptive attitudes against it. There is thus a period during which such a feature contributes to the gap between speaking and writing, but after which writing may catch up, reducing or eliminating the gap.

The Figure 2 pattern, exemplified by the shall-will dogma and by final prepositions, involves a feature which was once common in both speaking and writing, whose incidence in writing was decreased by prescriptivism, and which may subsequently be reintroduced into writing as the influence of prescriptivism wanes. Here the maximum differentiation between spoken and written language occurs during the period of maximum prescriptive influence.

The Figure 3 pattern, exemplified by split infinitives and dangling participles, presents the opposite picture. Here there was never a very significant occurrence of the feature in spoken language. These are features whose use is fostered by the extra planning time available to writers, although, from the point of view of a prescriptivist, they might be regarded as planning which has gone astray. During the period of maximum prescriptive influence the gap between speaking and writing was narrowed, not widened, and it is with the relaxation of prescriptivism that the gap is now increasing.

There is a sense in which each feature affected by prescriptivism has had its own history. On the other hand, there are sets of features which do seem to fall into repeated patterns of the kinds I have discussed. Studies of this sort can have some significance, not just for our understanding of certain differences between speaking and writing, but also for our understanding of the mechanisms of language change. From the small amount of work I have done in this area so far, I can report that it is frustrating--in part because of the diversity of the written data, in part because of the lack of satisfactory spoken data from earlier periods. Even so, it is certainly possible to do considerably more than I have done in this very preliminary study, and the results, as they come in, are likely to be intriguing and rewarding.

References

Alford, Henry. 1888. The queen's English. A manual of idiom and usage. Seventh ed. (Originally published in 1864.) London: George Bell and Sons.

Baron, Dennis E. 1982. Grammar and good taste. Reforming the American language. New Haven and London: Yale University Press.

Bolton, W. F. 1966. The English language. Essays by English and American men of letters 1490-1839. Cambridge: Cambridge University Press.

Brown, Goold. 1851. The grammar of English grammars. New York: Samuel S. and William Wood.

Campbell, George. 1963. The philosophy of rhetoric. Edited by Lloyd F. Bitzer. (Originally published in 1776.) Carbondale: Southern Illinois University Press.

Chafe, Wallace L. 1982. Integration and involvement in speaking, writing, and oral literature. In: Spoken and written language: Exploring orality and literacy. Edited by Deborah Tannen. Norwood, N.J.: Ablex.

Chafe, Wallace L. (in press) Linguistic differences produced by differences between speaking and writing. In: The nature and consequences of literacy. Edited by David Olson, Angela Hildyard, and Nancy Torrance. Cambridge: Cambridge University Press.

Chafe, Wallace L., and Jane Danielewicz. (in press) Properties of spoken and written language. In: Comprehending oral and written language. Edited by Rosalind Horowitz and S. J. Samuels. New York: Academic Press.

Finegan, Edward. 1980. Attitudes towards English usage. The history of a war of words. New York and London: Columbia University Teachers College Press.

Fowler, H. W. 1965. A dictionary of modern English usage. Second ed., revised by Sir Ernest Gowers. (Originally published in 1926.) Oxford and New York: Oxford University Press.

Fries, Charles C. 1925. The periphrastic future with <u>shall</u> and <u>will</u> in modern English. Publications of the Modern Language Association 40. 936-1024.

Leonard, Sterling Andrus. 1929. The doctrine of correctness in English usage 1700-1800. University of Wisconsin Studies in Language and Literature, No. 25.

Lowth, Robert. 1762. A short introduction to English grammar: With critical notes. London.

Murray, Lindley. 1795. English grammar. (Reprinted by The Scolar Press, Menston, England, in 1968.)

Quinn, Jim. 1980. American tongue and cheek. A populist guide to our language. New York: Pantheon Books.

Wilson, Edmund. 1971. Upstate. Records and recollections of northern New York. New York: Farrar, Straus and Giroux.

SUBSTRATE AND UNIVERSALS IN THE TOK PISIN VERB PHRASE

Gillian Sankoff
University of Pennsylvania

In previous papers on various aspects of Tok Pisin syntax and morphology (Sankoff 1977a, b; 1979; Sankoff and Laberge 1973; Sankoff and Brown 1976), I have tried to steer a course that founders neither on the lofty cliffs of universals nor on the hidden substrate reef. There are certainly those who see one or the other of these as a haven, and who would deny the viability of any third course, on the grounds that these two 'solutions' exhaust the universe of explanatory possibilities.[1] In my view, neither can constitute a full explanation of developments in Tok Pisin, because neither explains the dynamics of the processes involved. By this I mean something quite specific. Recourse to either substrate or universals, at least as employed in the creole literature, has generally been little more than an exercise in pattern matching. One observes how some part of the grammar of a creole language patterns, and then matches this pattern to some template, whether a putative universal or a part of the grammar of some other language.
    We need to do more than this. There may well be a 'natural semantax' (Bickerton 1974) in the brain, and people no doubt also carry in their brains the indelible structures of their first language grammar. But for either (or indeed any) pattern to surface and be sustained in the language, the discourse that it generates must prove viable in the everyday conditions of its production. The abstract rules or patterns that are usually thought of as generating discourse are in fact in a symbiotic relationship with it, because they will be altered if what they produce cannot survive in its natural environment: talk. Talk is in turn regulated by both the microinteractional and the larger sociohistorical context. Thus the reproduction of systems and subsystems in grammars depends on both aspects of what I have called the 'social life' of language (Sankoff 1980:xix-xxii).
    This paper examines the grammatical subsystem that has been at the heart of recent theoretical discussions of the nature of creole languages, i.e. tense, mood, and aspect marking (cf. Bickerton 1974, 1981; Muysken 1981, Givón 1982). In what follows, I steer a course that will throw neither universals nor substrate out with the bath water, but that is not

merely a compromise between the two. This course has been charted elsewhere, notably in Sankoff and Brown (1976) and Laberge and Sankoff (1979). It rests on the assumption that everything that becomes part of the grammar of a language must first appear in discourse.[2] A change in discourse patterns will be reflected in a change in the probabilities associated with the use of particular variants, which may lead to a reorganization of grammatical categories and rules.

Grammaticalization processes are, of course, by no means limited to pidgins and creoles: what is special is that typically many such processes are occurring at once. The result is that often we cannot rely on relating something we are trying to establish in one part of the grammar to some clearly established fact in some other part of the grammar, for that second fact will also be something that is in transition between two categories. We shall see an example of this in attempting to relate subject clitics to the establishment of an auxiliary.

1. Universals and substrate in the sociohistorical context. The sociohistorical context in which Tok Pisin evolved is fundamental to understanding the problems Tok Pisin presents to both the substrate and the universals lines of explanation. Tok Pisin is purportedly a bad candidate for universals because it was clearly not an 'early creolized' creole (Bickerton 1981:3-4). Though it had its roots in nineteenth century plantations (Mosel 1980, Mühlhäusler 1978), it was not a 'plantation creole' but rather a plantation pidgin. Its formative period occurred in a plantation system organized around relatively short-term indentured labor rather than slave labor. Workers stayed a few years rather than a lifetime. Thus the 'successive generations' of Tok Pisin speakers were successive cohorts of mainly young single men, each being replaced by another such cohort. Most of the children born to these men were born back home, into families with a Papuan or Austronesian home language. The fathers of such children may have introduced a little Tok Pisin into some of their talk with them,[3] but most of their mothers could not speak it,[4] with the result that those children who acquired it learned it in the same context their fathers had: as young adults away at work.

Now although Tok Pisin was formed in the plantation context, where speakers were removed from their home communities, it survived and flourished back in the New Guinea villages that workers returned to after their period of indenture was over.[5] In rural areas near European settlements, many people participated in the cash economy, where Tok Pisin was the lingua franca. And even in the more remote rural areas, initial recruitment of plantation laborers was usually concomitant with bringing an area into European control, with ensuing involvement with the civil authorities, the cash economy, and the missions. With the exception of some of the missions (cf. Sankoff 1977c:288-89), Tok Pisin was the lingua franca in all of these domains.

The creation of an infrastructure for Tok Pisin 'on the ground', in the places to which the plantation workers went home, has meant that the vast majority of Tok Pisin speakers have over the past hundred years spent most of their adult lives using Tok Pisin as a lingua franca in all sorts of dealings with the world outside of their natal villages, but have kept their first languages for home and local use (Sankoff 1971, Gilliam 1984). These would seem to be ideal conditions for the introduction of many substrate features into Tok Pisin. According to Bickerton, the introduction of such features while the language was still at the 'pidgin' stage would have blocked the development of a number of the putative universals he finds in 'early creolized' creoles. But there is also a major problem with invoking substrate as an explanation for anything to be found in Tok Pisin grammar: the vast number and diversity of languages spoken as first languages by speakers of Tok Pisin. Among the several hundred languages spoken in Papua New Guinea, one could surely always find at least two or three possible candidates for the source of anything less specific than a lexical item. Limiting the search to the first languages involved at the time when a given feature got established in Tok Pisin would reduce the number of possible substrate candidates,[6] but even so, one is left with a bewildering array of potential sources, and no principled reason for choosing among them.

Three unsatisfactory possibilities come to mind: (1) Tok Pisin has arbitrarily acquired feature x from language X, feature y from language Y, and so on; (2) Tok Pisin has incorporated only those substrate features with wide areal distribution; and (3) there is no unified grammar of Tok Pisin, only a set of versions or dialects, each of which reflects a different substrate, and which have enough surface resemblances to permit communication. The first of these possibilities, sometimes termed the 'cafeteria principle', is the least satisfactory and can, I think, be seriously invoked only in the case of particular lexical items. The problem with the second is that it is not sufficiently specific, but it contains a grain of truth which I extract and refine in the concluding section of this paper, where I also reexamine the third possibility.

2. The verb phrase in Tok Pisin. There is no current, unified analysis of the Tok Pisin verb phrase. Such an analysis is complicated at least by (1) the presence of so-called 'serial verb' constructions in Tok Pisin; (2) the uncertain status of many of the forms which seem to mark tense, mood, and aspect in Tok Pisin as modals, auxiliary verbs, full verbs, particles, adverbs, etc.; and (3) the lack of a clear understanding of the distribution and function of the so-called 'predicate marker' i. The present treatment is a first step toward unifying these questions.

There have been several attempts to analyze certain aspects of the problem. Hall (1943), Laycock (1970), Mihalic (1971), and especially Wurm (1971) all provide descriptions of each of the putative markers; Mühlhäusler (1976) discusses as part of his treatment of the lexicon those serial verb constructions analyzable as compounds. Woolford (1977) tries to unify an analysis of Mühlhäusler's 'compound' type serial constructions with other kinds of chaining, but her treatment is flawed by not taking into account the fact that some of the verbs she deals with should be analyzed as belonging to the auxiliary (cf. section 2.1). Finally, Mosel (1980), in her examination of the extent to which Tok Pisin exhibits substrate influence from Tolai, looks at both Mühlhäusler's 'compounding' chains and some of the tense, mood, and aspect markers, but in two quite separate parts of her analysis. In addition, given the gap in the literature on Tok Pisin, her treatment of tense, mood, and aspect is necessarily perfunctory. Some of the aforementioned sources also provide comments on i, which is also the subject of Woolford (1981) and Franklin (1980).

2.1 Serialization.

Although verb serialization, or verb chaining, is a feature not unique to pidgins and creoles, it is often said to be characteristic of them.[7] In Tok Pisin, we find examples such as those in (1) through (7).

(1) Em i <u>laik go hukim</u> pis.
    3S want go hook fish
    'He wanted to go {catch fish/fishing}.'

(2) Em <u>slip karai istap</u>.
    3S lie cry stay
    'He was lying there crying.'

(3) Mipela <u>igo swim igo</u>.
    1PL.EXCL go swim go
    'We went swimming.'

(4) Ol man <u>kam sanap lukluk</u> nau.
    PL man come stand look then
    'The people came and stood looking then.'

(5) Man ia <u>kirap amarim</u> em.
    man DET get-up hammer 3S
    'The man up and hammered him.'

(6) Na em i <u>salim</u> mi <u>kam</u>.
    and 3S send 1S come
    'And he sent me.'

(7) Yu yet <u>mekim kamap</u> long mi.
    2S INTENS make happen to 1S
    'You yourself made it happen to me.'

In my view, the verbs underlined in this set of examples should be analyzed as having different statuses, and as I develop the analysis, I will return to them at various points in this section and in the next two sections. First, however, let us examine Woolford's proposal (1977), which essentially treats them as all having the same status.

Woolford's analysis unites what she calls 'strictly defined' serial verbs, i.e. 'strings of two verbs with an intermediate noun such that the noun is the object of the first verb and the subject of the second' and 'other sorts of verb chaining' (p. 176). Her first type is exemplified by sentences such as (6) and (7), as well as by the second two verbs in (8) (Woolford's (2), 1977:176). In citing Woolford's example sentences, I use her glosses.

(8) Em i <u>save salim smok igo</u> antap long maunten.
    he know send smoke to up to mountain.
    'He sends smoke up to the mountain.'

Her mixed bag ('other sorts of verb chaining') contains two main types of sentences. Sentences of the first type are like (9) (Woolford's (7), 1977:177), consisting of two intransitive verbs with the same subject, the first a motion verb and the second what Woolford (1977:181) calls a 'directional verb'. The second two verbs of (3) also demonstrate this pattern.

(9) Em i kalap i go daun long si.
he jump go down to sea
'He dived into the sea.'

The second type contains sentences like (10) (Woolford's (8), 1977:177) and (11) (Woolford's (9), 1977:178). Though Woolford does not characterize them in any way, they seem to be chains of verbs with the same subject that take either NP or sentential complements.[8]

(10) Meri ia giaman pasim ai na em i lukluk.
woman pretend close eyes and she look
'The woman pretended to close her eyes and she looked.'

(11) Meri i holim pasim man bilong en.
woman hold fasten man of her
'The woman held her husband fast.'

Woolford proposes (1977:181) the phrase structure rule in (12) to account for at least the two main types of sentences she discusses.

(12) VP → V (NP) (VP)

Thus, (8) would be derived as in (8') and (9) would be derived as in (9').

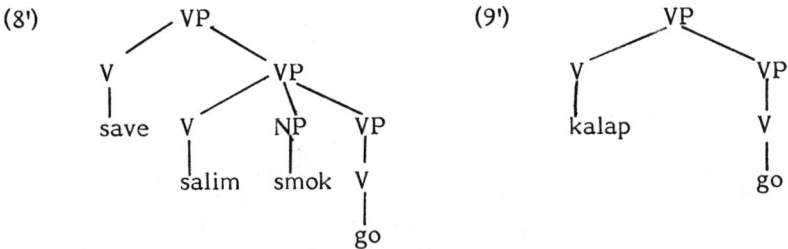

For chains of three or more verbs, Woolford's analysis gives us a right-branching structure. This would apply reasonably well to a number of verb chains found in my own data, e.g. (1') and (13) through (16). The nodes are labeled provisionally according to Woolford's analysis. Note, however, that the verb save in (16) is labeled a habitual marker rather than being glossed as 'know' as in Woolford's sentence, presented as (8).

Substrate and universals in the Tok Pisin verb phrase / 109

(1')
```
        VP
       /  \
      V    VP
      |   /  \
    i laik V   VP
           |  /  \
          go V    NP
             |    |
           hukim pis
```
'He wanted to go fishing'

(13)
```
        VP
       /  \
      V    VP
      |   /  \
    i laik V   VP
           |   |
          go   V
               |
             paitim
```
'He wanted to go hit (him)'

(14)
```
        VP
       /  \
      V    VP
      |   /  \
    i ken V    VP
          |    |
         go    V
               |
             istap
```
'He could go stay'

(15)
```
        VP
       /  \
      V    VP
      |   /  \
    i ken V    VP
          |    |
         go    V
               |
             wokim
```
'He could go make (it)'

(16)
```
        VP
       /  \
      V    VP
   mi save /  \
   (HAB)  V    VP
          |    |
         laik  V
               |
             toktok
```
'I like to talk'

Now consider sentence (17). The negative, <u>no</u>, occurs in the topmost VP node. Indeed, negation may occur only in this node, as illustrated in (16').

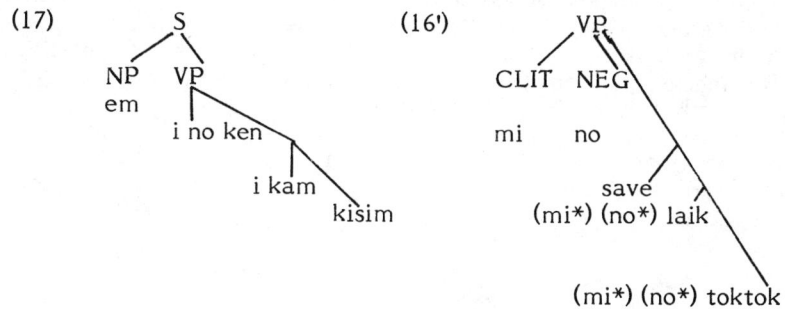

At the very least, this means that we would have to write a surface filter to rule out the application of no anywhere other than in the topmost VP. We also need to limit the application of the subject clitics--mi (1st sing.), yu (2nd sing.), yumi (1st pl. inclusive), ol (3rd pl.), and the -pela forms (various duals and plurals) in the same way.[10] Note that the third person singular em is not a clitic (cf. sentence (17)); I return to the subject of clitics in section 2.3.

Now notice the parallels in (1') and (13) through (15). All consist of a modal (laik 'want' or ken 'can'), followed by go 'go' or kam 'come', followed by a main verb. This is sketched in (18). Example (16), where save precedes laik, indicates that one might theoretically find sentences with more in the preverbal position. Other examples, however, lead us to order the three tentatively as follows: ken, save, and laik. And bin, marking past, or past-before-past, must occur prior to all of them, e.g. bin save wok 'had used to work' of bin go wok 'had gone to work', and so forth.

(18)

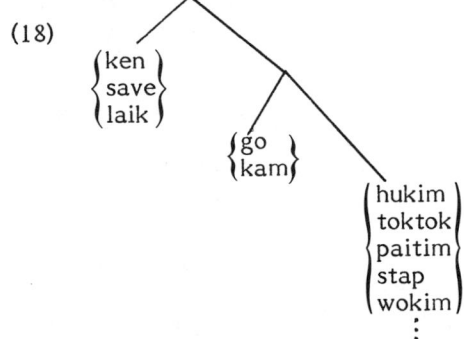

As (18) makes evident, it is clear that in all of these examples the rightmost verb in the string is the main verb, go or kam somehow modifies it, and ken, save, or laik has scope over the whole thing. In other words, a right-branching structure is appropriate.

It was seen earlier that the placement of clitics and the negative causes a problem which is perhaps minor and reparable for Woolford's analysis. But we are in more trouble with a VP like (19), for which a right-branching structure seems counterintuitive. In contrast with (1') and (13) through (18), where the rightmost verb is the main verb, here the main verb is the leftmost, with both i go and the completive or anterior marker pinis modifying it. The appropriate analysis would seem to be a left-branching one, as in (19').

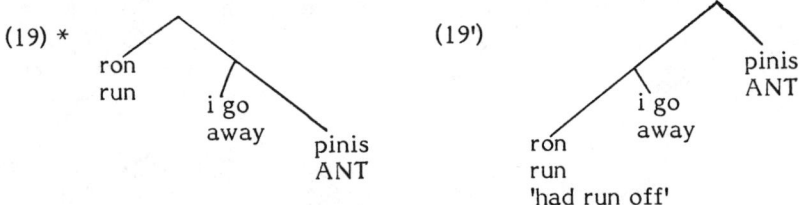

8 / Gillian Sa Substrate and universals in the Tok Pisin verb phrase / 111

A very similar sentence is illustrated in (20), but in this case the main verb <u>karim</u> 'to carry' is transitive, so a phrase marker is needed along the lines sketched there--again, a left-branching structure. Now note that Woolford's original sentence (8), rediagrammed here in its essential particulars as (8'), is very much like (20); however, it lacks the completive or anterior <u>pinis</u>, and contains instead the preverbal habitual marker <u>save</u>. I would suggest that (8") is a more correct representation of sentence (8): the habitual <u>save</u>, as in Woolford's analysis, takes scope over the whole predicate, but <u>go</u> is analyzed as a postverbal modifier rather than a main verb.

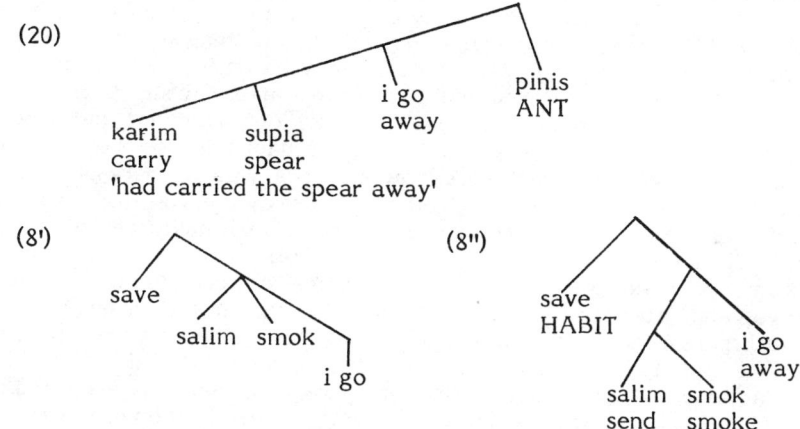

Looking back to Woolford's other sentences, one sees that in none of them is the rightmost verb unequivocally analyzable as the main verb. Sentence (8) is a good model for quite a number of sentences in my corpus where in a three-verb chain, the middle one is the main verb.

In summary, we have seen that Woolford's analysis fails to indicate that the topmost VP node is in any way different from later ones. We have also found that since the main verb may be modified both on the left and on the right, an analysis is needed that incorporates this fact in some way.

2.2 Tense, mood, and aspect. Taylor (1960) and Thompson (1961) noted that a range of creole languages had three preverbal particles: a past tense marker, a potential mood marker, and a durative aspect marker.[9] Bickerton (1974) changed the labels and their definitions slightly, and offered an interpretation in terms of cognitive universals to replace Taylor's and Thompson's essentially historical accounts. In addition, Bickerton made a basic distinction between stative and nonstative verbs, claiming that the unmarked interpretation of a nonstative will be simple past. The first marker then becomes 'anterior' rather than 'past', since it moves the unmarked reading back one stage to simple past for statives, and to past-before-past for nonstatives. The 'durative' aspect marker was relabeled 'nonpunctual', to cover both continuative and iterative. Finally, the 'potential' mood marker was redubbed 'irrealis', referring to futures, conditionals, etc. Bickerton's schema is, of course, an idealization, and as such does not account in a detailed and specific way for every occurrence or nonoccurrence of these markers in discourse. Givón (1982), for example, pointed out that many unmarked verbs in Bickerton's Hawaiian texts have neither of the two readings that Bickerton's schema allows for them.

I will not, however, dwell here on issues of accountability. Rather, I want to see to what extent the putative pancreole basic categories structure the Tok Pisin tense, mood, and aspect system. Though Bickerton specifically stated that Tok Pisin need not conform to the system he presented, it is tempting to see how far we can go with it. There are, however, some major obstacles. In several important respects, Bickerton's system is not sufficiently detailed for us to use, even in its most recent (1982) version. For one thing, he says nothing about negation, except to suggest that negative concord may be basic, despite its nonoccurrence in Hawaii. It does not, for that matter, occur in Tok Pisin either. But Bickerton is silent on the issues of placement and scope. Further, he tells us nothing about modals, perhaps because they are too variable in the creoles which he examined. In any case, there is no way in which modals can be omitted from the heart of the Tok Pisin system. Anterior and habitual markers, clearly part of verb modification, commonly take scope over them, as was noted in (16).

As far as the semantic categories themselves are concerned, Tok Pisin has two candidates for anterior: bin, which occurs first after negative in the verb phrase, and pinis, which occurs at the very end, even typically after the object NP if there is one. Irrealis is handled by bai, which, like lo in Papiamentu, occurs before the verb phrase (although as described in Sankoff and Laberge 1973, it has been moving closer to the verb over the past 60 or 70 years). Bickerton's third category, nonpunctual, is shared by the habitual marker save, which occurs preverbally, and the postverbal istap or igo, indicating continuative aspect.

Now what about placement? Muysken (1981) claimed that, theoretically, one could postulate two possible orders for the TMA markers within universal grammar, that is, either TMAV or VAMT. However, only the first seems to be attested in creoles. Muysken's two possibilities for representing TMA in universal grammar are given in (21).

(21a) TMA / __ VP, VP→V...
(21b) AMT / VP __, VP→...V

Muysken's two possibilities for representing TMA in attested creoles are shown in (22).

(22a)
```
        S
      / | \
    NP Aux  VP
       /|\   |
      T M A  V
```

(22b)
```
       V'''
      /  \
     T    V''
         /  \
        M    V'
            /  \
           A    V
```

Tok Pisin, as we have just seen, seems to have both left- and right-branching verb modifiers. The two possibilities for Tok Pisin that

Substrate and universals in the Tok Pisin verb phrase / 113

correspond to Muysken's suggestions are presented as (23) and (24), and (25) gives a linear representation of the major elements and their ordering.

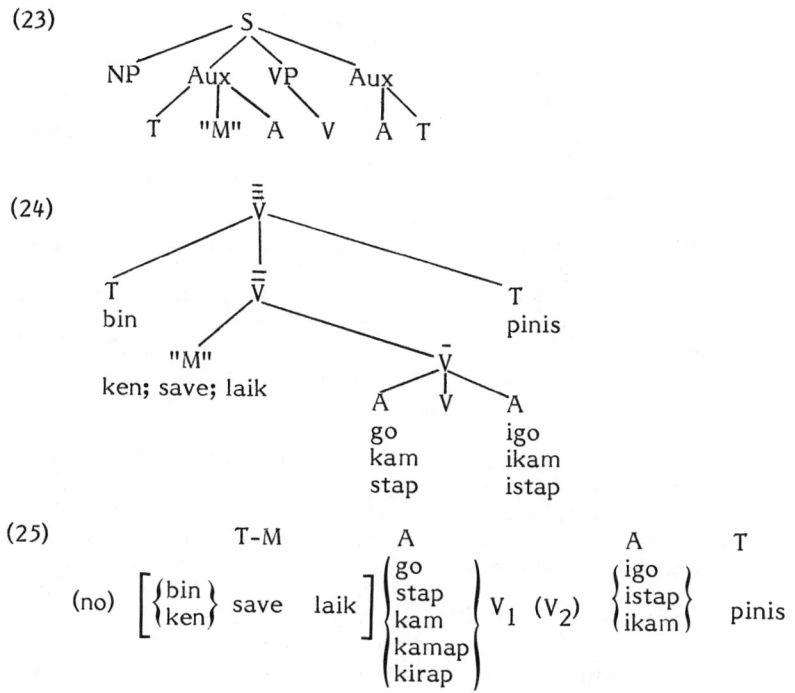

(23)

(24)

(25)

A few comments about this schema are in order, though a more detailed presentation will appear in Sankoff (in preparation). First, it is quite possible, and indeed frequently the case, that verbs occur without any of the TMA modification described here. Aspectual markers on both left and right are the most basic and most frequent, as in (3), for example; followed by modals; with the 'tense' markers bin and pinis clearly constituting the least important and least frequently marked grammatical category. Second, with the partial exception of bin and ken, all of the forms appearing in (24) and (25) can also occur as main verbs. Third, since, as has been explained, the irrealis marker bai does not appear in the verb phrase, the markers labeled 'M' are the modals ken and laik (both of which, however, sometimes indicate future and both of which can doubtless be considered as irrealis), as well as the habitual marker save. Lastly, I am considering the set of verbs Woolford referred to as 'directional' as being basically aspectual in character. When used after a verb of motion, igo and ikam certainly add direction to their marking of continuity, but igo in particular is basically, like istap, a marker of continuity, as illustrated in (26), where stap is the main verb, making postverbal istap infelicitous as a marker of continuity. Note that postverbal igo can be iterated to convey a longer time period.

(26) Mipela stap igo igo.
     1PL-EXCL stay CONT CONT
     'We stayed on (and on and on).'

Preverbal stap also conveys continuous aspect, and preverbal go, kam, kamap, and kirap are inceptive.
   Though having both left- and right-branching verb modification may seem unlikely, it is consonant with several other aspects of Tok Pisin grammar, as section 3 shows. But before discussing these typological issues, let us examine several facts about clitics and about the distribution of i- that support the analysis presented here.

2.3 The placement of i-. In a paper given at the 1977 Georgetown University Round Table on Languages and Linguistics (Sankoff 1977b), I analyzed two successive waves of cliticization of the subject pronouns in Tok Pisin. The first such wave washed i (originally the English third person subject pronoun) right up into the verb phrase, where it has remained ever since, being widely referred to in the literature as a 'predicate marker'. I prefer to regard it as a subject marker attached to the auxiliary.
   The postverbal markers virtually always appear as ikam, igo, and istap. (The latter two may be iterated up to four or five times to mark extremes of continuity and duration.) Thus i- is obligatory with the postverbal aspectual markers. Though in other environments i- is variable, some fairly strong trends can be discerned with respect to its distribution. The second most likely place for it to occur is the beginning of the verb phrase. On the other hand, it is very unlikely to occur before a main verb if that verb already has preverbal markers, unless the main verb is go, kam, or stap, as in (14). It never occurs between two main verbs: cf. (10) and (11) where, for example, (11') would be ungrammatical.

(11')   *Meri i holim i pasim man bilong en.

This supports Mühlhäusler's analysis (1976) of this kind of 'serialization' as belonging essentially to the lexicon. All of these facts suggest that i- is placed before the auxiliary, not the main verb. The right-hand auxiliary elements are marked more assiduously perhaps than the left because they occur in a place which is normally filled by something else, i.e. a noun phrase.
   When i became a subject marker within the verb phrase, its place as a subject pronoun was filled by em, derived from the English third person object pronoun him (perhaps also them). But whereas the tendency to copy noun subjects with pronouns, which was responsible for the original cliticization of i, had also resulted in the cliticization of the other subject pronouns, this did not happen again with em, leaving it in the subject noun phrase. Evidence for this analysis is to be found in the distribution of bai. Though it is variable in all positions, bai generally occurs to the left of all the subject pronouns, as in (27a) and (27b), but more frequently occurs to the right of full noun phrases and of em, as in (27c) and (27d). Em is alone among subject pronouns in showing this distribution, which Laberge and I observed a decade ago (Sankoff and Laberge 1973) but were unable to interpret at the time.

(27a) Bai mi go.
       IRR 1S go
       'I will go'

(27b) Bai ol i go.
       IRR 3PL SM go
       'They will go'

(27c) Em bai i go.
       3S IRR SM go
       'He will go'

(27d) Tupela meri bai i go.
       two girls IRR SM go
       'Two girls will go'

3. Left and right in Tok Pisin. Verbal auxiliaries are not the only things in Tok Pisin to show mirror image or nearly symmetrical structures. Nouns can have determiners on the left or right or both, as in (28); relative clauses can be marked on the left or right or both (cf. Sankoff and Brown 1976, Bradshaw 1979a), as diagrammed in (29); and quoted speech can be bracketed on either or both sides, as in (30).

(28a) wanpela man   'a man'
(28b) man ia   'the man'
(28c) ol man (ia)   'the men'

(29) NP ia [S ia]

(30) Na boi i tok, 'Mi no baim smok', em i tok olsem.
      and boy SM say 1S NEG buy cigarette 3S SM say thus
      'And the boy said, "I didn't buy cigarettes", so he said.'

As an SVO language, one would expect Tok Pisin to have all four of these--tense and aspect markers, determiners, relative clause, and quoted speech introducers--on the left, like Tolai. Mosel's (1980) schematization of the verb phrase in Tolai, an SVO Austronesian language, is shown in (31).

(31)   SM TM_1 TM_2 V_1 V_2 V_3 V_4

New Guinea's Papuan languages, however, are strongly SOV, and tend to have all of these on the right. Kaluli, for example, is a Papuan language with typical VAT ordering (Schieffelin, personal communication).

Tok Pisin has something for everyone. It is not the case, however, that those speakers with Papuan first languages have a version of Tok Pisin grammar that does all its modifying on the right, and conversely for those speakers with Austronesian first languages. Tok Pisin has not adopted the cafeteria approach to grammatical expansion, nor is its grammar simply a relexification of a number of very diverse substrates. Its left- and right-branching structures have some parallels, though, with languages in other areas where word order shift or contact between SVO and SOV languages is occurring. Bradshaw (1979b) has pointed to left- and right-bracketed negatives, relative clauses, and serial causatives in a number of New Guinea languages; serial verbs and left- and right-bracketed relative clauses also occur in a number of West African languages.[11] Such amalgams of 'typically SVO' and 'typically SOV' features are not, however, established in a pidgin language by fiat, overnight, by one or a number of speakers relexifying their native categories. Indeed, most of the features of Tok Pisin syntax that have been analyzed in any detail have been shown to have taken many decades to evolve. The amalgam, then, has involved forging new closed-class items and negotiating where to put them during a period when the grammatical glue of the original target, or superstrate, has dissolved. This has been done through talk, and has required some common metalevel understandings about communication, which I will call discursive practices. And such discourse patterns are, I argue, the most likely things for New Guineans of diverse language backgrounds to share. Along with some widely held prosodic and semantic features, discursive practices are better candidates for areal features than are the specifics of morphology or syntax. What Grimes (1972) calls 'outlines and overlays' in narrative conventions; rhetorical conventions used in the speech act known in Tok Pisin as rabisim ('rubbishing', or shaming); the copious use of sentence-final particles for asserting, seeking agreement, and so on; and clause-chaining patterns whereby only the last clause is finite, are found in one New Guinea language after the other.

My scenario for Tok Pisin runs as follows. It adopted SVO order not because, as Bickerton would claim, it 'needed' word order for case marking, but rather because of the clear and almost invariant English pattern. The open-class lexical items, largely of English origin, that eroded into closed-class items through ever-increasing use as glue, slowly became part of the grammar. They owed their initial placement to their placement in English, but some of them (like bai) subsequently began migrating to a place more befitting their emerging status. English words, however, were also pressed into service to do rhetorical work: reinforcing, asserting, questioning whether reference had been achieved, and so on. Much of this work, in New Guinea languages, is done by exploiting utterance-final position. Thus English words like the adverb here or the conjunction or that typically occur at the right-hand end of constituents or utterances, were enlisted, first on an ad hoc basis and then as members of the regular army.

As I pointed out several years ago (Sankoff 1979), in every area of Tok Pisin grammar that has been studied carefully, the grammar has been reinvented, not copied. Routinization of discursive practices provides the mechanism. And there is much that is shared about such practices, across a wide variety of substrate languages in Papua New Guinea. Substrate, then, enters at a metalevel, through discourse rather than by the relexifying of grammatical specifics. And in a sense, universals have to enter via the same quotidian path. Categories like the semantics of determiners or of tense, mood, and aspect may typically involve some basic, putatively universal characteristics, but they will interact with other elements in response to processing constraints involving things like ordering and memory, the input constraints provided by the superstrate model, and the subtle shaping of socially transmitted discursive practices.

Notes

This paper was begun in Vancouver, where I was a visitor in the Linguistics Department at the University of British Columbia, and finished in São Paulo. I thank my colleagues at UBC, especially David Ingram, Derek Nurse, Clifton Pye, and Michael Rochemont, and the student members of my seminar, for many helpful discussions. Talmy Givón, Bambi Schieffelin, and Fernando Tarallo contributed support, encouragement, and many fine insights. None of them, of course, is responsible for any errors that remain. I am grateful also to the many Papua New Guineans who helped me learn Tok Pisin and who worked with me during a number of visits to Papua New Guinea between 1966 and 1977. Lastly, I want to thank my mother, Marjorie Topham, the staff of the Lilliput Day Care Centre at UBC, and Ruth Elisabeth Lopes Moino of São Paulo for looking after Alice so well while I was working on this paper.

1. Superstrate influence is clearly not a serious contender as far as the morphology and syntax of Tok Pisin are concerned.

2. Note Benveniste's Latin motto: Nihil est in lingua quod non prius fuerit in oratione (1966:131).

3. In the late 1960s, I frequently heard Buang fathers joking with their small children in Tok Pisin. It seemed that what made this joking especially funny was the use of Tok Pisin itself.

4. Even today, more than twice as many men as women speak Tok Pisin (Sankoff 1977c:294).

5. Tok Pisin was used as a lingua franca in German New Guinea. According to Firth, 85,000 would be a conservative estimate of the number of New Guineans 'who went as indentured labourers to plantations in German New Guinea from villages within that colony' (Firth 1976:51).

6. Mosel (1980) appears to be correct in proposing Tolai in particular, and the Tolai-Patpatar language group in general, as the most important potential substrate source during the formative period of Tok Pisin's development.

7. Most authors who have done comparative work on creoles, including Bickerton, have noted this feature. Bickerton's (1981) explanation for it in terms of a 'need' to mark oblique cases is, I think, totally misguided and appears to neglect the existence of prepositions in all known creoles.

8. Woolford, however, explicitly rejects an analysis of a sentence like (10) as involving any kind of reduced sentential complement.

9. Though the markers occur only when expressing the particular semantic function with which each is associated, their ordering with respect to each other and to the main verb is always fixed, thus (Tense) (Modal) (Aspect) Verb.

10. Since the point of Woolford's (1977) analysis was to provide a phrase structure for serial verbs, rather than concentrating on details of negative and clitic placement, it is not clear how she would have solved the problems their placement would pose.

11. Bradshaw's (1979b) seminal paper on some of the consequences of SOV and SVO contacts in the Huon Gulf area of Papua New Guinea was an important influence in my thinking about the Tok Pisin verb phrase. I do not, however, agree with his view (1979a) that the double-bracketed

relative clauses in Tok Pisin have their origin in the syntax of any other language(s).

References

Benveniste, Emile. 1966. Problèmes de linguistique générale I. Paris: Gallimard.

Bickerton, Derek. 1974. Creolization, linguistic universals, natural semantax and the brain. University of Hawaii Working Papers in Linguistics 6.3:125-41.

Bickerton, Derek. 1981. Roots of language. Ann Arbor, Mich.: Karoma Publishers.

Bradshaw, Joel. 1979a. The origins of syntax in syntax: Tok Pisin relatives reconsidered. University of Hawaii Working Paper in Linguistics.

Bradshaw, Joel. 1979b. Causative serial constructions and word order change in Papua New Guinea. Paper presented at the annual meeting of the Linguistic Society of America, Los Angeles, December.

Firth, S. 1976. The transformation of the labour trade in German New Guinea, 1899-1914. Journal of Pacific History 11.51-65.

Franklin, Karl J. 1980. The particles i- and na in Tok Pisin. Kivung 12.2:134-44.

Gilliam, Angela M. 1984. Language and 'development' in Papua New Guinea. Dialectical Anthropology 8.303-18.

Givón, Talmy. 1982. Tense-aspect-modality: The creole prototype and beyond. In: Tense-aspect, between semantics and pragmatics. Edited by Paul J. Hopper. Philadelphia: John Benjamins.

Grimes, Joseph. 1972. Outlines and overlays. Lg. 48.513-24.

Hall, Robert A., Jr. 1943. Melanesian pidgin English: Grammar, texts, vocabulary. Baltimore: Linguistic Society of America.

Laberge, Suzanne, and Gillian Sankoff. 1979. Anything you can do. In: Discourse and syntax. Edited by Talmy Givón. New York: Academic Press. 419-40.

Laycock, D. C. 1970. Materials in New Guinea pidgin (coastal and lowlands). Pacific Linguistics D-5.

Mihalic, Rev. F. 1971. The Jacaranda dictionary and grammar of Melanesian pidgin. Port Moresby: Jacaranda Press.

Mosel, Ulrike. 1980. Tolai and Tok Pisin. The influence of the substratum on the development of New Guinea pidgin. Pacific Linguistics Series B.

Mühlhäusler, Peter. 1976. Growth and structure of the lexicon of New Guinea pidgin. Ph.D. dissertation, Australian National University, Canberra.

Mühlhäusler, Peter. 1978. Samoan Plantation Pidgin English and the origin of New Guinea pidgin. Pacific Linguistics Series A.54:67-119.

Muysken, Pieter. 1981. Creole tense/mood/aspect systems: The unmarked case? In: Generative studies on creole languages. Dordrecht: Foris Publications. 181-99.

Sankoff, Gillian. 1971. Language use in multilingual societies: Some alternate approaches. In: Sociolinguistics. Edited by J. Pride and J. Holmes. Harmondsworth, Middlesex: Penguin. 33-51.

Sankoff, Gillian. 1977a. Creolization and syntactic change in New Guinea Tok Pisin. In: Sociocultural dimensions of language change. Edited by M. Sanches and B. Blount. New York: Academic Press. 119-30.
Sankoff, Gillian. 1977b. Variability and explanation in language and culture: Cliticization in New Guinea Tok Pisin. In: Georgetown University Round Table on Languages and Linguistics 1977. Edited by Muriel Saville-Troike. Washington, D.C.: Georgetown University Press. 59-73.
Sankoff, Gillian. 1977c. Multilingualism in Papua New Guinea. In: New Guinea area languages and language study, vol 3: Language, culture, society and the modern world. Edited by S. A. Wurm. Fascicle 1, 265-307. Pacific Linguistics C-40.
Sankoff, Gillian. 1979. The genesis of a language. In: The genesis of language. Edited by K. Hill. Ann Arbor, Mich.: Karoma Publishers. 23-47.
Sankoff, Gillian. 1980. The social life of language. Philadelphia: University of Pennsylvania Press.
Sankoff, Gillian. (in preparation) The Tok Pisin verb phrase.
Sankoff, Gillian, and Penelope Brown. 1976. The origins of syntax in discourse: A case study of Tok Pisin relatives. Lg. 52.631-66.
Sankoff, Gillian, and Suzanne Laberge. 1973. On the acquisition of native speakers by a language. Kivung 6.32-47.
Taylor, D. 1960. Language shift or changing relationship? IJAL 26.144-61.
Thompson, R. W. 1961. A note on some possible affinities between the creole dialects of the Old World and those of the New. In: Proceedings of the Conference on Creole Language Studies. London: Macmillan.
Woolford, Ellen. 1975. Variation and change in the i predicate marker in New Guinea Tok Pisin. Paper prepared for the 1975 International Conference on Pidgins and Creoles, Honolulu.
Woolford, Ellen. 1977. Aspects of Tok Pisin grammar. Ph.D. dissertation, Duke University.
Wurm, S. A. 1971. New Guinea Highlands Pidgin: Course materials. Pacific Linguistics D-3.

THE PRAGMATICS OF REFERENTIALITY

Talmy Givón
University of Oregon, Eugene

1. Reference and existence. The treatment of referentiality (and coreference) in linguistics began as a by-product of a purely logical approach, whereby--to use the most extreme logical positivist formulation--terms have reference if there exists some entity in the so-called Real World (cf. Carnap 1958 or Russell 1905, inter alia). Thus, in (1a), the term the king of France does not refer, because there is no king in France, while the queen of England does refer because there is a queen in England.

(1a)   The king of France is bald.
(1b)   The queen of England is bald.

A more realistic linguistic approach would concede that what is at issue is not whether terms refer to individuals existing in 'the Real World', but rather whether they refer to those existing in some 'universe of discourse'. Thus, in (2), both (2a) and (2b) are equally referring expressions, regardless of the likelihood that in the so-called Real World the subject of (2a) does not exist while that of (2b) does.

(2a)   There was once a unicorn. The unicorn loved lettuce.
(2b)   There was once a rabbit. The rabbit loved lettuce.

By using the term 'universe of discourse', one could, of course, perpetuate the logic-bound tradition of viewing linguistic expressions as entities on their own (i.e. propositions or their concatenations), rather than as communicative acts performed by some speaker for a particular purpose. One consequence of adopting a more pragmatic approach to the problems of reference is that 'existing in some universe of discourse' in fact readily translates into 'meant by the speaker to have reference in some universe of discourse'. While this intensional reformulation of 'have reference' is indeed pragmatic--rather than logico-semantic--in some obvious sense, it nonetheless retains residual logico-semantic characteristics. The chief one of these is that the referential properties of terms can be determined strictly within the atomic proposition in which they are embedded, and without recourse to a wider extrapropositional context.

2. **Reference and propositional modalities.** The logico-semantic tradition is virtually silent about the systematic connections revealed in language between referential properties of NPs and the propositional modalities within whose scope those NPs reside. A brief summary of these regular correlations follows. Modern logicians recognize four major propositional modalities (cf. Carnap 1947), shown in (3).

(3a) Necessary truth [true analytically, by definition]
(3b) Factual truth [true synthetically, as fact]
(3c) Possible truth [possibly true]
(3d) Nontruth [false]

In human language it is possible to show that these same modalities may be redefined in terms of the communicative contract between speaker and hearer, as respectively (cf. Givón, 1982a):

(4a) Presupposition [true by agreement/convention; speaker assumes that (i) the hearer will not challenge this proposition, and (ii) no evidentiary support is required]
(4b) realis-assertion [strongly asserted as true; speaker assumes that the hearer may challenge this proposition, and is prepared to back it up with evidentiary support]
(4c) irrealis-assertion [weakly asserted as true; speaker is offering the proposition as hypothesis, expecting strong challenge and having little evidentiary support]
(4d) NEG-assertion [strongly asserted as false; with similar stipulations as in (4b)]

For the purpose of their systematic effect on the referentiality of NPs within their scope in human language, the four propositional modalities just given may be grouped into two larger macromodalities--fact and nonfact, as shown in (5).

(5a) FACT: presupposition and realis-assertion
(5b) NONFACT: irrealis-assertion and NEG-assertion

The correlation between propositional modalities and the referentiality of NPs under their scope can be then summed up as shown in (6) (cf. Givón 1973, 1983a:Ch.11).

(6)　　NPs <u>may</u> be nonreferential <u>only</u> when they are under the scope of some NONFACT modality. Otherwise they <u>must</u> be referential.

There are many sources in human language for the NONFACT modality, some taking the entire proposition under their scope, others taking only portions (such as the object or a sentential complement) under their scope. At this point I will not enumerate all of those, but rather illustrate the generalization (6) with a few representative examples,[1] using only indefinite NPs.

(7a)　　FACT, presupposition:
　　　　Mary regretted that she saw <u>an eagle</u>.
　　　　　　[⊃ Mary saw a <u>particular</u> eagle, one that the speaker is committed to assert: 'It does exist']
(7b)　　FACT, realis-assertion:
　　　　Mary saw <u>an eagle</u>.
　　　　　　[⊃ Mary saw a <u>particular</u> eagle, one that the speaker is committed to assert: 'It does exist']
(7c)　　NONFACT, irrealis-assertion:
　　　　Mary will see <u>an eagle</u>.
　　　　　　(i)　　[⊃ Mary will see a <u>particular</u> eagle, one that the speaker is committed to assert: 'It does exist']
　　　　　　(ii)　 [⊃ Mary <u>may</u> see <u>some</u> member of the <u>type</u> 'eagle', though the speaker does not have any particular one in mind]
(7d)　　NONFACT, NEG-assertion:
　　　　Mary did not see <u>an eagle</u>.
　　　　　　[⊃ The speaker does not have in mind any particular eagle that Mary didn't see, rather, he asserts that she did not see <u>any</u> member of the <u>type</u> 'eagle']

When I first discussed the systematic correlation between propositional modalities and referentiality properties of NPs in human language, one of the strongest supports I observed for such a formulation was the distinct morphological systems marking referential vs. nonreferential arguments in many human languages. In some, this is the major distinction within the article system, disregarding the further contrast of definiteness. Thus, consider examples (8)-(10) from Bemba (Givón 1973).

(8)　　　FACT, REALIS-ASSERTION:
(8a)　　a-à-somene <u>ici</u>-tabo　　　　　　　　　　　　　　　[REF]
　　　　he-past-read REF-book
　　　　　(i)　　'He read <u>the book</u>' [DEF]
　　　　　(ii)　 'He read <u>a book</u>' [INDEF]
(8b)　　*a-à-somene <u>ci</u>-tabo　　　　　　　　　　　　　　[*NONREF]
　　　　he-past-read NREF-book

(9) NONFACT, IRREALIS-ASSERTION:
(9a) a-kà-soma ici-tabo   [REF]
     he-future-read REF-book
     (i) 'He will read the book' [DEF]
     (ii) 'He will read a particular book' [INDEF]
(9b) a-kà-soma ci-tabo   [NONREF]
     he-future-read NREF-book
     'He will read some--unspecified--book'

(10) NONFACT, NEG-ASSERTION:
(10a) ta-a-à-somene ici-tabo   [REF]
      NEG-he-past-read REF-book
      'He didn't read the book' [DEF]
(10b) ta-a-à-somene ci-tabo   [NONREF]
      NEG-he-past-read NREF-book
      'He didn't read a/any book' [INDEF]

In some other languages, such as Spoken Israeli Hebrew, Chinese, Turkish, Sherpa, Persian, all Creoles, and many others, the numeral 'one' is used to mark referential-indefinite arguments, while nonreferential indefinites are most commonly left unmarked. Thus consider example (11), from Hawaii English Creole (Bickerton 1975, 1981).

(11a) He read one book   [FACT, REF]
      he read-past REF book
      'He read a book'
(11b) *He read book   [FACT, *NONREF]
(11c) He go-read one book   [NONFACT, REF]
      he future-read REF book
      'He will read a particular book'
(11d) He go-read book   [NONFACT, NONREF]
      he future-read book
      'He will read some--unspecified--book'
(11e) He no-read book   [NEG, NONREF]
      he NEG-read-past book
      'He didn't read a/any book'
(11f) *He no-read one book   [*NEG, REF]

The facts as described so far seemed rather clean and uncontroversial at the time, so that once 'semantically referential' was recast in terms of the speaker's referential intent, morphology in one language after another seemed to cooperate and thus uphold such a formulation (see e.g. discussion in Givón 1975/1979). Soon after, however, the ground suddenly shifted, when I noticed that in Hebrew one could in fact get semantically referential indefinite NPs to appear without the numeral 'one' under the scope of incontrovertibly FACT modalities. To illustrate this possibility, consider (12a-b) (originally from Givón 1976/1981; see further discussion in Givón 1982b, 1983a:Ch. 11).

(12a) ...az yatsati la-rexov ve-nixnasti le-xanut sfarim
       so I-exited to-the-street and-I-entered in-shop-of books
       '...So I went out and entered a bookstore

ve-kaniti sefer-<u>xad</u> she-himlitsu li <u>alav</u> meod,
and-I-bought book-<u>one</u> that-they-recommended to-me <u>on-it</u> very
and I bought a book that was recommended to me highly,

ve-ratsti habayta ve-hitxalti likro <u>oto</u>
and-I-ran home and-I-started reading <u>it</u>
and I ran home and started reading <u>it</u>,

ve-<u>ze</u> haya beemet sefer metsuyan...
and-<u>it</u> was truly book excellent
and <u>it</u> was indeed an excellent book...'

(12b)　...az yatsati la-rexov ve-nixnasti le-xanut sfarim
so I-exited to-the-street and-I-entered in-shop-of books
'...So I went out and entered a bookstore

ve-kaniti <u>sefer</u> ve-axar-kax ratsti habayta
and-I bought book and-after-that I-ran home
and bought <u>a book</u> and then I hurried home

ve-hitraxatsti ve-axalti ve-halaxti lishon...
and-I-washed and-I-ate and-I-went to-sleep
and washed and ate and went to sleep...'

Semantically, both (12a) and (12b) involve a realis-assertion--FACT--about buying 'a book', so that logically that particular book must have existed. However, the referential-indefinite marker 'one' marks that book only in (12a), where the particular referential identity mattered in the subsequent discourse, and where 'book' keeps recurring as topic in the subsequent discourse. In contrast, in (12b) the specific referential identity of the book seems not to matter; rather, the speaker 'did some book-buying' and then went home, with the particular book that was bought never mentioned again.

In assessing what such facts mean (Givón 1982b), I suggested that semantic referentiality is merely a special case of a more general phenomenon, pragmatic referentiality. It is, of course, not an accident that entities that tend to individuate strongly and have easily recognizable 'semantic' referential identity also tend to be more important--and recurrent--in discourse. Similar generalizations have been noted by Hopper and Thompson (1980, 1983). Thus, as I demonstrate shortly, the majority of arguments that persist longer in discourse are also semantically referential. But such a correlation is not absolute, and two types of crucial nonoverlaps are of great interest.

(i)　　As in (12b), the semantically referential NPs are nonetheless marked by the characteristic morpheme that tends to mark nonreferential NPs, just in case they are nonrecurrent and unimportant for the subsequent discourse.

(ii)　　Equally interesting are instances where semantically nonreferential NPs are nonetheless marked by the characteristic referentiality marker 'one' in those rare cases where they are of great thematic importance in the subsequent discourse.

In section 3 I report briefly on work done in two text studies, by Cooreman (1982, 1983) and Rude (1983), working on the discourse-conditioning of the antipassive construction in two ergative languages, Chamorro and Nez Perce, respectively.

3. **Semantic referentiality and discourse persistence.** It has been common knowledge that objects in the antipassive construction tend to be nonreferential, low on individuation (i.e. plural), low on topicality (i.e. indefinite), etc. (see e.g. discussion in Hopper and Thompson 1980; Kalmar 1979, 1980; Heath 1976, inter alia). What Cooreman has shown in her text-based study of Chamorro is that objects in the antipassive construction are lowest in topicality as compared to objects of the more common transitive ergative construction or to the patient-subjects of the passive. 'Topicality' was measured both anaphorically and cataphorically, and objects of the antipassive tend to be both primarily indefinite, i.e. have no anaphoric antecedence in discourse, and lowest in persistence in subsequent discourse. The comparison is summarized in Table 1. The measure of referential distance (RD) expresses anaphoric topicality, with a high value meaning low topicality. The measure of topical persistence (TP) expresses cataphoric topicality, with a high value meaning high topicality.

Table 1. Topicality properties of direct objects in Chamorro discourse.

Object type	Average RD	Average TP
in ERG-clause	4.35	0.81
in AP-clause	20.00[2]	0.00
in IN-passive	1.38	2.00
in MA-passive	3.33	1.44

Cooreman (1982) also notes that the patient in the antipassive construction does not appear at all--i.e. is 'deleted nonanaphorically'--70 percent of the time, and further, that the remaining 30 percent are predominantly semantically nonreferential.

Almost identical results are reported for Nez Perce by Rude (1983). The comparison between the topciality measurements of patient-objects in the ergative-transitive, antipassive, and passive constructions are given in Table 2.

Table 2. Topicality properties of direct objects in Nez Perce discourse.

Object type	Average RD	Average TP
in ERG-clause	5.25	2.64
in AP-clause	13.86	0.41
in PASSIVE-clause	2.86	1.71

In the Nez Perce text studies by Rude (1983), out of the total of 51 objects in the antipassive construction, 30 (or 59 percent) were indefinite, mostly full NPs (29 out of the 30), and most of those semantically nonreferential. While the percentages are not identical to those in Chamorro, the general direction is the same.

4. **Pragmatic referentiality and major participants in Krio narratives.** Krio is an English-based Creole language spoken in Sierra Leone. Its article system conforms to the normal Creole pattern described by Bickerton (1975, 1981), with a contrast between <u>di</u> 'the' (or <u>dis</u> 'this' and <u>'a</u> 'that') marking definites, <u>wan</u> 'one' marking referential indefinites, and the zero form marking nonreferentials (see example (11) for the Hawaii Creole illustrations). In this study, I have analyzed four stories taken from Hancock (1972). They are all short stories; the first, a joke, is given in section 4.1. In these stories, major participants are introduced for the first time as either REF-INDEF NPs marked by <u>wan</u> or names, or relational-definite NPs ('his wife', 'her brother' etc.). I have chosen only stories where at least some of the major participants are introduced as REF-INDEF NP, i.e. with <u>wan</u>. For each story, I divided all NPs/topics into two groups, major and minor participants. The major ones in these stories are either <u>wan</u>-marked or relational definites. The minor participants are either relational definites ('his neck', 'the window')[3] or zero-marked, with the majority of the latter being semantically NONREF, but an interesting minority being semantically referential.

Since the first story is short, I may as well illustrate the text analysis methodology used in this study by reproducing the story in its entirety.[4]

4.1 Story 1.

Na Kamfoh Wi Kam foh!
'It's Camphor That We Came for'

wan-dey-ya, <u>tu-pikin denh graní</u> sén denh na <u>wan mamí inh sháp</u>
one-day-here two child their grandma sent them to one woman her shop
'One day the grandmother of two children sent them to one woman's shop'

fo gó bái <u>kámfoh</u>. Wey denh rích déy, di mamí áks denh
for go buy <u>camphor</u> when they reach there the woman ask them
'to go and buy some camphor. When they arrived there, the woman asked them'

weytin denh kam foh; na-déy di pikín-denh séy, denh don-fogét.
what-thing they come for TOP-they the child-they say they done-forget
'what they came for; so those children said that they had forgotten.'

di mamí kól <u>ol di tin</u> na di shap; <u>ówri</u>, <u>simínji</u>, etc., denh til no memba.
the woman call <u>all the thing</u> LOC the shop <u>butter</u>, <u>clove</u>, etc. they still NEG remember
'The woman called (the names of) all the things in the shop: butter, cloves, etc., but they still couldn't remember.'

di pikín-denh jís dey-sáy, denh kám foh..., denh kám foh...
the child-they just PROG-say they come for they come for
'The children just kept saying, they came for...they came for...'

na-ính di mamí táya, en séy mék denh gó ówm en áks denh graní
TO-him the woman tired and say make they go home and ask their
   grandmother
'Well, so that woman got tired, and she told them they should go home
and ask their grandmother'

wéytin denh kám foh. As denh gó ówm nomóh, na-ính <u>wan di pikín-denh</u>
   mémba,
what-thing they come for as they go home nomore TO-him <u>one the child-
   they</u> remember
'what they were supposed to buy. As they went home, one of the children remembered,

en rón gó bák na di sháp en séy, 'Na-kámfoh wi kám foh, Má!'
and run go back LOC the shop and say 'FOC-camphor we come for,
   Ma'ame'
'so he ran back to the shop and said: "It's camphor that we came for,
Ma'ame!"'

The recurrence pattern of all participant NPs in this story is given in
Table 3.

Table 3. NP marking on first appearance in discourse, discourse
importance status, and recurrence in subsequent discourse
for Krio story 1.

NP and its marking at 1st occurrence	Semantic REF-status	Importance in discourse	Total occurrences in discourse
tu pikin 'two children'	REF-INDEF	major topic	18
wan mamí 'a woman'	REF-INDEF	major topic	6
wan di pikin 'one of the children'	REF-INDEF	major topic	3
denh graní 'their grandmother'	REL-DEF	minor, related to major	2
inh shap 'her shop'	REL-DEF	minor, related to major	3
kamfoh 'camphor'	NONREF	minor, but thematically important	2
owri 'butter'	NONREF	minor	1
siminji 'cloves'	NONREF	minor	1

As one can see, the correlation between the use of <u>wan</u> (or <u>tu</u>) to introduce an NP into the discourse and the discourse status of that NP is
rather striking. Only major participants, ones likely to recur through the
story more frequently, are introduced by the numeral-article. And all
the bare-stem NPs are both semantically nonreferential and

128 / Talmy Givón

pragmatically unimportant in the discourse--and thus recur little if at all after their initial entry into the discourse.

4.2 Story 2. <u>Wan Brokow Ows</u> 'A Tumbledown House.' The second story is somewhat longer. Table 4 presents an analogous analysis of its correlations. In this story we meet one more marking device of Krio, the suffixal -ya(-so) 'here...so', which is used to mark only important participants in the discourse when they are reintroduced, as full definite NPs, after a certain gap of absence.[5]

Table 4. NP marking on first appearance in discourse, discourse importance status, and recurrence in subsequent discourse for Krio story 2: <u>Wan Brokow Ows</u> 'A Rundown House'.

NP and its marking at 1st occurrence	Semantic REF-status	Importance in discourse	Total occurrences in discourse
a 'I'	speaker; REF-DEF	major	24
wan dey dey 'one there' / wan patikla wan 'a particular one'	REF-INDEF (pronoun)	major	13 (22)
di trit 'the street'	REF-DEF	minor	3
wan eykuru dog 'a mangy dog'	REF-INDEF	minor	2
yayam 'food'	NONREF	minor	1
di doti-boks 'the trash cans'	DEF-REF	minor	1
di oda pat 'the other side'	DEF-REF	minor, referring to 'street'	1
ows 'houses'	REF-INDEF	minor, prelude to major theme	2
denh ows-ya 'those houses-here'	REF-DEF	minor, prelude to major theme	
broko-ows denh 'rundown houses-they'	NONREF	minor, but attributive of major theme	1
di wol-denh 'the walls'	REF-DEF	minor, part of major	1
di winda 'the window'	REF-DEF	minor, part of major	2
winda-blain 'curtains'	NONREF	minor, part of major	1
da fain-fain gadin 'that beautiful garden'	REF-DEF	minor, part of major	1
di geyt 'the gate'	REF-DEF	minor, part of major	1
di do 'the door'	REF-DEF	minor, part of major	1

Table 4 (continued).

(1)	(2)	(3)	(4)
di step 'the steps'	REF-DEF	minor, part of major	1
ol di bowd 'all the boards'	REF-DEF	minor, part of major	1
gras-gras 'grassy'	NONREF	minor, attributive	1
maskita 'mosquitos'	REF-INDEF	minor	1
gows 'ghosts'	NONREF	minor	1
eni noiz 'any noise'	NONREF	minor	1
spirit 'spirits'	NONREF	minor	1
titi 'girl'	NONREF	minor, attributive of major	1
wan owl mami 'an old lady'	NONREF	minor; attributive of major; appear at thematic peak	1
wan mi fambul 'a family member'	NONREF	minor; attributive of major; appear at thematic peak	1
wan big noiz 'a big noise'	REF-INDEF	minor; thematic peak of story	1

Key: (1) NP and its marking at first occurrence; (2) semantic REF-status; (3) importance in discourse; (4) total occurrences in discourse.

Of the two major topics/participant NPs in this story, one is the speaker, coded as 'I'; the other, 'house' is coded as REF-DEF by the numeral <u>wan</u>. A host of minor participants are introduced as definite parts of a major participant, the house, and one may argue that in fact those constitute recurrences of the whole i.e. 'house' (cf. Linde 1974). Three types of interesting exceptions to the Creole morphological marking rules can be observed.

(i) Semantically referential NPs coded by bare-stem form. Two out of the total of nine bare-stem NPs--'houses' and 'mosquitos'--are semantically referential. However, they are thematically minor participants and low in individuation (cf. Hopper and Thompson 1980, 1983)--in fact, plurals.

(ii) Semantically nonreferential NPs marked with the numeral <u>wan</u>. There are two instances of these: 'an old woman' and 'a family member'. Both are similes predicating the major topic of this story, 'house'. And both come at the very thematic peak of the narrative, just prior to the old house crashing down.

(iii) Thematically nonrecurring--minor--NPs marked with <u>wan</u>. There are two of these, 'a mangy dog' and 'a big noise', and one of them--the latter--appears at the thematic peak of the story.

These exceptions--with only 'a mangy dog' remaining problematic[6]--in fact illustrate the underlying pragmatic nature of marking referentiality by the numeral <u>wan</u> in Krio:

(a) referential indefinites that are unimportant in the discourse do not get marked by <u>wan</u> in spite of their semantic referentiality;

(b) nonreferentials that are of central thematic importance in the narrative are marked by <u>wan</u> regardless of their semantic status as nonreferential;

(c) finally, although there is a strong correlation, statistically, between discourse importance of participants and their frequency of recurrence in the discourse, the bottom line is that thematic centrality overrides considerations of mere frequency.[7]

One last point concerns the use of the suffixal <u>-ya(-so)</u> in this story. It appears only twice, in <u>pan denh ows-ya</u> 'among those houses' and <u>dis ows-ya</u> 'this house'. Its appearance is thus limited to the central character or to the group of which the central character is member. As will be seen later on, in the two other--longer--stories, <u>-ya(-so)</u> is used with much higher frequency to reintroduce central characters into the discourse.

4.3 Story 3. <u>Tif Tif, God Laf</u> 'A Thief Steals, God Laughs'. The third story is still longer. The distribution of its NP participants, their morphological marking, their semantic referential status, and their discourse status and overall frequency, are all given in Table 5.

Table 5. NP marking on first appearance in discourse, discourse importance status, and recurrence in subsequent discourse for Krio story 3: <u>Tif Tif, God Laf</u> 'A Thief Steals, God Laughs'.

NP and its marking at 1st occurrence	Semantic REF-status	Importance in discourse	Total occurrences in discourse
Major participants:			
wan man 'a man'	REF-INDEF	major	74
wan fam 'a firm'	REF-INDEF	major	12
inh bos onh pikin sef 'the boss's own son'	REL-DEF	major	29
plenty moni 'lots of money'	REF-INDEF (mass noun)	major	18
wan kobod 'a cupboard'	REF-INDEF	major	5
Minor participants:			
inh wok 'his work'	REL-DEF	minor, related to major	1
inh bodi 'his body'	REL-DEF	minor, part of major	1

Table 5 (continued).

(1)	(2)	(3)	(4)
inh main 'his mind'	REL-DEF	minor, part of major	1
inh grachuiti 'his gratuity'	REL-DEF	minor, related to major	1
inh at 'his heart'	REL-DEF	minor, part of major	1
di sai 'the place'	REF-DEF	minor, loca-tional[8]	1
son sai 'some place'	REF-INDEF	minor	1
son denh big man-denh 'some of the important men'	REF-INDEF[9]	minor	1
maneyja 'manager'	NONREF	minor; attribute of major	1
grachuiti 'gratuity'	NONREF	minor	1
meseynja 'messenger'	NONREF	minor; attribute of major	1
pey 'pay'	NONREF	minor	1
penshon 'pension'	NONREF	minor	1
bris 'breeze'	NONREF	minor	1
wowk 'work'	NONREF	minor	1
ol sai 'every place'	REF-INDEF	minor	1
no sai 'nowhere'	NONREF	minor	1
ol man 'everybody'	NONREF	minor	1

Key: (1) NP and its marking at first occurrence; (2) semantic REF-status; (3) importance in discourse; (4) total occurrences in discourse.

Of the five major participants in this story, three are introduced initially with <u>wan</u>, a fourth with the quantifier 'plenty', since it is a mass noun, and the fifth is relationally definite, thus related to 'firm' via 'the boss'. Not a single minor participant is introduced by <u>wan</u>.

All minor participants appear only once in the discourse. They are further divided into two major types: (1) relational-definite referential ones, largely related to either major participants or to the location, thus indirectly to the major participant 'firm'; or (2) zero-marked NPs, overwhelmingly nonreferential semantically, and only one marginally referential ('everywhere'). These facts again underscore the use of <u>wan</u> to introduce only referential arguments that are of major importance for the discourse.

Only two NPs are marked by the suffixal -ya-so. Both are major participants, the messenger (dis meseyna-ya-so, dis man-ya-so) and the money (dis moni-ya-so). The main participant in the story, the messenger, appears 13 times in the story as full definite NP. Of these, 12 occurrences are marked with -ya-so. The money, the other major participant, occurs 10 times in the story as full definite NP. Of these, only 2 are marked with -ya-so. The correlation between the use of -ya-so to reintroduce a topic back into the discourse and the thematic importance of that topic is again rather striking.

4.4. Story 4. Weytin Du No foh Tros Uman 'Whatever you do, Don't Trust a Woman'. Our fourth story is the longest. The same analysis done for the first three stories is presented, for this story, in Table 6.

Table 6. NP marking on first appearance in discourse, discourse importance status, and recurrence in subsequent discourse for Krio story 4: Weytin Du, No foh Tros Uman 'Whatever You Do, Don't Trust a Woman'.

NP and its marking at 1st occurrence	Semantic REF-status	Importance in discourse	Total occurrences in discourse
Major participants:			
wan big man 'an old man'	REF-INDEF	major	66
inh wef 'his wife'	REL-DEF	major	29
wan vileyj 'a village'	REF-INDEF	major	5
wan oda vileyj 'another village'	REF-INDEF	major, related to major	1
tri jownk 'three braids'	REF-INDEF	major	3
tri minin 'three meanings'	REF-INDEF		12
di vileyj inh chif 'the village's chief'	REL-DEF	major, related to major	14
wan switat 'a lover'	REF-INDEF	major	11
wan pikin 'a child'	REF-INDEF	major	17
wan lapa 'a wrapper'	REF-INDEF	major	6
Minor participants:			
dis pikin inh pipul denh 'this boy's relatives'	REL-DEF	minor, related to major	2
son di ia na inh eyd 'some of the hair on his head'	REF-INDEF	minor, part of major	1
inh eyd 'his head'	REL-DEF	minor, part of major	2

Table 6 (continued).

(1)	(2)	(3)	(4)
ol man 'all the men'	REF-GENERAL	minor, related to major (village)	1
blok 'cell'	REF-INDEF	minor	2
inh nek 'his neck'	REL-DEF	minor, part of major	3
dis man inh sikrit 'this man's secret'	REL-DEF	minor, related to major	2
uman 'woman'	NONREF	minor, but related to major theme	2
slip 'sleep'	NONREF	minor, but related to major theme	2
pipul-pikin 'other people's child'	NONREF	minor, but related to major theme	2

Key: (1) NP marking at first occurrence; (2) semantic REF-status; (3) importance in discourse; (4) total occurrences in discourse.

The correlation between morphological marking with wan and the importance of an NP participant in discourse is again obvious in this story. In most cases this is also reflected in the frequency of occurrence of the NPs. In one exceptional case--wan oda vileyj 'another village'--wan participates in a fixed expression for which there is no easily accessible morphological alternative, given that oda vileyj could only mean, as indefinite, the plural 'other villages', but never the singular 'another village'. Another apparent exception, 'three braids', with only three occurrences in the story, is thematically of critical importance.

Of the bare-stem NPs, two are technically semantically referential, 'all the men' and 'cell'. The first may actually be considered anaphoric-referring, and thus definite. It is also of obviously low individuation (cf. Hopper and Thompson 1980, 1983). And the second, 'cell', is clearly unimportant in the story, so that its thematic unimportance overrides its semantic referentiality, and it is not marked by wan.

The distribution of the uses of -ya-so as marking reintroduced definite NPs in this story is given in Table 7.

Of the 10 major participants listed in Table 7, 7 get subsequently marked upon reintroduction as full DEF-NPs--i.e. when reintroduced into the discourse following a considerable gap of absence or a thematic break--by -ya-so, at least once. Not a single minor participant ever gets reintroduced as full NP with -ya-so. Finally, of the 7 participants reintroduced at least once with -ya-so, 6 were introduced originally by a numeral, either wan or tri. While these correlations are not absolute, they are nonetheless again striking. They illustrate how the grammar, of at least this Creole language, not only marks major participants in a special way upon first introduction into the discourse, but also upon subsequent reintroductions.

Table 7. Distribution of the use of -ya-so in marking reintroduced full DEF-NPs in Story 4.

Participant NP	Importance status	Total occurrences: As full DEF-NP	With -ya-so
denh tri jownk-ya-so 'those three braids'	important	1	1 (100 %)
di tri minin-ya(-so) 'those three meanings'	important	10	4 (40 %)
dis man-ya-so inh wef 'this man's wife'	important	10	2 (20 %)
dis switat-ya-so 'this lover'	important	2	1 (50 %)
dis man-ya-so 'this man'	important	18	8 (44 %)
na inh dis chif-ya-so 'it was this chief'	important	8	1 (12 %)
dis lapa-ya-so 'this wrapper'	important	4	1 (25 %)

5. Discussion

5.1 Semantics vs. pragmatics of referentiality. It is perhaps not an accident that in a broad way, the history of the treatment of referentiality by philosophers, logicians, and linguists follows a similar course as the history of the treatment of propositional modalities. For the latter, one began with strictly deductive approaches to isolated propositions or truth relations between them in terms of only two modalities--true and false. By Kant's time, it was already clear that two more modalities must be contemplated in order to account for the more complex facts of human language and human cognition. The mode of 'truth' was thus split into analytic truth and synthetic truth, and this is very clearly an antecedent--once one recognizes 'definition' or 'rules' as products of a communicative pact between speaker and hearer--to the later distinction between presupposition and assertion, respectively. Somewhere between Kant and Peirce 'synthetic truth' was split into factual truth--our realis-assertion, and possible truth--our irrealis-assertion. And again, although the logicians adopted this as a purely semantic-logical distinction, it is easy to see how in human language what is really involved is the communicative contract in terms of evidentiality, challenge, and their interaction with subjective certainty (Givón 1982a).

In a similar vein, purely logico-deductive approaches first recognized only the problem of 'existence', mapping onto one Real World. Variables bound by the existential quantifier referrred to some entities existing in that Real World, while those bound by the universal quantifier did not likewise refer, but rather 'pertained to classes/types'. The introduction of the Universe of Discourse to replace the Real World as locus where terms found their reference was, in fact, as I have argued earlier, a move toward making reference a matter of the speaker's referential intent although still within the scope of atomic propositions--and thus retaining residual 'semantic' coloration. What I have suggested here is that if one is to account for the referential properties of natural language, one has no choice but to take the next step and recognize that the speaker's referential intent is not restricted to whether he 'means an actual entity in the discourse universe', but rather, whether that entity is important enough thematically in the communication so that its unique referential identity actually mattered. What I have broadly traced here is the historical progression given in (13).

(13) OBJECTIVE <u>REFERENCE</u> IN 'THE' REAL WORLD ⟶
SPEAKER'S <u>INTENT OF REFERENCE</u> IN SOME DISCOURSE ⟶
SPEAKER'S <u>INTENT OF IMPORTANT REFERENCE</u> IN THE DISCOURSE

In human language, at least so far as the evidence of structural coding seems to suggest, the relevant context for determining reference is not the Real World, nor even the Universe of Discourse per se, but rather the thematic organization of that universe of discourse. Within the discourse universe, then, entities are considered 'referential' only if the nature of their participation in the thematic organization makes their unique referential identity important enough. Otherwise, they are consigned to the same nondistinct grab-bag of masses, plurals, objects of habit, groups or types, all of which may or may not exist at some meta level, but whose individual identity does not matter in this particular thematic context.

5.2 Correlations between physical, semantic and pragmatic referentiality. With all that has been said here, one cannot fail to recognize the rather privileged position that semantically referential entities occupy within the pragmatics/thematics of reference. As noted, the vast majority of entities that were marked by <u>wan</u> in our Krio narratives were indeed semantically referential. And conversely, the vast majority of entities that were marked by bare-stem (zero) morphology were semantically nonreferential. One could also go on and note that--if the discourse is about the normal themes of human affairs, everyday life and the nuts-and-bolts of human existence and struggle for survival--a very large frequency of overlap exists between semantic referentiality in the universe of discourse and physical referentiality in the Real World. Neither of these facts is accidental. And neither takes away even one iota from the contention made earlier, namely, that reference in human language is essentially a pragmatic-thematic matter. Human discourse does not have to revolve around human affairs in the Real World. But the fact that such discourse is both ontogenetically and phylogenetically privileged is well motivated by the evolution and use of our communication system as a tool for survival in this particular world. However, the pragmatics of perspective, saliency, and the assignment of thematic importance in a particular task-context governs our use of language. In other words, communication is never task-neutral or context-free. And the systematic 'exceptions' in the Krio linguistic code, miniscule as they are in terms of frequency,[10] nontheless illustrate how, when semantics and pragmatics are in conflict, the coding system goes with pragmatics.

5.3 Possible psycholinguistic and neurological correlates of pragmatic referentiality.

Almost all human languages make a coding distinction between a referential noun introduced into the discourse for the first time (REF-INDEF) and one already introduced previously, by whatever means (DEF). In addition, as we have seen, many languages--perhaps most--also code nouns in a special way if they are likely to be thematically important in the discourse. While thematic importance is not a totally objective and measurable property, it is nonetheless real. Further, quite often--as noted here--it correlates with straightforward measures of frequency of occurrence in the text. Perhaps the most universal device crosslinguistically for coding pragmatically important entities is that of 'naming'. Tagging a participant by name is a way of filing it in the permanent memory--but in a particular fashion, thus making it instantaneously available in a way that is independent of lower level thematic contexts. In other words, it tags the participant/entity as belonging to a higher thematic level/unit.

In a recent experimental study, Anderson et al. (1983) show that the processing of referents that belong to a higher--more general--thematic level in the narrative is easier, faster, more efficient. Such referents are thus clearly 'more available', as compared with referents pertaining to lower, smaller, and more limited thematic contexts. Such results point to an exciting field of empirical study of discourse, whereby the grammatical coding of referents in discourse as 'more important' will be shown to have processing consequences, in terms of making such referents more readily available to the language processor.

Notes

1. For a complete list, see Givón (1973, 1983a:Ch.8)
2. The average 20 (clauses), for referential distance measurements, represents terminating the count at 20 clauses, i.e. either RD larger than 20 clauses or--as is most likely here--no anaphoric reference at all. The choice of 20 is motivated by considerations that are not important here (see Givón 1983b), but some limit has to be imposed arbitrarily to avoid dealing with infinity.
3. See Linde (1974) for the definiteness of parts-of-whole in locational expressions.
4. I have used the same transcription as in Hancock (1972), but added hyphenations of grammatical morphology as well as lexical stress marks. The traditional Krio writing system renders all grammatical morphemes as separate words.
5. When topics/participants remain in the discourse continuously, they are marked as pronouns or occasionally, and in these Krio texts only following the conjunction en 'and', as zero anaphora. The -ya-so marker never appears with pronouns, but only with full NPs. It thus involves the reintroduction of important participants. For the systematic, cross-linguistic description of the role of full definite NPs vs. pronouns or zeros, see Givón (1983b).
6. One may, of course, propose that 'a mangy dog' was thematically important in terms of the narrator's choice in describing the utter desolation of the scene, which is the crucial backdrop for visiting the old house, the major topic in the narrative.

7. One may argue that in both exception cases here, the nonreferential NP was attributive of the central participant in the discourse, the old house.
8. This could also be an anaphorically based reference to 'firm', in which case it should be counted there. But see also Linde (1974).
9. Given the context of 'firm' and normative assumptions--culturally based--about men working in the firm, this may be also counted as relational-definite and thus containing some anaphoric reference to a major topic.
10. The justification for considering discourse about human actions and doings as in some sense the ontologically prime mode of language requires no further comment. The generalizations made by Hopper and Thompson (1980, 1983) with respect to how concreteness, physical saliency, individuation, compactness, and agentiveness of nouns correlate with their so-called 'discourse manipulability' and their prototype properties qua nouns, all pertain to taking this fundamental assumption for granted. Similarly, the statistical correlations recorded by both Cooreman (1982) and Rude (1983) concerning the low discourse topicality of objects that are semantically nonreferential were all recorded in this 'basic' discourse mode.

References

Anderson, A., S. C. Garrod, and A. J. Sanford. 1983. The accessibility of pronominal antecedents as a function of episode shifts in narrative text. Quarterly Journal of Experimental Psychology 35A.427-40.
Bickerton, D. 1975. Creolization, linguistic universals, natural semantax and the brain. MS. Honolulu: University of Hawaii.
Bickerton, D. 1981. Roots of language. Ann Arbor, Mich.: Karoma.
Carnap, R. 1947. Meaning and necessity. Chicago: University of Chicago Press.
Carnap, R. 1958. Introduction to symbolic logic and its applications. New York: Dover.
Cooreman, A. 1982. Transitivity, ergativity and topicality in narrative discourse: Evidence from Chamorro. In: Givón (1983b: 427-89).
Givón, T. 1973. Opacity and reference in language: An inquiry into the role of modalities. In: Syntax and semantics, vol. 2. Edited by J. Kimball. New York: Academic Press. 95-122.
Givón, T. 1975/1979. Negation in language: Function, pragmatics, ontology. WPLU no. 18, Stanford University. Reprinted in Givón (1979).
Givón, T. 1979. On understanding grammar. New York: Academic Press.
Givón, T. 1976/1981. The development of the numeral 'one' as an indefinite marker. Folia Linguistica Historia 2.1: 35-53.
Givón, T.1982a. Evidentiality and epistemic space. Studies in Language 6.1.: 23-49.
Givón, T. 1982b. Logic vs. pragmatics, with human language as the referee: Toward an empirically viable epistemology. Journal of Pragmatics 6.1.: 81-133.
Givón, T.1983a. Syntax: A function-typological introduction, vol. 1. Amsterdam: J. Benjamins.

Givón, T., ed. 1983b. Topic continuity in discourse: A quantitative cross-language study. Typological studies in language, vol. 3. Amsterdam: J. Benjamins.
Hancock, I., ed. 1972. The Journal of the Krio Literary Society 1.1.
Heath, J. 1976. Antipassivization: A functional typology. Berkeley Linguistics Society, vol. 2. Berkeley, Calif.: Berkeley Linguistics Society.
Hopper, P., and S. Thompson. 1980. Transitivity in grammar and discourse. Lg. 56.4: 251-99.
Hopper, P., and S. Thompson. (in press) The communicative basis for lexical categories. Lg.
Kalmár, I. 1979. Case and context in Inuktitut (Eskimo). Ottawa: National Museum of Man (publication no. 49).
Kalmár, I. 1980. The antipassive and grammatical relations in Eskimo. In: Ergativity: Toward a theory of grammatical relations. Edited by F. Plank. New York: Academic Press.
Linde, C. 1974. The linguistic encoding of spatial information. Unpublished Ph.D. dissertation, Columbia University.
Rude, N. 1983. Topicality, transitivity and the direct object in Nez Perce. MS. University of Oregon, Eugene.
Russel, B. 1905. On denoting. Mind 14.479-93.

WHITHER RADICAL PRAGMATICS?

Jerrold M. Sadock
University of Chicago

1. Pragmatic theory in general. A pragmatic account of a linguistic datum is one which refers the fact not to independent structural or semantic principles, but to principles concerning the use of the language. Whereas the units of structural syntax and semantics are abstractions like 'sentence' and 'proposition', 'verb phrase' and 'predicate', those of a pragmatic theory are factual entities like 'utterance' and 'conversational contribution'. The principles that are invoked in syntactic and semantic accounts have no independent existence outside the language system, and include, for example, statements like 'PRO must be ungoverned' and 'variables must be properly bound'. But pragmatic principles, such as the principle that one should not do more than is necessary to achieve a certain goal, or that one should consider the feelings of others, would seem to exist regardless of the existence of a linguistic system.

Thus there is a sense in which a pragmatic account of a fact of linguistic behavior is a deeper explanation than is an account of that fact in terms of syntax or semantics. A pragmatic treatment reduces a phenomenon in one sphere to general principles of another sphere; syntactic and semantic treatments do not. When we explain the chemical behavior of an element in terms of quantum-mechanical physics, we have, in a real sense, explained it more deeply than when we point to the position of the element in the periodic table.

Putting it somewhat differently, pragmatic accounts, because of their nonlinguistic nature, are capable of genuinely simplifying the account of natural language behavior by eliminating--not just renaming--structural features that would otherwise be required to model the facts.

To take a simple case, consider the well-known pragmatic treatment of exclusive or in English (Horn 1976, Gazdar 1979). It is a fact that or can be used to indicate something like 'exactly one of...' or something like 'at least one of...' Now since there is no doubt that use can reflect meaning (we use alligator to refer to alligators only because it means 'alligator'), and since ambiguity, both lexical and structural, is an undeniable fact of natural language, one observationally adequate theory of or is that it is ambiguous, an accidental phonological merger of two distinct words with distinct meanings, and hence uses.

But a highly satisfying account of the bifurcated use of or can also be given, relying on only one meaning (identical to the weaker, inclusive sense) and pragmatic principles with an independent motivation. In particular, an account can appeal to the very general notion that where the language provides expressions of the same type and degree of complexity which differ in that one is more contentful than the other, then not using the more contentful expression in a context that provides no apparent reason for not using it can indicate that the user believes the stronger expression to be false. So, since and and or are expressions of the same type, and and is stronger and no more complex that or, saying P or Q where I might well have said P and Q can come to indicate roughly the same thing as P or Q and not (P and Q), i.e. exclusive negation.

A serious question that needs to be asked about this or any similar account is whether we really have simplified anything by invoking it, or whether, in fact, the same constructs have just taken up residence in another locality under assumed names. In this particular case, that does not seem to be so, because as it turns out, exactly the same pragmatic mechanism is needed, even if we adopt the ambiguity theory of or.

Suppose or is ambiguous. Still it is the case that when the word is used, there rarely is any unclarity as to how it was intended. We must therefore have some pragmatic means of calculating the intended meaning of an ambiguous sentence used in a particular context. It turns out that the pragmatic sketch of the range of understandings of or that I have given is exactly what we would need to explain how hearers will choose the right meaning of a presumably ambiguous or (and how speakers will be able to calculate whether their utterance will be taken in the intended fashion).

Suppose we are discussing John's moral character and you say, 'Well, he either smokes or drinks.' Supposing still that or is ambiguous, then what you have said is either (1) or (2), and it is my job to figure out from the context which one you intended.

(1) (John smokes) V inc (John drinks)
(2) (John smokes) V ex (John drinks)

How can we account for the fact that you are likely to be taken as having intended (2) in this context? In general, we will take an utterance as having as much relevant content (or just 'relevance', cf. Sperber and Wilson 1983) as is consistent with the context. Now we know that (2) is stronger than (1), that the stronger statement would be relevant in the context of this discussion of John's habits, and finally that there is nothing in the form of utterance that would give an indication that the weaker reading was intended (in particular, that the longer unambiguous form and/or has not been chosen). So we conclude that (2) was intended.

But note that this account of the disambiguation of the sentence contains all the details of a pragmatic account that would be sufficient, in and of itself, to account for the way the sentence is understood without the need for a postulated ambiguity. So the account that makes use of ambiguity is seen clearly to be one that ought to be sent to Mr. Occam's shop for a trim.

2. **Radical pragmatics.** Because of the hope that pragmatic accounts hold out for actually explaining (and thereby doing away with) structural assumptions and principles, there has been an understandable tendency during the last ten years or so to render as many facts in pragmatic terms as possible, and, in the process, to simplify the structural system perhaps to the point of invisibility. The big idea in radical pragmatics is that many of what were conceived of as essentially inexplicable structural facts of language are really reflections of the fact that natural language is used by real speakers in real contexts to accomplish real goals. The hope is that by taking into account the appropriate aspects of the use of expressions, the structure becomes otiose and can be dispensed with in explaining the primary linguistic datum, namely, that a certain expression can be used on a certain occasion with a certain effect.

Pragmatic accounts of natural language data are, in other words, quite seductive; so what I wish to do here is be a linguistic Ann Landers and try to answer the question, 'How do we know when we've gone too far?' Like the columnist, I believe that it is not only possible to go too far, but that many young people nowadays are doing so.

Two fairly distinct traditions of pragmatic explanations are in evidence today, one based squarely on Grice's (1975) notions of the role of cooperativity in language use, and the other based more on discourse-functional notions reminiscent of the thinking of the London School of Firth and Halliday, and the Prague School of Firbas and Sgall. In general, a Gricean pragmatist is not averse to the employment of discourse notions in his/her accounts, nor is a functionalist opposed to the invocation of Grice's maxims; but the brunt of the explanatory effort does differ between these two schools. A characteristic difference between the two modes of explanation is that the result of Gricean reduction is ordinarily an impoverishment of the semantic system of the language, while reduction in the functionalist mold is usually at the expense of the syntactic system. But both camps can be indicted for failure to exercise moderation in their pragmatic proselytizations. In an effort to be fair, I will discuss one example of excessive pragmatism from each.[1]

Whereas some extreme structuralists can be criticized for adopting an unjustifiably negative view of function in the description of natural language data, pragmatists of both stripes can be chided for the opposite error: the radical structuralist says that there is nothing of value to be gained by considering the functions that natural languages serve; the radical pragmatist takes the same dim view of structure.

But Saussure (1966) was right: human languages have structure.[2] Therefore there are correct and incorrect descriptions of their structures. While it is true in a sense that a purely formal account of the structure of a natural language is 'merely a recapitulation of the data', or 'merely a statement about correlations to be found in the data', it does not follow that no differences of any kind attach to differences in formal description. It is a true fact about English that [h] and [ŋ] are in complementary distribution, but it would be just plain wrong to describe English as presenting a significant generalization here by, say, making [h] and [ŋ] allophones of the same phoneme. It is a fact that the regular third person nominal plural morpheme in English and the regular third person singular verbal inflection are phonologically identical; but it would be wrong to claim that this is a principled fact of English by, say, postulating a morphological analogue of the liver fluke, a motile morpheme that swims from one host to another.

A language system is not simply a collection of facts, but rather a collection of generalizations obtaining among these facts. To describe a language formally in such a way as to make one generalization is not to do exactly the same thing as to describe it in such a way as to make another, for in the two cases we are describing different systems. And to describe structure without making any generalizations is the equivalent of claiming that there is no structure at all.

3. Function and structure. The radical pragmatic stance is that once we know the 'why', we need no longer be concerned about the 'what'. To pursue a biological metaphor that has become rather popular lately,[3] the radical pragmatist would be like an anatomist who, realizing that birds fly, loses all interest in the structure of their wings. Since fly they must, he says, then wings they must have and those wings must be as they are, else the birds could not fly. But this thinking is faulty. Bats fly with very different wings, and helicopters and rocket ships fly without benefit of wings. In fact, to predict the wingedness of birds, we must bring autonomous structural considerations to bear. Independent structural knowledge of the articulation of animal appendages rules out the possibility of birds with rotors, and independent structural knowledge of their digestive systems makes jet-propelled birds at least highly unlikely. The appropriate point of view is to examine structure in the light of functional requirement and function in the light of structural requirement, and this holds of linguistics every bit as much as it does of biology.

In fact, one of the strongest motivations for the independent study of linguistic structure is exactly that it is needed to support any reasonable functional theory. The structural features of natural language are what support the raiments of natural language function. Ann Landers would probably advise us to keep our raiments on.

4. Radical Griceanism. Let me now present a case in the tradition of Grice where it is clear that a pragmatic explanation can be taken so far as to undermine its own structural foundations.

Consider the elegant and convincing treatment of the understanding of scalar expressions originally given by Horn (1976) and elaborated by Gazdar (1979). The fact that a scalar expression, e.g. a cardinal number expression, can be variably understood as indicating 'at least n' or 'exactly n' was claimed by Horn not to be the result of a systematic ambiguity in such expressions, but rather the result of Gricean rules of pragmatic inference. In particular, Horn argued that such expressions are lower bounded semantically, that is by entailment, but upper bounded only pragmatically, that is by implicature. Thus (3) is false if John makes $10,000, but only misleading in some contexts of use if he makes $20,000.

(3) John makes $15,000.

Horn also observed that the direction of the scale on which such expressions lie can be pragmatically adjusted. To break 100 in golf means to have a score of less than 100, while to break 100 in bowling means to have a score of more than 100. An utterly pragmatic interpretation of this situation (not, incidentally, Horn's[4]) would be that the natural numbers have no meaning in and of themselves, but are merely ordered with respect to each other by entailment. Thus <u>three</u>, for example, would not mean 'three', but any expression containing it would imply the truth of a similar expression with <u>two</u> substituted for <u>three</u>, but not one with <u>four</u> substituted for it.

On this theory, the natural number words we have in English would mean hardly anything at all. They would achieve their effective ability to communicate information about cardinality in an entirely pragmatic way. Such a result might offend our sense of propriety, but what is really wrong with it is that it cannot work. There is simply not enough conventional content left in the number words for any pragmatic theory to use as input. On a theory that gives the natural number words a semantic lower bound, the precise use of these words (e.g. <u>Three is the square root of nine.</u>) can be modeled as a contextual setting of an indeterminate upper bound equal to a semantic lower bound. But if there is no precise upper or lower bound, it is not at all clear how we could ever account for the precise use.

Surprisingly, there is actually an advantage to the outrageously pragmatic theory of number words in that it treats them differently from the inexact quantifiers like <u>some</u>, <u>many</u>, <u>most</u>, and <u>all</u>. With these we find exactly the same upward dual understanding as with the numerical quantifiers (<u>some</u> being variably 'some only' or 'at least some'), but we do not find any scale reversal. It does not seem possible to use <u>some</u>, for example, in such a way as to implicate 'at most some'.

In order both to capture the correct range of contextual understandings of the various quantifiers and to account for the asymmetry between the exact and inexact ones, it seems to me that a less radical pragmatic theory than even Horn's might be required. His theory of the inexact quantifiers can remain, but I suggest that the exact quantifiers have exact meanings. The pragmatic principle involved in their interpretation as one-way unbounded is one of loose-speaking, the same principle that allows us to describe France as hexagonal (see Austin 1962). A speaker using <u>three</u> to indicate 'three or more' would then be conveying less than his words imply, rather than more.[5]

5. Radical functionalism.
The second case[6] I want to describe is an example of overboard functionalism. It has to do with the treatment of Eskimo sentence types and case marking. There are four sentence patterns that we will be immediately concerned with which are traditionally called the intransitive, the transitive, the antipassive, and the passive. These are illustrated in that order by (4)-(7).

(4) Angut sulivoq.
 man work-3sg
 'The/A man works.'

(5) Angutip nannut takuai.
    man-erg bears see-3sg/3pl
    'The man sees the bears.'
(6) Angut nannunik takuvoq.
    man bears-inst see-3sg
    'The/A man sees bears.'
(7) Nannut angummit takusaapput.
    bears man-abl see-passive-3pl
    'The bears were seen by a man.'

There is clearly a strong association in this language between the form of a sentence and discourse-functional dimensions such as old information-new information, and theme-rheme, as the definiteness of the noun phrases in the glosses in these examples is meant to suggest. Ivan Kalmår, in a study of the North Baffin Island dialect (Kalmår 1979), suggests that these notions are all we need to understand the fundamental facts of Eskimo grammar, and provides the following (mostly pragmatic) flow chart as a scheme for selecting sentence type in Eskimo. In this chart, what I have called the transitive Kalmår calls the 'ergative', and what I have called the antipassive, he calls the 'accusative', reflecting his belief that the ergativity of Eskimo is an artifact of functional concerns and that the antipassive is really another sort of transitive clause. For the same reason, he calls the case that I have labeled instrumental in (6) the accusative case.

(8)

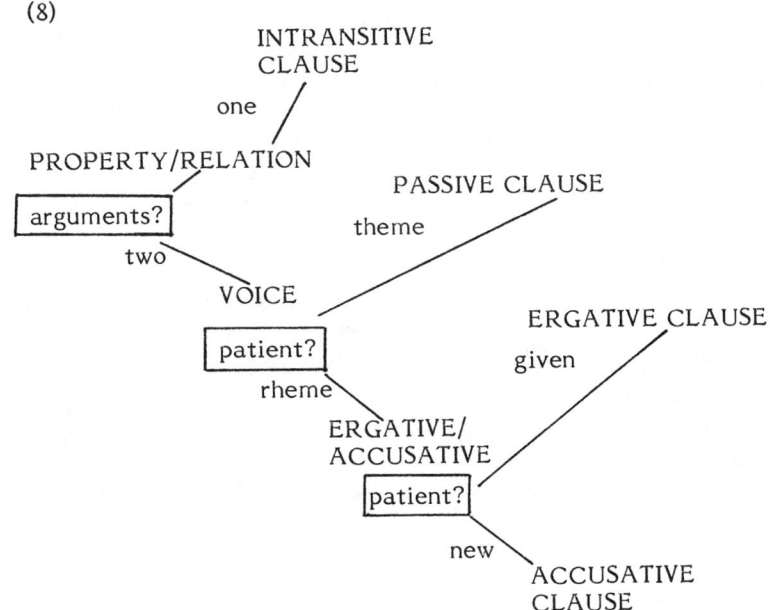

While Kalmår is surely onto something, his form-follows-function doctrine leads him to the claim that the very obvious syntactic principles of Eskimo do not, in fact, exist. However, the following are

Whither radical pragmatics? / 145

among the structural facts that characterize not only the four sentence patterns illustrated, but the whole language. (1) Every clause contains exactly one absolutive case noun phrase and at most one ergative case noun phrase. It may contain any number of oblique case arguments which are always optional. (2) The Eskimo verb agrees with its absolutive and ergative arguments only, thus producing two sentence patterns, an intransitive with single agreement and a transitive with double agreement. (3) The language is ergative in case marking. (4) There are a large number of relation-changing affixes in the language, including those that detransitivize transitive verbs and those that transitivize intransitive verbs. Whatever else these do, they do not produce exceptions to (1)-(3).

Kalmår's functional treatment misses these facts entirely and in fact, he specifically denies (2). Any or all of these strictly structural facts of the language could be different and Kalmår's scheme would come through unscathed. For example, associations between clause type and discourse function could simply be scrambled in a diagram like (8), if the facts warranted it.

But, of course, the facts could not warrant it. We sense that it is not accidental that the oblique case passive agent and the oblique case antipassive patient are nonthemes, in Kalmår's terminology. Nor does it seem accidental that these arguments are optional, whereas the absolutive arguments in these patterns and in the transitive are obligatory.

There is, in other words, a rigid structure to this language. What we see, then, is that the road connecting form and function is not a one-way street as the radical functionalists seem to imply. Not only does form follow function, but function also follows form, a fact that cannot be captured without recognizing the essential independence of the structural layer of language.

Having stated these structural verities explicitly, it becomes possible to observe that one functional principle accounts for roughly what Kalmår's purely functional scheme does, but does it both better and more generally. This is the principle that arguments with which the verb agrees are, ceteris paribus, more topical (thematic) than other arguments which could stand in contrast with them.

First of all, this generalization extends to the other sentence patterns of the language, some of which Kalmår worries about, but cannot deal with. To take just two examples, the structure-dependent functional principle directly handles the fact that the incorporated object in (9) is nontopical, and that the promoted object in (10) is much more topical than the nonpromoted argument in (11). But the direct matching between discourse properties and surface form that Kalmår proposes will not extend to these since (9) and (11) are not antipassive (i.e. accusative) clauses in any obvious sense.

(9) Kaali illoqarpoq.
Karl house-have-3sg
'Karl has a house.'
(10) Kaalip meeraq oqarfigaa.
Karl-erg child speak-to-3sg/3sg
'Karl spoke to the child.'

(11) Kaali meeqqamut oqarpoq.
Karl child-allat speak-3sg
'Karl spoke to a child.'

Furthermore, Kalmår's scheme is empirically inadequate in several ways. For one thing, the discourse-functional differences among sentence types disappear where the grammatical system of the language forces a choice of one form. For example, factive nominalizations in -neq are formed from the intransitive stems only, and thus for transitive verbs must be formed from the antipassive clause rather than from the transitive. Thus, whereas (12) is odd compared to (13) because unique entities like nature, the sun, and so forth are automatically topical in Eskimo (just as they are automatically definite in English), the nominalization of (12), namely (14), is not odd because it is the only possible form.

(12) ??Qallunaat pinngortitamik mingutittipput.
Danes(abs) nature-inst make-dirty-antip-3pl
'The Danes despoil nature.'
(13) Qallunaat pinngortitaq mingutippaat.
Danes(erg) nature(abs) make-dirty-3pl/3sg
'The Danes despoil nature.'
(14) Qallunaat pinngortitamik mingutittinerat
Danes(erg) nature-inst make-dirty-antip-nom-3pl
'the Danes' despoilation of nature'

Kalmår also observes that there are clear exceptions to his principles in his own very brief corpus. Examinations of longer texts would surely turn them up in great numbers. Consider the following two snatches of connected text from a Greenlandic children's book (Schwaerter 1961).

(15) Ullut ilaanni Suulut karsikoq nassaaraa.
days one Suulut-erg old-box find-3sg/3sg
'One day Suulut finds an old box.'
Aamma qisualunnik nassaarpoq.
also wood-piece-inst find-3sg
'He also finds some pieces of wood.'
(16) Ullut ilaanni Suulut allunaasamik nassaarpoq.
days one Suulut string-inst find-3sg
'One day Suulut finds a piece of string.'
Aamma nassaaraa kikiak.
also finds-3sg/3sg nail
'He also finds a nail.'

Both of these pairs of sentences consist of one transitive and one antipassive. In (15) the transitive is first and in (16) the antipassive precedes. But there is clearly no difference in terms of givenness between the patients in each pair. What this shows is that the pragmatics of case and transitivity, being pragmatics and not grammar, is much more subtle than a functionally driven account of natural language could accommodate.[8] While there are clearly pragmatic ramifications to the choice of sentence type in this language, the choice is not absolutely mandated by the context. Sometimes the choice is motivated merely by a desire to avoid repetitious sentence patterns and this is precisely what I suspect is going on in the little Greenlandic texts cited here.

6. Conclusion. What I have tried to show here is, first, that the grammar of a language, while clearly suited to the purposes for which its speakers want it, is essentially independent from function; and second, that the recognition of this fact is essential to a correct functional description of the language. To the extent that the goal of radical pragmatics is the elimination of independent structural descriptions, it is misguided and will eventually prove unworkable. To the extent that its goal is a detailed and correct account of the intricate symbiosis that characterizes the association between structure and function in natural language, it is an important and exciting linguistic enterprise that deserves to flourish.

Notes

1. Other examples that might have been discussed include Atlas (1977), Kempson and Cormack (1981), Garcia (1979), and my own Sadock (1976).
2. For a recent defense of this time-honored fact, see Newmeyer (1983).
3. The anatomical metaphor is employed by both radical structuralists and radical functionalists. Compare Chomsky (1977:86):

> How does it [the heart] grow in the individual from the embryo to its final form? The answer is not functional: the heart does not develop because it would be useful to carry out a certain function, but rather because the genetic program determines that it will develop as it does.
> Let's go back to linguistics: here comparable remarks can be made...suppose that someone proposes a principle which says: The form of language is such-and-such because having that form permits a function to be fulfilled--a proposal of this sort would be appropriate at the level of evolution (of the species, or of language), not at the level of acquisition by an individual...

with Givón (1979:5):

> Imagine an anatomist describing the structure of the human body without reference to the functions of various organs. But this is precisely what happened in transformational-generative linguistics...an attempt has been made to describe the structure of human language...without reference to natural explanatory parameters.

The value of my own use of this metaphor should be considered in the light of its apparent flexibility.
4. Horn theorizes that the quantifiers remain lower bounded, but the high end of the scale becomes the low end.
5. This is a perfect example of the pragmatic paradox: the less something means in fact, the more it signifies in practice. The more precise

quantifiers have greater contextual latitude (one-way unboundedness and scale reversal) than the less precise ones (one-way unboundedness only).

6. John Richardson (1984) presents some cogent arguments along somewhat different lines. In particular, he points out Kalmår's (and by extension, other radical functionalists') grave misunderstanding of the role of optionality in a structural theory.

7. 'One' and 'two' in this diagram refer to the number of semantic arguments in the clause. Kalmår uses 'theme' to refer to 'what the sentence is about', and 'rheme' to indicate the comment made about the theme.

8. There are also clear pragmatic correlates of the choice of passives and actives in English, as shown in various studies such as Givón (1983). But these studies also show that the correlation is not perfect and that it is, in other words, a use of the structure of the language rather than a substitute for it.

References

Atlas, Jay D. 1977. Negation, ambiguity, and presupposition. Linguistics and Philosophy 1.323-36.
Austin, J. L. 1962. How to do things with words. London: Oxford University Press.
Chomsky, Noam. 1977. Language and responsibility. New York: Pantheon Books.
Cole, Peter, and Jerry Morgan, eds. 1975. Syntax and semantics, vol. 3: Speech acts. New York: Academic Press.
Garcia, Erica C. 1979. Discourse without syntax. In: Syntax and semantics, vol. 12: Discourse and syntax. Edited by T. Givón. New York: Academic Press. 23-49.
Gazdar, Gerald. 1979. Pragmatics: Implicature, presupposition, and logical form. New York: Academic Press.
Givón, Talmy. 1979. Understanding grammar. New York: Academic Press.
Givón, Talmy, ed. 1983. Topic continuity in discourse: A quantitative cross-linguistic study. (Typological studies in language, vol. 3.) Amsterdam: John Benjamins.
Grice, H. P. 1975. Logic and conversation. In: Cole and Morgan, eds. (1975). 43-58.
Horn, Laurence R. 1976. On the semantic properties of logical operators in English. Ph.D. dissertation, Yale University. Reproduced by Indiana University Linguistics Club, Bloomington.
Kalmår, Ivan. 1979. Case and context in Inuktitut (Eskimo). (National Museum of Man Mercury Series paper no. 9) Ottawa: National Museums of Canada.
Kempson, Ruth, and Annabel Cormack. 1981. Ambiguity and quantification. Linguistics and Philosophy 4.259-310.
Newmeyer, Frederick J. 1983. Grammatical theory: Its limits and possibilities. Chicago: University of Chicago Press.
Richardson, John. 1984. An Arctic afternoon: Pragmatic correlates of grammatical processes in Eskimo. University of Chicago course paper.

Sadock, Jerrold M. 1976. Larry scores a point. Pragmatics microfiche, fiche 1.4.
Saussure, Ferdinand de. 1966. Course in general linguistics. Edited by Charles Bally and Albert Sechehaye in collaboration with Albert Reidlinger, trans. with an introduction by Wade Baskin. New York: McGraw-Hill.
Schwaerter, Adolf. 1961. Suulut. Godthaab: Det Grønlandske Forlag.
Sperber, Dan, and Deirdre Wilson. 1983. Relevance: Foundations of pragmatic theory. MS, working draft.

A PSYCHOLOGICALLY AND SOCIALLY PLAUSIBLE THEORY OF LANGUAGE STRUCTURE

Richard Hudson
University College, London

1. An introduction to word grammar

1.1 Background. In this paper I want to do two things. First, I shall tell you something about a linguistic theory called word grammar, which I have been working on for the last few years--since finishing the textbook on sociolinguistics (Hudson 1980) which some of you may know. Then I shall take a particular problem that faces those with an interest in both sociolinguistics and the theory of language structure, and explain how word grammar helps to solve it. The fact that word grammar is useful for the sociolinguistically inclined is not unconnected with the fact that I started developing the theory just after I had finished working on the sociolinguistics textbook. I was tired of having to criticise theories of language structure for being asocial, and decided to try and do something about it.

However, I do not want to give the impression that word grammar is especially designed for sociolinguists, because it is meant as a stab at the true nature of language, and I for one do not believe that truth for sociolinguists is different from truth for psycholinguists or for linguists interested solely in language structure. Admittedly, they are all interested in a different part of the truth, but their findings must be compatible with one another, so that they could in principle be fitted together into one giant jigsaw puzzle, whose bits all mesh. So word grammar is meant to be a theory of language structure which will accommodate everything I know as a linguist, plus the things I've read by sociolinguists, psycholinguists, and cognitive psychologists. This is what I mean when I describe it as 'psychologically plausible' and 'socially plausible'--at least, it is not blatantly at odds with what psychologists, psycholinguists, and sociolinguists believe.

I shan't be able to tell you much in this paper about the theory, but you can make up your own mind about its plausibility by looking at a book-length account which is due out soon (Hudson 1984). Meanwhile, I shall try to persuade you that the effort of reading the book will be worthwhile. To be honest, I must make it clear that the book is mainly about language structure, so it has a chapter on morphology and lexical relations, a longer one on syntax, and an even longer one on semantics. The first chapter says something about psychology, and the last one is a brief discussion of the structure of utterances, but it doesn't develop these areas in any detail. On the other hand, I have a fair idea about how they might be developed, given enough personpower, and I'm not aware of any fundamental problems waiting for those who try to develop them. So the book and the theory are primarily aimed at linguists, and the most well-developed suggestions are in the area of language structure. This is just because I am a linguist, and language structure is what I am most interested in--and what I have thought and written about most.

I hope you will agree that at least the more mainstream theories of language structure are not very plausible either psychologically or socially--I have in mind theories as diverse as government-and-binding, relational grammar, generalised phrase-structure grammar and Montague grammar. Of course, their proponents would say that they do not care, because they were only concerned with linguistic structure, and from that point on I should have to concentrate on showing them that even with their restricted aims, word grammar could do better-- which it could. But it seems to me very shortsighted to restrict one's aims in this way, knowing that sooner or later the crunch will come and all the details of your theory, which you have worked out with such loving care, may need to be changed drastically. For example, it is all very well to say that you are not interested in words like hullo, but you should at least have some idea of how they fit into your theory of language structure, even if you leave the details to be worked out by others.

What I have just said about the well-known mainstream theories is equally true of the little ripple that I caused in the mainstream by a theory called daughter-dependency grammar, which I described in a book some years back (Hudson 1976). This was a nontransformational theory which made much use of arbitrary syntactic features. It is hard to think of parallels for syntactic features of this kind outside language, so they are suspicious from the point of view of psychological plausibility; but there are good internal linguistic reasons for avoiding them too, namely, that if a feature only relates to a single fact, then it is always better and easier to state that fact directly, rather than use the clumsy device of a feature to mediate it. And daughter-dependency grammar was not very promising from the social point of view, either, because it made no provision for referring to the nonlinguistic context, as one would have to do in dealing with words like hullo.

Word grammar is a radical alternative, by any standards. You may not like radical alternatives, so this is not meant to impress you. It is just a fact. Word grammar has no transformations, no phrase structure, no distinction between the rules and the lexicon, or between semantic and pragmatic structures, or between sentences and utterances. It is called word grammar because most of the grammar is about words, taken either as particular lexical items, or as general types (such as 'noun' or 'plural'); but there are no references in the grammar to phrases, clauses, or sentences. In spite of this, we can write word-grammar accounts of relative clauses, unbounded dependencies, extraposition, and so on--all the tricky areas of grammar against which linguists like to test their theories. At the moment you just have to take my word for it, but if you read the book, you will find a full account.

1.2 Instantiation. One of the main features of word grammar is that generalisations are made in terms of a hierarchy called instantiation hierarchy. For example, <u>dog</u> is an instance of a 'noun', and 'noun' is an instance of a 'word'--nothing very radical there, of course. The interpretation is not very controversial, either: certain generalisations about distribution and inflections are made in relation to the category 'noun', and we say that <u>dog</u> is a noun because these generalisations are also true of <u>dog</u>. So we can say that if X is an instance of Y, X has the properties of Y among its properties (along with other properties, such as being pronounced /dog/ and being used to refer to things that bark). I call 'noun' the 'model' and <u>dog</u> the 'instance', and I find it is helpful to connect the instance and its model in a diagram by means of a double-shafted arrow, as in Figure 1. You can think of the double shaft as a kind of tube for conveying information from the model to its instance, because the instance takes some of its properties from its model, but not vice versa. In the terminology of some cognitive scientists, the instance inherits properties from the model.

Figure 1.

word ⟹ noun ⟹ <u>dog</u>

The theory becomes more controversial when we add the word 'normally' to the principle that an instance has all the properties of its model. This proviso is needed because the properties of the model can be overridden by properties of the instance. For example, the inflectional peculiarities of an irregular noun will override the normal rules for making nouns plural, as in the case of <u>goose</u>. Provided we specify in the grammar that the plural of <u>goose</u> is <u>geese</u>, the normal way of forming plurals will not apply. Linguists have known this for thousands of years, and have even given the principle a name--the Proper Inclusion Precedence Principle (Pullum 1979:82). The effect is that we can say that <u>goose</u> is a noun, although it does not share all the properties which a typical noun has--it is not as typical a noun as <u>dog</u>. You can see that the category 'noun' acts like the 'prototypes' studied by Rosch and her colleagues, so that we could rank words for 'nouniness', in true Rossian fashion (Ross 1973). Some nouns are more typical than others regarding their inflections; others are more typical regarding distribution--e.g. <u>today</u> is a noun, but it can occur in places where nouns typically cannot occur. And so on.

Even more controversial is the claim that the relation of a particular occurrence of the word <u>dog</u> to the stored word <u>dog</u> is the same as that of the latter to the category 'noun'. Suppose someone says <u>My dog is bigger than your dog</u>. This utterance contains two instances of the word <u>dog</u>, so it seems fairly reasonable to say that the relation between each of these instances and the stored word <u>dog</u> is that of instantiation; but that is the relation we have assumed between stored <u>dog</u> and 'noun', and between 'noun' and 'word'. So unless you can find some fundamental difference between these two cases, we have to accept that the relation is the same. That may seem easy to agree to, but if you do agree, then you have lost the boundary between sentence and utterance, because the logical relation between an utterance of an expression and the stored representation of that expression is a relation which is also found between stored elements. Let us call the two occurrences of <u>dog</u> in <u>My dog is bigger than your dog</u> 2 and 7, respectively (to show their position in the utterance). Figure 2 shows how they fit into the pattern started in Figure 1. Of course, as we should expect, their properties include those of the stored word <u>dog</u>, plus others (e.g. the properties of being uttered as second and seventh words of this utterance).

Figure 2.

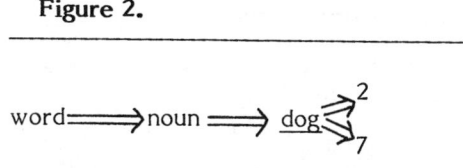

If we take the step that I have just described, then the stored representations for linguistic expressions can be seen as normalised models for uttered expressions. This is an important point because utterances have just the properties that sociolinguists are interested in-- they occur at particular times and places, they are said by particular people to particular other people, and their speakers have purposes and see their utterances as fulfilling particular social functions. In the mainstream tradition of linguistics, all these properties have been simply left out of the normalised stored representations, whereas other properties such as pronunciations have been left in. No general principles are ever offered to explain why this particular distinction is made. It is not because pronunciations are always as specified in the normalised representation; they often are not (e.g. the normal <u>n</u> at the end of <u>in</u> is often represented by a quite different pronunciation as a result of assimilation). Nor is it because words are never restricted in relation to these situational properties; for example, <u>good morning</u> is restricted to use before lunchtime. I conclude, then, that unless good reasons can be found for excluding such information from the permanently stored representation of a word, it may be stored.

1.3 Companionship. The relation of instantiation is often called the 'isa' relation by cognitive scientists, because <u>dog</u> is a noun, and so on. We can match this relation with a 'hasa' relation, which I call companionship--the relation between one entity and another which may (or must) occur with it. This is the relation in language between a word and the words with which the grammar allows it to occur. For example, the subject is a companion of the verb, and so are the various objects and other complements, because all these relations are directly sanctioned by the grammar. So, in <u>cows eat grass slowly</u>, <u>cows</u>, <u>grass</u>, and <u>slowly</u>

are all companions of eat, but grass and slowly are not companions. We can say that the verb has a subject and an object, and that is why I call this the 'hasa' relation.

The companion relation is asymmetrical, so we can link companions by an arrow pointing from the 'haver' to the 'had'--from the verb to its subject and object, for example. This relation is well known in traditional grammar, and is called dependency; and it is because we can exploit dependency that we have no need for phrase structure. When used in syntax, arrows can be left without further labels (except in the cases of subjects and other preverbal elements), since we only need to show the direction of dependency. Figure 3 is an example of a dependency structure, combined with the instantiation structure which shows which lexical items the words are instances of.

Figure 3.

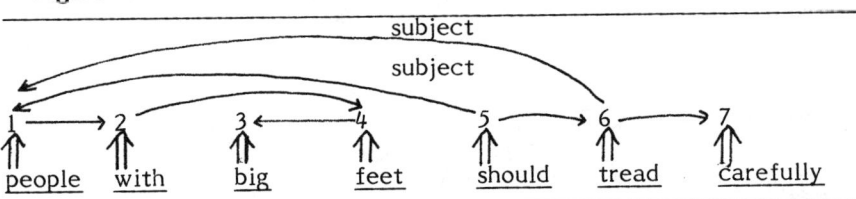

In semantic structure we need companions too, to link arguments to their predicates, and generally speaking, the semantic companion relations match the syntactic ones; there are enough exceptions, though, to make it clear that the two levels are distinct. For example, the semantic element corresponding to tread has the referent of its subject as a companion, and the referents of people and feet in the last example are linked as companions. In semantics, I think it is clear that we need to distinguish different kinds of companions, but it does not matter whether we call the distinct categories semantic roles, semantic functions, deep cases, or theta roles; the idea is the same behind all these different names. For example, we should label the subject-based semantic companion of tread 'actor', but this would be the wrong label for the referent of feet in relation to people. There is a partial semantic structure in Figure 4, where a star attached to a number is the name for the semantic element corresponding to the word with that number; so, for example, 1* stands for the referent of the first word, which is people.

Figure 4.

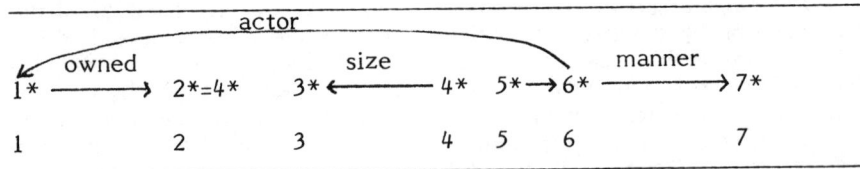

A plausible theory of language structure / 155

One of the main uses of the companion relation is that it allows us to impose restrictions on potential companions, in order to show which combinations of words are possible and which are not. This applies both to syntactic and to semantic components. For example, we can require subjects to precede the verb, or to be in the nominative case, or whatever the facts demand; and we can require actors to be animate, and to provide the energy used in the action, or again whatever the correct analysis is. These restrictions can be imposed in relation to very general categories, like 'verb' or 'action', and in effect they provide a definition of the companion types concerned. This is important because it means that there need be no undefined labels in a word-grammar analysis, in contrast with many other theories where semantic roles, in particular, are left extremely short of definition.

Just to make the point clear, take the category 'subject'. Suppose we want to require subjects to be nouns and to precede their verb; we can show this diagramatically, as in Figure 5. By the way, I should explain that there are two notational systems to choose between in word grammar; if you do not like diagrams, you can use algebraic formulae. I think diagrams are easier for the reader, but formulae are certainly better for the writer. Figure 5 shows that a verb takes a companion called 'subject', which must be an instance of 'noun' and which must precede the verb (this is shown by the 'is less than' sign, which refers to the numbers that are used to name words, and that get larger with time). Since this is a property of the general category 'verb', it will automatically be inherited by any instance of 'verb', so there is no need to state separately for a particular verb, such as <u>tread</u>, that it takes a subject with these properties.

Figure 5.

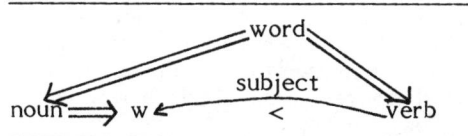

Since I shall be using the companion relation as applied to semantic structures, I shall give a semantic example as well. Suppose we take 'action' as a particular instance of 'event', in which there is an actor. We could say that an event must, by definition, have a time and place, so by inheritance an action must have these companions too. Further down the instantiation hierarchy, we could say that a deed is an action, in which the actor is a person. All this information is contained in Figure 6. So if we say that the meaning of <u>tread</u> is a kind of deed, then we automatically predict that it will have a doer who is also an actor, and who is a person and an energy source, and that it will have a time and place. We could even require the actor to be the referent of the verb's subject, as it normally is.

At the moment, I do not want to dwell on the linguistic advantages of having word meanings structured in this way. Instead, I should like to point out that Figure 6 could quite reasonably be taken not just as an account of a part of semantic structure, but as a hypothesis about part of general cognitive structure--i.e. of the mental structures which we use when we process our experience, nonlinguistic as well as linguistic. Suppose I hear a creaking floorboard. I interpret this bit of experience as an instance of treading, which automatically means it is a deed, so there must be a human actor, and there must be a place (namely, on the floorboard). We need not worry about the order of operations in this bit of processing; the point is simply that I could not take it as an instance of treading without including the other elements in the analysis.

Figure 6.

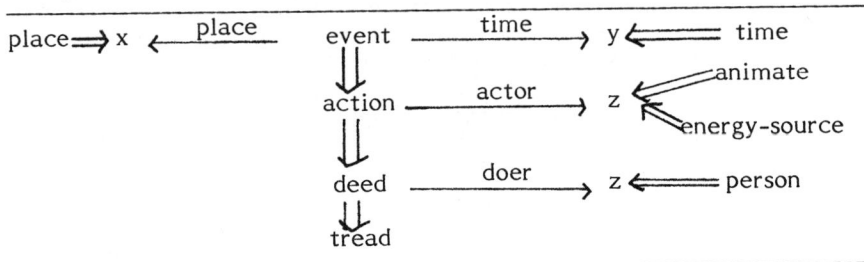

2. Help for the sociolinguist

2.1 The problem. I have now given you enough information about word grammar to be able to move to the main point of this paper: how word grammar can help bridge the gap between theories of language structure and the findings of sociolinguistics. The problem is that we know all sorts of things about the ways in which words interact with the situations in which they are used, but none of the mainstream theories provides a slot into which this information can be put, in contrast with the rich provision that they make for information about syntax, morphology, phonology, and semantics. It may not be a coincidence that the same is true, more or less, of conventional dictionaries, which provide just ad hoc labels like 'slang' or 'greeting'.

Let us suppose that someone wanted to write a grammar for my competence, and that he came to the word cookie. Now, as you probably know, we in Britain use biscuit instead of cookie, but we know that Americans use cookie, so this is part of our competence, in the sense of 'knowledge of linguistic expressions'. It certainly affects our linguistic behaviour, because we do not use the word, although we know it; and, of course, the reason why we do not use it is because we know that it is used only by Americans, and we are not Americans. But how do you fit this information about cookie into, say, a transformational lexical entry for cookie? The best you could hope for would be some kind of uninterpreted diacritic feature like [+American], but without an interpretation, that might as well not be there. But this problem is surely ridiculous because the fact to be stated is so straightforward: all we want to say is that the word is used only by Americans.

As you are all well aware, this problem is the thin end of a very large wedge indeed, and we could make similar points in relation to register differences in vocabulary (e.g. try versus attempt), regional and social variation in pronunciation, politeness forms, greetings, and many other phenomena. What they all have in common is that they require some kind of reference to situational elements such as speaker, addressee, time, place, and genre of speech activity. Even if you are not into sociolinguistics, you still have an interest in solving this problem because the same is true of words with deictic meaning, and speech act categories.

What we need, then, is some kind of principled account of the structure of speech situations, or rather, of our mental representations of speech situations. Once we have this, we can combine it with our account of mental representations of word structures, and we shall be able to say just what we want. Of course, I am not the first person to say that we need an account of speech situations, and there are a number of analyses already on the market to choose from--for example, Hymes' list of 16 components of speech (Hymes 1972). But these are not principled, in the sense that they could be fitted together with a linguistic analysis as part of a unifying theory. So at best we need to adapt them before using them in a generative grammar.

2.2 The word-grammar solution. I think word grammar provides the basis for a solution. First, ask yourself what kind of a thing a word is. Admittedly, we are used to thinking of words as static objects or patterns, because of writing; but when you think of spoken language and ask what a word is, the answer is clear: it is an event. But we have just been discussing events, in our classification of knowledge, and related the general category to more specific categories, 'action' and 'deed'. In terms of this system of categories, we can improve on the description of words as events: they are deeds. This means that we can join up Figure 2 and Figure 6, via the link in Figure 7, so that automatically 'word' inherits all properties of 'deed': every word has a human doer, a time, and a place.

Figure 7.

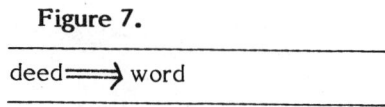

This immediately gives us three of the elements we are looking for: speaker, time, and place. So if we want to impose some restriction on the speaker of a word, such as being American, we can do it in just the same way as we did in requiring that a doer should be a person. You can see how the restriction on <u>cookie</u> would be stated in Figure 8, and Figure 9 gives the meaning of <u>now</u>, by using the variable x inherited from 'event'.

Figure 8.

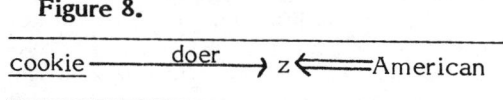

Figure 9.

---
now*=y
  |
now

    To bring in the addressee, we have to refer to a more precise model for 'word', namely, 'communicative deed', which is in turn an instance both of 'deed' and 'communication', where 'communication' would include static forms of communication like writing and pictures as well as dynamic forms. We can assume that, by definition, a communication has a source and a goal, or addressee, so 'word' inherits this companion from 'communication'. The details are not too important at the moment; the main point is that by linking words to more general cognitive categories for kinds of event, we can provide a principled theoretical basis for our analysis of the structure of the situation.

    Let me finish with a few words about speech acts. As I have already pointed out, there is an interesting connection between semantics and situational analysis, because we referred to general categories like 'deed', 'action', and 'event' in our analysis of situation structure, but there is no obvious reason why we should not take these concepts as the meanings of English words deed, action, and event, respectively. So we have actually killed two birds with one stone: we have found a theoretical framework for a cognitive analysis of situation structure, but at the same time we have given ourselves the basis for semantic analysis of three English words. My assumption is that we have only a single conceptual structure corresponding to any given bit of experience; the alternative would be to assume that we have one cognitive representation for processing deeds themselves, and a different one for processing the word deed. We would need very strong evidence for such a perverse assumption.

    Now much the same seems to me to be true of speech-act categories. I assume that we classify particular bits of speech in terms of categories like 'invitation', 'promise', and so on; presumably, such categories are further subdivisions of 'communication'. But we also have words like invitation and promise to deal with, and we need to provide some kind of conceptual analysis of their meanings. The logic of what I have just said about deeds and so on is that the meaning of the word invitation is the concept 'invitation' which I described as a speech-act category, and similarly for promise and so on. If this is true, then we can see speech-act theory as a branch of lexicography, concerned with the meanings of words like invite and promise. Once we have worked out what these words mean, we can be sure that at least these meanings exist, as conceptual categories, in our minds, and the natural assumption to make is that these are the concepts that we use in distinguishing one speech act from another. If so, then there can be no conflict between truth-conditional semantics and speech-act semantics, because the latter is one particular area of the truth-conditional analysis of word meaning.

    3. Conclusion. The main point that I have tried to make is that word grammar is the kind of theory of language structure that sociolinguists and their friends need, because it provides a view of language into which our knowledge of situations of utterance can be integrated in a very satisfactory way. I could have made similar points about the attractions of word grammar for those interested in language acquisition, where I think there is very clear evidence that the child's understanding of the situation of utterance plays a crucial part (e.g. Barrett 1984). But even if you are not keen on sociolinguistics or language acquisition work, word grammar should help you in your work on language structure, and I hope I have said enough to make you want to find out a bit more.

References

Barrett, Martyn D. 1984. Early semantic representation and early word-usage. In: Semantic development. Edited by S. A. Kuczaj and M. D. Barrett. New York: Springer.
Hudson, Richard. 1976. Arguments for a non-transformational grammar. Chicago: University of Chicago Press.
Hudson, Richard. 1980. Sociolinguistics. Cambridge: Cambridge University Press.
Hudson, Richard. 1984. Word grammar. Oxford and New York: Blackwell.
Hymes, Dell. 1972. Models of the interaction of language and social life. In: Directions in sociolinguistics. Edited by John Gumperz and Dell Hymes. New York: Holt, Rinehart and Winston. 35-71.
Pullum, Geoffrey K. 1979. Rule interaction and organisation of a grammar. New York and London: Garland.
Ross, John R. 1973. A fake NP squish. In: New ways of analyzing variation in English. Edited by Charles-James N. Bailey and Roger Shuy. Washington, D.C.: Georgetown University Press. 96-140.

THE MAKING AND BREAKING OF CONTEXT IN WEST TEXAS ORAL ANECDOTES

Richard Bauman
University of Texas at Austin

Linguistically and sociolinguistically informed approaches to context have had a significant effect on the study of oral narrative in recent years, to the considerable enrichment of our understanding of the patterns and functions that organize the place of narrative in social life. But this has been a recent development; traditionally, for most folklorists and anthropologists interested in oral narrative, a concern with context has directed attention to the institutional context of expressive forms, in the Malinowskian tradition, or to the context of cultural meaning--what one has to know about the ethnographic particularities of a society in order to understand what is going on in its stories--a more Boasian concern (Bauman 1983).

As early as 1926, to be sure, Malinowski exhorted students of oral narrative to attend to the situational context within which stories are actually told (Malinowski 1926), but the call was never fully taken up until comparatively recently. Under the impetus of the ethnography of speaking, however, and the performance-centered approach to oral forms that developed under its stimulus, the analysis of storytelling as situated verbal activity--as part of the process by which the ongoing conduct of social life is verbally accomplished--has burgeoned (Bauman 1977). Such studies have involved as well the examination of the ways in which oral narratives are contextualized by the surrounding discourse within speech situations (e.g. Bauman 1981), and the ways in which stories may be collaboratively accomplished in conversational interaction (e.g. Roemer 1980).

I have invested a lot in the promotion and practice of these analytical approaches and I continue to believe strongly in their productiveness, both for narrative studies and for linguistics. They have become reasonably well established as part of our analytical repertoire, however, and I would prefer to use this opportunity to advance another line of language-centered contextual analysis that is as yet less fully developed in narrative studies.

The making and breaking of context in West Texas oral anecdotes

In a paper presented at the 1981 Georgetown University Round Table on Languages and Linguistics, William Labov (1982) examines the dynamics of speech actions and reactions, as portrayed in narratives of personal experience, as a means of elucidating relations of speech and action in the social world reported by such narratives. Although he is ultimately--and I think most usefully--concerned with the performance and effects of speech actions in social life, Labov's use of narratively framed accounts of social interaction requires of him a consideration of the ways in which speech actions are endowed with social meaning by their contextualization in the narratives themselves; the narrative discourse creates a context for the reported discourse and renders it meaningful.

For present purposes, the point I draw from Labov is that insofar as acts of speaking are of focal importance in certain kinds of narrative, an understanding of the ways in which these speech acts are contextualized within the narrative can enhance our understanding both of how speaking operates and is understood to operate in social life, and of how narratives are constructed.

My interests in this regard are stimulated also by Bakhtin's suggestion (1971:195) that:

> the orientation of the word among words, the various perceptions of other speech acts, and the various means of reacting to them are perhaps the most crucial problems in the sociology of language usage, any kind of language usage, including the artistic.

Of the various forms Bakhtin identifies by which speech may be oriented toward another utterance, he is most interested in reported speech. I share Bakhtin's interest in reported speech as social process and artistic resource, but with special reference not to written, but to oral narratives.

I propose to examine in this paper two oral narratives I have recorded--a sample of a larger corpus--in which reported speech is not only an artistic device but the very esthetic focus of the story; the reported speech is the maximally reportable act recounted in the narrative (Labov 1982). In generic terms, the narratives I examine are anecdotes; the anecdote may be defined as a short, humorous narrative, purporting to recount a true incident involving real people (Bødker 1965:26, Botkin 1949, Röhrich 1977:6-8, Taylor 1970). The characteristic formal features of the genre include a focus on a single episode and a single scene, and a tendency to limit attention to two principal actors. As a corollary, perhaps, of this last feature, anecdotes also tend to be heavily dialogic in construction, often culminating in a kind of punchline, a striking, especially reportable statement rendered in direct discourse. That is to say, quoted speech is a significant stylistic feature of the genre; accordingly, the anecdote would seem to offer itself as an especially apt focus for investigation of the formal and functional role of reported speech in oral narrative.

The stories under study were recorded in 1972 from a West Texas rancher, then 70 years old, whom I will call (pseudonymously) Caswell Rogers. Here are the texts we will examine; the titles are my own, supplied for convenience in referring to specific stories.[1]

NOT THAT YOUNG

CR: Jack was a good worker and a good cowboy too. He was...

Mrs. R.: And a good drinker...

CR: ...but he was a little heavy on the bottle. And the old man ...uh...he wanted him to work all the time, and Jack just didn't see any use in that, workin' so much.

One day we were workin' cattle and they had a pole corral...a pretty hot day and there's a bit of shade right around the edge of this pole corral.

Ol' Man Trimble came out and said, 'Say,' said, 'come here, sit down and rest a little bit,' says, 'those boys out there are younger'n you are.'

I sat down there and Jack was doin' 'bout twice much work as anybody else out there, and I knew the ol' man and he was...been havin' a pretty hard time, so I told him...well, I thought it would help Jack a little. I said, 'Now you see Jack is doin' twice as much work as anybody out there.'

The ol' man said, 'Yeah, he sure is, and he's a good hand. I try to help him and every time I try to help him, why he gets off on one of these big sprees,' and said, 'I just can't help a fella like that.'

I said, 'Well, Mr. Trimble, Jack is young,' I said, 'probably you was young one time.'

He said, 'Hell, yes, but not that young!'

PASTURE FULL

Int.: What's that story, that Lawr-...that...when you and Lawrence were on the jury and...and Shorty Hammond was being tried for cattle rustling?

CR: Oh, they's tryin' Shorty. Shorty was always into something, and he'd stole four calves from a fella, so they was tryin' 'im. Lawrence and I was a prospective jury--they'd already picked the jury, and...but we had to stay there.

So, uh, 'bout the time they picked the jury, why, Shorty decided, or his lawyer decided, maybe he better plead guilty; that might be the easiest way out, because they had the evidence against him. So he decided to plead guilty, so the Judge put him on the stand and got to questioning him and said, 'Mr. Hammond, is it true that you stole those calves from Mr. Bales?' (Stole 'em from Ira Bales).

Said, 'yes.'

'Well, Mr. Hammond, don't you know that's wrong to steal cattle?'

Shorty said, 'yes.'

'Well, why did you do it?'

He said, 'Oh, I got drunk, so I didn't know what I's doin'.' Said, 'I do that every time I get drunk.'

Lawrence said, 'Aw, that's no excuse.' Said, 'I'd have a pasture full if I stole cattle every time I got drunk.'

The making and breaking of context in West Texas oral anecdotes

Let us attend first to the structure of the stories. In both, we may observe, the maximally reportable act--that is, the point of the story, is an instance of quoted speech. This bit of reported speech always occurs at the end and brings the narrative to closure. Goffman has noted (1974:559) that in informal talk, 'tales told about experience can (and tend to) be organized from the beginning in terms of what will prove to be the outcome.' Taking our lead from this observation, we may profitably examine the organization of the highly end-oriented stories before us in terms of the way in which they set up the climactic reported utterance, that is, in terms of the way in which they accomplish the creation of a context for the quoted speech that brings them to closure. As we shall see, however, the punchlines of these stories are reflexive: they loop back to reconstitute, or rekey (Goffman 1974:79-81), what has come before. In this process, the antecedent portion of the narrative, which has built up a context for the punchline, is itself recontextualized. Accordingly, we need to determine both how the punchline is set up and how the portion of the story antecedent to the punchline is made available for such subsequent rekeying.

We may begin by observing that these are stories about morality--proper and improper behavior, responsible and irresponsible action, and attitudes toward them. The moral tenor of the stories is introduced from the beginning; the first piece of narrative business that is performed in these texts is the introduction of the central actors by reference to the problematic, morally loaded attributes that will make for the focal conflict of the story. While the establishment of character adumbrates the moral tension of the story, the character attributes that are introduced are not bound to the event recounted in the narrative but are antecedent to it, elements of character by which the individuals portrayed are more generally known in the community. While the central actors are presented from the beginning in terms of morally colored attributes, the initial section of the stories also serves to bring onto the stage all other interactants in the narrated event, who may be implicated in a variety of ways in the central moral conflict.

In addition to the introduction of the dramatis personae, the other function performed by the opening section of the narratives is the setting of the scene for the narrated event to follow. This involves the establishment of the time and place of the central encounter and the occasioning acts or circumstances that bring the dramatis personae into the interaction that will in turn set up the concluding punchline (cf. Chafe 1980:42, Colby 1973:654, Labov and Waletzky 1967:32).

I draw the introduction of the central actors and the setting of the scene into a single section because they are not always separate and sequentially ordered in the stories. While an element of character is always presented first, not all the dramatis personae are necessarily brought forward before the narrator moves to the setting of the scene. Elements of time, place, or occasioning action may intervene before all the principal actors are finally introduced.

In 'Not That Young,' the dimension of moral conflict is made explicit in the introduction of Jack and 'the old man,' who is his grandfather. Jack is a drinker--publicly known as one, as witness Mrs. Rogers' interjection--and while he is capable of good work, his moral worth is compromised by the fact that he often chooses to go off on binges instead.

Thus, because the old man wants him to work all the time and Jack goes off on sprees, his drinking brings about conflict within the family, a serious problem. The old man is a cattleman, a cattle owner, which implies a certain economic substance and status, while Jack, who simply works for him, goes off on sprees. The moral contrast between the two is strongly implicit. Mr. Rogers himself is the third character in the story, and one of the two central interactants.

The scene of the story is set by references to time ('One day'), place (Mr. Trimble's cow-lot, made up of pole pens), and occasioning action. The latter, which functions to bring together the principal actors in the narrative, is the 'working' of Mr. Trimble's cattle: the branding, ear-marking, dehorning, inoculation, and castration of his new calves.

In the 'Pasture Full' story, Shorty is identified at the beginning as a cattle thief, the moral valence of which needs no comment in this cattle ranching community. His character as a trouble maker is amplified by identifying him as someone who is 'always into something,' a euphemism for always doing things that cause trouble. He is, in short, identified as a disruptive person. Lawrence is set up as the morally contrasting figure. That he is a prospective member of the jury for Shorty's trial implies that he is a respectable, upstanding member of the community.

The scene is set in the courtroom and the presence of the interactants is accounted for: Shorty as defendant, Lawrence and Mr. Rogers as prospective jurors required to remain after the jury has been selected. The particle _so_ marks a sequential movement toward the central narrated event: 'So, uh, 'bout the time...' begins to situate the narrative event temporally and leads into the further occasioning act represented by 'so he decided to plead guilty.' The next _so_ ('so the judge put him on the stand') marks the transition from the setting of the scene to the onset of the narrated event itself.

Let us summarize. We have seen that the initial section of both of these anecdotes is devoted to the fulfillment of two complementary functions: the introduction of the dramatis personae and the setting of the scene for the narrated event to follow. To this point in our examination of the narratives:

(1) the central actors have been introduced in terms of morally weighted attributes that they bring with them to the narrated event, and most of the secondary characters have been introduced as well;

and a variable combination of the following scene-setting functions have been accomplished:

(2) the narrated event has been situated in place;
(3) the dramatis personae have been brought onto the scene of the narrated event by certain occasioning actions or circumstances;
(4) the story has been situated in time by the use of time markers such as _one day_;
(5) in one of the stories (and others in my corpus) a process of narrative sequentiality has been set in motion toward the onset of the narrated event, marked by the sequential particle _so_.

We are ready, then, to turn to a consideration of the narrated event itself, the sequence of actions and reactions that is actually replayed for

The making and breaking of context in West Texas oral anecdotes / 165

us in the narrative and toward which the introductory section has led. We have already noted that the essential part of the narrated event is the conversational encounter that culminates in the punchline, but this portion of the narrative may include other elements as well. Thematically, the narrated event implicates a moral offense, which then provides the focus for the conversational encounter that concludes the narrative. The narrated event concludes with a dialogic exchange culminating in the quoted speech of the punchline.

The moral offense around which the narrated event revolves has already been adumbrated in the opening section of the story in which the principal actors are presented in terms of particular morally weighted attributes. In the two stories before us, the morally offensive actions have taken place antecedent to the narrated event, namely, Shorty's stealing of the cattle in 'Pasture Full' and Jack's going off on sprees when he should have been working in 'Not That Young.'

In 'Pasture Full,' the narrated event consists wholly of the reported or quoted speech of the trial proceedings. Part of the account is very summary; 'the Judge put him on the stand' may not be readily apparent as reported speech, but it is in fact a summary of the verbal routine by which the defendant is called to the stand. The next action, 'got to questioning him,' is also summary, but here the speech act involved is explicitly named. From this point on, the story consists entirely of quoted speech with its associated framing devices.

'Not That Young' is somewhat more complicated. After the opening act of quoted speech, in which Mr. Trimble calls Mr. Rogers over to sit down, followed by Rogers' response to the summons, the story momentarily shifts away from the conversational interaction as Mr. Rogers tells us more about the background of the exchange to follow. The essential point here is that Mr. Rogers is a spokesman for Jack's position in the conflict between Jack and his grandfather; Jack is not a direct interactant in the reported encounter, but his present behavior within the frame of the narrated event does influence the conversational interaction between Mr. Trimble and Mr. Rogers. Accordingly, we are given an account of Jack's relevant action within the narrated event. This additional information is to account for Mr. Rogers' motivation for taking the tack he does in the ensuing dialog with Mr. Trimble. The information is reserved for this point in the narrative because it does not become relevant until Mr. Trimble calls him over. Only then does his idea of smoothing things out between the old man and his grandson come into play.

We arrive, then, at the conversational encounter itself, the core of these anecdotes. As we move into the conversational encounter, an important shift takes place in the presentational mode of the stories, a shift from the recounting of circumstances and actions--telling about them--to replaying the actions, reenacting them to a degree by ostensibly repeating what was done in the original past event of which the narrative is an account. In the terminology of classical rhetoric, this may be seen as a shift along the continuum from diegesis to mimesis, from telling to showing. The great majority of the reported turns at talk in the stories is rendered as direct discourse. The central encounter in 'Not That Young' has five turns at talk, all in direct discourse, while 'Pasture Full' has seven turns, all once again in direct discourse. To be sure, the mimetic closeness with which the original dialog is replayed is attenuated by the quotative devices that frame the direct discourse, but the retention of the tense of the original quoted utterance--a basic feature of direct discourse--enhances the sense of reenactment by transposing the past into the present. And in 'Pasture Full,' the framing devices fall away and the quoted speech is left to stand on its own.[2]

As suggested earlier, even direct discourse is kept at a remove from full reenactment of the purported dialog of the original event by the quotative devices with which it is framed. Reported speech, especially quoted speech, involves special problems of communicative management, because the narrator is actually speaking for other people in addition to himself. Accordingly, there is a need for ways of marking the difference between the voice of the narrator in the present storytelling context and the reported speech of the actors in the original event being reported (one of whom, of course, can be the person who later tells the story, but in a different voice), and of marking speaker change within the conversational dialog that is the core of the narrated event. The quotative frames are an important means of accomplishing these tasks. An essential constituent of the quotative frames is the verbum dicendi, the verb of saying. In the stories before us, the verba dicendi used to introduce the quoted speech are all said, with a single exception--one instance of told, as a false start in 'Not That Young.'

In addition to the verba dicendi, there is a further range of devices which serve to organize the reported speech of these stories. In fact, the organizing system for reported speech in these texts is highly redundant, with multiple devices operating concurrently to indicate who is speaking and when. Most of these can be illustrated from the dialog in 'Pasture Full':

> ...so the Judge put him on the stand and got to questioning him and said, 'Mr. Hammond, is it true that you stole those calves from Mr. Bales?' (Stole 'em from Ira Bales).
> Said, 'yes.'
> 'Well, Mr. Hammond, don't you know that's wrong to steal cattle?'
> Shorty said, 'yes.'
> 'Well, why did you do it?'
> He said, 'Oh, I got drunk, so I didn't know what I's doin'.' Said, 'I do that every time I get drunk.'
> Lawrence said, 'Aw, that's no excuse.' Said, 'I'd have a pasture full if I stole cattle every time I got drunk.'

First of all, reported speech may be attributed. The speaker may be identified by a variety of means: by pronoun (he said), by name (Shorty said), or by some other identifying term (the Judge...said). Similarly, reported speech may be addressed to an identified addressee, as in Well, Mr. Hammond... Third, the beginnings of quoted utterances may be marked by particles such as Well, Oh, or Aw, that tend to occur only in this initial position, while the ends of these utterances are marked by transitional pauses that are longer than those that may occur within quoted utterances. And fourth, the conversational encounter may be organized by recognizable conversational structures and routines, such as the routine of courtroom interrogation in the passage above, made up of question and answer adjacency pairs. This routine serves so well in assisting us to differentiate among speakers that two of the quoted turns at talk are replayed without recourse to any quotative frames at all.

While cohesive ties such as this may be found throughout the replayed dialogs in these stories, helping to give coherence to the interactions portrayed, cohesion assumes special stylistic importance when we get to the punchline that brings the narratives to closure: the last lines of the stories are saturated with anaphoric ties to the lines that precede them to a far greater degree than at any other point in the stories. A demonstration of these ties (based on Halliday and Hasan 1976) will open the way to a more extensive discussion of the role of the punchline in these anecdotes, toward which much of our analysis has been directed.

In 'Not That Young,' the patterns of cohesion show up especially clearly when we note that the penultimate line is itself made up of two segments, marked by the repetition of the quotative frame, I said. If we break the line down into the two resultant shorter segments, we find that the punchline has strong anaphoric ties to both of them, intensifying the sense of cohesion across the concluding lines of the dialog.

> I said, 'Well, Mr. Trimble, Jack is young.'
> I said, 'probably you was young one time.'
> He said, 'Hell, yes, but not that young!'

An inventory of the cohesive ties between the punchline and what precedes it would include the following:

(1) the parallelism of the opening quotative frame: I said (2x)/He said;
(2) the rhyme of the particle that opens the quoted utterance: Hell:Well;
(3) the assent marked by yes, probably to both parts of Mr. Rogers' statement, but certainly to the suggestion that he 'was young one time';
(4) the contradiction marked by the adversative conjunction but, qualifying the assent of the yes that precedes it;
(5) the contrastive demonstrative not that, qualifying the assent concerning his earlier youth still further;
(6) the lexical repetition of the key word young.

Like the penultimate line in 'Not That Young,' the quoted utterances in both concluding turns at talk in 'Pasture Full' are divided into two segments, each introduced by the quotative frame. Here, though, despite the fact that both lines are relatively long, the patterns of cohesion extend across the whole lines.

> He said, 'Oh, I got drunk, so I didn't know what I's doin'.' Said, 'I do that every time I get drunk.'
> Lawrence said, 'Aw, that's no excuse.' Said, 'I'd have a pasture full if I stole cattle every time I got drunk.'

The ties include:

(1) the parallelism of the initial quotative frame;
(2) the parallelism of the particles Oh and Aw that open the quoted utterances;
(3) the demonstrative reference that's which points back to the preceding line;
(4) the word no, which repudiates an aspect of the preceding line;
(5) the naming of the illocutionary force of Shorty's preceding statement, namely, excuse;
(6) the repetition of the medial quotative frame, said;
(7) the substitution of stole cattle for that in Shorty's statement;
(8) the parallelism of the entire concluding phrase, varying only the tense of get;
(9) the lexical repetition of drunk which is tied to both uses of the word in the penultimate line.

Let us examine the effect of the strong cohesion between the punchlines of the stories and the preceding lines that set them up. It would not be too strong to say that density and multiplicity of the ties between them set the concluding lines of the stories off to a degree from the rest of the text and give them the quality of a kind of closing couplet. The multiple repetitions, parallel constructions, and other forms of anaphora contribute directly to the strong sense of closure that is achieved by the punchlines (Smith 1968:158-71). When the punchline is spoken, we know that the story is complete simply in formal terms.

The cohesion between the punchline and the line that comes before it is such that the punchline impresses us as a transformation of the preceding line--similar to it and modeled upon it, but transforming it in the process. The punchline contains within it two voices--its own and that of the preceding speaker upon which it has wrought a transformation. Most important, this double-voicedness is a correlative on the formal level of the double-voicedness of the punchline on the level of meaning as well. That is, the formal nature of the punchline is a correlative of its fundamentally ironic function. To demonstrate this, we need to examine the content and social interactional structure of the reported conversational encounters that lead up to, and culminate in, the punchlines of the stories.

We may begin by recalling that these anecdotes are moral stories; the conversations are about moral issues: decorum, responsibility, work, order. How are these issues developed in the interactions between the principal actors?

In 'Not That Young,' we find that the story is artfully constructed from the very beginning in terms of a set of paired contrasts between youth and age, and working and avoiding work. In the narrated events, these contrasts are evoked by the old man, Mr. Trimble, when he calls Mr. Rogers over to rest in the shade while Jack, who is 'younger'n you are' and doing 'twice as much work as anybody else out there' continues to work. While Mr. Rogers, knowing of the friction between grandfather and grandson, takes the opportunity to speak on Jack's behalf, Mr. Trimble, from his place in the shade, criticizes Jack, who is working especially effectively, for occasionally going off on sprees; this is one of the major ironies of the story. Rogers, in turn, attempts to account for Jack's irresponsibility by attributing it to his youth, the same youth that enables him to work so vigorously. Young men will be irresponsible at times, but at least this is compensated for in Jack's case by his ability to do the work of two men when he does work. Then, using the rhetorical strategy of identification, Rogers points out that Mr. Trimble was young once too, and here Mr. Trimble is caught, for he was known in the community for his own escapades and was fully as *young* as Jack. What is more, people knew it.

From this vantage point, the latter half of Mr. Trimble's response, 'but not that young,' appears on the surface as an after-the-fact gesture at upholding the position he has been taking as a spokesman for sobriety and responsibility, but it is understood by Mr. Rogers as an acknowledgment by the old man of the inconsistency of his attitude toward Jack. In explaining the story to me, Mr. Rogers made clear that he sees Mr. Trimble in the punchline as in effect stepping back from the line he has sustained throughout the exchange, and rereading the situation and his own stance toward it. The punchline amounts to a concession that he knows he is taking the situation too seriously; it objectifies the situation and assumes a relativist stance. Not that work and responsibilty aren't valid ideals--they are--but one has to recognize that life doesn't--perhaps shouldn't--always work that way.

'Pasture Full' works to similar effect. In this story, the interaction of the narrated event is organized in terms of the routine of interrogating a defendant in a court of law. There are clear contrasts operating in the story between the agents of morality and the legal order, namely, the judge and the jury, and the morally culpable defendant, a confessed thief.

The interaction proceeds with the judge doing the questioning and Shorty, having decided to plead guilty, doing the remedial work of acknowledging the wrongness of his act. Ironically, though, what Shorty offers as a mitigating factor in his guilt actually casts him in a light that is worse yet: not only is he a thief, but a drunkard as well. We have already established the strong tension surrounding drunkenness in this region.

Right after Shorty's confession of his double moral lapse comes the response by Lawrence that serves as the punchline. Lawrence, as a prospective juryman, aligned with the agents of morality and order against the hapless defendant, says 'Aw, that's no excuse. I'd have a pasture full if I stole cattle every time I got drunk,' suggesting, though with some joking exaggeration, that he often gets drunk himself. At one level, this statement plays on the ambivalence felt in this region toward alcohol; Lawrence likes to drink, sometimes even to excess, but he doesn't let himself get out of control like Shorty. Most important, however, his statement shifts the moral alignment in the courtroom: Lawrence is now identified with Shorty, as someone who gets drunk, even while denying the validity of Shorty's excuse, which is, of course, truly 'no excuse.' By his words, he has broken the moral alignment that has prevailed and rearranged it, reframed the situation. Again, he does not deny that Shorty is guilty and behaved wrongly--he just sets up a relativistic alternative concerning what can be morally acceptable in real life, regardless of ideal public standards.

Now that our analytical path through these anecdotes has led us to an understanding in formal and functional terms of the efficacy of the punchlines that bring them to closure, we can see more clearly just how tightly structured these stories are. The punchline is the crucial element, the point of the story. But the punchline in turn depends closely upon the line that precedes it and on the social interactional and substantive thrust of the entire replayed conversation that constitutes the core of the narrated event. All of these elements are rooted in a particular moral tension that is the subject of the conversational interaction and gives the punchline its ironic and relativistic impact; this tension is adumbrated from the very beginning of the story in the introduction of the dramatis personae. Thus, from the introduction of the principal actors, to the setting of the scene that brings them to the central encounter, to the conversational interaction between them, to the punchline that caps it off, the parts of these anecdotes constitute a markedly tight structure.

In both cases, the anecdotes achieve their effect by rekeying the situation, recontextualizing it, overturning the apparent direction of the interaction and the moral alignments and attitudes that have seemed to control it, and establishing an ironic alternative, not as a substitute but as a coexistent perspective. The effect of the punchline is to that extent subversive, a breakthrough both on the part of the one who is reported to have spoken it, and on the part of the narrator, into a kind of skepticism and relativism that takes pleasure in refusing to take ideal, normative moral expectations too seriously--a 'comic corrective,' in Burke's apt phrase, 'containing two-way attributes lacking in polemical, one-way approaches to social necessity' (1937:213).

This, in fact, is the essence of much humor. Indeed, upon examination, these stories may seem to have some basic affinities with other humorous expressive forms. The punchline in many narrative jokes built upon reported speech, for example, works by reframing what has come before it (Sherzer 1982). In all, the 'successful subversion of one form by another completes or ends the joke, for it changes the balance of power' (Douglas 1968:365). To carry the correspondences still further, traditional verbal jokes also represent a form of reported speech. They are often introduced by reference to the person from whom they were learned, as in 'Wanna hear a joke my sister told me?' (cf. Sacks 1974), and insofar as they are known to be in oral tradition, they are in a sense reported out of the abstract collective voice of tradition. And again, as noted, many narrative jokes employ fictional reported speech both as stylistic device and as punchline.

Given all these correspondences between jokes and other humorous routines and the anecdotes of our West Texas storyteller, what are the differences among them? Part of the answer to this question is suggested by a consideration of the context in which these stories occur. They are conventionally told in a variety of small group sociable settings in which the conversation deals with the members of the local community and the surrounding region. In recent years, they have figured most prominently during visits by the narrator to members of his family who have moved away from home, or on occasions when those relatives have come back on visits of their own. Conversation on such occasions often involves catching up on the people of the community--births, deaths, marriages, divorces (in recent years), and other significant activities. The community is small and the ranching and farming region around it is rather thinly populated. People are still identified in terms of residence ('Cal lived back this side of Johnny's') and kin connections ('Ms. Brown, you know was one of 'em--Joe Bob's mother'), with the latter providing one of the major organizing principles by which successive people are brought up for mention and discussion. Of course, kinship is not the only salient social feature by which people are known; as in most small, traditional, agrarian communities, the personal and social identity of individuals is also defined in part by their actions and experiences, elements of their local social biography. It is here that narrative comes into play; stories are the major means by which such actions and experiences are memorialized and given expression. Thus, the mention of a given individual may evoke a story about him or her, either a personal narrative in which the teller figures with that individual, or a third person narrative about the individual in question that has been told to the narrator by someone else at varying degrees of remove from the original event. That is, the chain of transmission may be of varying length, but there is always a sense of locality and familiarity about the dramatis personae of the stories--they are all known personally or in terms of their connections within the community: kinfolk, neighbors, friends.

Because these stories are about known and familiar individuals and constitute a part of their social biographies, they are densely indexical in a concrete social sense. That is, part of their meaning derives from the great complex of indexical associations that they evoke--the individuals portrayed, other known aspects of their lives and characters, and potentially all the other people in the community, including those present at the storytelling event, with whom they are linked by the kinds of social and communicative ties that give cohesion to the conversations in which the stories are told.

To be sure, these stories, like all literature used as equipment for living (Burke 1941), have a certain metaphorical as well as metonymic meaning, as a kind of extended name or label for the recurrent social problem situations they portray: the embarrassment occasioned by publicly visible immoral behavior, the damaging of someone else's property through careless incompetence, and so on. And to extend the Burkean perspective still further, the stories also convey an attitude toward such situations and a strategy for dealing with them. The attitudes will vary depending upon the situation, but there is always an attendant unease about the public moral conflict the stories portray, and the favored strategy that emerges from the stories is to alleviate the resultant tension by ironically transforming the ongoing situation into something else. It is here that we see the importance of the crucial bits of quoted speech that bring the stories to closure; what is highlighted in these anecdotes is the transformative capacity of speech. Bakhtin maintains that 'The speaking person in the novel is always, to one degree or another, an _ideologue_, and his words are always _ideologemes_...It is precisely as ideologemes that discourse becomes the object of representation in the novel' (1981:333, italics in the original). So too in these anecdotes, but the ideology to which the last speaker gives voice is ultimately ironic and skeptical (White 1973:37), showing how the normative pressures of morality that lead to social tension may be evaded by those with the verbal wit to do so.

Traditional punchline jokes, as many have pointed out, have the same subversive potential. Unlike our anecdotes, however, jokes are not at all rooted in community; they are anonymous, impersonal, generalized. Indeed, if one were inclined toward speculation, one might suggest that the modern punchline joke, which emerged as a recognized form only in the nineteenth century (Röhrich 1977:4, 8), might have evolved out of the punchline anecdote under the social conditions of the modern industrial era. Anecdotes of the kind we have been examining thrive in the intimate social environment of the small local community, whereas jokes belong preeminently to the impersonal milieu of urban industrial society (Röhrich 1977:9). As imaginative products ungrounded in a known community of real individuals, jokes can only be metaphorical and speculative in their relationship to actual experience. They tell us in abstract terms about how structures <u>might</u> fall apart or be overturned, while the true anecdotes are told to keep us aware of the vulnerability of life as it really <u>is</u> and the capacity of speech both to make this vulnerability apparent and to bring it under control.

Notes

1. Concerning the transcriptions: my representation of spoken language is, frankly, intended to have more expressive than linguistic accuracy in a strictly formal sense. I am more interested here in the narratives as oral literature than as dialectological data. No words have been added or deleted (ellipsis indicates pauses, not deletions), no grammatical constructions 'corrected', no eye-dialect introduced, but I have been concerned to convey that this is a record of language in a spoken, not a written mode, and to preserve something of the quality (however vague and impressionistic that term may be) of oral discourse. To this end, I have selectively employed a variety of devices, some of them in themselves conventions for representing oral speech in print, some of them attempts to capture certain features of local pronunciation as employed by the speakers. Above all, I would emphasize that no pejorative connotation of any kind is intended by the mode of presentation I have employed (cf. Preston 1982).

2. I am using the term 'mimetic' here solely to identify a presentational mode, with no claims implied concerning the degree of actual correspondence between the original event and its representation in narrative discourse. In the process, I am begging some very large issues, for an excellent discussion of which see Sternberg (1982).

References

Bakhtin, M. M. 1971. Discourse typology in prose. In: Readings in Russian poetics. Edited by L. Matejka and K. Pomorska. Cambridge, Mass.: MIT Press. 176-96.

Bakhtin, M. M. 1981. The dialogic imagination. Transl. by C. Emerson and M. Holquist; edited by M. Holquist. Austin: University of Texas Press.

Bauman, R. 1977. Verbal art as performance. Repr. ed. 1984. Prospect Heights, Ill.: Waveland Press.

Bauman, R. 1981. 'Any man who keeps more'n one hound'll lie to you': Dog trading and storytelling in Canton, Texas. In: And other neighborly names. Edited by R. Bauman and R. D. Abrahams. Austin: University of Texas Press. 79-103.

Bauman, R. 1983. The field study of folklore in context. In: Handbook of American folklore. Edited by R. M. Dorson. Bloomington: Indiana University Press. 362-68.

Bødker, L. 1965. Anecdote. In: International dictionary of regional European ethnology and folklore, vol. 2. Copenhagen: Rosenkilde and Bagger. 26-27.

Botkin, B. 1949. Anecdote. In: Standard dictionary of folklore, mythology, and legend, vol. 1. New York: Funk and Wagnalls. 56.

Burke, K. 1937. Attitudes towards history, vol. 1. New York: The New Republic.

Burke, K. 1941. Literature as equipment for living. In: The philosophy of literary form. Baton Rouge: Louisiana State University Press. 293-304.

Chafe, W. L. 1980. The deployment of consciousness in the production of narrative. In: The pear stories. Edited by W. L. Chafe. Norwood, N.J.: Ablex. 9-50.

Colby, B. N. 1973. A partial grammar of Eskimo folktales. American Anthropologist 75.645-62.

Douglas, M. 1968. The social control of cognition: Some factors in joke perception. Man 3.361-76.

Goffman, E. 1974. Frame analysis. New York: Harper and Row.

Halliday, M. A. K., and R. Hasan. 1976. Cohesion in English. London: Longmans.

Labov, W. 1982. Speech actions and reactions in personal narrative. In: Georgetown University Round Table on Languages and Linguistics 1981. Edited by D. Tannen. Washington, D.C.: Georgetown University Press. 219-47.

Labov, W., and J. Waletzky. 1967. Narrative analysis: Oral versions of personal experience. In: Essays on the verbal and visual arts. Edited by J. Helm. Seattle: University of Washington Press for the American Ethnological Society. 12-44.

Malinowski, B. 1926. Myth in primitive society. London: Kegan Paul, Trench, Trübner.

Preston, D. R. 1982. 'Ritin' fowklower daun 'rong: Folklorists' failures in phonology. Journal of American Folklore 95.304-26.

Roemer, D. 1980. Interjected routines as metanarrative commentary. Working Papers in Sociolinguistics 68. Austin: Southwest Educational Development Laboratory.

Röhrich, L. 1977. Der Witz. Stuttgart: Metzler.

Sacks, H. 1974. An analysis of the course of a joke's telling in conversation. In: Explorations in the ethnography of speaking. Edited by R. Bauman and J. Sherzer. New York: Cambridge University Press. 337-53.

Sherzer, J. (in press) Puns and jokes. In: Handbook of discourse analysis. Edited by T. Van Dijk. London: Academic Press.

Smith, B. H. 1968. Poetic closure. Chicago: University of Chicago Press.

Sternberg, M. 1982. Proteus in quotation-land: Mimesis and the forms of reported discourse. Poetics Today 3(2).107-56.
Taylor, A. 1970. The anecdote: A neglected genre. In: Medieval literature and folklore studies. Edited by T. Mandel and B. Rosenberg. New Brunswick, N.J.: Rutgers University Press.
White, H. 1973. Metahistory. Baltimore: Johns Hopkins University Press.

ENTER TEXTUALITY: ECHOES FROM THE EXTRATERRESTRIAL

Thomas A. Sebeok
Indiana University

Jorge Luis Borges once observed that every writer of fiction creates his own precursors by modifying each of his reader's conceptions of the past. The same retrospective axiom surely constrains every other sort of text fabricant, from scientist to, in the case at point, cinematic auteur. For purposes of this presentation, a 'text' will be regarded as any significant object, or, more technically, as any coherent string of signs. Although the internal simplicity or complexity such a string may display is not at issue here, multistranded strings tend to be more fascinating than single filaments, and syncretic aggregations--of which film offers a conspicuous example--even more so.

The Janus-faced concept of 'intertextuality', which, in contrast with Borges' dictum, works as much prospectively as it does in a retrograde scape--by extension of M. Baxtin's original, although hardly precise, formulation of heteroglossia, dialogism, and polyphony--denotes ways in which works of art (especially of literature) are produced in response not to social reality but to previous works of art and the codes and other conventions governing them. In Kristeva's reformulation (1969:146), 'tout texte se construit comme mosaïque de citations, tout texte est absorption et transformation d'un autre text. A la place de la notion d'intersubjectivité s'installe celle d'intertextualité...' Intertextual codes, which Barthes characterized (1974:10) as a 'mirage of citations', are ultimately insubstantial, every reader having become a more or less representative embodiment of a vague, generalized intertextuality; as he went on to write in 1970: 'This "I" which approaches the text is already itself a plurality of other texts, of codes which are infinite or, more precisely, lost (whose origin is lost).' To the degree to which a work of art is 'intertextual', it becomes distorted, opaque even, a darkly specular reflection of actuality--as, for instance, a myth. It becomes a lattice of signposts, regressing into, effectively, infinity, and thus capable of sustaining many alternative interpretations. Yet it may become a dialectical (vs. sequential) tool for furthering the study of typological goals far more tellingly than the more indeterminate conception of 'influence', and, as such, may assume various shapes, including, notably, allegorical.

I once argued (Sebeok 1979:xiii), modifying Samuel Butler's famous brocard about a hen and an egg, that a sign is only a sign's way of making more signs. I learned only recently that B. F. Skinner (1983:30) made an analogous claim, 'that a poet is only a literary tradition's way of making more of a literary tradition, and...that a scientist is only science's way of making more science.' It is in line with these views that all texts must be regarded as 'intertextual', although, of course, variations, by definition, do occur on all levels. These are the mechanisms for increasing information, the measure of novelty, with the passage of the ages.

In 1859, Darwin instructed the readership of his Origin of Species that 'all the living forms of life are the lineal descendants of those which lived long before the Silurian epoch', and we now have an impressive body of evidence that the direct-filiation hypothesis, as it has since come to be called (Margulis 1981:37), applies universally to the patterns of evolution of all animals and plants, indeed of all genomes; (true, the evolution of eukaryotes from prokaryotes seems to require the invocation of an additional principle of symbiosis, but, even so, the combined effects lead to the formation of precisely the same phylogenies). Note that the concept of 'intertextuality', with its actual or implied groping for ultimate codes whose origins are lost, postulates a body of discourse assumed to be already in place and thereby allows for the creation of the works in posse, envisaging the signifying practices of texts to be produced by some future weaver of yet another text. In fact, it is a tacit extension into the cultural sphere of the canon of direct filiation, so well recognized in the domain of our biosphere. If, as Pierce taught, man is a sign, or a text (Sebeok 1979:60f., 1981:6), then each and every one of us is the 'intertextual product', in quite a literal sense, of myriad prior biochemical developments and innumerable precursors--minimal self-replicating entities, leading to polygenomic cells--that populated the Earth since the common ancestors of life arose, more than three billion years ago, from organic compounds on the surface of our planet, organizing themselves into macromolecular systems of signs capable of storing and transmitting information.

In this paper, I propose to examine Steven Spielberg's artful and entrancing transfiguration of the archetypally familiar boy-and-his-pet story (the everyday carnal) into a sci-fi fantasy (the mythic supernal), as enacted in E. T. The Extraterrestrial, and attempt to decipher how the unfamiliar trappings, transcendental reverberations, and subliminal currents thereof come into focus in consequence of a consistent application of intertextual techniques and effects (the déjà-vu, as well as the déjà-lu, and even the déjà-entendu).

The march of variegated visual and auditory metonyms--disembodied footsteps and jangling keys, unoccupied moving swings and toy soldiers, ominous breathing and musical notes, Reese's pieces and clinical charts--which, together, and more, constitute the organizing pith of this picture, its energetic armature, if you will, is punctuated by Elliott's and E.T.'s ligamentary emblematic geranium: it wilts, but, in the end, it re-effloresces in its pot. The tropes are carefully balanced out on multiple planes, one of which is cast in a botanical idiom. The visitors, who touch down on a California forest clearing, densely begirded by tall trees and lush foliage, are back, we learn, on a plant-gathering field trip. As the crew of this peaceable expedition is about to be captured by depersonalized but ill-boding government agents, the aliens take off in their pumpkin-shaped spaceship (the film's texture is ingrained with carnivalesque images of, particularly, Halloween and Christmas), inadvertently abandoning one of their kind. The focal meaning of the geranium was underscored by Kotzwinkle (1982:183), who wrote a novel based on Melissa Mathison's screenplay, as he ends his book with this pregnant sentence: 'He went into the misty light, with his geranium.'

The marooned 'old botanist' (an epithet sometimes used to characterize E.T.) is left shuffling through the grass as the ship's hatch shuts, petals folding inward. He finds his way to the vegetable garden of Elliott and his family, rounded out by a teenage brother, a younger sister, and their mother, lately singled (dad having taken off for Mexico with Sally, a girlfriend). The lonesome alien, yearning for his home, three million light-years distant, and the fatherless (i.e. 'alienated') boy are united by a natural bond of companionship.

The movie is obviously a direct, although undeclared, continuation of Spielberg's Close Encounters. Kael (1982:119) remarked that 'that's partly because this film has the sensibility we came to know in that picture, and partly because E.T. himself is like a more corporeal version of the celestial visitors at the end of it.' The link, moreover, is non-verbally signaled by John Williams' variations on an unmistakable theme, the scores serving to enhance both scripts as well as those of the tripartite Star Wars saga released so far.

With palpable deliberation, Spielberg intersows self-references to his own and kindred previous works. During the Halloween scene, among the costumed children fanning out to go haunting, there is a little figure dressed up as Yoda, the gnostic gnome introduced in The Empire Strikes Back. E.T., an 'old monster' now in ghostly disguise, turns his head in recognition of the Jedi, along with the complicit members of the audience, as a colleague who has, as it were, strayed into this picture from a neighboring set.

Jaws puts in a brief synecdochical appearance in the guise of a scoop in Elliott's fish tank, while the tub of live frogs he liberates during biology class to prevent the chloroforming and dissection of these Kermit-like creatures, themselves reminiscent of the eye-boggling apparition of the extraterrestrial ('Are you a Muppet?' Elliott's sister, Gertie, asks), evokes the episode featuring Marion, the heroine in the snakepit, from Raiders of the Lost Ark, underlined by a comic shot of a schoolmate of Elliott's standing as if she were paralyzed in midst of the pandemonium of escaping frogs, crawling over hands and feet. The climactic big chase sequence, the children and the space-goblin fleeing military vehicles on bicycles that sometimes fly high in the sky, by application of a low-level antigravity formula, recalls several high-powered cliff-hanger pursuits from the same 1981 film and similar tricky effects from still earlier Spielberg pieces. The contrast between the sophisticated military vehicles and other lethal equipment at the disposal of the uniformed members of the search party--their space-travel gear, especially their gleaming head masks, bring to mind the terror of Darth Vader in carapace and his undifferentiated metallic troops--with the kids' ordinary yet bewitched bikes, is neatly captured as Elliott and 'the ancient fugitive' soar in the dusk against the moonlight. This remarkable shot is another icon of Halloween, and the one that instantly made me think of the Good Witch from The Wizard of Oz, with which the film shares still further implicit but deep figurations (as it does, if more tangentially, with Meet Me in St. Louis). In preparing for Halloween, by the way, Mary, Elliott's mother, actually plays the Good Witch: looking beautiful, like a star-creature, she carries a star-wand to touch trick-or-treaters on the head.

E.T. shares paradigmatic qualities perhaps most explicitly with J. M. Barrie's Peter Pan, passages from which are read aloud in the movie. Tink's dying and getting well again if children do and declare that they believe in fairies--E.T. himself avers his belief--prefigures the extra-terrestrial's own revival.[1]

Such intertextual lineages are rooted, I believe, in Spielberg's sensibility; they could easily be traced out further: to Robinson Crusoe, for example (Kotzwinkle 1982:125), or Humperdinck's Hansel and Gretel (again, the Reese's Pieces), and selected passages from the imagination of Jules Verne and H. G. Wells. Although Spielberg supplied the idea for the picture, the screenplay was developed by three writers, among them Melissa Mathison, who was one of the scenarists for Carroll Ballard's 1979 film, The Black Stallion. She is probably responsible for the emphatic development of the boy-and-his-pet theme, sparked by Walter Farley's 1941 novel, which inseminated numberless sequels. She also seems fond of lonesome boys who are bereft of their father, a motif that is autobiographically congenial to Spielberg as well.

The fatherless ten-year-old Elliott and his forsaken unearthly familiar are, however, much more than friends. In a profound sense, they are identical, as the boy's very name, ElliotT, insinuates. Communication between the two of them progresses rapidly from sign language to Earth language: 'the language center of his marvelous brain came fully on, a thousand stored tongues reappearing, as reference and cross-reference took place, so that Earth's language could be viewed in the round. He grasped its fundamentals, and then its delicate edges' (Kotzwinkle 1982:75). It continues via two-way telepathic connections. When E.T. gets plastered on a six-pack of beer at home while his telepathic sender is in full force, Elliott suffers bizarre effects in school, along with the loaded source. When E.T.--who, by the way, is constituted of DNA like all the rest of us--becomes mortally sick, Elliott does so in analogous fashion, as reflected by electronic scanners and displays. Kotzwinkle (1982:167) comments: 'The boy and the monster were linked somehow, as if the monster were feeding on the child's life. The child came in and out of consciousness, hallucinating, babbling, sinking under again. I'd cut the cord that ties them, thought the doctor, if only I knew where and what it was.' E.T., of course, recovers ('Do you believe in fairies?'), and so does Elliott; the wilted geranium blooms again, simultaneously.

The 'intertextual' pedigree of E.T., traced out so far to literary, filmic, musical, and autobiographical lines of descent, crisscrossing but controlled in a highly craftsmanlike manner by the omnipresent director, must be regarded as a pattern that works only skin-deep. Notwithstanding that these interwoven elements of its surface structure may suffice to convey the gratification derived from wonted up-beat narrative constituents distanced by exotic trappings, they do not, by themselves, I think, account for either the genuinely tearful cathartic enchantment many viewers report experiencing during this movie, or its record-breaking box office success. These must be ascribed to the archetypally subliminal religious infrastructure in which the film is soaked. It is thus turned into a calculated yet unpretentious allegory.

Before ascending to this level of inspection, however, it might be worth pointing briefly to yet another reason for E.T.'s lachrymose allurement. The physical design and traits of E.T. enable us to descry him as an idealized bundle of what ethnologists call biological 'releasers'. Although, to be sure, E.T. is not actually an animal, he is, as mentioned, a very special pet of Elliott's, exemplifying to perfection Morris' (1967:230) first law of animal appeal, which states that 'The popularity of an animal is directly correlated with the number of anthropomorphic features it possesses.' E.T. does so, in superoptimal degree.

A preternatural creature descends to the Earth from his unearthly orb, inscribed with a delicate gothic design ('as if an enormous Christmas tree ornament had fallen from the darkness...the greatest heart-light the world has ever seen'--Kotzwinkle 1982:182). He is found in a tool shed, arguably a suburban Southern California rendition of a manger. He is adopted and protected by a family, the mother of which is named Mary; (it is, incidentally, worth noting that Mary is the sole adult female in the picture, like Princess Leia Organa was in Star Wars). The visitor proceeds to perform magical deeds, like making mundane balls float in the air and rotate in orbit. He executes wonderful healings and levitations. Indeed, his presence is referred to several times as 'miraculous'.

Love is the message E.T. brings to Earth, and, among the Earthlings, it is the children he attracts as his immediate disciples. He is hounded and persecuted by sinister legions of faceless pursuers, undergoing suffering, death, resurrection, and, at last, ascension, to his home. Holding onto his geranium, he embraces Elliott, and delivers an intricate wave-sign of benediction, 'to release the child from the narcosis of the stars' (Kotzwinkle 1982:182). 'I'll be right here,' he finally pronounces, as his luminous fingertip glows over the boy's chest.

We, who are left behind, can look forward to a Second Coming.

Postscript. This essay was finished before the release of Ron Howard's entrancing comedy, Splash. While its lyrical surface sheen has seemingly nothing in common with E.T., a detailed analysis of the underlying structure reveals that this film is almost a point-for-point transform of the earlier masterwork. As the extraterrestrial descends from outerspace, so the Thalassic creature ascends from below, both to master language in identical fashion. Both plots are about all sorts of love, although Allen's is consummated both sexually and romantically with the ravishing mermaid, whom he finally joins (after a compulsory chase scene), forever after, in her maritime abode. Although space will not allow me to particularize my argument here, the dense 'intertextuality' between these two movies needs at least to be pointed out, and, elsewhere, to be explored much further.

Note

1. Several auditors of this lecture have called my attention to a scene where E.T. hides from the children's mother in a toy-filled closet. As she opens the door, he blends so well with the dolls that she fails to notice him. I am told that this sequence is intended to recall a mirthful pause in Chaplin's 'The Circus', which opened in 1928, but which I have never seen. The sequence is briefly described by Huff (1951:213) thus: 'Charlie freezes into a wooden statue among other figures on a Noah's Ark, as the cop dashes past.' The principle involved, in both cases, is, of course, that of Poe's 'The Purloined Letter'.

References

Barthes, Roland. 1974. S/Z. New York: Hill and Wang.
Culler, Jonathan. 1981. The pursuit of signs: Semiotics, literature, deconstruction. Ithaca, N.Y.: Cornell University Press.
Huff, Theodore. 1951. Charlie Chaplin. New York: Henry Schuman.
Jefferson, Ann. (in press) Intertextuality. In: Encyclopedic dictionary of semiotics. Edited by Thomas A. Sebeok et al. Berlin: Mouton.
Kael, Pauline. 1982. The pure and the impure. The New Yorker, June 14.
Kotzwinkle, William. 1982. E.T. The extra-terrestrial. New York: G. P. Putnam's Sons.
Kristeva, Julia. 1969. Semiotike: Recherches pour une semanalyse. Paris: Seuil.
Margulis, Lynn. 1981. Symbiosis in cell evolution: Life and its environment on the early earth. San Francisco: W. H. Freeman.
Morris, Desmond. 1967. The naked ape: A zoologist's study of the human animal. New York: McGraw Hill.
Sebeok, Thomas A. 1979. The sign and its masters. Austin: University of Texas Press.
Sebeok, Thomas A. 1981. The play of musement. Bloomington: Indiana University Press.
Skinner, B. F. 1983. Origins of a behaviorist. Psychology Today 17.9:22-33.

ON THE PRAGMATIC 'POETRY' OF PROSE: PARALLELISM, REPETITION, AND COHESIVE STRUCTURE IN THE TIME COURSE OF DYADIC CONVERSATION

Michael Silverstein
The University of Chicago

The natural, public habitat of linguistic structure is in the intersubjective complexities of communication. This is the realm of interactional pragmatics. Regularities in such communication that can be formally described might be termed pragmatic structures; many linguists have been seeking to account for them within linguistics, or to explain why one should not or even cannot. My discussion is aimed at demonstrating one such kind of structure by example, a 'poetic' structure of linguistic forms that develops coherence in the realtime work of dyadic conversation. Such poetics of prose has fundamental importance, I believe, for clarifying some of the issues emerging in debates concerning the integrity of grammatical form, the varieties of meaning, and the contextualization of language use. Perhaps this relevance will be more vivid when cast in terms of current linguistic controversy over self-styled 'functionalist' and 'formalist' approaches.

For linguistics in recent years, the sentence has been the hero for the orthodox, whose functional and formal autonomy are to be celebrated-- or, for nonbelievers, the villain whose grammatical riches, only apparent, are to be reattributed to other phenomena. Assumed to be a transcendent unit of abstract theory, the autonomy of the sentence is generally defended as being tantamount to the autonomy of linguistics as a science with pretensions to real 'explanation' in its own terms. (Note the echoes of Saussure and of Bloomfield.) Assumed to be a self-contained totality of theoretically relevant structures, the formal integrity of the sentence in consistent structural terms is seen to mark the most significant dividing line of a structural hierarchy of inclusiveness, and hence of types of scientific accountability for language. Assumed to be a syntactic structure of uniquely determinate (or at least decidable) propositional value, the sentence condenses and interrelates numerous functional speculations: on the modeling in logic of some hypothesized system of individual cognition; on its structured mirroring in intersubjective representational forms (for example, in surface syntax); and on the dependence of distinctly verbal communication and hence of linguistics on isolating some unifunctional meaningfulness in an abstract logical model. The sentence, then, is--like the taxonomic phoneme of yore, to some--at a triple intersection of epistemological, formal, and functional assumptions. No wonder the frequently heated debates have been so concerned to attack or to defend its specification in particular!

Here, the problem of linguistic form is approached in a manner somewhat different from the 'text grammatical', 'functional', or 'discourse grammatical' points of view, as these have been represented in much contemporary work.[1] My demonstration here is based on distinguishing, first, principles of sentence-grammatical form, possibly equivalent to the transcendent ('second-order' mental), autonomous ideal structures that the model-fitting strategies of orthodox syntacticians seek to characterize. Let us agree that, however partial in specifying public, surface-structure forms, these principles define the sentence as a grammatical entity. These principles, however ultimately minimal, would determine something of the recursive structure of unboundedly complex, logically relevant ideal forms said to underlie the 'conceptual creativity' of syntax. This level is not much in evidence in the following conversational material.

Second, we should identify surface forms of what we might call sentence-scope, as these unfold in realtime discourse. By the first assumption, these are at least partly instancing or realizing the principles of syntax, and at most partly something else. Syntax in the earlier sense almost certainly cannot specify everything about such sentence scopes; however, what is syntactic in the strictly autonomist-formalist-logicist sense must be definable on evidence only within the bounds of sentence-scopes. Anything larger as the data-base would threaten the triplex of assumptions that divide abstract, transcendent, formal sentence syntax from actual realtime, immanent, functionally multiplex discourse.

To be sure, syntacticians have now 'clarified' their positions to mean that most likely certain realtime, perhaps cognitive-psychological, or even actor-strategic 'functional' principles operate with respect to production/reception of some aspects of the ultimate shapes of sentence-scopes as occurring performance units. (The interactions between these and autonomous syntax are decidedly vague, however.) But strict syntacticians do not countenance formal, abstract, and transcendent principles of the very same order as syntactic ones determining structures larger than the sentence-scope in occurring discourse.

The problem of formal ordering, on which my demonstration centers, illustrates the opposition rather nicely. For, in the public domain, discourse unfolds in a time-bound, linear 'sequentiality'; ever since Saussure's postulate on the matter ([1916] 1960:103), this sequentiality has been explicitly differentiated from the concatenational 'syntagmaticity' of the transcendent domain of grammar. Syntagmatic order of elements is, of course, a common syntactic principle, one even in our own English language relating to Agent-Patient relationships. Compare also enclisis, as in Wackernagel's Law in Indo-European, and similar positional restrictions on specific classes of syntactic constituents.

But such regularities seem to be based on qualitative principles of relative order. They can always be formulated with respect to some particular level of syntactic/morphological constituency--and hence, to this degree, are always 'structure dependent', note--in terms of which an ordinal (or positional) rather than cardinal (measured), and local (within constituency-defined scope) rather than global (defined on the entire scope), principle can be formulated. By contrast, as Jakobson (1960:358) so brilliantly and oracularly formulated it, 'poetic function [of language pragmatics] projects the principle of equivalence from the axis of selection into the axis of combination.' This means that formal units, as units of a poetic order of language structure, depend for their very definition and special kind of meaningfulness--'equivalence' or any of its variants, including antonymy, in the Jakobsonian idiom--on the fact of their cardinal combinatory positions within the sequential order of actual, linear discourse. The fundamental poetic principle, then, is sequential measure, or meter, in terms of which the linear signal can be measured off into units of whatever sort.

In the most highly developed poetry--to be distinguished, of course, from poetic principles as these apply to language in general (Jakobson 1960:359)--the aesthetic form generally consists of multiply overlaid, hence both cyclic and hierarchy-generating, measurements, frequently at several different structural planes of propositional linguistic form simultaneously, e.g. several phonological measures concurrent with morphosyntactic and lexical ones. However, meter, in the sense of the basic fact of poetic organization, need not rest on specifically phonological measure; rather, anything in linguistic form can serve as the basis for poetic pragmatic structure, such form being defined with respect to the metric principle(s). The data here, for example, illustrate such poetic structure in the referential-and-predicational sentence-scope forms of a developing dyadic conversation.

To follow the demonstration, one must understand a few principles and concepts from our heritage of semiotic functionalism. First, I will be using some reasonably uncontroversial proposals about English surface grammatical constituency within the sentence-scope, with no ultimate claim implied about their reducibility/autonomy as sentence-grammatical. Second, I will be using the concept of parallelism, involving a measured repetition that serves as the metered frame for positional variability. This very elementary type of poetic structure (see Jakobson 1966; Bricker 1974; Fox 1977) can be developed in a purely sequential fashion, continued or not whenever a significant unit boundary is reached, and hence nicely merges the notions of local and global measurement. It is perfect as a form developed through strategic contingency. Third, I will make reference to the theme/rheme status of linguistic units (see Firbas 1964; Daneš 1970). These can be identified in the meter-framed variable portions of sentence-scope within the poetic structure. Hence, these are relative to English surface structure, including stress-level phenomena, within the sentence-scope stretch of discourse.

The use of these few tools gives us the ability to understand several aspects of how this conversation is integrated as a developmental structure in time, an 'inter'-subjective, publicly negotiated creation in which poetic organization plays a central role both in cohesion or 'texture' (Halliday and Hasan 1976:1-30) and in what have been termed 'speech acts' (Searle 1969) and illocutionary/perlocutionary effects (Austin

[1962] 1975). The mutually entailing cooccurrences of forms--special, text-internal indexical relationships that make text part of the context of occurrence of any sign--induced by the way forms have positions in the induced or constituted poetic organization privilege the construal of 'topics', denotata that, once introduced, can be maintained as true referents with pro-forms or even zero explicit linguistic forms. The parallelisms and repetitions of the material that remains in poetic sequence contribute the determining structure, independent of any sentence-level contribution to surface sentence-scopes. In this view, the syntactic problem of 'recoverability'--or reconstitution of grammatical and referential identity--of empty, absent, or deleted elements of would-be sentence-scopes, is an artifact of the grammar-level perspective on the way poetic organization determines a discourse structure of topics and comments.

In the material that follows, in fact, it is interesting to see that as conversation moves forward in its linear time frame, certain momentarily ambiguous pro-units and 'deletions' are resolved by implication as part of the conversational work much later than at the point at which they first occur. But that is as we would expect, since the sentence-scope fragments that occur in parallelistic structures develop certain thematic elements by rhemes that have linear ordering relationships. Conversation moves through a specification of its unique and topical referential content from among whatever is the residual set of possibilities at the moment of ambiguity, in due course the specification being the explicit thematic base for a rhematic form that serves as comment on the topical referent.

This linear progression of syntactic poetics played out in time achieves the semblance of what some would reconstruct as 'indirect speech acts' (Searle 1975). Rarely in this conversation, as in the rest of our experience outside of formal occasions, does anyone issue an explicit metapragmatic formula of canonical 'performative' shape, or even of recognizably conventionalized sort. What we find, rather, is that the poetically established sequence of thematic/rhematic elements sets up a dynamic, analogical quasi-syllogism of concepts in realtime. The playing out of this quasi-logic is differentially contributed to by the two participants, and shows differential cohesion within vs. across interlocutors. From such a public, emergent structure, not necessarily from the propositional interpretations of sentences implied by sentence-scopes plus vague canons of so-called implicature, can any interpretability of speech act 'moves' (or any equivalent actor-centered reconstitution of intents in a psychological philosophy) proceed on an empirical basis.

Were we to view abstract sentence grammar as an immanent, rather than transcendent, cognitive psychological mechanism--a 'first-order mental structure'--as some are unfortunately wont to do, we would constitute the problem of discourse coherence in terms of the tension between the hierarchical organization of information, as revealed in syntactic structures, and the apparent linearity of realtime-bound productive/receptive discourse performance. But there is no direct tension of this sort. For to make this leap is to forget the triple 'decontextualization' that sentence-syntax constitutes vis-à-vis public linguistic data. For example, the hierarchical 'chunking' of conceptual information, whatever its cognitive reality, is not merely reflected in hierarchical forms, such as super-/subordinate syntactic structures of surface sentence-scopes, which are at a completely different order of phenomena, regardless of the fact that the superordinate and subordinate portions of sentence-scopes occur in certain language-particular ordering relationships. Poetic pragmatics, I would maintain, mediates among these orders. It is a transcendent structure in exactly the same sense as syntax, but it is developed in realtime through principles that are inherently linear, yet abstract and formal. Along this poetic dimension of structure, some true understanding of immanent 'functional' constraints may be forthcoming.

Let me illustrate this in an example. The data I discuss come from the set of dyadic conversations induced, videotaped, transcribed, computer-stored, and in several respects analyzed by my colleague Starkey Duncan and his associates at The University of Chicago, as material for studies of nonverbal interpersonal turn-taking behavior (see Duncan and Fiske 1977 for documentation[2]).

The transcript as organized and presented here needs some explanation. I have organized the contributions of the two subjects, labeled A and B, into two parallel columns. I have labeled the explicit questions (Q) and responses (R) in pairs, with a numerical subscript index of its position within the total conversational sequence of each respective speaker. Thus Q_{A6} labels A's sixth explicit question form in the transcribed conversation. The temporal dimension is represented from left to right on every line of transcript, and vertically down the transcript for sequential utterances. Every line represents talk no earlier than the line above it. When there is an overlap in the conversation, this is indicated by putting braces two lines high around the overlapping segments; material appearing on the resulting upper line of a two-line brace is simultaneous with that on the lower line of the next occurring brace according to the temporal dimension conventions. Thus, in (6), ...cation chánged [700msec] a... spoken by B is simultaneous with ...overwhélming. spoken by A. I give a section number, in the left-hand margin, to each explicit Q—R sequence, or to each whole poetic structure of a subject, plus its associated material. Speech is continuous, and silences in the range of ca. 20-30 msec are indicated with an em-dash; long pauses are indicated by specifying their approximate length in brackets.

Linguistic material is indicated in a close-to-standard English orthography, indicating only unusual stress and intonation-height characteristics, i.e. those distinctive in degree and/or placement given surface syntax. Since participants refer to each other with the personal deictics I and you, these have been indexed with subscripts, i = subject B, j = subject A. Unambiguously restorable material is, in a few cases, necessary for the transcript in English orthography to make sense; this is indicated in square brackets. Also indicated, by $\emptyset$, is material that, relative to the parallelistic structure of sentence-scopes, would be reconstituted as missing constituent(s) by a sentence-syntactic view of sentence-scope completeness.[3] Finally, according to the method of maximizing parallelism and poetic structure in a determinate earlier-to-later (i.e. realtime) fashion, I have used outline-style indentation to various margins to highlight units of equivalent relative status in the poetic structures that develop.

A   B

(1) Hu?úh, An' Q_A6 how do you_i like Chicago compared [to ∅]
    Q_A7 did you_i go to school thére ór uh, [wa
                                              [I_i] díd go to school there
                                        R_B7
                                              I_i went to school hére álso, [úm

    {Óh}, uh-húh

    Óh, uh-húh   ...there...
                                              um, so I_i came back kind of
                                              I_i wa[s]

(2) Q_A8 An' you_i wént to undergraduate ∅ hére ór
                                              R_B8 ∅ in Chicago át, uh, Loyola

(3) Óh óh óh óh I_j'm an óld Jesuit boy myself_j, (unfortunately
                                              (Oh áre ya_j ∅   Q_B1 Where'd you_j gó [to ∅]

(4) R_A1 ∅ [at] Georgetown, down (in Washington
                                              (O:h yéah), yeah
    (It's) too bád
    Í_j— [710 msec]   Q_B2 Did you_j finish ∅
                                              Óh, úh— [huh

(5) R_A2 Úm Yéah Wéll this is my_j second yéar here
    (And), uh, Í_j don't know,
    It was níce
    {X_i}

On the pragmatic 'poetry' of prose / 187

(6)
```
          Íj sorta enjóyed it —
             Ìj
      This place is réally — dì different —
           Ìj mu' —
                              Ij must sáy
                                           Yeah
Bùt. uh. [710 msec]
     Ìj don't know,
          Íj Ij enjoyed the educátion there
{x₂}
     And it réally was góod
        It [wasn't]
              [overwhélming]
                             {Ii think} —
                                          Jésuit edu[cation chánged [700 msec] a]
                                                     lót in the lást five or six yéars
                              An' Ii think
                                          Ii just caught
                                          Ii caught the tail end of uh — óf the — really óld
                                                     schóol —
                                          Ít was
                                          Ii — was really
```

188 / Michael Silverstein

I_1 mean —

   'cause $\acute{I}_1$ $\acute{I}_1$ did my$_1$ úndergraduate work

      I_1 fínished that líke four yéars a [690 msec] go

         fíve years ago

Ánd —

  I_1 thínk

    Nów — próbably Loyola is a lót different

      an' a lot bétter [690 msec]

        y'$_j$ knów

         a lót more — variety of courses

          being offered et cetera

      ánd —

        yóu$_j$ know

I_1 — I_1...

On the pragmatic 'poetry' of prose / 189

The two participants in this excerpt are males in their 20s not before acquainted; they have been asked to sit facing each other and to converse. Subject A is a graduate student in the Law School, B in the School of Social Service Administration. Their conversation moves through several phases, from (i) mutual introductions, to (ii) self-conscious mutual excuses, through (iii) trying to find mutual topics of discourse. In searching for topics, A and B start with mutual prior acquaintances; it turns out that each had previously participated in a similar conversational dyad with a female student known to the other (relative participant gender was a variable in the study). Their search continues in question (Q) and response (R) sequences about prior, current, and future experiences. We enter during the first of these, when A has been asking about where B came from 'before', i.e. before coming to graduate school at The University of Chicago. Up to the point at which we enter, it has been exclusively A's role in the interaction to ask explicit questions, B's role to respond to them.

At the point we enter, it appears that A had just been trying to find out at what school B had been, but had gotten, instead, a response about where B had lived. (Up to this point, the ambiguity of the form Chicago as denoting both place and institution has allowed this room for maneuvering.) B's introducing his prior residence, Iowa, prompted several sequences of 'Trivial Pursuit' about the state, its towns and cities, geographical loci last referred to by B with the pro-form there, as indicated on the transcript. A then begins anew to clarify B's origin in the sense of establishing old school ties, making the conversational seam in an ingenious way.

In (1), A brings the conversation's informational structure back to the main rank of questions-responses instanced some turns back (A: Where did you come from before? B: Um, Iowa. I lived in Iowa.) A poses his sixth such question in the conversation (labeled Q_{A6}), How do you like Chicago compared ⊂ ⊐ ? which is a conventionalized conversational follow-up, complete with stressed like, to the piece of information on where the interlocutor had lived before, taking Chicago as the name of a place, the deictic here and now/after, as compared with the place Iowa, the deictic there and then/before. Note that A's question lacks completely any syntactically expected coda, ...to there/...to Iowa, which is of course fully recoverable from the thematic status of Iowa/there in preceding discourse.

Immediately, without any pause to give B the turn to respond, A focuses on the now-locational reading of Chicago vs. Iowa (= there). Formulating it with the stressed rheme thére, A once more asks his question about prior education in the seeming guise of clarifying the rheme like Chicago compared ⊂ ⊐ with a parallel rheme of an almost parenthetical nature (By the way, did you...), stressing and thereby making focal the recoverable topic there in an ambiguous--and thus perhaps 'politely indirect'--yes/no and either/or structure: Q_{A7} Did you go to school thére ór...? Note that the utterance indexically presupposes that B went to school somewhere as asked. The material that might complete the disjunction introduced by ór is, of course, entirely unimportant to reestablishing the question on the table (though leaving room for the possible response that B had lived in Iowa for some other reason). B responds now to the pointedly defocused (and hence, for polite conversation, more compulsive) specificity of the predicate <u>go to school</u> with its emphatic, confirmatory form, including the stressed auxiliary <u>do᷄</u> (in past tense). Abstracting syntactically from the assertorial <u>di᷄d go</u>, we find that B's utterance R_{B7} is otherwise the precise syntactic counterpart to A's question Q_{A7}, changing only the personal deictic from <u>you</u>$_{\text{i}}$ to $\underline{I}_{\text{i}}$, because of the shift of deictic origin relative to the speech-event roles. We should also observe that the form $\underline{I}_{\text{i}}$ <u>went to school there</u> is also precisely parallel to B's earlier remark at the same information-rank, $\underline{I}_{\text{i}}$ <u>lived in Iowa</u>, formally contrasting <u>go to school</u> with <u>live</u> and specifying it further. (In the instance, the form <u>there</u> has its precise interpretability from the long-standing thematic status of <u>Iowa/there</u>, maintained by both A and B in exactly analogous syntactic positions since an earlier part of the conversation.)

The participants have both been maintaining reference to Iowa with the form <u>there</u>. <u>There</u> vs. the implicit deictic origin <u>here</u> (included in the denotation of <u>Chicago</u> so far) is now to be established as a major, explicit contrast in rhematic position. Speaker B continues his response, reintroducing Chicago vs. Iowa as two geographical loci in the final, contrastive portion of an entirely parallel sentence, $\underline{I}_{\text{i}}$ <u>went to school he᷄re a᷄lso</u>. Observe that B's new information is in the contrast of locatives, and hence he uses a sequence of stresses in the rhematic portion, <u>he᷄re a᷄lso</u>, and the nonassertorial <u>went</u> instead of <u>di᷄d go</u>, as in his previous utterance. This is followed by some space-filling pause forms (<u>u᷄m um...</u>) during which A indicates his registration of the utterance turn (<u>O᷄h, uh-hu᷄h</u>), and then B continues. He gives a summary statement that establishes a time sequence, <u>so I_{i} came back kind of</u>. With its normal stress peak on the rhematic final portion, the verbal <u>came back</u>, this utterance unit concludes with a modalizing parenthetical, <u>kind of</u>. In this way, the deduced conclusion is highlighted, in a way that, for example, $\underline{I}_{\text{i}}$ <u>came back here, kind of</u> would not do, except with extra heavy stress on the phrasal verb <u>came back</u>. Given the perspectival deixis of the verb, one can, of course, <u>come back</u> only if <u>here</u>--i.e. as established, Chicago--both preceded and followed <u>there</u>--i.e. as established, Iowa. B begins to make this coming back more precise, in the context of questions about going to school, saying I_{i} <u>wa⟨s⟩...</u>, but A interrupts, registering B's utterances with <u>Oh, uh-hu᷄h</u> and then continuing to pursue his line of questioning about prior education.

In this eighth question-and-response sequence, A uses a form that is again parallel to the utterances in Q_{A7}--R_{B7}, now uninverted in order, asking for a confirmation of a particular deduction about the time sequence of B's here-and-there-and-here education that B has just set up. The operative predicate, in parallel utterances, for most of the interaction has been <u>go to school</u>, and A continues to use this, asking more particularly if undergraduate school is to be paired with the first location <u>here</u> of the sequence entailed by R_{B7}. The utterance <u>an' you</u>$_{\text{i}}$ <u>we᷄nt to undergraduate he᷄re o᷄r</u> has form parallel both to A's previous question and to B's responses; it deletes the repeated noun <u>school</u> and uses merely its would-be modifier <u>undergraduate</u>--this has ben the focus of A's questioning all along--and uses a final stressed <u>he᷄re</u> in the maximally rhematic position; for B's having gone to undergraduate school here, i.e. at or in Chicago, is one way of understanding <u>coming back</u>. So note that there is a certain implicative continuity of this confirmatory question, following as it does upon the came back rheme. But its form is cast into the proper syntactic mold of the unfolding structure of parallelisms in utterances that establish the specific here and there reference points.

The next utterance, B's, labeled R_{B8}, is at once a perfect structural reply to the question and the continuation/conclusion to B's last, interrupted syntactic unit in (1). In Chicago át, uh, Loyola specifies two things and at last definitively disambiguates thereby locational and institutional referents. First, it specifies with in Chicago that Chicago is indeed now intersubjectively to be taken in the geographical-locative sense, in keeping with the sequence of heres and theres just developed. Second, it confirms that going to (undergraduate) school here can no longer be taken to be Chicago, The University of (which would be at Chicago). Third, it specifies the long sought-after information, át--note the contrastive and disambiguating stress--uh--note the pregnant hesitation--Loyola. (As we shall see, throughout the rest of this portion of the interaction, as indeed beyond it to the conclusion of the videotape, B demonstrates considerable tension about this datum.) So this phrase is properly a syntactic conclusion either to the recoverable I_i went to undergraduate school... or to the earlier, interrupted I_i wa[s]... Given the tight parallelisms determining the sequences of syntactic forms, it is irrelevant for us to try to decide/determine if one or the other may have ben 'intended'; the seeming structural ambiguity of cohesion--or the double determination of the syntactic fragment by rich parallelism--does not affect its information content in the flow of the discourse.

At this rhematic news of Loyola, subject A jumps in, further to introduce himself, making the discovered commonalty between B and himself an intersubjective reality. I:'m an óld Jesuit boy myself, he remarks, with mock-humorous qualification unfortunately uttered simultaneously with B's response to this revelation.[4] B's response is the inverted rhetorical question form of discovery, Oh áre ya:? deleting the entire recoverable predicate noun phrase of A's utterance, but otherwise perfectly parallel with it, stressing the finite verb. B then continues without interruption to deliver the expected information question, Q_{B1}, beginning interactional segment (4), Where'd you: góɛ ɔ? Observe that the by now well established to undergraduate school is not necessary to the explicit signal to keep the sense of go here the specific one in use, i.e. 'attend'. The syntactic form is thus precisely parallel to A's questions and B's responses in (1) and (2), with a preposed WH-form. A's answer here, R_{A1}, is the perfect counterpart to B's earlier R_{B8}, moreover, with a discourse chiasmus in the explicit material. Deleting all would-be Subject and Predicate material except the rhematic essentials, A's utterance is equivalent to '[I_i went to (school at)] Georgetown, down in Washington.' Note the mirror-image syntactic symmetry between R_{B8} and R_{A1}: in Chicago at, uh, Loyola vs. [at] Georgetown,...in Washington.

This exchange, in the rhetorical figure of a syntagmatic cross (X-Y...Y-X), is in fact the crux of the interaction. Up to this point, only A has posed questions. At this point B, having once asked his first, now keeps the interrogator's role for the rest of the transcribed conversation. A's volunteering of his own personal information in (3) shifts the roles by letting B assume the questioner's role in (4).[5] Indeed, after B registers the response to this with the assenting O:h yéah, yeah of recognition, A begins to formulate another comment, and hesitates, leaving a silence of some 710 milliseconds, relatively long for this interaction. (He seems to be waiting for B to pose a question, having exchanged interaction roles with him.) Before he desists, A begins the syntactic outline of a comment he will fully develop, it turns out, in segment (5), a discourse structure with finite clauses of form it [be] [Evaluative]$_{Adj}$ and clauses with Subject I_j in a complex and regular pattern.

But, A having hesitated, B offers his next question, Q_{B2} Did you$_j$ finish[ᴐ]? where the syntactic completion with either a quasi-object or a locative again is fully recoverable in any of a number of ways: Did you$_j$ finish... school/undergraduate school/at Georgetown [now equal to A's there, we should observe]/down in Washington/there/etc. All these are possible sentence-level completions fully in keeping with the thematic cohesion of the particular syntactic unit in Q_{B2}, but here again it is irrelevant to the structure of discourse at this point to make a unique syntactic determination.

Observe how, whatever the 'correct' conclusion to B's question Q_{B2}, the suppressed reference sets up an equivalent there for A, i.e. where he was before or then, parallel to the there vs. here distinction that has been the emerging contrast for subject B in the conversation thus far. So, in answer to B's question, A replies in R_{A2} affirmatively to having finished there, and then he goes on to prepare for the continuation of the utterance he began but interrupted in his earlier turn. Wéll thís is my second year here, he remarks. This introduces in maximally rhematic position the explicit contrast between a current here, which can only be the institution, The University of Chicago, and the former there, Georgetown University, of two years earlier and more. (It should be noted too that this affirmative utterance is precisely the syntactic parallel of A's own earlier question Q_{A4}, not included in our sample transcript, Is this your$_j$ first year here, or? Note additionally the consistency of question style, a blend of (optionally inverted) yes/no question and disjunctive (either)/or question, exactly as in Q_{A7} and Q_{A8} discussed earlier.)

Óh, úh-huh, B registers, finishing the last syllable as A continues. And--perhaps A rushes so as not to lose the opportunity through turn-transition to express what he hesitated on before--I_j don't know / It was nice / I_j sorta enjóyed it. Let us term this sequénce of three clause structurés with no explicit connectives a_1-b_1-c_1. After an unstressed misfire (I_j), A continues with a fourth unconnected affirmative clause--let us call it d_1--with a heavy stress on both initial deictic topic and final rhematic portion, thus: Thís place is réally réally--di dífferent-- emphasizing the contrastive value of both.

Then comes a parenthetical. The structure of this parenthetical is interesting, since it appears to demonstrate in its misfired first portion, I_j mu'--, something of the compulsive rhythmic or metrical nature of sentence-scope discourse units, considered in phonological terms. The expected parenthetical stress contour, when achieved, would of course have predicate stress, I_j múst say or, as here, I_j must sáy. A begins to use a discourse unit stressed initially on I_j, just like units a_1 and c_1, which form, with this unit--let us term it e--a pattern of alternating sentence-scope discourse units. After B's intercalated registration of

A's discourse so far, Yeah, A repairs the stress contour by redoing the full-clause parenthetical, I̬ must sáy.

Let us look a bit more closely at the sequence a_1-b_1-c_1-d_1-e. It is a sequence of full, simple clauses, every odd-positioned clause beginning with I̬. Read together, these give a rather hedged judgment about personal experience, I̬ don't know, I̬ sorta enjoyed it, I̬ must say. The form it here clearly refers to something in the past, perhaps the same thing as the it of clause b_1, It was nice, if we wish to make a cohesive totality of a_1 through e. On the other hand, out of context, the sentence-scope b_1 could possibly include the initial form it just as a place-filler for the predicate be nice. Just from the sequence b_1-c_1, on which such cross-sentence local cohesion relations are definable, it is not clear how to take the subject it of b_1 in relation to the object it of c_1; they may be coreferent, they may not be.

However, once we look at the overall structure of the sequence of poetic units, things are clarified. Units b_1 and d_1 have a structure with parallel be + [Evaluative]$_{Adj}$, b_1 with past tense was and d_1 with present tense is. Having already established his prior there and his current here, A is clearly contrasting these explicitly in topical position in b_1 vs. d_1, it vs. this place, corresponding to the deictic tense differentiation, was vs. is. This leaves no room for doubt as to what A is driving at. The contrast of the evaluative adjective nice in b_1 with really really different in d_1 shows that different here is a value-laden index of speaker disapprobation, heard in colloquial usage in some parts of the country (This sure tastes/smells/feels/etc. dífferent means$_{nn}$ 'I don't really like the way this tastes/smells/feels/etc.')

Now A continues his development with a contrastive Bút, uh--compare the And, uh with which he began this whole sequence--and then pauses for a significantly lengthy time before plunging ahead. I̬ don't know, he continues, using a unit we can term a_2 to emphasize its poetic identity with a_1, I̬ I̬ enjoyed the educátion there, a unit parallel to c_1 and so termed c_2 here. It is this unit that finally clarifies the reference of object it in c_1, when we consider it in its poetic position and in light of the contrastive rhematic stress on the educátion. (Observe: What was it you liked / Why'd you like the place? I (sorta) enjoyed the educátion there.) It in c_1 and there in c_2 seem to be coreferential.

And it réally was góod, continues A, with a unit we can label b_2. This unit parallels the form of b_1, It was nice, with the addition of the adverb really from d_1. Observe that, as b_1 is to d_1 in the earlier sequence, b_1 about the past there and d_1 about the present here, d_1 having the incremental really on its evaluative adjective, here the position of really is shifted to the evaluative of b_2. And then A concludes with a unit d_2 that contrasts with b_2 just as d_1 contrasts with b_1. Since b_1 and b_2 are, in essence, the same, ultimately d_2 contrasts with d_1 by three pairs of parallelisms: this place vs. it, is vs. was, and really really different vs. not overwhelming, whence different is (by contrastive poetic logic) not not overwhelming or overwhelming. The ultimate message of contrast in d_1 vs. d_2 is that 'this place' (The University of Chicago) is what it/there (Georgetown University) is not, really really different, i.e. overwhelming. Things have gone from good to bad.

Observe, by the way, that B has already begun segment (6), following upon the explicit form of A's c_2-b_2, as A is uttering the last unit of (5),

194 / Michael Silverstein

d_2. Observe also how B pauses during the utterance of <u>overwhelming</u> simultaneous with his own speech.

Subject A has thus developed a sequential structure of the form a_1-b_1-c_1-d_1-e-a_2-c_2-b_2-d_2, with an internal chiasmus -b_1-c_1- : -c_2-b_2- within the basically bipartite structure of repetitions. The <u>there</u> of <u>then</u> in the past tense is characterized as good, nice, and enjoyable; the <u>here</u> of <u>now</u> in the present tense is characterized by contrast as different, overwhelming. And all this has been achieved not with explicit logical connectives, as with principles of poetic parallelism, determining a verse-like structure for privileged rhetorical contrasts and cohesive anaphoric continuity. Hence, in the transcript, the various corresponding units are aligned according to the overall structure, and the chiasmus is noted with a marginal Greek χ. A complete structure, it forms a segment by itself.

In (6), B takes up a commentary on the portion of A's turn (5) that has preceded his entry into speaking. A's turn culminated, then, at d_1 in the rheme <u>réally réally dífferent</u>. (For note that a_2-c_2-b_2 essentially recapitulates the content of the first 'verse', making some of the references clearer.) B proceeds to give a reading of the opposition set up between <u>then</u> and <u>now</u> as enjoyable vs. <u>different</u> that is of a piece with the hesitation and avoidance we noted in his introduction of his own undergraduate educational experience prior to being at The University of Chicago. He proceeds to fashion a discourse about the <u>then</u> and <u>now</u> of his own <u>it/there</u>, Loyola University, in a sequence of units that form a remarkable continuation of the style of A in (5), independent declaratives structured by parallelism and rhythmic repetition, containing but a single quasi-logical connective ('<u>cause</u>), and that only in an explanatory subsection.

<u>I̭ think,</u> B begins, overlapping with A's last sentence, and mirroring A's <u>I̭ don't know</u> of $a_{1,2}$. Let us call this unit a'_1, so as to emphasize the structural parallelism. B further mirrors A's <u>education there</u> (i.e. at Georgetown) of c_2, the last referent mentioned in the rhematic portion of A's utterances, in making the thematic seam to his own conversational contribution. And, for the rhematic portion of his observation, he mirrors the rheme of A's culminative d_1, <u>(be) different,</u> only in its processual equivalent: <u>chánged,</u> including even an equivalent of the intensive <u>réally réally</u>, namely, <u>a lót</u>. Given the processual formulation of the 'difference' between <u>then</u> and <u>now,</u> this time shift needs an interval formulation, such as that B supplies in his utterance. Thus: <u>Jésuit education chánged...a lót in the lást five or six yéars.</u> Notice how the time interval, the last five or six years, is highlighted as the focal portion of the rheme, and how, in so doing, the stressed <u>lást</u> brings us up to the conversational <u>now</u>. As an utterance unit, the whole is a statement about an <u>it/there</u> but making rhematic continuity with d_1; it has properties akin to A's $b_{1,2}$ and to A's d_1. Let us term it b'_1/d'.

<u>An' I̭ think,</u> B continues, introducing an experience of his own in his old school, <u>I̭ just caught/I̭ caught the tail end of uh--óf the--really óld schóol.</u> Such a structure mirrors A's clauses with personal deictic Subject in $c_{1,2}$, and hence can be termed c'_1. If we termed <u>I̭ think</u> a'_1, <u>An' I̭ think</u> would be <u>An'</u> + a'_1, or a''_1. Thus, the sequence so far in (6) is a'_1-b'_1/d'-a''_1-c'_1.

At this point B demonstrates an interesting disfluency, going into an 'it' statement, then going into a 'I$_i$' statement, then attempting to repair with the clarifying frame I$_i$ mean --, structurally equivalent here to I$_i$ think of a'$_1$. B continues to clarify the time interval separating then and now with another personal statement constituting his then experience of having caught the tail end of the old school. He says, 'cause I$_i$ I$_i$ did my undergraduate work I$_i$ finished that like four years a--by comparison with b'$_1$/d', we see that this falls short of the interval that B had himself set up there for the process of 'change', and there is a long, perhaps computational pause--...go five years ago--the numbers now being perfectly to scale.

This a'$_2$-c'$_2$ sequence is then followed by And--I$_i$ think, parallel to the second sequence-opener he used, and hence a"$_2$, and then by a complex 'it' statement about Loyola University, B's it/there, bringing the whole structure back to explicit use of the predicate be different of A's d$_1$ in (5). But here, the predicate glosses change--as it turns out, for the better--rather than glossing overwhelming, as in A's earlier segment. This b'$_2$/d' unit is itself highly complex in internal parallelistic form, illustrating the fact that the poetic subsequences are hierarchically embedded in other, superordinate ones.

Nów--próbably Loyola is a lót different, starts out the segment, with an undifferentiated b'$_2$/d' parallelistic form. But it continues with a parallel to the last, rhematic element, an' a lot bétter, explicitly clinching the equivalence of [now] different [sc., through change] = better [than then]. After a long pause, B adds a parenthetical to introduce further explication, y'$_i$ knów (compare A's own parenthetical in (5) e, I$_i$ must say), followed by another parallel unit. A lót more--variety of courses being offered et cetera, continuing in the comparative form, gives the specific sense of 'different' = 'better'.

With the ánd--, B continues with a perfectly parallel stressed conjunction, such as that linking the lot different-lot better-lot more units. But this is not quite correct from a discourse structure point of view, and after a hesitation, B frames what he has said so far with another parenthetical, you$_i$ know, which demonstrates the essence of the kind of composition such interaction consists of. For this now serves not so much as a parenthetical, an afterword-boundary for something just uttered, as a prospective framing device for what follows. B fashions in this way what we can regard as a formal seam, leading on to the next section, in which he will speak of his dissatisfaction with the Loyola of there-and-then, in pointed contrast to the idyllic memory of A's Georgetown, his there-and-then. From the point of view of B's discourse so far, Ánd--yóu$_i$ know here looks like a failed unit of form [And]$_{Conj}$ [a lot [Compar]$_{Adj}$...], you$_i$ knów. But from the point of view of how it figures in introducing further discourse, it is precisely equivalent to the various a' and a" structures, with the substitution of you$_i$ know for I$_i$ think. Observe how the parenthetical y'$_i$ knów contrasts with the presentational yóu$_i$ know, just as the unstressed an' of the comparative phrases contrasts with the stressed ánd like those joining major sequence segments. Hence, the very parallelistic structure internal to b'$_2$/d', slightly violated, becomes the seam to the next major structure B will develop. Having distinguished a view of then and now in which it/there gets better, B will go on to distance himself from there-then, i.e. Loyola in terms of dissatisfaction, confirming for us the underlying tension surrounding the comparison of Loyola to Georgetown developed in the interactional structure.

In (5), then, A has introduced a very tight structure of a_1-b_1-c_1-d_1-e; a_2-c_2-b_2-d_2. In (6), B responds with an equally tight structure, of the form a'_1-b'_1/d'-a''_1-c'_1; a'_2-c'_2-a''_2-b'_2/d'. The last unit, b'_2/d', is itself internally complex, consisting in its final, rhematic section of d''-b''_1-e'_1-$b''_2 \neq e'_2$, where d" is <u>Loyola is a lot different,</u> the b" units are the equivalent comparative evaluations (cf. the $b_{1,2}$ units of A's disquisition), and the e' units are the parentheticals, the last poetically ambiguous in metric structure. B will then go on to emphasize the contrasts to A's $c_{1,2}$ units in his next section.

We must emphasize once again the distinctiveness of the organization of the linguistic material we have analyzed. In this, as in any dyadic conversation, we have discovered a poetic organization that has its seemingly adirectional, atemporal, 'structural' aspect--once we describe it--and also its seemingly directional, temporal, 'functional' aspect-- which we as well as the interlocutors seem to understand. The atemporal or 'structural' looks hierarchical, almost constituency-like; the temporal or 'functional' looks transformative, accomplishing the semiotic work. But the structure identified is transcendent in exactly the same sense as syntax, though as native speakers in a certain tradition we may not have any intuitions about it in the same fashion as we do for the latter. And the function, about which we have many intuitions, seems to involve interpersonal social acts, accomplished in some realm of beliefs, intents, thoughts, rather than being merely a time-bound formal structure, in which we are participants, but to which we are not really parties.

One's 'heroes'--and 'villains'--may be a matter of unexamined, and ultimately irrelevant, perspectival assumptions.

Notes

I am grateful to Jerrold Sadock and James McCawley for comments on oral presentation of an earlier draft of this paper, and to Anthony Woodbury for extensive commentary on its earlier written form.

1. These recent debates with syntactic formalism have been unconvincing, I think, at least partly because they have not been paying attention simultaneously to all three areas of assumptions surrounding the inviolability of the sentence-scope boundary for true grammar. For example, one of the concerns of work professing a 'text grammatical' and similarly global text-orientation to larger-than-sentence scopes of language (cf. van Dijk 1977; Givón 1979), has been to extend the analysis characteristic of sentence-scope syntax to stretches 'higher', as it were, in a constructed hierarchy of forms (cf. also earlier tagmemic work). As orthodox syntacticians have been quick to point out, the coherence, or putative well-formedness, of stretches of language 'above' the sentence may well not be formulable in strictly comparable autonomous, and abstract terms. Rather, such entities as the topical period, the paragraph, and the whole text seem to be content units--from the perspective of referential-and-predicational analysis of language--consisting of causal or temporal event sequences, narrative scenes and plots, etc. The

relationship of these content units to formal abstract sentence structure, or even to the propositional schemata associated with sentence-scope chunks of language, is quite problematic (see Morgan and Sellner 1980).

Similarly incomplete have been attempts at various types of psychological or communicational reductive functionalism--demonstrating that within-sentence formal units are the local exemplars of speaker-oriented and/or hearer-oriented human information-processing strategies, disambiguation requirements, etc. The long known alignment of theme/rheme, old/new information-coding, and topic/comment of the surface sentence-scope, a chunk of discourse, with the Subject/Predicate distinction of abstract sentence structure, is an intriguing unmarked situation in many languages, to be sure. But, as orthodox grammarians have pointed out (see Morgan 1982; Newmeyer 1983), teleological, actor-centered, one-factor explanations of these and other language-particular formal facts or universal statistical tendencies do not (some would argue cannot in principle) constitute reduction of syntactic categories and regularities in the normal sense. We might note, then, correspondence of grammar-determined portions of surface sentence-scopes with function-driven distinctions, both 'localizable', as it were, in the same segments. But such facts need something more like multivariate statistical models of competing functional requirements, given structure in the normal sense, than alternatives to it, the argument goes, playing upon the residual 'arbitrariness' of much of sentence-syntax as a still function-independent or unmotivated realm of structural regularity in languages.

But the house of autonomous formal sentence-propositional grammar is hardly inwardly calm and ordered. It is not difficult to understand in the terms of these debates the recent history of orthodox syntax. On the one hand, portions of sentence-scope facts have been ceded to functionalists and text-theoreticians, while on the other, ever more abstract autonomous principles are being formulated that redefine, in effect, what is still contained in grammar in the orthodox sense. Nevertheless, no real theory has been forthcoming of just _how_ the multiplicity of now-recognized factors interact, making this, mutatis mutandis, as empty a 'modularized' structural-functionalism (as opposed to a reductive one) as one might imagine.

I doubt that real clarity will emerge until all sides of the discussion recognize the full set of dimensions of the problem of isolating sentence syntax, and become more honestly semiotic (see Silverstein 1984 for some proposals).

2. The computer-generated transcript available to me includes, in addition to segmental linguistic forms, for each participant, transcription of head and hand kinesics, and paralinguistic features such as smiles, laughs, drawl, etc., all displayed against a time measure in milliseconds, for synchronization. The data are used with the permission of Starkey Duncan, to whom I am grateful for encouragement.

3. To say that full sentences are, or can potentially be, 'understood' from what then emerge as sentence-fragments, is only to say that sentence-scopes with certain grammatically specifiable forms are reconstructible 'off line', as it were, by a kind of secondary reflection upon the occurring material (with contextual cues), plus various default

prescriptions based on hypotheses about the way sentence-scopes code propositionality. This reconstructive procedure gives the illusion that decontextualization is equivalent to abstraction (in the syntactician's canonical sense). From this confusion, sentences can then be viewed as pure, complete forms of ideal theory, while what from this perspective appear as sentence-scope fragments are merely contextualized reductions. Decontextualization, abstraction, and idealization are not simple equivalents; this is not what is intended in sentence-syntax, nor here, though mistakenly identifying them has generated much confusion in the literature about ideal speaker/hearers and the like.

4. We may add that there seems to be something of an asymmetric and manipulative quality to A's interactional style, culminating at this point. Were we interpreting the interaction, rather than giving a formal analysis based solely upon syntactic form in discourse context, we would see this as a game of One Upmanship. A, the Law School student, has led B, the lower-status Social Services student, to reveal his background in some detail. He may well be responding in an aggressive manner to the noticeable hesitancy with which B, the student at the academically and professionally lower-ranked division of The University of Chicago, has at first avoided as long as possible taking the 'where-did-you-come-from-before' line of questioning as directed to schooling. At last, having been worked into this corner, he very hesitantly reveals that his undergraduate school was not indeed The University of Chicago (one continuing possibility for the reference of here), but Loyola University of Chicago. But A reveals first off only that he, too, has gone to a Jesuit institution (as an undergraduate, presumably, else the formal parallelism established in the interaction is a misfire). His mock humor here has a slightly aggressive connotation, as he sets B up to ask him which Jesuit institution. A will now be able to increase his situation-relevant status even more, when he reveals his undergraduate institution.

5. Compare Irvine's (1974) discussion of Wolof (Senegal) dialogic greetings, in which the roles of initiator and respondent have status and caste connotations, and entail certain further relations of bestowal action. One of the strategic moves of greeters is to shift their dialogic role from the one to the other by certain interesting formulaic repetitions, hesitations, and readjustments.

References

Austin, J. L. [1962] 1975. How to do things with words. 2nd edition. Cambridge, Mass.: Harvard University Press.

Bricker, Victoria R. 1974. The ethnographic context of some traditional Mayan speech genres. In: Explorations in the ethnography of speaking. Edited by Richard Bauman and Joel Sherzer. Cambridge: Cambridge University Press. 368-88.

Daneš, František. 1970. One instance of Prague School methodology: Functional analysis of utterance and text. In: Method and theory in linguistics. Edited by Paul L. Garvin. Janua linguarum, Series maior, 40. The Hague-Paris: Mouton. 132-46.

Dijk, Teun A. van. 1977. Text and context: Explorations in the semantics and pragmatics of discourse. Longmans Linguistics Library, 21. London: Longmans.
Duncan, Starkey, and Donald Fiske. 1977. Face-to-face interaction. Hillsdale, N.J.: Lawrence Erlbaum Associates.
Firbas, Jan. 1964. On defining the theme in functional sentence analysis. Travaux linguistiques de Prague, 1. L'Ecole de Prague d'aujourd'hui. Prague: Editions de l'Académie Tchécoslovaque des Sciences. 267-80.
Fox, James J. 1977. Roman Jakobson and the comparative study of parallelism. In: Roman Jakobson, Echoes of his scholarship. Edited by Daniel Armstrong and C. H. Van Schooneveld. Lisse: Peter de Ridder Press. 59-90.
Givón, Talmy, ed. 1979. Discourse and syntax. Syntax and semantics, 12. New York: Academic Press.
Halliday, Michael A. K., and Ruqaiya Hasan. 1976. Cohesion in English. English Language Series, 9. London: Longmans.
Irvine, Judith T. 1974. Strategies of status manipulation in the Wolof greeting. In: Explorations in the ethnography of speaking. Edited by Richard Bauman and Joel Sherzer. Cambridge: Cambridge University Press. 167-91.
Jakobson, Roman. 1960. Closing statement: Linguistics and poetics. In: Style in language. Edited by Thomas A. Sebeok. Cambridge, Mass.: MIT Press. 350-77.
Jakobson, Roman. 1966. Grammatical parallelism and its Russian facet. Lg. 42.399-429.
Morgan, Jerry L. 1982. Discourse theory and the independence of sentence grammar. In: Georgetown University Round Table on Languages and Linguistics 1981. Edited by Deborah Tannen. Washington, D.C.: Georgetown University Press. 196-204.
Morgan, Jerry L., and Manfred B. Sellner. 1980. Discourse and linguistic theory. In: Theoretical issues in reading comprehension. Edited by Rand J. Spiro, Bertram C. Bruce, and William E. Brewer. Hillsdale, N.J.: Lawrence Erlbaum Associates. 165-200.
Newmeyer, Frederick J. 1983. Grammatical theory: Its limits and its possibilities. Chicago: University of Chicago Press.
Saussure, Ferdinand de. [1916] 1960. Cours de linguistique générale. 5th ed. Paris: Payot.
Searle, John R. 1969. Speech acts, An essay in the philosophy of language. Cambridge: Cambridge University Press.
Searle, John R. 1975. Indirect speech acts. In: Speech acts. Edited by Peter Cole and Jerry L. Morgan. Syntax and semantics, 3. New York: Academic Press. 59-82.
Silverstein, Michael. 1984. The functional stratification of language and ontogenesis. In: Culture, communication, and cognition: Vygotskian perspectives. Edited by James V. Wertsch. New York: Cambridge University Press. 207-37.

THE POLITICS OF POLITENESS: SOCIAL WARRANTS IN MAINSTREAM AMERICAN PUBLIC ETIQUETTE

Thomas Kochman
University of Illinois at Chicago

This paper begins with two propositions: first, there is a distinct political character to mainstream American public protocols; and second, this political character is often lost on mainstream Americans who tend to see the standards they set for social interaction as impartial, that is, serving the political interests of all participants equally. I want to deal briefly with the second proposition before turning more attention to the first.

Mainstream Americans do not see themselves as being politically shrewd, or disingenuous, when they ask members of minority groups who have felt themselves aggrieved to stop being angry as a prerequisite to negotiations aimed at discussing the nature and/or resolution of those grievances. Rather, mainstreamers simply see themselves as invoking what society has established as conventional procedures for handling disputations and disagreements. Such procedures require that individual negotiators on all sides remain calm and 'rational' (i.e. unemotional) in presenting their views. They also require that negotiators be predisposed to acknowledge at the outset that the parties to the negotiation may not be altogether correct in their respective assessments of the situation. Furthermore, mainstream Americans also believe that (1) there are multiple sides to an issue, (2) no side has a monopoly on the truth, (3) the more firmly one side believes that it is right, the less likely it is to be flexible enough (to be predisposed) to acknowledge the 'truth' in the other side's position, and/or to agree to accept compromise as the proper resolution of differences. Moreover, to the extent that one side or the other is angry or otherwise emotional, its perspective on matters is also likely to be commensurately distorted.

All of these views are applied a priori to mainstream social interactions, such as negotiating sessions, rather than being empirically tested for their accuracy. Thus, mainstreamers do not actually consider whether the thinking of opposing parties really does become fuzzy or incoherent when they behave emotionally, or even--in a relative sense for any one person--more fuzzy or incoherent. Nor do they actually examine qualitatively the 'truths' being advocated by opposing sides to consider whether one side may well have a greater claim on reason, human feeling, and/or justice than the other (Marcuse 1965:85 calls this nonpartisan stance 'abstract' or 'pure' tolerance.) And because these mainstream views are not tested empirically, they can hardly be said to be 'scientific', but rather must be classified as part of mainstream American cultural folklore or ideology. Thus, we find folk sayings which encode such views: 'People are less rational when they are emotional', 'Compromise, or "agreeing to disagree", is the proper way to deal with differences that cannot be resolved in any other way.'

Yet, upon closer examination, one might see that mainstream American protocols might not, in fact, be all that impartial. Rather, as with most established systems, such protocols can be seen as serving the interests of those who have installed them, even if the individuals whose roles are regulated and behavior defined within and through the system do not see the self-interest within that system. After all, participants need not be aware of their complicity within a system for the system to have its effect. Indeed, it may be better both for them and for the system if they are not. For how can they maintain a sense of themselves acting in 'good faith' if they know that by asking aggrieved parties to stop being angry as a prerequisite to negotiation, they may well, in effect, be requesting that the aggrieved parties weaken their bargaining stance, thus preparing them to accept less than they might otherwise be willing to accept if they were to remain angry?

Moreover, one might see a political strategy in mainstreamers asking aggrieved parties to assume a posture of nonanger before having been given a substantive reason for doing so (such as a change in the conditions that produced the anger). The assumption of such a posture would allow mainstreamers to gain a pacified adversary as a prerequisite to negotiation, although from their own perspective of self-interest, this might well have been regarded as the desired consequence of negotiation. Mainstreamers' requests for pacification as a prerequisite to negotiation, however, free them from having to make any substantive concessions to get it. For example, some years ago a White House official said, with regard to the American Indian Movement's takeover of Wounded Knee, 'The White House will not negotiate while guns are pointed at federal officers at Wounded Knee' (Christian Science Monitor, April 9, 1973). One might well wonder why the federal government would have any further need to negotiate if they were able to get the American Indians to surrender their arms as a prerequisite to negotiation, since that result may well have been the motivation for the government's agreement to negotiate with the Indians to begin with.

Or, one might also see a political motivation behind the mainstream promotion of compromise, or 'agreeing to disagree', as the proper way to deal with 'differences'. For do not 'compromise' and 'agreeing to disagree' ultimately establish a priority of peace over conviction, truce before 'truth'? And is not 'truce' much easier for established societies to manage than the disorder that is often produced from commitment by political adversaries to irreconcilable 'truths'?

In any event, I am less concerned for the moment about mainstreamers' awareness (or lack of awareness) of the political character of their public protocols than I am about the actual political nature of those protocols. Consequently, what I would like to do here is to develop and document further the proposition that mainstream American protocols have this political bent, above and beyond what I have already said. I am going to do this by examining the notion of social warrants within the framework of mainstream American public etiquette. This is an especially useful way of revealing both the cultural and social norms of mainstream American communication (or for that matter, of any sociocultural group), and their distinctive political character.

Social warrants. The term 'social warrants' is especially apt in connoting the entitlements to which individuals can lay claim in social interaction, since these entitlements bear directly upon the degree of leverage that individuals can hope to muster in establishing parity for their point of view, or, more generally still, in influencing the course and outcome of encounters and transactions in which they are participants. These entitlements themselves have a social basis--consequently, the term 'social' warrant. However, when people typically consider the social basis for such entitlements, they look to ascribed characteristics of age, sex, and family position, both apart from, and in conjunction with, achieved characteristics, such as rank, title, or social position.

Rarely do people see social warrants or entitlements in terms of the cultural norms that society has set to regulate social interaction. Yet, social warrants do have a cultural basis. Although culturally defined, etiquette systems exist ultimately to govern social interaction. For example, they do more than define parameters for proper and improper conduct: they also contain within them the means to command conformity with these norms. In socially symmetrical public transactions, these means are in the form of social warrants; in the context of social interaction, such warrants are the entitlements that enable individuals to claim respectful consideration for themselves from others with whom they are interacting.[1]

Unlike entitlements that derive from an individual's social position, however, these culturally based entitlements are conditional upon situated performance, and the very pattern of this performance serves to maintain the standards that society has set for social interaction. And unlike other social warrants, which individuals can be said to own permanently, these warrants accrue to individuals only so long as they deserve them--and they continue to do so only as long as they behave in ways that society has established as appropriate. As long as people deserve and receive each other's respectful consideration, their sense of themselves as bearers of social warrants tends to recede. (This may be yet another reason why mainstream Americans tend to be unaware of the political character of their public social interaction.) But should individuals forfeit respectful consideration for themselves, it is likely that they will become immediately aware of their loss of political leverage, because this loss will be translated interactionally into their lost capacity to influence further the course and outcome of the encounter or transaction which engages them. Thus, it is in the self-interest of those who would wish to maintain their political leverage not to forfeit the social warrant that grants them that leverage. And it is in protection of this warrant that people often work to behave in ways that conform to society's prescriptions of how to act.

The political character of mainstream American public etiquette is expressed not only in the form of the leverage that it generates in any given transaction. This political character is also expressed, in a larger social sense, in the kind of behavior that the norms wish ultimately to produce. Thus, there is a political motivation behind those mainstream norms that discredit presentations that are argumentative, confrontational, and emotional; presentations that reflect or display the degree to which an individual believes in what s/he says; or presentations that might rely upon force of individual personality or verbal skill in order to succeed. Such presentations are defined as either irrelevant to, or threatening to undermine, the social basis upon which decisions are reached in mainstream public social life. The reason such presentations are so defined is that one concern of mainstream public life is the maintenance of a social order in which power is by nature administrative, invested in office, rank, and social position, or, to borrow Hacker's (1979:52) phrases, 'corporate' rather than 'corporeal'. With respect to this corporate nature of power, individuals are socialized to act in ways that would effectively enlist their cooperation in the official exercise of administrative power.

Mainstream American social etiquette also acts as a principal socializing agent: it promotes mainstream American communication and discredits that of other social or cultural groups (e.g. the lower classes or ethnic minorities), at least insofar as their patterns of behavior are incompatible with the way power is promoted and exercised in mainstream social life. Consequently, I would argue that mainstreaming in a cultural sense, that is, as part of Americanization, is first and foremost a process of political socialization, concerned with behavior that relates to people's willingness or ability to cooperate with the official exercise of established administrative power, and with other matters that directly or indirectly relate to that power. Principal among such forms of behavior are those concerned with individual allegiance, especially divided allegiance and matters that deal with the priorities that individuals have set as to what, and whose, interests they shall serve, and with what measure of zeal and devotion.

I do not have time to develop all of these matters here. Indeed, I have yet to establish adequately my first proposition that along with its rules of conduct, mainstream American public etiquette generates a strong political bent. Consequently, I would like to show this by looking more closely at the specific etiquette governing the mainstream American notion of 'showing consideration for the feelings of others', especially as this notion is realized in mainstream public occasions and/or transactions. I am going to do this by considering the cultural significance of such expressions and terms as 'showing consideration', 'feelings', and 'others' to show both the distinctive character of the mainstream American cultural pattern, and its fit and function within the larger mainstream public contexts.

Showing consideration. Public consideration is typically shown negatively by avoiding actions or statements that others might find offensive. This is opposed to more positive demonstrations of consideration, e.g. actively doing things that might give another pleasure or satisfaction, that one might show in more private personal contexts. But in public, consideration is shown by keeping one's behavior at the non-arousal level: not only by not doing or saying things that might prove offensive, in terms of content, but also by not providing a stimulus so powerful that it might arouse others beyond the level that their defenses can comfortably manage. As Slater said (1976:115) about mainstream American public occasions generally: 'Clothes must be drab and inconspicuous, colors of low intensity, smells nonexistent...sounds should be quiet, words should lack affect.'

Thus, polite conversation avoids issues or topics about which individuals are likely to have strong feelings: traditionally, sex, religion, and politics. Consequently, polite conversation is also a way of showing consideration for other people's feelings, that is, not saying or doing anything that might unduly excite or arouse. The 'gentleman's agreement' (though hardly confined to adult males) is and was, 'You don't do or say anything that might arouse my feelings, and I won't do or say anything that might arouse yours.' 'Considerate' topics are therefore safe (nonarousing) topics. Like Trevor Pateman's notion of 'idle discourse', polite conversation is static rather than dynamic: 'Once begun it aims only to stay where it is' (Pateman 1975:40). Ultimately and essentially, then, mainstream consideration is a form of protection, not really of feelings, but rather of sensibilities, as will be argued next.

Feelings. I want to consider now the term 'feelings' as part of the mainstream American notion of 'showing consideration for the feelings of others'. This term is somewhat of a misnomer if one tends to equate feelings with emotions, since emotions are precisely what mainstream Americans do not show consideration for in everyday public social interaction. On the contrary, the public expression of emotions such as anger, joy, and sorrow is supposed to be muted, if they are to be expressed publicly at all. Again, I think this is primarily because of their potential to arouse and involve others, and in so doing, actively to charge and heat up public occasions and events. Emotions in this regard are double edged and, consequently, also doubly frowned upon, connoting the existence of an already aroused state, but in that state, also possessing a capacity to arouse others. Thus, a person often feels compelled to apologize to others when an emotion (such as grief or joy) erupts beyond his or her ability to contain it. And the reason one feels so compelled is that social etiquette considers such a public expression of emotions to be an imposition on other people's consideration, where even among known others--as at the workplace, for example--their expression often needs to be justified. ('Other people's consideration' is here being limited to avoiding undue arousal, but not to showing commiseration or other empathetic involvement.) In fact, showing strong emotions in public may well forfeit for those individuals the social warrant that entitles them to receive respectful consideration for their feelings--their feelings here obviously not being charged emotions. But not only are individuals not entitled to receive respectful consideration from others when they express strong emotions; they actually risk being accused of being inconsiderate of other people's feelings. The result is that they then risk forfeiting the consideration of others for their own feelings.

But if not emotions, what are the feelings for which mainstream Americans show consideration? I would argue that these feelings are inactive or inert states, which is to say, unaroused states. And again, public consideration is shown for these feelings by not activating them in any potent way. And what are these feelings qualitatively? That is hard to say. Being inactive and uncharged, they are also undifferentiated and difficult to identify. Because of these qualities, I prefer to call them 'sensibilities'; I can then reserve the term 'feelings' for those that are more actively charged, that is, emotions (even though I recognize that the term 'sensibilities' may also connote more than just a state of inactive, undifferentiated feelings). I also believe that the term 'sensibilities' characterizes the internal state accompanying the interactional role that mainstreamers occupy when they are deemed most deserving of respectful consideration from others. This last point becomes clearer in the next section, where I discuss the mainstream cultural meaning of the term 'others'.

Others. Upon hearing for the first time the expression 'showing consideration for the feelings of others', one might be likely to construe the word 'others' as referring to another person, that is, someone other than oneself. In this regard, individuals are often taught to consider themselves 'selfish' if they 'place their own feelings before those of others.' But a closer examination of this expression reveals an apparent contradiction in that interpretation. For are not we ourselves also 'others' in other people's consideration, just as they are 'others' in ours?

And what about behavior that we consider socially unacceptable, as in the case of a young man playing a radio loudly on a bus? Are we not then also the 'others' who should be receiving respectful consideration, even as we are also 'ourselves'? And if it is for 'ourselves' that we request that the radio be turned off, are we not then also being 'selfish'? Objectively speaking, yes, but culturally speaking, no. We are not being 'selfish' because social etiquette has determined that 'we' are the 'others' in that situation, not the young man who played the radio loudly. Consequently, this example shows that oneself can also be an 'other' and moreover, as an 'other', can insist upon receiving respectful consideration for oneself, even preemptively, without being considered 'selfish'.

But what does this do to our first interpretation, in which the term 'others' referred to other people, not to oneself, and which defined as 'selfish', the placing of one's own feelings before those of another? Clearly, that interpretation needs to be qualified. For as we have discovered, the term 'other' (or for that matter, 'self') does not refer socially to a person per se, that is, a 'who', but in reality to a 'what': a social category or status, for which individuals must qualify, which they must continue to deserve, and for which they can also become disqualified, or can forfeit, by behaving improperly.[2]

But that, of course, does not explain why mainstream etiquette considered 'us', the nonradio-playing bus passengers to be, preemptively, the 'others' in that situation, or why the behavior of the radio's owner disqualified him from that category. This explanation must come from a closer look at the process of accommodation that is expected within mainstream public etiquette. According to such etiquette, individuals in their interactional role as assertors are expected to mute or otherwise moderate their level of self-assertion to a point which individuals as receivers can tolerate. That is, individuals as assertors are socially accountable in this regard to individuals as receivers, but not vice versa.³ A failure by assertors to acknowledge such accountability by modifying their behavior accordingly makes them 'selfish'. Thus, it was the interactional role that each party (assertor or receiver) played on the bus that allowed us to make the determination that, even though both parties were promoting their own self-interest, only the young man was being 'selfish'.

This relationship between interactional role and the attribution of selfishness exists for the following reasons. While receivers always qualify as 'others' in mainstream American public etiquette, assertors continue to qualify as 'others' only if the level of their self-assertion conforms to public norms respecting 'good taste'. Recall that in mainstream public etiquette, 'good taste' invariably requires the application of individual self-restraint, since powerfully arousing presentations are generally considered to be in 'bad taste'. And individuals who do not show adequate self-restraint in their assertiveness risk forfeiting consideration for their sensibilities. Once that happens, those individuals' sensibilities are regarded as no longer deserving public protection. Thus, an adult passenger on the bus, in brusque and hostile fashion, may order the young man to 'turn his damn radio off'. Note that this other passenger can do this without being considered 'rude', since one can only be 'rude' to people who still retain the status of 'other'. But, culturally speaking, one cannot be 'rude' to those who have forfeited the social warrant that grants them the right to claim respectful consideration from others. Note, however, that a mainstream sense that 'the punishment should fit the crime' may still be operative; but because this last notion falls within the mainstream American sociocultural realm of 'fair play', not 'politeness' per se, I will leave it for another time.

It seems that one can almost claim that the role of 'other' is always that of receiver in mainstream social interaction. Thus, even when assertors have not disqualified themselves as 'others', as when they keep their self-assertiveness within proper bounds, their sensibilities still deserve protection. But the social frame which shows that assertors have not forfeited consideration for themselves--that they retain their respective statuses as 'others'--requires that they be placed on the receiving end of an interaction, for it is essentially as receivers that we demonstrate the concept of 'consideration' within the mainstream notion of 'showing consideration for the feelings of others'. And because it is essentially only as receivers that individuals can and do receive consideration for their feelings, it again seems more appropriate to call the internal state that is being protected by such 'consideration', 'sensibilities' rather than 'feelings'. To show consideration for feelings, that is, emotions, others would also have to show consideration for the role of assertor, since it is this role that people play when they are expressing their feelings.

As I have stated, mainstream culture does not show such consideration. Black culture, by way of contrast, does. Consequently, black social etiquette is obliged to promote a process of accommodation whereby receivers also accommodate assertors, for example, by granting them culturally sanctioned outlets for an unrestrictive expression of those feelings. In short, the kinds of feelings that we show are directly tied to the kind of role that we assume in social interaction. And the kinds of feelings that receive 'consideration' are directly tied to the status of that role within the culture in which those feelings are displayed.[4]

A further point needs to be made to show that within mainstream etiquette, there is a sociocultural bias, or predisposition, in favor of low-keyed assertive public behavior. Note that individuals forfeit consideration for themselves as 'others' only when their behavior becomes more intense than cultural norms allow, that is, when they are being irresponsibly self-assertive. But what happens when individuals are being irresponsibly nonassertive, as when they refuse to participate in a group discussion, notwithstanding the need to hear from everyone? Under those circumstances, individuals do not forfeit consideration for themselves as 'others'; they are still entitled to receive respectful consideration for their sensibilities, because according to the prevailing rule governing social etiquette, they have a 'right' not to speak if they do not want to do so. Thus, those who might otherwise be able to influence a person's behavior in a situation where he or she is behaving irresponsibly, might find that they only have a preemptive social warrant vis-à-vis that individual only when his or her behavior is in the direction of being irresponsibly active, but not when it is being irresponsibly passive. In short, we can order a person to 'keep quiet', but not to 'talk'. Mainstream American society grants social warrants to others only for the purpose of generating a quiet public climate, but not to induce more forceful self-assertive behavior, even when such would clearly be in the interests of producing more responsibly active social participation.

The role and function of individual sensibilities. Individual sensibilities have a vital role in maintaining social standards for public behavior, for socialization works only to the extent that individuals internalize social norms as to what constitutes proper and improper behavior. Indeed, this shared sense of what is, and what is not, appropriate is what is conveyed by individual sensibilities. And, as already pointed out, sensibilities can function as regulators and custodians of public order in social interaction only if the role in which sensibilities are brought to bear-- namely, the receiver role--is granted a preemptive social claim for consideration in public social interaction.

However, simply granting preemptive status to the receiver role in order to enable sensibilities to exercise their custodial function does not, in and of itself, ensure the production of only low-keyed presentations. It is also necessary to keep sensibilities relatively sensitive and/or susceptible. This is where the reciprocal nature of the process of accommodation, discussed earlier, makes its contribution. Assertors' reduction of the power of their self-assertion to the level that can be withstood by their receivers, ensures--through the reciprocal nature of accommodation--that the sensibilities of receivers will remain susceptible, precisely because they are not being confronted with those more forceful presentations to which, through repeated exposure, they might well become inured. This, in turn, might well have the effect of making them less personally sensitive and/or susceptible, and consequently, also more socially tolerant of more forceful public behavior. Thus, just as low defense produces low offense within an etiquette system that requires that assertors moderate the level of their self-assertion to the level that receivers can comfortably manage, so, too, does low offense maintain low defense by moderating the level of assertive behavior only to the level that receivers can already comfortably manage.

And so mainstream American etiquette accomplishes socially what mainstream American society wishes to accomplish politically: public behavior is kept sufficiently low-keyed so that established authority can exercise its power with a minimum of resistance and/or risk, no doubt a consummation devoutly to be wished by mainstreamers in societies all over the world.

Notes

1. Of course, the ascribed or achieved qualities also have a bearing on the extent to which individuals, in fact, do or do not forfeit consideration for themselves, especially in socially asymmetrical situations where one side has prerogatives that the other side does not, and where consequently there may also be present a different accountability for one's behavior. In this paper, so as to reveal the particular bias that only the behavioral norms themselves generate (reflected in the way social warrants are maintained or forfeited), I assume that prerogatives growing out of ascribed or achieved status are equal for all social interactants, or, said another way, that the risk or accountability to the norms regulating social interaction is the same for all participants.

2. In different cultures, status as an adult 'other' may itself have to be earned, rather than being considered a 'given'. An American white middle-class couple who lived in New Zealand for five years made an interesting distinction between life there and in America which bears upon this point. They said that in America you are presumed to be 'all right' until/unless you prove yourself otherwise. In New Zealand, you are assumed not to be all right until you prove yourself otherwise. In the American system (at least for white middle-class adults), respectful consideration for oneself, or status as a qualified 'other', is given. One is innocent until proven guilty. Thus, the American etiquette system can be regarded as one in which others disqualify themselves. In the New Zealand system (and probably the English one), respectful consideration for oneself must be earned. There, one is presumed guilty and must prove oneself innocent. That etiquette system may well be regarded as a more severe system of qualification for 'other' status, and, consequently, as one in which some individuals, in the eyes of others, may never get to be quite 'all right', a situation similar to that of children and members of minority groups in the United States.

3. Receivers, of course, may accommodate forceful self-assertiveness, but they are not required by mainstream public etiquette to do so. Consequently, that they should do so is seen as a matter of individual choice. And, because receivers are not required to accommodate immoderate assertor behavior, only receivers can get public credit for being 'tolerant', tolerance here being understood as an individual's willingness to endure behavior that society would consider to be in bad taste. But assertors would not be seen as being especially tolerant of receivers who, for example, were not being properly attentive to what the assertors were saying. Nor could assertors hold receivers to be socially accountable for that behavior since, even though it falls within

the general category of social etiquette, it makes no impact on public order. Consequently, such a matter of etiquette would not become an issue for the courts. But publicly cursing a policeman would--and, in fact, did, in the case of Lewis v. City of New Orleans (40 U.S. Law Week 3614), cited in Haiman (1972a). (See also Haiman 1972b.)

4. This should not imply that the status of the feelings being 'considered' derives from the status of the role. Rather, it may be the opposite: the status of the role derives from the kinds of expression that people manifest while in that role.

References

Hacker, Andrew. 1979. Two 'new classes' or none? Society 16.2:49-54.
Haiman, Franklyn. 1972a. The fighting words doctrine: From Chaplinsky to Brown. Iowa Journal of Speech 3.1:3-31.
Haiman, Franklyn. 1972b. Speech v. privacy: Is there a right not to be spoken to? Northwestern University Law Review 67.153-99.
Kochman, Thomas. 1981. Black and white styles in conflict. Chicago: University of Chicago Press.
Marcuse, Herbert. 1965. Repressive tolerance. In: A critique of pure tolerance. Edited by Robert Paul Wolff, Barrington Moore, Jr., and Herbert Marcuse. Boston: Beacon. 81-123.
Pateman, Trevor. 1975. Language, truth and politics. Nottingham: Stroud and Pateman.
Slater, Philip. 1976. The pursuit of loneliness. Revised edition. Boston: Beacon.

TALK AND ITS OCCASION: THE CASE OF CALLING THE POLICE

Don H. Zimmerman
University of California, Santa Barbara

0. Introduction. Erving Goffman has proposed (1974:500) that 'utterances--whether formal or informal--are anchored in the surrounding, ongoing world'. The degree to which they are anchored varies, to be sure, for utterances inhabit and are responsive to a domain of face-to face conduct--the 'interaction order' (Goffman 1983b)--and may be only 'loosely coupled' to some more encompassing scene. The point of Goffman's observation is nevertheless clear: whatever the relevant world, talk is to some extent part of it, and this connection cannot be ignored when we consider language as it is deployed in the conduct of both everyday and extraordinary affairs in society.[1]

Though it bears repeating, this insight is not exactly new. Linguists concerned with semantic issues have come to recognize the limits of reliance on semantic structures alone for the interpretation of utterances. While they can be assigned a reading, utterances taken in isolation do not provide sufficient clues to the meaning and use of similar locutions fully situated in a live setting. Natural languages like English cannot profitably be made to behave like formal languages, and thus recourse is necessary to the circumstances and manner of utterance production in order to settle--if so definite a term is possible--matters of meaning and function. One must, in short, appeal to context--indeed, to the social context, the occasion of speaking.

To speak of context is, of course, to speak of many things: the preceding or surrounding discourse--the 'co-text' (Brown and Yule 1983:46); the situated identities of participants and their knowledge of the world, particularly of the social world, brought to 'focal consciousness' (Goffman 1983b) by the play of those identities--the list is potentially lengthy and the selection of contextual features for consideration somewhat arbitrary. Here, those features are selected which appear to figure in the organization of a particular instance of talk as a social activity, both 'internally' as discourse and 'externally' as action, the springs of which originate in and ultimately rebound on a 'surrounding world'.

A small segment of the world is examined in this paper--citizen phone calls to an emergency number for police or medical assistance. These calls, developed over a sequentially ordered and organizationally structured series of utterances and turns, constitute a recurrent social occasion, 'calling the police'.

Inspection of the calls reveals a definite underlying organization with distinct segments, each of which performs specific functions. For example, the opening of the call, like telephone call openings more generally (cf. Schegloff 1979), provides the site and marshals the tools for routinely addressing and resolving the 'identity' issue posed in part by the lack of visual access in this mediated form of face-to-face contact. The initial alignment of situated identities (e.g. 'citizen'-'police') thus achieved projects a framework within which structurally relevant understandings of subsequent utterances can be achieved.

Other aspects of the organization of the call to be discussed here include the complaint/remedy (or request/response) bracket--an adjacency pair organization in which the first and second pair parts are routinely separated by a type of insertion sequence (Schegloff 1972), termed here an 'interrogative series', which addresses response contingencies relevant to the police (cf. Merritt 1977; Maynard and Wilson 1980). The calls also exhibit a closing sequence which, like the opening, is closely fitted to a particular type of transaction--a request for service--as well as reproducing the essential features of conversational closings noted by Schegloff and Sacks (1974). The overall shape of the calls appears to be quite comparable to that of calls to other types of service-oriented organizations, suggesting that the issues and contingencies involved in calling the police are general to a whole class of telephone transactions (cf. Frankel 1977, 1981; Merritt 1977).

The contextual features important to an analysis of the production, comprehension, and consequentiality of these packages of talk point to a world outside the discourse, indeed, a world brought into it by callers' descriptions of distant events (cf. Whalen and Zimmerman forthcoming). But description is language at work, and its workplace is, among other things, an occasion brought into being, in part, by the talk itself. This paper outlines the work talk does in fashioning the occasion of calling the police.

Finally, the overall organization of the calls and their contextual features described here, along with their observed similarity to 'service calls' in general, is viewed as the contingent accomplishment of unnoticed but nevertheless skilled work by callers and service personnel. That is, the calls' evident orderliness is not the product of following a known-in-common prespecified format or plan.[2] Rather, the organization emerges as the working through of issues--both internal to the discourse and resident in the affairs to which the discourse is addressed--using culturally distributed procedures as ordinary and pervasive means of getting on with and getting through the call.

1. The setting. The 'Mid-City' police department[3] is located in a large metropolitan area in the midwestern United States. At the time of the research, the department used a centralized, two-tiered computer-based dispatching system, offering the public an emergency number to call for reports of trouble, or requests for police or emergency medical assistance.

Civilian employees, henceforth 'complaint-takers' (CT), answered calls distributed via a rotary system and entered information derived from their interaction with callers (C) into a computer terminal. While the system provided prompts for the required information, it could be entered in any order. The information acquired was then transmitted electronically to dispatchers (sworn officers) who had the responsibility of sending police units to the scene of the trouble. Ambulance and paramedic assistance were sent by an ambulance dispatcher who was contacted by the complaint-taker by phone.[4]

The task of the complaint-taker was to collect and codify the information necessary to dispatch the police or ambulance to the scene of a reported incident. This generally involved ascertaining and coding the nature of the reported problem, that is, its character as 'policeable business', e.g. a 'burglary', 'domestic', and so forth; its location, and other pertinent information such as the presence of weapons or numbers of persons involved in the incident. The demand for information of this type in large part makes up the 'contingencies' of police response discussed later.

A small number of calls are transferred to some other office (e.g. to a particular precinct at which crime reports are to be filed, or to some division such as homicide or internal affairs). With few exceptions, incoming calls are processed and forwarded electronically to the dispatcher for ultimate disposition.

The 125 calls[5] examined in this paper represent a two-hour (11PM-1AM) segment of tape from the first weekend of the month, which complaint-taker folklore designates as busier than usual since it is payday for many, with a consequent increase in drinking and drinking-related incidents. There was also a rainstorm this night, which increased the number of accidents and reports of (false) burglary alarms from security organizations. It is worth noting that the volume of 'business' on this evening was a feature attended to by at least one complaint-taker, as revealed in a personal call also recorded on the tapes.

(1) [MCE 21-26:36][6]

```
1    CT: Hello
2    C:  Hello what ur ya doin'
3    CT: Oh god (.) busy as shit
4    C:  Is it still.
5    CT: Yes. Between storms, accidents (.) you name it it's goin'
         on.
```

Thus, the discussion to follow deals with a collection of calls that may most directly reflect the activities of late night, weekend hours, as well as the contingencies of weather. Different troubles--or at least, different frequencies of occurrence for particular problems--may characterize different time periods. The interests of this paper, however, are in the achieved organization of the calls which, for reasons to be developed further on, is assumed to be largely independent of their specific content, rendering the selectivity of the collection less problematic than it might otherwise be. Moreover, other studies of citizen calls to the police in Canada and in the northeastern United States provide examples of calls with essentially the same organization as that discussed here (cf. Sharrock and Turner 1983, Meehan 1983).

2. Calling the police. While telephone calls to a police emergency number have their own specificity--they are usually requests for assistance of the type that the police in particular have the responsibility to provide--they are, nevertheless, telephone calls. Moreover, even first-time callers of the police will probably have little difficulty in working their way through such calls, suggesting that some rather general social organizational principles bear on the management of this particular kind of encounter. In this regard, it appears that calls to the police are one member of a class of telephone transactions here termed 'service calls'.[7] The alacrity and precision with which they are generally conducted is likely the consequence of the application by both complaint-taker and caller of methodic procedures appropriate to calls of this type, suitably adapted to the specific feature of a 'call to the police'.

The interactional work of a call, then, addresses issues posed in the first instance because it is a telephone encounter. Such work is also responsive to issues that emerge because placing the call is by that very act a 'request' for service of a particular sort. Moreover, in some but by no means all of the calls, caller makes a fairly explicit request for assitance, as in (2).

(2) [MCE 21-21:28]

C: Yes if ya gotuh squad car could ya send one over tuh Beach an Owen Avenue.
CT: What's the problem there.

But just as commonly, callers simply report a trouble.

(3) [MCE 21-23:32]

C: Yes, I'd like tuh report uh loud party.
CT: Where is it ma'am.

If the caller requests assistance, as in example (2), the result will be a query from the complaint-taker concerning the nature of the problem which, obviously, is not required in the case illustrated by example (3). The 'request' format explicitly projects the remedy or response to an as yet unvoiced 'complaint' to an organization whose business it is to know about and respond to it, concerning some state of affairs that is in need of redress.

What is being made focally relevant in the opening segment of the call is the division of labor in our society with regard to matters of social control. In Sharrock and Turner's terms (1978:187), a socially organized resource--police power--is being mobilized to deal with a problem that others cannot or choose not to deal with by other means. This mobilization raises certain issues, i.e. the policeable nature of the problem and its urgency (see the discussion of the 'contingencies of response', Section 2.3). The point to be noted here is that the hearability of an utterance as a 'complaint' draws on its location within an institutional framework--

that of policing--which touches the interactional realm through the organization of the call. That organization provides a place, just after the alignment of identities in the opening sequence, the 'first topic' slot (Schegloff and Sacks 1974, Schegloff 1979), which is where the reason for the call is ordinarily provided.

Figure 1 presents this proposed general organization; it consists of five major components which, it is suggested here, characterize not only calls to the police but the broad class of service calls that occur in this society.

Figure 1.

Opening/Identification

Complaint/Request

Interrogative series

Remedy/Response

Closing

In terms specific to the subset of service calls addressed in this paper, the police complaint-taker and citizen-caller must (1) accomplish a proper 'opening', that is, align their respective identities and thus project the nature of the call; (2) provide and/or elicit a reason for the call, e.g. by making a 'complaint' or a 'request' for assistance; (3) arrive at a mutually acceptable description of the reported trouble, including the caller's stance toward or involvement with it (Whalen and Zimmerman forthcoming) and an adequate formulation of the trouble's location--a process involving what is called here an 'interrogative series', ordinarily initiated and directed by the complaint-taker; (4) the offering of a 'remedy' or 'response' to the complaint or request for assistance; and (5) the achievement of 'closing', that is, a coordinated exit from the call.

Example (4) displays this organization rather starkly.

```
(4)   [MCE 21-9:12]

1     CT:       Mid-City Emergency.
2     C: Um yeah (.) somebody jus' vandalized my car,
3     CT:       What's your address.
4     C:        [Gives address]
5     CT:       Is this uh house or an apartment.
6     C:        Ih tst uh house
7     CT:       Uh-your las' name.
8     C:        Minsky
9     CT:       How you spell it.
10    C:        M-i-n-s-k-y
11    CT:Wull sen' someone out to see you.
12    C: Than' you.
13    CT:       umhm bye.
14    C: Bye
```

The opening segment is accomplished in turn 1 and in the first component (Um yeah) of turn 2; the complaint is delivered in the second component of turn 2, with the interrogative series initiated in turn 3 and running through turn 10. (Here, and in segments 5, 6, and 14, the interrogative series is indented for expositional purposes.) The complaint response occurs in turn 11, closing the complaint-response bracket and serving also as a 'pre-closing' move (Schegloff and Sacks 1974), with turns 12 through 14 occupied with the closing.

A virtually identical organization is evident in a call from C (caller) to an operator (O) at a county animal control agency, reproduced in example (5). The organization of the opening (lines 1 and 2), the complaint (line 2), the interrogative series (lines 3 through 16), the remedy (line 17), and the closing (lines 19-20) are all remarkably comparable. The indented utterance pair in lines 8 and 9 is a nested insertion sequence (Schegloff 1972) within the interrogative series.

(5) [TAS 2:83:DB]

```
1    O:  Coun' animal control?
2    C:  Yes Uhm (.) There's uh an injured cat at the corner of
         Jackson an' Matthews?
3    O:      Is it alive?
4    C:      Mm yeah I think so    ⌈cuz
5    O:                            ⌊Ok
6    C:      it's bleeding from the mouth
7    O:      Which corner? Near the hospital?
8    C:      Uh no   It's like uh    Y'know where the flower
                                     stan' is?
9    O:                              Uh huh
10   C:      Jus' there˙ In thuh gutter
11   O:      Your name?
12   C:      Sandy Hillman?
13   O:      Wher're y'calling from
14   C:      Home
15   O:      Number?
16   C:      869-8606
17   O:  Okay I'll get thuh man on call t'check it out
18   C:  Thanks
19   O:  Bye
20   C:  Bye
```

A call to an airlines reservation number (A) provided in example (6) differs only in the feature that caller's request for assistance involves the provision of information, with the response (the information delivery) in lines 11-13 and 15 (caller's line 14 being, perhaps, an acknowledgment of the receipt of information to that point and an invitation to continue). Note that caller in line 16 requests further information, resulting in a brief interrogative series (lines 17-18) and a further response (line 19) before the call is closed.

(6) [LL: Air]

```
1   A:  Federated Airlines Reservations Joanne
2   C:  Hi  Could you tell me what your cheapest fare would be
        from Portland to Washington, D.C.?
3   A:        Mmhm?  Your travelling one way or round trip?
4   C:        Round trip
5   A:        And when are you planning on travelling
6   C:        Uh probably in the summer sometime
7   A:        Okay  So it would be after the fifteenth of June
              you'd be leaving?
8   C:        Yes
9   A:        All right  About how long 'r your planning on stay-
              ing
10  C:        Um two or three weeks?
11  A:  Okay  Okay I can tell you right away the lowest rate that
        we can offer um would be our Super Saver fare (.) You
        would have to make your reservation at least a week
        before you travel       Okay for the
12  C:                          Mhm
13  A:  lowest fare (.) you'd have to stay at least seven days (.)
        and not more than fourteen days
14  C:        Okay
15  A:        'Kay  An' that's going to be a round trip of three ninety-
              nine
16  C:        'Kay an' what is your cheapest fare one way
17  A:            On a one way?
18  C:            Yeah
19  A:        That would be (.) three oh nine
20  C:        Okay  Thank you very much
21  A:        Uh huh bye bye
```

Examples (4) and (5) are typical of the service calls collected to date, and point quite clearly to the strong kinship among calls of this type. The operators working these diverse numbers do not appear to be given specific training on how to organize a call. Rather, they are instructed in organization policy and goals and the type of information needed to advance these aims. It seems likely, then, that the common discourse features these calls exhibit are achieved by the use of methodic procedures generally available not only to the operator but also--at least in part--to the caller, the call's actual features being an interactional accomplishment. The achieved structures of this concerted effort are considered next.

2.1 Opening identification. Openings, like closings, bear upon 'the distinctive characteristics of various "types" of conversations' (Schegloff 1979:25). They provide a place where 'the kind of conversation this is', is indicated, negotiated, and ratified.

In face-to-face conversations, one may speak of processes prior to a conversational opening, a 'pre-beginning' in Schegloff's terminology (1979:27), where the issue of identification is salient. The identity of the person with whom one is about to speak determines how the conversation will be initiated (i.e. the components of initial turns at talk) as well as what 'type' of conversation will be projected.

Identification is both 'categorical' and 'recognitional', the latter referring to the recognition of 'particular, known others' (Schegloff 1979:25) in face-to-face encounters. Identification is ordinarily accomplished through visual means, and has both cognitive and social status, the latter when identification is 'prospectively reciprocal' (Schegloff 1979; cf. also Schiffrin 1977) and displayed in some form (e.g. a mutual turning toward, approach, etc.).

In telephone conversations, identification/recognition cannot routinely occur prior to the initiation of a conversation, nor can it be a condition for its occurrence. Thus, a distinctive feature of telephone call openings is the identification/recognition 'problem' and its solution; callers and answerers can be shown to orient to the problem and to attempt to resolve it in and through, and in some instances parallel with, other activities in their talk.

Space does not permit a detailed review of the management of the identification/recognition issue in casual telephone contacts (Schegloff 1979). It is sufficient here to point out that in calls to service agencies in general, and to Mid-City police as a case in point, answerers employ categorical self-identification. Three different forms of categorical self-identification were employed by complaint-takers in the Mid-City Police Department in their opening turn: (1) Mid-City Emergency; (2) Mid-City Police and Fire; (3) Emergency Center. These designations may be considered to be the first component in answerer's first turn; in Mid-City, they are the only components. Meehan's (1983) 'Big City' police sometimes employed one or more additional suborganizational identifiers.[8] Example (6) illustrated the practice of using three components (Federated Airlines Reservations Joanne on line 1). Thus, the answerer's opening can vary in the depth and detail of the identification. The pattern of the callers' response to complaint-takers' opening is exemplified in example (7).

(7) [MCE 21-2:1]

1   CT: Mid-City emergency.
2   C: Yes I'd uh like tuh report uh disturbance...

The caller's first turn typically offers a yes or other acknowledgment marker, which may be characterized as confirmation that caller has reached the number intended and as a preface for additional components which will ordinarily complete the alignment between complaint-taker as an 'agent of the police' and caller as 'citizen/complainant'.[9]

That callers are oriented to answerer's self-identification and its possible implications for the call is evident in the fact that each answerer variant carries with it its own problematic: the use of the term emergency can draw responses such as Oops, this isn't an emergency, while the use of the pair Police and Fire can evoke the 'switchboard' request, Police, please. Note here that caller withholds an acknowledgment[10] if such an alignment issue does occur, but in its place addresses that issue, as shown in (8).

(8) [MCE 21-25:35]

```
1    CT:  Mid-City Emergency.
2    C:   Can I 've the police, please.
3    CT:  This is police.
4    C:   Oh uh there's some loud music over on...
```

(9) [MCE 21-8:10]

```
1    CT:  Mid-City emergency ((silence)) Hello?
2    C:   Hullo Is thuh ((unintelligible)) sherf's deparmen
3    CT:  Uh yes (an) what
4    C:   Is this thuh Marlin Count-⌈sheriff depar
5    CT:                            ⌊No: it's the Mid-City police.
6    C:   Uh I would like tuh make uh (hones') phone call.
```

Caller in example (8) apparently hears complaint-taker's opening as a 'switchboard' situation—the term <u>emergency</u>, as Meehan (1983:82-88) has suggested, is by design rather broad in its coverage, and caller specifies the particular 'emergency' organization she wishes to contact. In example (9), caller does not respond to complaint-taker's opening, leading to her <u>Hello?</u> (line 1) to determine if there is anyone on the line, and caller's confirmatory <u>Hullo</u>. Caller's first turn is devoted to checking out the identity of answerer and is followed by complaint-taker's mistaken answer to caller's query, quickly corrected by her repeat-request (<u>what</u>) in line 3. The confusion is resolved in line 5 with the caller offering a preface to his subsequent complaint.

Other types of service calls illustrate the same sort of identification issue. In a call to a pottery shop, Caller (C) encounters from Answerer (A) an unexpected personal rather than categorical identification.

(10) [AR: Pottery]

```
1    A:   Irene
2    C:   Uhm (.) let's see is this the pottery retail place?
3    A:   Uh yes uh huh
4    C:   Uhm I was wondering if...
```

A partially cut off identification from Answerer leads to the same 'identity checking' from Caller.

(11) [LL: Train Reservations: 2]

```
1    A:   'svations Miss Ghent speaking
2    C:   Is this Train Reservations?
3    A:   Yes it is
```

A call, then, does not proceed to further business until the type of call projected by complaint-taker's opening is 'recognized' by the caller, that is, reconciled with the caller's sense of who the recipient of the upcoming complaint or report should properly be. While the point cannot be pursued in detail here, it seems evident that the care taken by participants in crafting an opening, that is, in aligning their situated identities, provides a working framework which commits participants to the nature of the occasion summoned up by the initiation of the call and thereby provides for the presumptive hearability of utterances as relevant to the purposes of that occasion of talk (cf. Meehan 1983:88-97).

2.2 Complaint/request. The complaint-request component (line 2 in examples (4), (5), (6), and (7)) is ordinarily the next event following the caller's acknowledgment of complaint-taker's categorical self-identification. The examples cited to this point display a 'single utterance format' for delivering the complaint (Sharrock and Turner 1978:175-77) although the report of trouble can be delivered in a 'multiple utterance' format, as in example (12).

(12) [MCE 21-7:8-9]

```
1    CT:  Mid-City Emergency.
2    C:   This is thuh Kit-Kat Club on ten one three oh Williams?
3    CT:  Mmhm
4    C:   and thuh laundrymat (.) Jim's laundrymat?
5    CT:  Mmhm
6    C:   it's down the street here a bit (.) tst anyway it's lef' open.
         It's wide open.
7    CT:  Mmhm
8    C:   An it's supposed to be locked at nine a clock so I don' know
         if somebody broke in there or what's goin' on
9    CT:  We'll get somebody there.
```

In this call, caller provides a categorical self-identification (Kit-Kat Club) and a location delivered with a question contour, or 'try-marker' (line 2), which solicits acknowledgment or recognition and is followed by complaint-taker's recognitional Mmhm in line 3. The continuation of caller's utterance in line 4 then identifies another establishment, again offered with a try-marker (Jim's laundrymat?) followed by caller's specification of its location relative to that of caller's establishment (lines 4 and 6). The trouble (it's wide open) is then reported in lines 6 and 8, with complaint-taker's continuer (Schegloff 1982) in line 7 and followed immediately in line 9 by complaint-taker's promise of assistance.

The example just described, example (12), is one of the very few calls in which the caller, building her designedly multiple-utterance turn with the collaboration of the complaint-taker, provides a connected account of the candidate policeable trouble (i.e. the situation that is potentially a problem for police to handle) and its location without any interrogation (and hence, without any insertion sequence). The caller's use of try-markers in lines 2 and 4 elicits acknowledgment—not only of understanding but of the prefatory character of the utterance to that point, an utterance which is displaying both how the caller might have come to know of the trouble, and why she might be interested, as a context for the report (cf. Whalen and Zimmerman forthcoming). The presentation of the complaint (including locational information) is directly followed by the remedy, or response to the complaint, which occurs at the turn-transition beginning on line 9.

There are two points to be stressed here. The first is that the complaint or request for assistance--the reason for the call--is hearable as a matter requiring response or remedy (Sharrock and Turner 1978:174-75). In those calls where the citizen's 'complaint package' (Meehan 1983:101-8) is developed without intervention by the complaint-taker, this response is found in the next turn adjacent to the reported trouble, as in example (12). The other point is that other talk--sometimes a good deal of it--routinely intervenes between the initiation of a complaint and the delivery of a remedy, as in example (13), where both location and the problem are elicited by a course of questioning inserted between the request/response bracket.

(13) [MCE 21-24a:33]

```
1    CT: Mid-City Emergency.
2    C:  Yeah we'd like ya tuh send an ambulance out
3    CT: Where to.
4    C:  Uh: sixty- uh sixty five and uh: ((background voice))
         um ((background voice))
5    CT: Tuh where?
6    C:  Eighty second=
7    CT:                =Sixty five what  Sixty five an what
8    C:  Ninety second. Sixty fifth street an ninety second
9    CT: Ninety second Avenue?
10   C:  Yeah
11   CT:      What's thuh problem.
12   C:  Uh there's been un accident.
```

The work accomplished by this elicitation defines the next major component of overall organization--the interrogative series.

2.3 The interrogative series. It is by now fairly clear that in a call to a 'service agency' like the police, caller's request (or complaint) routinely elicits responses which are not responses to the request itself, but to the issues that it raises. This was evident, for example, in (6), in which the reservation desk had to know caller's travel dates to determine the cheapest fare.

Of particular interest here is the fact that making a request engages an organization rather than simply an individual, and thus, varying with the circumstances of the call, encounters contingencies of response which are evident to the organizational personnel receiving the request, but are perhaps unknown or only vaguely perceived by caller. Thus, a complaint or request routinely involves some processing, that is, some course in which its features--many of which have yet to be made evident--are fit to the requirements of organizational response (cf. Merritt 1977; Frankel 1977, 1981).

In their study of calls to the police, Sharrock and Turner (1978:175) speak of a 'police-initiated fact-seeking sequence' dealing with matters preliminary to police response. In their corpus, as in the Mid-City materials, a series of question-answer pairs characterize this 'fact-seeking sequence' or interrogative series, which appears to function as an insertion sequence between a complaint and its remedy. Schegloff

(1972:76-79) discusses insertion sequences in terms of embedded or nested sequences of questions and answers, as in the following adapted from Schegloff (1972:78-79).

Q base	S1:	Are you coming tonight?
Q1	S2:	Can I bring a guest?
A1	S1:	Sure.
A base	S2:	I'll be there.

As evident in this example, the nested Q/A pair deals with a contingency of response to Q base, namely, whether S2 can bring a guest or not. Additional nested Q/A pairs could conceivably be inserted, ultimately motivated by Q base and coming to rest in A base. There appears to be nothing in the logic of the insertion sequence, however, to prohibit the deployment of a series of chained (as opposed to nested) Q/A pairs addressed to a set of more or less discrete contingencies of response (cf. Merritt 1977).

Example (14), taken from Maynard and Wilson (1980:301-5), provides an interesting illustration of an insertion sequence consisting of just such a series of Q, A pairs in the context of sentencing procedures in a municipal court.

(14) [RSS: 301-301]

1	P.D.:	Your Honor, we request immediate sentencing and
2		waive the probation report.
3	Judge:	What's his record:
4	P.D.:	He has a prior drunk and a GTA [Grand Theft Auto].
5		Nothing serious. This is just a shoplifting case.
6		He did enter the K-Mart with the intent to steal.
7		But really all we have here is a petty theft.
8	Judge:	What do the people have?
9	D.A.:	Nothing either way.
10	Judge:	Any objections to immediate sentencing?
11	D.A.:	No
12	Judge:	How long has he been in?
13	P.D.:	Eighty-three days.
14	Judge:	I make this a misdemeanor by P.C. article 17 and
15		sentence you to ninety days in County Jail, with
16		credit for time served.

The circumstances in this interrogative series of example (14) are different, of course; it is face-to-face, and involves three participants. It is, moreover, a request from one sector of an organization, represented by the Deputy Public Defender (P.D.), to another sector (the Judge) over a matter that is also the professional concern of a third, the Deputy District Attorney (D.A.). Nevertheless, this brief interaction is interesting because the P.D.'s request also engages an organization and its contingencies of response (although the latter are undoubtedly known to the P.D. and figured in his request) which are elicited by the Judge.

Requests (or complaints) that are followed by insertion sequences like the interrogative series can thus be seen to occur in a variety of organizational contexts. These episodes of questioning address a series of contingencies associated with the particular organization's response to a request for its service and appear to be understood as so addressed by persons initiating the request. That is, most callers in the Mid-City corpus appear to recognize what the person on the other end of the line is doing and grant it legitimacy, a comprehension and acceptance which facilitates their delivery of a response.

It is in this moment between the request and its response that two rather major issues are addressed and, in most instances, resolved without marked trouble. First, in the case of the call to the police, caller must furnish an account or description of some occurrence so that complaint taker can hear the incident as policeable trouble. Descriptions are answerable to criteria of adequacy that vary by socially structured circumstances (e.g. gossip, courtroom testimony, ethnographic reportage, etc.) and are thus particularly vulnerable to contingencies of response (Whalen and Zimmerman forthcoming, Sharrock and Turner 1978, Frankel 1981). The second issue involves the achievement of an adequate locational formulation (usually in terms of specific addresses or street intersections). In Mid-City, for example, complaint-takers required street addresses or intersections in order to process a complaint. This information was entered into their computer and verified. The race, sex, number, and location of persons involved in a reported incident may also be asked for, as well as whether weapons are present.

The completion of the interrogative series is marked by the complaint-taker's delivery of a promise of assistance, i.e. the remedy or response to the complaint. This promise has structural equivalents in other service calls, e.g. the reservation clerk's provision of the requested fare information (example (6)) and the judge's sentencing (example (14)). It is important to point out that the promise to send assistance is adjacent to the closing sequence, and itself can be analyzed as a pre-closing move (Schegloff and Sacks 1974, Zimmerman and Loseke 1981). Its role as an initator of closing--particularly the closing of a telephone call--furnishes a powerful structural motive to withhold it until the information deemed necessary for the police reponse is elicited.

2.4 Remedy/response and closing. The fourth segment of the call is the remedy/response move by the complaint-taker in the form of a promise of assistance, e.g. <u>Wull sen' someone out to see you.</u> As already suggested, utterances of this general format following the interrogative series are hearable both as the response to the initial complaint and as a pre-closing move. That complaint-takers and callers are oriented to this type of utterance as a response to the complaint, and hence as the occasion to terminate the call, is indicated by the fact that complaint-takers will 'abort' its production by an abrupt cut-off (indicated in example (15) by the hyphen), followed quickly by the reinstitution of questioning if they are uncertain of some item.

(15) [21-16a:21-22]

13   CT: We'll get somebod-   are you sure it's Southeast and not Northeast.

Likewise, callers will withhold acknowledgment of the promise of assistance to pursue some feature of the complaint presumably not yet dealt with to their satisfaction, as example (16) shows.

(16) [21-7:9-9]

9   CT: We'll get somebody there.
10   C: <u>We</u> do not have thuh owner so you must have it on file at thuh Northside station.

Upon receiving the promise of assistance, callers typically provide some form of acknowledgment (as in example (1), where caller says <u>thank you</u> (line 11)). The promise thereby furnishes the response to the caller's complaint and initiates a pre-closing move completed by caller's acknowledgment (cf. Schegloff and Sacks 1974). It is upon the completion of this pivotal sequence that a terminal-exchange (Schegloff and Sacks 1974) ensues by which the call is brought to a fairly rapid conclusion.

Calls to the police--like other service calls--have a single purpose: they have an expectably focused matter to bring to the attention of the police, and then project by their very initiation the expectation of police response to that matter, i.e. the dispatch of a squad car. It is this feature of the call that provides for the status of the promise, or 'action announcement' by the complaint-taker (<u>we'll get somebody there</u>) as the initial turn in the terminal sequence.

Like exit from ordinary conversations and ordinary calls, exit from police calls is managed with reference to speaker's rights to resume or initiate various lines of talk, the actual exchange of the farewells being preceded by a closing section in which speaker willingness to forego further talk is coordinated and displayed.

3. Conclusions. If talk is indeed anchored in the world--a world which includes the social world--then the nature of this connection surely cannot be ignored when considering the meaning of utterances. It would miss the point, however, to treat this proposal as yet another call to respect 'the context'. Every utterance is interpreted in some context, however impoverished. Even the contemplation of isolated utterances contrived by the linguist, alluded to in the opening remarks, draws on a context formed by the existence of a scholarly community sharing many of the presuppositions about language, speakers, and the world, and which is disposed to treat such an enterprise as sensible. The issue is not whether context is considered, but how, from what perspective, and with respect to which features?

Something else is implied then, namely, that talk for and between persons is social in character, that it occurs within and with respect to social occasions, occasions which are coupled to a greater or lesser degree to some larger institutional arena or some series of such arenas.

The talk is not independent of its occasion, and merely set down in it, but rather is coconstitutive of it.[11] A framework is progressively erected for the comprehension of what is said and, in being said, done. Talk, by bringing into focus a particular type of occasion, summons up the context of its interpretation as well.

Calling the police was the case in point here. These calls were viewed as instances of a more general class of service calls, displaying a definite achieved organization. The term 'achieved' was employed to emphasize a particular view of the stable, recurrent features exhibited by these calls. The organization of these calls was treated as a situational accomplishment of callers and service operators' applying general interactional skills and specific social knowledge to tasks and issues posed by the nature of the telephone encounter as such, as well as the contingencies involved in securing and providing the particular service in question.

Thus, callers and operators--complaint-takers, in the case of the Mid-City police--have to achieve an opening, which involves, among other things, the alignment of identities appropriate to the occasion and consequential for further inference and action in the call. A request for service--which can be accomplished in a number of ways--must be made and understood as such, and a course of work initiated, in the form of an insertion sequence, through which the contingencies of providing (or promising to provide) the service requested, can be addressed and satisfied. A closing attuned to the specificities of the call must be jointly accomplished. Although the circumstances displayed by each police call were varied, each was managed in light of its individuality and with respect to the resolution of the issues posed by the mediated encounter and the jointly acknowledged purpose of the call. The interactional order (e.g. caller vis-a-vis complaint-taker) and the institutional order (e.g. citizen-complainant vis-a-vis the police) are articulated within the unfolding organization of telephone exchange.

Two further points bear emphasis here. First, if the lineaments of a social occasion and its linkages to a larger institution and context are brought to focus in these calls, then both the occasion and its relevant institutional site are as much the achieved outcome of encounters as the context for interpreting the discourse occurring within them. From the vantage point of the completed call (or any species of discourse), the dynamic reflexive nature of what transpires may easily be overlooked. For that matter, the importance of a practical comprehension of utterances by participants sharing the responsibility for managing the outcome of the encounter may also be overlooked, and this raises the second point.

The production of most discourse is fundamentally interactive (cf. Schegloff 1981). Each 'move' in a discourse establishes some kind of understanding of the previous move, and of the larger context, and is subject to acceptance, modification, or reconstitution, depending upon the subsequent move by another that it motivates. These 'scenic interpretations' are structurally relevant in that they are requisite for addressing and accomplishing the purposes of the encounter, for working it through, as it were. The issue for interactants is to understand enough to proceed (which is a principle of practical interpretation), rather than understanding for its own sake (a principle of theoretical interpretation).

3.1 A final note. The problem of context, of the relationship of talk to its occasion, can barely be posed, much less addressed, in one investigation or in a short paper. It does seem likely, however, that the issues involved will require some concession to sociological sensibilities, as well as recourse to sociologically sensitized studies of talk in actual settings. It appears particularly strategic to examine those places in society where talk is patently a major instrument for the accomplishment of the setting's work, as in the case of calling the police.

Notes

This paper is based on work undertaken with several persons. I should like to acknowledge and thank Donilene Loseke, Deirdre Boden, Marilyn Whalen, Lynda LaFontaine, Terri Cook, Judy Blum, and Audrey Rice. Thomas P. Wilson provided helpful comments. Deborah Schiffrin also gave particularly helpful suggestions. Responsibility for this paper, and most particularly for its shortcomings, is mine. Thanks are also due Mary Wiemann for her patient and efficient preparation of the manuscript.

The research reported here was supported by the Center for the Study of Violence and Anti-Social Behavior (Grant No. 34616-03). Portions of the analysis reported here were begun while I was guest professor at the Center for Survey Research, Mannheim, West Germany, June-July 1981.

1. In this paper, language behavior, or talk, is viewed as a form of social interaction.
2. This is not to say that service calls do not employ explicit formats. As pointed out further on, specific items of information may be required by the organization in question, and the elicitation may be guided by written or computer-prompted instructions (cf. Frankel 1981). The point stressed here is that the overall structure common to classes of this type is not achieved by reliance on an explicit format.
3. The calls were obtained by Donilene Loseke during a brief period of field observation at Mid-City. The analysis reported here had its roots in a co-authored, unpublished paper (Zimmerman and Loseke 1981). This section, and other parts of the study, borrow from portions of that earlier work which drew heavily on Loseke's field notes and observations.
4. With two exceptions, the 26 complaint-takers employed by Mid-City were female. All dispatchers were male. The sex of callers was imputed by transcribers from informal assessment of voice qualities. Accordingly, all pronouns referring to persons are used in a specific rather than generic sense.
5. Segments from transcripts of those calls are presented in simplified form. The notation (.) indicates a very brief pause; words enclosed in parentheses indicate transcriber uncertainty.
6. All transcript segments are identified as to their source. 'MCE' denotes 'Mid-City Emergency'; the next digits, e.g. 21-26, designate tape channel number and call number; the last digits indicate page number of the transcript. Segments from other sources are denoted or identified by similar coding.
7. In speaking of service calls, reference is intended to those telephone contacts in which callers have recourse to a telephone 'service port' (Goffman 1983b) for the purpose of securing some assistance or

service, whether in the form of simple information (such as determining bus or train schedules or the cost of some commodity), or of accomplishing some transaction (such as ordering from a catalog, making a travel reservation), or securing the promise of assistance (such as arranging for the plumber to come to the house or for the police to be dispatched). See Merritt (1977) and Frankel (1977), for a discussion of service transactions.

8. Meehan (1983:81-82) reports a range of openings involving up to three components: (1) an organization identifier; (2) a subunit identifier; and (3) answerer's organizational identity. Components (2) or (3) are deletable, whereas (1) is not. Thus, actual calls to the Big City police may be answered with the organization identifier alone:

[BC 44:2]
P: Big City Police Emergency

Or calls may combine component (1) with other components:

[BC 18-2]
P: Big City Police Emergency three thirty five

[BC 32-2]
P: Big City Emergency Dispatcher McGrew

Meehan provides a perceptive and useful discussion of the relevance of a call's opening to the nature and problematics of the business to be transacted within it. His analysis of the Big City calls and the analysis reported in this paper are remarkably convergent, although done independently and without knowledge of the other. Space precludes discussing Meehan's findings here.

9. The relationship between complaint-taker's opening and that of the caller is fairly complex, and has been simplified here for reasons of space. For example, in some calls, caller's first component consists of a frame, <u>This is</u>, followed by a categorical self-identification, usually a business or organization. It should be noted, moreover, that the identities involved in the opening, particularly the identity of the caller, are subject to transformation over the course of the call. Callers may become 'victims', 'passers-by', 'neighbors', 'interested parties', etc. The negotiation of identities in calls to the police is the subject of another paper in progress.

10. The term 'withhold' might refer to the fact that when identification issues emerge, acknowledgment is absent and talk directed to the issue proceeds directly. A stronger sense is intended, however, as suggested in (i) and (ii).

(i)   [MCE 17-5:105]
1   CT: Mid-City police an' fire
2   C: Cu Yeah uhm I'd like tuh

(ii)   [MCE 17-6:69]
1   CT: Mid-City police an' fire
2   C: Hi oh I want thuh police

In (i), caller's opening word is self-interrupted, or at least is left unfinished, and is followed by an acknowledgment token. This suggests an orientation to the appropriateness of the latter's occurrence as a first component of the turn. Acknowledgments can be 'retracted' by use of 'surprise' markers like oh in (ii), followed by an utterance 'explaining' the contravention of caller's original expectations. Acknowledgment is thus not merely present or absent but accountably present or absent.

11. Saying does not of itself necessarily make it so. In the present case, calling the police, while it initiates a state of talk, also brings into play an apparatus which was already 'there', e.g. the police organization, its division of labor, the occupational role of 'complaint-taker', policy, procedure, accumulated experience, etc. But the call itself is what achieves the instantiation and integration of these elements into the recurring occasion, 'calling the police'.

References

Brown, Gillian, and George Yule. 1983. Discourse analysis. Cambridge: Cambridge University Press.

Frankel, Richard M. 1977. Between client and server: Aspects of the organization of conversational exchange during service. Unpublished Ph.D dissertation, The City University of New York.

Frankel, Richard M. 1981. 'I wuz wondering-uhm could Raid uhm affect the brain permanently d'y'know?': Record keeping in the context of communicative interaction. Paper presented at the annual meeting of the American Sociological Association, Toronto, Canada.

Goffman, Erving. 1974. Frame analysis: An essay in the organization of experience. New York: Harper Colophon.

Goffman, Erving. 1983a. The interaction order. American Sociological Review 48.1-17.

Goffman, Erving. 1983b. Felicity's condition. American Journal of Sociology 89.1-51.

Maynard, Douglas W., and Thomas P. Wilson. 1980. On the reification of social structure. In: Current perspectives in social theory, vol.1. Edited by Scott G. McNall. New York: JAI Press. 287-322.

Meehan, Albert T. 1983. For the record: Organizational and interactional practices for producing police records on juveniles. Unpublished Ph.D. dissertation, Boston University.

Meehan, Albert T. 1984. Assessing the police-worthiness of citizen's complaints to the police: Accountability and the negotiation of 'facts.' Unpublished paper.

Merritt, Marilyn. 1977. On questions following questions in service encounters. Language in Society 5.315-57.

Schegloff, Emanuel. 1972. Notes on a conversational practice: Formulating place. In: Studies in social interaction. Edited by David Sudnow. New York: Free Press. 75-102.

Schegloff, Emanuel. 1979. Identification and recognition in telephone call openings. In: Everyday language: Studies in ethnomethodology. Edited by George Psathas. Boston: Irvington. 23-78.

Schegloff, Emanuel. 1982. Discourse as an interactional achievement: Some uses of 'uh huh' and other things that come between sentences. In: Georgetown University Round Table on Languages and Linguistics 1981. Edited by Deborah Tannen. Washington, D.C.: Georgetown University Press. 71-93.

Schegloff, Emanuel, and Harvey Sacks. 1974. Opening up closings. In: Ethnomethodology. Edited by Roy Turner. Harmondsworth, England: Penguin. 233-64.

Schiffrin, Deborah. 1977. Opening encounters. American Sociological Review 44.679-91.

Sharrock, W. W., and Roy Turner. 1978. On a conversational environment for equivocality. In: Studies in the organization of conversational interaction. Edited by Jim Schenkein. New York: Academic Press. 173-98.

Zimmerman, Don H. and Donilene Loseke. 1981. Citizen calls to the police. Unpublished paper.

Zimmerman, Don H., and Marilyn Whalen. (forthcoming) Telling trouble: Citizen calls to the police. In: Language in institutional settings. Edited by Richard M. Frankel. Norwood, N.J.: Ablex.

IDEALIZATION IN SOCIOLINGUISTICS: THE CHOICE OF THE STANDARD DIALECT

Alan Davies
University of Edinburgh

0. Introduction. In this paper, I argue that idealization is as necessary in sociolinguistics as it is in linguistics. In so doing, I assume that notions of the Speech Community and of the Standard Language are part of that idealization. I discuss a recent British example of the ongoing debate over Standard and Dialect in education; I conclude that on educational issues, sociolinguistics may advise but not judge.

Before I begin, I suggest four 'truisms' about language to set the scene. (Truisms, of course, are other people's false ideas.)

0.1 All languages are equal. This is a frequent statement in introductory linguistics textbooks but it has an Orwellian penumbra about it. It means that all languages (all language 'codes') have equivalent (not the same) devices like grammars and vocabularies, and that they are all capable of doing the same things, e.g. expressing intimacy, poetry; telling jokes, writing novels; teaching science, engineering, medicine; running governments, operating air traffic controls and computer systems; maintaining genealogies and oral traditions. But surely this is a statement of linguistic potential; in terms of sociolinguistic suitability--that is, choosing a language for a particular function, use, or set of uses--languages are certainly not equal. Of course, they can develop, but at any point in time they are not equally developed. An example is languages that currently lack writing systems, and therefore swiftly become less and less developed, while those already developed in terms of domain of use, in terms of types and tokens of use (e.g. English), snowball on to greater and greater developments.

0.2 Political change favours dialectal maintenance. The idea here presumably is that revolutions are perpetrated on behalf of minorities or underdogs, and that, therefore, their interests and identities gain in strength and respectability. It is, of course, more complicated: the Irish language served as a symbol for Irish independence, but when Ireland achieved independence the language was, in effect, abandoned. It was the Irish example against which Saunders Lewis (1962) warned Welsh nationalists. Make sure of the language first, he urged, before aiming for political freedom. Indeed, it has been suggested (and the low vote in Wales in favour of devolution (11%) is evidence for this) that in an independent Wales, the Welsh language would get far shorter shrift than it presently does from London. France illustrates the same trend of abandonment of minorities. At the time of the French Revolution, the Convention decided that only one language, French, was revolutionary, and that others (Basque, Provencal, etc.) were living remembrances of feudalism and therefore counter-revolutionary. France has a well-known tradition of monolingual policies both in France itself and in its colonies. Minority languages and dialects do not survive revolutions.

0.3 Different language functions require different language codes. The argument behind this is that there is a linguistic virtue in having more than one dialect code (the bidialectal, tridialectal...policy) available in order to carry out a wide range of functions. Now there may be other grounds for a bidialectal policy, but it is not the case that different functions (home, work, school, religion, etc.) need different codes, though of course they may require different uses of the same code. Confusion about code and function did disservice to Bernstein's work. In any case, my first truism, 'all languages are equal', and my third cannot both be true.

0.4 Speech communities have unique membership. This is the identity argument again, that in language and dialect, as in life, we have to choose. But things are not like that. Indeed, if this statement is true, then no one can be bilingual or bidialectal--which is manifestly absurd. The fact surely is that speech communities, like other social groups, overlap, and link up in a multiplicity of ways; we are, most of us, members of more than one speech community.

1. Standard or dialect: An educational choice. The standard-vs-dialect issue is not an old problem which is now resurfacing in contemporary contexts of varieties of world English and maintenance of ethnic minority languages. Rather, it is an old solution to the permanent educational problem of the best medium for curriculum efficiency. Educational systems have typically assumed, not always correctly, that the speech community is a pretheoretical political primitive and that it is not the business of education to promote or create potential speech communities. Fishman (1977) reminds us that if we accept a pluralistic model, as advocated, for example, by Kjolseth (1973), then we immediately face the practical standard-dialect issue: which Arabic? which Chinese? which Italian? which Punjabi? In some speech communities, the issue may be resolved by choosing a superposed standard, e.g. Urdu in place of 'standard' Punjabi or English in place of 'standard' Tok Pisin. Such a choice is curiously easier than attempting to resolve competing claims among home dialects.

Educational choices about language, the medium for writing and for speech (which may be different), and the selection of foreign language options, are neither linguistic nor sociolinguistic choices. Although linguistic and sociolinguistic ideas and research inform those choices, they do no more; they provide evidence about distribution, attitudes, elaboration, and codification which are taken into account in the court of educational decision--a court which is primarily a political one. In that court, what determines the final decision is an educational philosophy about the kind of society we wish ours to be, with the recognition that for the advantage of pluralism in dialect and language maintenance, there is the price of fragmentation, nonintegration through one standard, and lack of proficiency for many in that standard. On the other hand, for the advantage of efficiency, of proficiency in and integration through one standard, there are the disadvantages of alienation, overall cultural loss, and possible cognitive dissonance.

Of course, the choices that educational systems make will attempt to secure as many advantages and as few disadvantages as possible for all members, but in my view there is no escape from making these choices on the basis of somewhat idealized models (getting the best for most) and making provision for individual exceptions and special cases on an ad hoc basis. As always, revelations about special problems--e.g. the deaf, the illiterate, the minority language--take us back to a reexamination of the provision for the majority, and to our general educational philosophy. If our choice falls on minority dialect and language maintenance, then the majority must be involved.[1]

My concern here is with the debate over institutionalised language variety. This debate has recently focussed on the issue of which dialect to use for language maintenance in bilingual education programmes (Tosi 1982, Rosen and Burgess 1980, Trueba and Barnett-Mizrahi 1979). Cummins' (1979) interdependency hypothesis provides a psychological rigour to this debate, but if indeed he is right about the necessity to cognitive/academic language proficiency of the home language, then our conclusion can only be pessimistic since many, perhaps most, children in the world's schools learn to read in a superposed code.

2. Language vs. code: Enter linguists. The language/code debate began a generation ago in the 1950s, when a connection was made between language deprivation and disadvantage--a development of earlier attempts to connect intelligence to educational disadvantage. The issues in the language debate seem to be as follows: children in certain social and ethnic groups (e.g. the working class and blacks) are disadvantaged, and they do not do as well as they should or could in education. Such children also employ different language varieties. They are thus seen to suffer from deprived language.

Through the late fifties and sixties, in work such as that of Bereiter and Engelmann (1966) and of Bernstein (1971), and in the Head Start programs and the Educational Priority Areas, the theory was developed and remedial action was taken to provide enriched language. At the same time, there was the more linguistic debate as to the nature of the deprived language--was it a language deficit (the groups in question speaking an impoverished variety) or was it a language difference (their variety was not impoverished, just different)? Notice that I have deliberately used the term 'variety', not 'dialect', because I wanted to avoid committing myself as to whether this argument was about code (i.e. the structure of language) or about the use of code. In general, those who saw the argument as being about code supported the deficit view; those who saw it as being about the use of code supported one or other version of the difference view.

It is at this point that linguists entered the argument, largely in order to present specialist advice on the nature of those alternative minority varieties, which I will here call dialects. A united front is presented by, for example, Labov (1969), Trudgill (1975), maintaining that nonstandard dialects, i.e. those of the working class, the blacks, and, by implication (explicitly so in Trudgill's work) the Scots, are equal, fully structured, and in no way impoverished.[2] In this view, Standard English in not a superior or primary dialect, but is one dialect among others. In switching to this sociolinguistic view, it is as though the obviousness that is accorded to the necessary idealization in linguistics (dealing only with well-formed, decontextualised, written sentences) is forgotten. Sociolinguists, whose very data are contextualised language and language variety, can easily forget that they too are describing and analysing data at a distance, not the authentic data of a realistic speech community, but partly contextualised, partly destandardised data. Otherwise, they could not analyse, they could not study. Reflection, analysis, and academic research must always deal with somewhat idealized data transcribed according to some imposed system, analysed according to some other system, etc., while judgements and pragmatic decisions about educational questions and problems must deal with realities.

2.1 Sociolinguistic idealization. I now want to take further the question of idealization in relation to the problem of data. It was axiomatic in linguistics (as distinct from sociolinguistics) that the data of actual speech were not amenable to analysis since they were too variable, 'fairly degenerate in quality' (Chomsky 1965:31), consisting of 'fragments and deviant expressions of various sorts'. Linguistics has therefore chosen to describe a more idealized form of data ('langue, competence'), and, within this area, has achieved success.

The sociolinguist is very much concerned with destandardising and contextualising, i.e. de-idealizing the linguistic data, and with a wider definition of data, one which may permit a correlation of linguistic form with social function. So what are the sociolinguist's 'primary data'? Not, obviously, linguistic competence, nor the 'degenerate' data of actual speech, but something in between. If it is 'communicative competence' as suggested by Hymes, etc., this is presumably some kind of idealization of both language and social structure. Bell (1976) suggests that it is 'socially meaningful behaviour within a given society'.[3] There is, further, the problem of the degree to which the data are already idealized by the very process of collection; there is also the problem of the relationship between data and theory.

Bell (1976) argues, as far as the data-theory relationship is concerned, that sociolinguistics can only be inductive (like structural linguistics but unlike transformational grammar). Therefore, its task for the moment is to discover, first for the specific speech communities and ultimately for the universal notion 'speech community', the system which contains 'the set of community norms, operating principles, strategies and values which guide the production and interpretation of speech, the community ground rules for speaking' (Bauman and Sherzer 1974:7).

As for the idealization problem, we have already observed that it is impossible to collect raw data. Collection and transcription already impose partial analysis: a problem that cannot be avoided by any activity which attempts to describe nondiscrete events in terms of discrete units of analysis. The sociolinguistic view seems to be that a level of idealization lower than that in linguistics can and should be accepted. Labov (1972:203) has argued that the ungrammaticality of everyday speech is 'a myth with no basis in actual fact', that 'the great majority of utterances--about 75%--are well-formed sentences by any criterion' and that if you take ellipsis and universal editing rules into account, you are left with less than 2% of ungrammatical or ill-formed sentences. If that is so, then introspection is less appropriate a method than empirical investigation. Labov further argues that what is of interest to the sociolinguist is the vernacular in which the speaker's utterances are well-formed because he is not as preoccupied with his speech as he might be in formal contexts. To some extent, then, we can accept that the primary linguistic data of sociolinguistic concern may be less idealized, i.e. closer to the reality which the description is intended to model.

The basic model with which sociolinguistics works is that of the Speech Community. Of course, the Speech Community is not homogeneous, but neither is it variable in an unlimited way; its variability must be assumed to be systematic and not individually based. The Speech Community is an idealization in sociolinguistics analogous to the Standard language idealization. What sociolinguistics emphasizes in its concern with variability is parts/groups/minorities vs. wholes/states/ majorities; but idealization away from individual behaviour still takes place. This holds true even for such radical sociolinguistic approaches as ethnomethodology, where the data are transformed by a residue of 'common-sense operation' (Labov 1969:201, quoting Garfinkel). What this means is that within the majority group/minority group view, sociolinguistics is/can be just as normative as the standard language view: if indeed a language is a dialect with an army, arming the dialect does not make it less normative than the language it seeks to challenge.

3. Language vs. code: The reaction of educators. I want now to present the opposing views in the language/code debate, as they have been dramatically represented in recent publications. What I shall suggest is that the apparent permissiveness of the linguistic views has led to a stern rebuttal from an educational standpoint, an antithesis which, bizarrely, seems to say many of the right things but for the wrong reasons.

Trudgill (1975) makes a strong case for the use of nonstandard dialects in education. But I will quote one of his more recent publications (1983) to make the point that we are dealing with an issue of present concern. Trudgill writes (1983:193): 'In educational circles this contrast between Standard English and the non-standard dialects is currently the focus of some considerable debate. To what extent, the question has been asked, are we justified in continuing to encourage and reward the use of Standard English in British schools?' It appears that he is referring to spoken English since he does say (pp. 194-95): 'It is certainly true that all reading materials are written in Standard English and that many children learning to read have also to cope with a new and different dialect.' But even here he is ambivalent, suggesting that even Standard written English does not need to be 'taught' since the 'differences' (from what? other varieties?) are 'not sufficient to cause great difficulties, and most children appear to become skilled at "translating" as they go along, at a very early stage' (p. 195). Trudgill points out (p. 205), quite correctly, that 'Grammatical forms which are most typical of working-class dialects have low status, because of their association with groups who have low prestige in our society,' and comments (p. 206): 'If children suffer because of attitudes to non-standard dialects it is the attitudes that should be changed and not the dialects'. Trudgill also suggests that society is becoming more relaxed about accents, as witness a wider range of accents among radio and television presenters, announcers, etc., and sees this as a sign that our attitudes have relaxed, the implication being that if attitudes to accent can change, so can attitudes to dialect. But I query whether society's attitudes to accent have changed. Macaulay's account of self-stigmatizing Glaswegian children (Macaulay and Trevelyan 1975) still rings true. We now accept a wider range of accents on television and radio because we now have a much wider variety of programmes, and on the entertainment slots (the majority of the output), regional (not strong regional) and class (again not very marked) accents are, as it were, licensed. But on the 'serious' news and comment slots, the presenters (including the ethnic talking heads) use modified RP or Scots.

Trudgill proposes slightly different treatments for various minority groups. For working-class children, he says that society's attitudes must change. For West Indian or Caribbean children, he suggests (1983:194) that what would be helpful is a recognition, especially by teachers, that some WI children in British schools may be faced with what is perhaps best described as a semi-foreign language problem; that is, while they have a problem, it is a problem not with Standard English but with British English as a whole. This is an odd position to take in view of the fact that most 'Caribbean' children now in our schools were born in the UK. And for Scottish children, Trudgill says (1983:190-91) that 'while social dialect continua ranging from local dialect to Standard English are found in much of England, in lowland Scotland...there is discontinuity because of the greater linguistic differences involved...Many Scottish children...are well aware that they have one dialect for school and another for other situations.' Trudgill concludes that while 'translation' is possible from nonstandard to standard dialect, and children learn early how to do it, the 'problem' must be a question of social attitudes. The only reason, he claims, for teaching Standard English is that it is socially advantageous, i.e. not linguistically or cognitively so. To dismiss linguistic advantage in this way implies either that children do not need access to the range of written material, most of which is in Standard English, or that they will acquire Standard English anyway--in which case, what is the fuss about? It isn't linguistic, says Trudgill, it's social attitudes; it's a matter of giving prestige to the children's home speech, and not denigrating it explicitly or by implicitly denying it a school role. He is presumably (it is not clear) talking here only about spoken, not written English. In the case of writing, there are, of course, two major problems. First, there are no accepted conventions, in most cases, of how to write down dialect forms; second, in the absence of sophisticated linguistic training, trying to distinguish between correct and incorrect dialect forms would be an impossible burden on teachers. How would one write, for example: <u>mi asks di man fi put mi moni iina him pakit</u> 'I asked the man to put my money in his pocket' (Sutcliffe 1982)?

Trudgill is game enough to quote in his recent book some of the fierce attacks made on him, such as: 'Some poor children already suffer from progressive teachers anyway who think it wrong to make them read. They are now threatened with a rash of Trudgills who won't correct their grammar. Yet nothing could penalise the working-class more than to be denied the right to knowledge' (<u>Sunday Telegraph</u>, 28 November 1975; Trudgill 1983:198). Whatever Trudgill has actually written, however subtle his qualifications, I think it understandable that he should be popularly interpreted in this way.

Let me turn now to his antagonist, John Honey, who earlier in 1983 published Number 3 in the Black Paper series (Honey 1983); it is one of the Kay-Shuttleworth Papers on Education, published by the National Council for Educational Standards.

Honey's premises are to me rebarbative: he considers that standards have declined, that civilisation is collapsing and the barbarians are at the gate. It's the 'law and order' issue in language education. 'It is a serious matter', he says, 'that our educational system...continues to turn out...an annual crop of total illiterates' (p. 3). The responsibility, he claims, lies not only with the schools, but with 'a group of specialists in linguistics' (yes, you, Trudgill) propagating the notion 'that for schools to foster one variety of English is contrary to the findings of the science of linguistics' (p. 3). 'What we are dealing with', he tells us, is 'the theory of functional optimism', which seems to be a way of representing the linguistic view that all languages are equal. I have to say that Honey's strictures against linguistics are often ill-informed. He uses as a clinching argument against the 'all languages are equal' position that you cannot translate an academic paper on physics from English into Masai. But nobody ever said you could! Such flatulence does not help his cause; as I said earlier, he does have a cause, alas! Again, he shows his lack of understanding on the same point when he remarks: 'we have not been given any evidence that all languages or dialects have a grammatical structure of equal complexity' (p. 17). But what on earth does 'equal complexity' mean? How would you show that English and French, say, have equal complexity?

However, when he comes to his 'cause', he has my attention (Honey (1983:21-22):

> For schools to foster non-standard varieties of English is to place their pupils in a trap. To persuade such speakers that their particular non-standard variety of English is in no way inferior, no less efficient for purposes of communication, but simply <u>different</u>, is to play a cruel trick. All the evidence we have suggests that listeners filter the messages they receive from utterances of other speakers in accordance with perceptions of those speakers which are heavily influenced by the standard or non-standard nature of the language of the utterance in question. Quite apart from this filter mechanism, we know that the use of non-standard English has the power to <u>distract</u> from the speaker's intended message. The 'adequacy for

communication' of any language or dialect is therefore, at least in part, a function of those sociolinguistic factors which we have seen dictating the acceptability of such a language or dialect in specific situations, for specific functions, and specific audiences.

It is difficult, says Honey (correctly), to change attitudes to dialects. Furthermore, the local dialect is not necessarily romantic; it can be given a sentimental value which puts limits in advance on children's 'ability to express themselves...outside their immediate subculture, and to slam the door on any real opportunity for social mobility' (pp. 24-25). And he blames linguists for their support of linguistic diversity (1983:27):

> To sociolinguists [sic] like me, for whom all the speech forms of the dialects and other varieties of English in contemporary Britain are a source of fascination and joy, it is hard to face the sad but true fact that in a plural society the handicaps of disadvantaged groups can be increased by promoting linguistic diversity, as they can be reduced by fostering greater linguistic uniformity.

Honey favours a bidialectalism (or bilectalism) approach--a policy 'which is designed to foster the child's use of his own non-standard language while giving him competence in a second dialect--standard English--whose use he will need for certain specific functions' (p. 30).

4. Conclusion: Bridging the gap? In this final section I want to ask whether these two positions ((1) Standard English does not need to be taught, even for writing (Trudgill), (2) Standard English only should be recognised in schools (Honey)) are really as far apart as the polemic suggests. Let me first quote Richards (1978:55-56):

> The task of promoting Standard English is not the mammoth undertaking it is sometimes made out to be. Nor need its practice prevent the use of dialect in conversation where its adequacy for conveying meaning is not in question...Such problems as do arise are comparatively small in relation to those of countries in which the dialects are so deviant from the standard that they almost constitute other languages; or where within the country, more than one language is in common use. Attempts to promote dialects as alternatives to Standard English can only exacerbate what problems there are. To contemplate such action in an area as small as the British Isles is altogether ludicrous.

And on the problem of alienation, Richards says: 'The danger lies in believing the problem to be solely educational and thus expecting a cure to be effected through this agency alone' (ibid.).

Whether or not linguistics is normative (and Haas 1982:3 argues that it always is: 'It is well known that all the descriptive linguistic disciplines owe their origin to demands for their normative application'), sociolinguistics certainly studies language in normative institutions, and education is in essence normative. Societies need standard languages in order to function as societies; as social agencies, schools have to accept and teach standard language if only because one of the primary purposes of education is literacy. What gets lost in the language/code debate is, paradoxically, the individual. Although society as a whole requires Standard English, individuals may well gain and grow through sympathy for, and attention to, their home language variety--which in many cases is not the spoken standard. (For children beginning school, of course, it is never, or very rarely, the written standard.) Between an individual idiolect and the social standard there are certain dialects which are nonstandard. To promote these as a school policy is (and I agree with Richards) ludicrous, an essentially divisive procedure; but to accept them is not ludicrous. On the contrary, to attempt to eradicate spoken dialect forms from individual speech (as against a bidialectal policy of adding standard forms) is a vain and hopeless policy: it will not work. The goal in schools must be decided educationally, not linguistically: it must surely be to promote production and understanding of written Standard English, and understanding of spoken Standard English; and it must tolerate production, where appropriate, of non-Standard dialect English in the spoken form. Milroy (1981:18), in a recent study of Belfast, reminds us that 'the standard is actually an ideal, a norm which speakers may have in mind...perhaps there is no speaker of English who actually speaks the standard in all its levels (grammar, vocabulary, phonology) at all times'. And he quotes normal code switching in Lowland Scots:

JJ to me - 'Dae ye ken ocht aboot thon stane abune the hoose...'
JJ (later to my wife) - 'I was askin yer man (i.e. husband) if he knew anything aboot that stone above the house?'

A recent discussion by Coates (1982) recognises that standardisation is an attempt to solve and not to create a problem. Coates makes the excellent point (1982:41) that standardisation has an inevitability and that 'it symbolises integrative aspiration towards the social group whose norm is represented by distributions of SPFs'. (SPFs are Standard Pronunciation Features.) 'For those involved in education', he says, 'standardisation can be seen as a litmus paper for a pupil's self-identification with the demands of school and a willingness to meet them practically even at the possible cost of distancing him or herself from the (language of the) peer group.' He then helpfully distinguishes features 'for which there is no shift within a given community from those for which certain individuals display shift.' An example of the first might be intervocalic glottal stop and of the second, rhotacism ($\pm$ /r/). This is a most helpful approach. 'My plea is', he says, 'that thought should be given before a linguistic feature is condemned or corrected' (p. 47). Exactly! And as a coda, 'One may applaud or regret the impact of standard accents as one's conscience dictates; acknowledging that it is there, we should evaluate in an understanding way the linguistic tensions that it gives rise to in real people' (p. 47). Amen to that!

In summary, the argument is more about identity than about language. Language teaching needs to steer wisely between Scylla and Charybdis. If the child's or student's home dialect or language is ignored or scorned, s/he may suffer alienation. If the home dialect or language is given official status--as the medium of spoken interaction--there is the danger of functional divergence and eventual diglossia for those bidialectal groups for whom the written language, for example, may thus become fossilised, static, not amenable to change, and therefore not something with which they can identify.

Sociolinguistics idealises just as linguistics does, but less so. To put it another way, sociolinguistics is a wider linguisitics, still idealising. One aspect of that idealisation is the notion of standard language. My argument has been that sociolinguists must advise that for teaching the written language, the standard dialect is the only choice. Anything else would be trahison de clercs.

Thus, as students of language, linguists, sociolinguists, language teachers, we may (no one can stop us) use our knowledge of language to inform our judgements and our advice on language in education. But the decision is really an educational one which has to do with balancing two apparently conflicting values, those of society and those of the individual. Balance demands cost, on both sides, and it is the measure of a just society that the cost should be one we are prepared to pay.

Notes

1. Current developments of teaching materials for 'language awareness' (Hawkins 1984) may be one way of creating that involvement.
2. Trudgill goes further, recommending that such nonstandard dialects be used in education (to be usually interpreted as L1 in English teaching).
3. This itself raises questions about generality since sociolinguistics is presumably concerned to generalize across societies while, of course, using data from particular societies.

References

Bauman, R., and J. Sherzer, eds. 1974. Explorations in the ethnography of speaking. London: Cambridge University Press.
Bell, R. T. 1976. Sociolinguistics. London: Batsford.
Bereiter, C., and S. Engelmann. 1966. Teaching disadvantaged children in the pre-school. Englewood Cliffs, N.J.: Prentice-Hall.
Bernstein, B. 1971. Class, codes and control, vol. 1. London: Routledge and Kegan Paul.
Coates, R. 1982. How standard is standard? In: Languages for life. Edited by T. Pateman. Brighton: University of Sussex.
Chomsky, N. 1965. Aspects of the theory of syntax. Cambridge, Mass.: The MIT Press.
Cummins, J. 1979. Linguistic interdependence and the educational development of bilingual children. Review of Education Research 49.
Fishman, Joshua A. 1977. Standard versus dialect in bilingual education: An old problem in a new context. Modern Language Journal 61.7. Reprinted in Trueba and Barnett-Mizrahi, eds. (1979).
Haas, W. 1982. Standard languages: Spoken and written. Manchester: Manchester University Press.
Hawkins, E. 1984. Language awareness. London: Cambridge University Press.
Honey, J. 1983. The language trap. Kay-Shuttleworth Papers on Education, No. 3. Kenton, Middlesex: National Council for Education Standards.

Kjolseth, R. 1973. Bilingual education progress in the U.S.: For assimilation or pluralism? In: Bilingualism in the South West. Edited by J. A. Turner. Tucson: University of Arizona Press.
Labov, W. 1969. The logic of non-Standard English. In: Georgetown University Round Table on Languages and Linguistics 1969. Edited by James E. Alatis. Washington, D.C.: Georgetown University Press. 1-43.
Labov, W. 1972. Sociolinguistic patterns. Philadelphia: University of Pennsylvania Press.
Lewis, Saunders. 1962. The fate of the language (Tynged yr laith). BBC radio speech of 13 February. Trans. by G. Aled Williams. In: Presenting Saunders Lewis. Edited by A. R. Jones and G. Thomas. Cardiff: University of Wales Press. 127-41.
Macaulay, R. K., and G. Trevelyan. 1975. Language, education and employment. Edinburgh: Edinburgh University Press.
Milroy, J. 1981. Regional accents of English. Belfast: Blackstaff Press.
Richards, J. 1978. Classroom language: What sort? London: Unwin.
Rosen, H., and T. Burgess. 1980. Languages and dialects of London school children. London: Ward Lock.
Sutcliffe, D. 1982. British Black English. Oxford: Blackwell.
Tosi, A. 1982. Between the mother's dialect and English. In: Language and learning in home and school. Edited by A. Davies. London: Heinemann.
Trudgill, P. 1975. Accent, dialect and the school. London: Edward Arnold.
Trudgill, P. 1983. On dialect. Oxford: Blackwell.
Trueba, H. T., and C. Barnett-Mizrahi, eds. 1979. Bilingual bicultural education and the professional. Rowley, Mass.: Newbury House.

LANGUAGE AND THE LAW: REFERENCE, STRESS, AND CONTEXT

Ellen F. Prince
University of Pennsylvania

1. On linguists as expert witnesses. The presence of linguists as expert witnesses in courtroom proceedings has grown in the past few years from a newsworthy rarity to a not uncommon event (see, for example, Levi 1983). At the present time, however, it is still not as commonplace, compared, for example, with the presence of physicians or civil engineers as expert witnesses. The reason for this disparity is, I believe, twofold.

First, and most obvious, it is probably the case that most lawyers simply do not think of calling upon linguists, due to the fact that their participation is still a relative novelty. Second, and more important, is the fact that the domain of the linguist--language--is viewed by the courts, both implicitly and explicitly, in a qualitatively different way from those of the physician or engineer, and this difference militates against the use of linguists as experts. The difference, as I see it, is basically as follows. Domains such as medicine or engineering are seen, both by the layman and by the courts, as clearly outside the ken of the average individual; there is no sense, among any sector of the population, that an ordinary person of average intelligence and education will have reliable intuitions about whether, for example, the ingestion of a certain chemical will have an adverse effect on a patient who has a certain disease, or whether the substitution of one grade of concrete for another in the construction of a building will impair the structural soundness of that building. In contrast, the domain of language is, in a manner of speaking, in everyone's ken; we do not need an advanced degree to know what some English sentence means.

From a linguist's point of view, this position is on the surface unimpeachable. After all, is it not that very competence that we are in the business of studying? However, a consideration of some of the questions that arise in legal proceedings reveals that a linguist's expertise is often very much in order. First, certain questions call not for linguistic competence so much as for what we call linguistic 'metacompetence': the knowledge that linguists have about linguistic competence. For example, the competence of any normal speaker will enable him/her to assign an interpretation to an utterance in a context, but it is a linguist's metacompetence that is required to determine how the interpretation might be affected as the context is varied, say, by positing different tacit assumptions that the hearer may have. Second, in our society at least, laymen, including the courts, are susceptible to holding certain folk theories of language which may be brought to bear on their analyses, along with their linguistic competence. Thus, in a sense, the situation is not that laymen use linguistic competence while linguists use metacompetence; rather, both make use of metacompetence, but it is only the linguist's that is subject to scientific inquiry and testing.

In what follows, I am going to recount a situation in which I served as an expert witness and which, I believe, illustrates the need for a linguist's expertise both to show how an interpretation of a text depends on its interaction with its context, and also to counter a deeply entrenched folk theory held by society and incorporated into legal practice: namely, the notion that the written language is the 'true' language and, consequently, that a written transcript of an oral discourse is a perfectly adequate representation of that discourse--if not the best representation.

2. The case. In February 1980, a United States District Court held grand jury proceedings investigating police corruption in a state capital. Among those testifying under oath was the former chief of police of the city, henceforth the Chief. Two months before that, in December 1979, the FBI had covertly taped a personal conversation between the Chief and the then assistant chief of police, henceforth the Assistant Chief, but this tape was not transcribed until November 1981, or 21 months after the grand jury proceedings.

Three days later, on the basis of a comparison of the transcript of this tape with a transcript of the grand jury proceedings, an indictment was filed charging the Chief with having committed perjury during the grand jury proceedings. At this point, I was asked by the defense lawyer to look at the materials and see if there was anything that I, as a linguist, could contribute to the case. The materials given to me were the transcript of the grand jury proceedings, a copy of the tape made of the personal conversation between the Chief and the Assistant Chief, and the FBI transcript of that tape. I examined them and found out that, indeed, there was much to be said from a linguistic point of view.

2.1 The problem. The utterance for which the Chief was indicted for perjury is his response to the district attorney (D.A.) in (1).

(1) D.A.: And you are not familar with any other police officer on your force accepting money from anyone?
    Chief: I am not.

The motivation for this indictment was the revelation, in the transcript of the covertly taped personal conversation, that the Chief had been told by the Assistant Chief at that time that the latter had received some money from someone, henceforth the Gambler. Therefore, the argument was that since the Chief knew that the Assistant Chief, a police officer on his force, had accepted money from someone, his answer in (1) was false.

I shall now present the analysis that I presented in court.

2.2 The analysis. Linguistic theory construes the problem of interpreting a linguistic utterance not as trying to discover what the sentence 'really means', but as discovering what understandings of the utterance competent and cooperative language-users may predictably construct, following the various linguistic principles and strategies that they have (unconsciously) at their disposal.[1] The basis for this point of view is that a sentence in vacuo may 'mean' very little, and the interpretation of an utterance, i.e. a sentence at some time, in some place, by someone, to someone, varies with the linguistic and situational context in which it occurs and with the beliefs, assumptions, and hypotheses of the interpreter. Fortunately, this variation is neither arbitrary nor idiosyncratic: language-users operate in a rule-governed way, employing various conventional principles and strategies as they go about constructing an understanding of a linguistic utterance.[2]

Let us now consider the question shown in (1), the crucial question in this case. Out of context, this question could presumably be answered in a variety of ways. Consider, for example, the possible answers in (2).

(2a) Yes, Joe Smith received $25 as a wedding gift from his aunt in Peoria. (Joe Smith is a member of the police force.)
(2b) Yes, my wife and I gave our son $50 for his 25th birthday.
(2c) Yes, Sam Jones won $5 in the instant lottery.

But, presumably, if one could have answered (2a), (2b), or (2c), and gave instead the answer in (1), that alone would not be considered to constitute perjury. The reason is simply that the answerer must construct an understanding of the question that is appropriate to (his understanding of) the context. The prior context, in this case, consists of two questions and the answers given to them; thus we have a subtext consisting of three question-answer pairs.

(3) Q1: Now, all the names that I have just read to you, I am going to ask one more time. Are you familiar with any of those individuals ever making any payments to any police officers on the police force, either while you were the Captain of Detectives or the Chief of Police?
A1: No, sir.
Q2: Have any of those individuals ever paid you any money?
A2: No, sir.
Q3: And you are not familiar with any other member on your force accepting money from anyone?
A3: I am not.

Let us now analyze the prior context to see how it influences the understanding of Q3 that a cooperative answerer would presumably construct.

2.2.1 Question 1. Question 1 explicitly evokes a set of previously named individuals--those local gamblers whose names have just been read to the defendant--and asks whether any member of this set made any payments to any police officers during a certain time interval.

The only serious potential for difference in understanding here, given a single, unambiguous prior list of names, concerns the interpretation of make any payments and any police officers. Making a payment, or paying, is conventionally understood not as a synonym for giving money, but as a special case of it. That is, one makes a payment for something.³ On the other hand, it is conceivable that one may construe the giving of money to a policeman by a nonintimate in his district as something approaching a payment, even if there is no explicit discussion of goods or services rendered, just so long as the potential for such a rendering is salient.

The potential for difference in understanding any police officer relates to whether the Chief understands himself to be included in the set of police officers evoked. On the one hand, he might construe that he is so included, in accordance with the definition of police officer and the fact that he fits that definition. On the other hand, he might invoke the linguistic convention of referring which says that speakers should refer to coparticipants (i.e. speaker and addressees) explicitly if they mean to refer to them at all. Thus it is bizarre and misleading, though not false, for A to say to B the sentence in (4) if someone is meant to refer to A or B.

(4) A: Someone has been spending a lot of time with your wife.

That is, if the someone is A, he has not lied; but, by not saying I, he has misled B into thinking 'not-A.' Likewise, if the someone is B, A still has not lied, but, by not saying you, he has misled B into thinking 'not-B.' (The situation is actually more complex: even if someone is a third party, if A thinks B knows that party, A is conventionally obligated to indicate who it is, and the lack of such an indication leads B to infer that he does not know the individual in question.) With respect to Q1, then, the Chief may construe any police officer to include him, following a technical, definitional understanding; or, he may construe any police officer to exclude him, following the linguistic conventions of referring.

Thus, there are four possible understandings of Q1.

(5) Q1:

		PAY	
		+Service...	-Service...
ANY POLICE OFFICER	+Chief	Q1a	Q1b
	-Chief	Q1c	Q1d

(6) Q1: During a particular time interval T, has any of a previously mentioned set of individuals I given money...
  Q1a. ...to you or any other police officer in exchange for something?
  Q1b. ...to you or any other police officer?
  Q1c. ...to any police officer other than you in exchange for something?

Q1d. ...to any police officer other than you?

As will become relevant later, the Gambler from whom the Assistant Chief claimed to have taken money was not among the set I, and the time at which the Assistant Chief claimed to have taken the money was not during T.

2.2.2 Question 2. Now consider Q2. <u>Have any of those individuals ever paid you any money</u>? It is a very basic, perhaps universal, convention of language that one does not ask for information one already has. This convention is known as the Gricean Maxim of Quantity (Grice 1975). This is not to say that one cannot do so: it simply says that, without any explicit reason for thinking the contrary, a cooperative answerer assumes that new information is being requested when one is asking him/her a question. Thus the understanding of Q2 will presumably vary according to how the answerer understood Q1. Put simply, the answerer will try to find some difference between Q1 and Q2. Since the same morpheme, <u>pay</u>, is used in both questions, it is highly unlikely that a difference will be found to lie in the sense of that term. That is, however <u>pay</u> was understood in Q1, it will presumably be understood the same way in Q2. Likewise, the set of individuals (I) referred to in Q1 is explicitly referred to again in Q2 (<u>any of these individuals</u>) and cannot account for the difference being sought.

One possible difference lies in the possible understanding of <u>ever</u>, especially for individuals who had chosen Q1a or Q1b. However, how the word was actually stressed by the speaker is relevant, if not crucial. If <u>ever</u> is phonologically destressed in Q2, it would normally be understood as anaphoric, i.e. as referring back to something already mentioned, in this case presumably the time interval T referred to in Q1. If, on the other hand, <u>ever</u> is phonologically stressed, it would generally be understood as nonanaphoric and would presumably be understood as 'at any time at all' (see Ladd 1978). Consider examples (7) and (8), where A is a job interviewer and B is a job applicant.

(7a) A: What was your grade point average in college?
(7b) B: 3.3, a B+.
(7c) A: Did you <u>ever</u> get an F?
(7d) B: No.
(7e) A: Did you <u>ever</u> make Dean's List?
(7f) B: No.
(7g) A: Did you <u>EVER</u> receive any scholastic distinction?
(7h) B: Yes, in high school I was class valedictorian.

(8a) A: What was your last job?
(8b) B: I was a piano teacher at the Powell School.
(8c) A: Did your students come for lessons one at a time or did you <u>ever</u> teach a large class?
(8d) B: I taught them just one at a time.
(8e) A: Did you <u>EVER</u> teach a large group?
(8f) B: Yes, in 1975 I taught music appreciation at the Lee School. There were about 30 students in each class.

Note that ever in (7c) and (7e) is destressed and is normally understood as being anaphoric to the time interval previously mentioned: in college. That is, CG would not be taken to have lied in (7d) if he had, in fact, received an F in high school. In (7g), however, ever is stressed, the stress marking its nonanaphoricity, and the high school episode mentioned in (7h) becomes relevant. Likewise, in (8c), destressed ever is taken to refer to the time interval previously evoked: last job, while in (8e) the stressing of EVER releases it from anaphoricity and induces the understanding 'at any time at all'.

Thus, depending on how Q1 was understood and on how ever is understood--which in turn depends to a very large extent on how it was uttered--we find the following four plausible understandings of Q2.

(9) Q2:   Has any individual in I given money to you...
     Q2a: ...in exchange for something during T?
     Q2b: ...in exchange for something at any time?
     Q2c: ...during T?
     Q2d: ...at any time?

(See the Appendix for a list of the possible understandings.) Note that two routes are redundant, i.e. Q1a → Q2a and Q1b → Q2c, in that no new information is requested in Q2. Conceivably, such redundancy might prompt a hearer to reject these understandings of Q2 for those in which ever is nonanaphoric, even if it is destressed; however, little is known about how language-users deal with such infelicities. Another, perhaps more plausible, possibility is that a hearer, arriving at the redundant understandings of Q2a and Q2c, might remove the redundancy by backtracking and reanalyzing Q1a or Q1b as Q1c or Q1d, respectively. It should be noted that such a reanalysis would not affect the truth-value of the answer given to Q1 and so, presumably, would not be mentioned. Thus, there is a slight statistical edge in the likelihood of the understandings of Q1c or Q1d being chosen. In any event, if the hearer had chosen, immediately or via reanalysis, Q1c or Q1d, and if ever is destressed in Q2, then a choice of Q2a or Q2c is more likely than a choice of Q2b or Q2d. That is, there is no reason to change the understanding of ever so long as there is something new asked for. Thus, assuming ever is destressed, Q2a and Q2c are the most likely understandings of Q2.[4]

If, on the other hand, ever is stressed, the situation is quite different: Q2b and Q2d are highly favored.

2.2.3 Question 3. Finally, Question 3 is highly complex: Now, all the names that I have just read to you, I am going to ask one more time. Are you familiar with any of those individuals ever making any payments to any police officers on the police force, either while you were Captain of Detectives or the Chief of Police? First, there is the matter of the change from pay to accept. This may reflect merely a change in point of view, e.g. give/take, in which case accept is understood as the inverse of pay. On the other hand, for those who had the more restricted understanding of pay (i.e. Q1a, c; Q2a, b), accept may be broader or it may not.

Second, there is the matter of the understanding of <u>any other police officer</u>. This is a necessarily anaphoric term, in that <u>other</u> indicates that the individual in question is different from some previously evoked individual or set of individuals. There are two possible candidates for that previously evoked individual or set thereof: either <u>you</u> or <u>any police officers on the police force (during T)</u> in Q1. (Note that, since the latter has two possible understandings, there are in fact three candidates for that previously evoked individual or set thereof. Due to Q2 and to the Referring Principle mentioned earlier, however, one of these--the one where <u>any police officers on the police force</u> is understood as excluding the Chief, leaving <u>any other police officer</u> to refer to the Chief--is extraordinarily unlikely.) In any event, <u>any other police officer</u> can be plausibly understood as referring either to a police officer other than the Chief, or to a police officer other than those on the police force during T.

Third, and perhaps the most crucial, is the understanding of <u>anyone</u>. Here again there is a problem of stress. If <u>anyone</u> is destressed, its most plausible understanding is anaphoric, i.e. anyone among the previously evoked set I. If it is stressed, however, it is not likely to be construed as anaphoric and then would include anyone at all. Consider examples (10) and (11).

(10) A: Have you hired someone yet?
B: I've interviewed 12 people but I don't like anyone.
A: I think you don't like ANYONE.

(11) A: How was your high school reunion?
B: Oh, lots of people showed up, but I didn't remember <u>anyone</u>.
A: Good grief! If you don't remember your old classmates, you won't remember ANYONE!

Note that destressed <u>anyone</u> in (10B) is anaphoric to the set of 12 people interviewed, while the stressed ANYONE in A's response is nonanaphoric, understood as 'anyone at all'. Likewise, destressed <u>anyone</u> in (11B) is anaphoric to the set of people who showed up, while stressed <u>anyone</u> in A's response loses its anaphoricity, being understood as 'anyone at all'. Notice how bizarrely redundant A's response would be in both (10) and (11) if <u>anyone</u> were destressed.

Thus there are three binary variables in Q3, leading to eight possible understandings. Furthermore, as no new time interval is stated, one would infer that the same time interval that held in Q2 still holds. But Q2 could be understood as involving one of two different time intervals, T and any time at all. Thus Q3 has 16 possible understandings, shown in (12). (See also Appendix.)

(12) Q3A: Has, during time interval T,...
Q3Aa: ...any I given any police officer other than you money in exchange for something?
Q3Ab: ...any I given any police officer other than you money?
Q3Ac: ...any I given any police officer not on the force during T money in exchange for something?

Q3Ad: ...any I given any police officer not on the force during T money?
Q3Ae: ...anyone at all given any police officer other than you money in exchange for something?
Q3Af: ...anyone at all given any police officer other than you money?
Q3Ag: ...anyone at all given any police officer not on the force during T money in exchange for something?
Q3Ah: ...anyone at all given any police officer not on the force during T money?
Q3B: Has, at any time at all,...
Q3Ba: ...any I given any police officer other than you money in exchange for something?
Q3Bb: ...any I given any police officer other than you money?
Q3Bc: ...any I given any police officer not on the force during T money in exchange for something?
Q3Bd: ...any I given any police officer not on the force during T money?
Q3Be: ...anyone at all given any police officer other than you money in exchange for something?
Q3Bf: ...anyone at all given any police officer other than you money?
Q3Bg: ...anyone at all given any police officer not on the force during T money in exchange for something?
Q3Bh: ...anyone at all given any police officer not on the force during T money?

Note once again that these are all merely theoretical possibilities, if we ignore stress. If <u>EVER</u> was stressed in Q2, then Q3B is favored over Q3A; if <u>ever</u> was destressed in Q2, then Q2A is favored. Likewise, if <u>ANYONE</u> was stressed in Q3, then Q3Ae-h and Q3Be-h are favored; if <u>anyone</u> was destressed, then Q3Aa-d and Q3Ba-d are favored. The interaction of these two variables is shown in (13).

(13) Favored understandings of Q3, depending on stress:

	ever	EVER
anyone	Q3Aa-d	Q3Ba-d
ANYONE	Q3Ae-h	Q3Be-h

In any event, we have found 4 plausible understandings for Q1, 4 for Q2, and 8 for Q3, allowing for 128 theoretically possible routes, some of which would likely be favored by a hearer seeking nonredundancy, and some favored according to how certain items were stressed.

2.3 Understanding of <u>take</u>. In order to determine whether the Chief's response to Q3 was consistent with his beliefs, one must, among other things, make some hypothesis about what his beliefs in fact were. In this respect, part of his conversation with the Assistant Chief, covertly taped two months before the grand jury proceedings, seems to shed light on his beliefs about the Assistant Chief's taking of money.

At the trial, the judge did not permit me to present this section, stating that the personal conversation was not 'relevant' to the perjury issue--in spite of the fact that it was this conversation that led to the perjury indictment. However, as it was included in my report to the lawyer, which report the judge read, I include it here.

Following is a corrected transcript of the pertinent part of the conversation, where C = Chief and A = Assistant Chief.[5]

(14) C: What the fucking hell's the MATTER with you?
A: I don't know. Whew...I don't know. I don't know what they got. (Tape cut) I didn't want to say nothing yesterday, I didn't want to upset you. So when X says--I called X last night: so he called me early this morning: and he said, Your phone must be tapped: and they're watching your place. He said, when he came out, they--he had somebody in the car with him: and he seened somebody pull in: and uh I don't know whether he said HE followed THEM or THEY followed him when he left there. I don't know.
C: They can't have anything.
A: I don't know.
C: What the hell can THEY have? <u>You never took anything</u>.
A: I did, yeah.
C: From what?
A: From Y up there--
C: Yeah, but you went to the track with that money.
A: Well, yeah, but you know, I used to stop in there and--
C: That's right but--
A: He'd give me: like ten dollars, twenty dollars, something like that usually--
C: So, what the hell?
A: a week or a couple of weeks. There was never really any-- serious uh--
C: <u>You never did him any favors</u>.
A: No.

The crucial line here is <u>You never took anything</u>. If one assumes that one's statements in private conversation reflect one's beliefs--an assumption which presumably underlies the government's covert taping of private conversations such as this one--one must infer that, at this point in time, the Chief believed that the Assistant Chief had not taken any money.[6]

The next question is whether there is evidence that he changed his belief. As it appears here, there is none. First, the transfer of money in question appears to be one that he already knew about, since he volunteers that the Assistant Chief 'went to the track with that money.' Thus he either lied when he said <u>You never took anything</u> or else he did not consider this transfer of money to the Assistant Chief to constitute taking. Second, and equally important, is the statement <u>You never did him any favors</u>. By a very basic principle of linguistic interaction, the Gricean Maxim of Relation (Grice 1975), utterances are intended to be relevant to their context. Thus one infers that this statement is intended to be relevant to the issue at hand, i.e. whether the Assistant Chief took money from Y. Since the Chief has been arguing that he did not, the relevance of this statement appears to be as evidence for that position. Taking money, from the Chief's point of view as it is represented here, crucially involves the notion of receiving money in exchange for something.

2.4 Finding. It is my understanding of the case that the Chief, in order to have perjured himself by answering Q3, had to have understood Q3 as Q3Bf: <u>...anyone at all given any police officer other than you money</u>?, rather than as one of the other 15 possible understandings. That is, I am assuming he believed the following: Assistant Chief, a member of the police force during T, was given money at some time not in T, by someone not in I. If both <u>ever</u> and <u>anyone</u> were stressed, these are plausible understandings. However, if neither or only one were stressed, other understandings are more plausible.

3.0 Discussion. As I have tried to show, a finding of perjury in this case hinged largely on how two words uttered by the D.A. during the grand jury proceedings were stressed. Interestingly, the proceedings had, in fact, been taped and so the answer to this question should have been available. However, as I was told, such proceedings are taped only to ensure that a transcript can be made; once the transcript is finished, the tapes are destroyed, the transcript serving as the official record of the event. I should add that there are no fine-tuned legal conventions for indicating stress or intonation in the transcripts.

A courtroom anecdote may be relevant here. In the course of my testimony, I read the examples shown in (7)-(8) and (10)-(11) and, noticing a distraught look on the court stenographer's face, I said jokingly to her, 'Hope you can handle this.' As soon as court was adjourned, and even before the jury had left the jury box, the stenographer jumped up and said to me something along the lines of: 'Oh, it's impossible to transcribe that! They tell you just to punctuate it as you hear it, but it's not like punctuation.' The stenographer had obviously learned what linguists know but what the courts have a real problem with: written language and oral language are different, and the former cannot be taken to be simply a representation of the latter.

In conclusion, the Chief, who was, I am sorry to say, a most distasteful character, was acquitted after a very brief deliberation. Given that the only other witness for the defense was a clergyman testifying to his philanthropy, I infer that my testimony played an important role in the acquittal. If the courts could adopt a more enlightened attitude about language, perhaps by consulting linguists when deciding on general practices such as keeping records of speech events, it is possible either that such a trial would never take place (with a large saving to the taxpayer) or that it would lead to a conviction. But I guess we have progressed if a linguist's testimony can prevent a conviction where the evidence is missing.

Appendix

Possible understandings of Q1-3

Q1: During a particular time interval T, has any of a previously mentioned set of individuals I given money...
Q1a: ...to you or any other police officer in exchange for something?
Q1b: ...to you or any other police officer?
Q1c: ...to any police officer other than you in exchange for something?
Q1d: ...to any police officer other than you?

Q2: Has any individual in I given money to you...
Q2a: ...in exchange for something during T?
Q2b: ...in exchange for something at any time?
Q2c: ...during T?
Q2d: ...at any time?

Q3A: Has, during time interval T,...
Q3Aa: ...any I given any police officer other than you money in exchange for something?
Q3Ab: ...any I given any police officer other than you money?
Q3Ac: ...any I given any police officer not on the force during T money in exchange for something?
Q3Ad: ...any I given any police officer not on the force during T money?
Q3Ae: ...anyone at all given any police officer other than you money in exchange for something?
Q3Af: ...anyone at all given any police officer other than you money?
Q3Ag: ...anyone at all given any police officer not on the force during T money in exchange for something?
Q3Ah: ...anyone at all given any police officer not on the force during T money?
Q3B: Has, at any time at all,...
Q3Ba: ...any I given any police officer other than you money in exchange for something?
Q3Bb: ...any I given any police officer other than you money?
Q3Bc: ...any I given any police officer not on the force during T money in exchange for something?
Q3Bd: ...any I given any police officer not on the force during T money?
Q3Be: ...anyone at all given any police officer other than you money in exchange for something?
Q3Bf: ...anyone at all given any police officer other than you money?
Q3Bg: ...anyone at all given any police officer not on the force during T money in exchange for something?
Q3Bh: ...anyone at all given any police officer not on the force during T money?

Notes

I should like to thank Joshua D. Lock, Esq. for his confidence and cooperation, without which this work would most certainly never have been done. I am grateful also to Tony Kroch and Debby Schiffrin for their help.

1. As was pointed out to the court, the term 'cooperative' is a technical one following the Gricean model, indicating that the individuals are engaged in rational, goal-directed behavior and are assuming the same of their coparticipants. It does not, of course, suggest that they are being friendly, nice, or affable in any way.

2. See, among others, Horn (1972), Bolinger (1977), Clark and Haviland (1977), Kuno (1978), Morgan (1978), Gazdar (1979), Green (1980).

3. Webster's Third International Dictionary defines payment and pay as follows:

payment: 1. the act of paying or giving compensation : the discharge of a debt or obligation. 2. something that is paid : something given to discharge a debt or obligation or to fulfill a promise. 3. archaic:...

pay: v.i.: 1. to give a recompense : make payment : discharge a debt or obligation. 2. to make suitable return for expense or trouble : be worth the effort or pains : be profitable. 3. to be amiss or afoot.

v.t.: 1. (obsolete)... 2a. to satisfy (someone) for services rendered or property delivered : discharge an obligation to : make due return to. b. to engage for money : HIRE. 3a. to give in return for goods or service. b. to discharge indebtedness for : SETTLE. c. to assume the charge of. d. to make any agreed disposal or transfer of (money). 4. to give or forfeit in expiation or retribution. 5a. to make compensation for : make up for : RECOMPENSE. b. to make retaliation for--usually with back. c. to requite (someone) according to what is deserved : get even with--usu. with back. d. (archaic)... 6. to give, offer, or make freely or as fitting. 7a. to return value or profit to. b. to bring in as a return. 8. to slacken (as a rope)...

4. Note, of course, that this is simply a probability of likelihood and not a statement about what is possible or which one is 'better'.

5. Working with a Sanyo transcriber, I found an average of 12 substantive mistakes per typewritten page in the FBI transcript of the conversation. This was analogous to the situation I had found in two previous cases where FBI transcripts of private conversations were used. Moreover, in at least one instance in the present case, a mistake introduced a sense of culpability that the spoken text did not contain. That is, the Chief was recounting to the Assistant Chief that all the local gangsters had been calling him since he came home from the hospital; one, in fact, had said, 'Do you need anything?', to which he had responded, 'No, I don't need nothing.' This was transcribed as: 'Do you know anything?', 'No, I don't know nothing.' The conspiratorial flavor of the transcript version was no doubt responsible for the question-answer being quoted in the local newspaper during the trial. It should be noted, of course, that tapes of private conversations are generally of very poor quality; the jury is, therefore, generally given a transcript to read along and it is highly unlikely that they will detect any errors in it. Thus there is a grave responsibility to provide as accurate a transcript as possible, a responsibility which, in my opinion, the government has not appreciated.

6. Of course, the notion that private social conversation is for the purpose of transmitting objective information and, therefore, that the speakers are committed to the truth of the propositions they are expressing, is not supported by studies of social conversation. See, for example, Goffman (1967), among others. However, it is a fact that utterances made in covertly taped private social conversations have figured prominently in Federal court cases as evidence of the utterer's beliefs and knowledge, analogous to utterances made under oath. The seriousness of this problem cannot, in my opinion, be overestimated.

References

Bolinger, D. 1977. Meaning and form. London: Longmans.
Clark, H., and S. Haviland. 1977. Comprehension and the given-new contract. In: Discourse production and comprehension. Edited by R. Freedle. Hillsdale, N.J.: Erlbaum. 1-40.
Gazdar, G. 1979. Pragmatics: Implicature, presupposition, and logical form. New York: Academic Press.
Goffman, E. 1967. Interaction ritual. Garden City, N.Y.: Anchor Books.
Green, G. 1980. Linguistics and the pragmatics of language use: What you know when you know a language...and what else you know. Center for the Study of Reading. Urbana: University of Illinois.
Grice, H. P. 1975. Logic and conversation. In: Syntax and semantics, vol. 3. Speech acts. Edited by P. Cole and J. L. Morgan. New York: Academic Press. 41-58.
Horn, L. 1972. On the semantic properties of logical operators in English. Ph.D. dissertation, University of California, Los Angeles.
Kuno, S. 1978. Generative discourse analysis in America. In: Current trends in textlinguistics. Edited by W. Dressler. Berlin and New York: de Gruyter. 275-94.
Ladd, D. R. 1980. The structure of intonational meaning. Bloomington: Indiana University Press.
Levi, J. 1983. Language and the law: A bibliography. Bloomington: Indiana University Linguistic Club.
Morgan, J. L. 1978. Toward a rational model of discourse comprehension. In: TINLAP-2. Edited by D. Waltz. New York: Association for Computing Machinery.

PERSONAL, GROUP, AND COUPLE IDENTITIES: TOWARDS A RELATIONAL CONTEXT FOR THE STUDY OF LANGUAGE ATTITUDES AND LINGUISTIC FORMS

Howard Giles
University of Bristol

Mary Anne Fitzpatrick
University of Wisconsin-Madison

It is a central argument of this paper that although scholars have explored both personal and group identities as salient contextual parameters of language attitudes and behaviors, a crucial point on the individual-group continuum has been neglected. While it is true individuals have relatively enduring personal and group identities, we also know that individuals have dyadic and/or couple identities as well. Just as individuals define themselves and are defined by others as upper class and female or Welsh and Catholic, so too they define themselves as husband, lover, and girlfriend. Such relational identities, while of some import for social actors, are largely ignored by language scientists. To begin our exploration of dyadic identities, we have chosen to focus on the couple, particularly the marital dyad. Marriage is an important 'nomos-building' institution in our society (Berger and Kellner 1975) because it creates for people the sort of order in which they can experience their worlds as making sense. It is through conversations with one another that married partners construct a shared reality and subsequently define their identities. Through these marital conversations, a couple identity is not only built but also kept in a state of repair and ongoingly refurbished. As Berger and Kellner (1975:226) so eloquently phrase it:

> The nomic instrumentality of marriage is concretized over and over again, from bed to breakfast table, as the partners carry on the endless conversation that feeds on nearly all they individually or jointly experience.

To place our emerging interest in couple identities within the framework of our past work, we will first survey some of the research conducted on the relationships between social meanings, particularly personal and group identities, and various linguistic forms.

Personal identities. Within the study of personal identities and language, a ubiquitous finding has been that listeners rate standard accented speakers on audiotape more favorably across competence (or status-related) traits than their nonstandard counterparts (Ryan and Giles 1982; Giles and Edwards 1983). Recently, and in line with other workers (e.g. Romaine 1980; Ryan and Bulik 1982), we have been examining some contextual riders to this, and other, effects. For instance, in one study, we found that the typical status upgrading of British standard RP (Received Pronunciation) was attentuated significantly when the sociophysical setting for the investigation was an evening youth club rather than the usual, more formal, classroom setting (Creber and Giles 1983). Perhaps more surprising (see, however, Myers and Lamm 1976; Taylor and Royer 1980) was another of our findings that the status connotations of RP were <u>accentuated</u> when informants were asked to discuss their speaker evaluations with each other for approximately 90 seconds before making their ratings (Giles, Harrison, Creber, Smith, and Freeman 1983). In a further study, we found a tendency for Welsh bilingual respondents to make evaluative distinctions between standard RP English and nonstandard Welsh-accented English on status traits when the experimental procedure was conducted in English, but not when it was in the Welsh language. When the rating task was in the latter language, however, listeners would make social attractiveness comparisons between standard and nonstandard voices that would not be apparent in an English judgment setting (Price, Fluck, and Giles 1983). Hence, not only can the status connotations of a standard variety be diminished or exaggerated, depending on the nature of the context, but the evaluative criteria brought to bear in them can also vary.

Another ubiquitous finding in the language attitudes domain has been the positive linear relationship between speech rate and perceived competence (e.g. Brown 1980; Stewart and Ryan 1982; Street, Brady, and Putnam 1983); that is, the faster you talk, the more competent you sound. The effect was obliterated, however, when the rating task was moved out of its social vacuum. In this instance, allowing listeners access to information that a speaker was taped while helping a naive audience comprehend an unfamiliar topic, made him sound just as intelligent and competent as when he was heard to talk much faster (Brown, Giles, and Thakerar 1983).

But not only does contextual knowledge affect one's evaluations of linguistic forms; it can also influence people's perceptions of those very same features. Guided in part by Snyder (1981), we found that telling people the speaker they had just listened to on tape was a high status person induced them to rate him as having spoken at a faster rate and with a more standard accent than those provided with no such information who, in turn, rated him more positively on these linguistic dimensions than did a third group provided with low status information (Thakerar and Giles 1981). This phenomenon, which we subsequently labelled the 'retrospective speech halo effect' (Ball, Byrne, Giles, Berechree, Griffiths, Macdonald and McKendrick 1982), suggests that what we think someone should sound like can sometimes be more influential in determining our linguistic judgments about them than what can be measured objectively as such.

Furthermore, this rather robust phenomenon, which we recently replicated in Australia (Ball et al. 1982), has implications beyond mere cognitions to actual speech behaviors. In this respect, another vein of our research has been concerned with showing how and why individuals converge their linguistic and vocal forms toward each other in cooperative or integrative frames of mind, or when they desire each other's approval (see, for example, Street and Giles 1982; Giles 1984). There is, of course, no problem here if there is isomorphism between where people's speech styles actually are objectively, and where others believe them to be subjectively. Recently, we found that people converge toward where they believe others to be linguistically rather than where they are in physical reality (Thakerar, Giles, and Cheshire 1982). In this study, members of dyads who had each agreed about the relative statuses of their partners were required to talk about a problem task they had just solved together. At the commencement of their discussion, they were judged to possess highly similar accents and speech rates. During the course of their conversations, however, lower status partners in the dyads standardized their accents and talked faster while the higher status speakers nonstandardized their accents and talked slower. Although, in objective linguistic terms, this might seem like 'divergence', in actual fact, data were gathered indicating that speakers believed they were moving toward each other linguistically. This process of so-called 'linguistic divergence but psychological convergence' (Thakerar et al. 1982) has been noted independently (albeit in different conceptual terms) in a number of cultural settings (see Beebe 1981; Bell 1982; Caporael 1981). These mutual apparent divergences could be potentially the interpretive breeding ground for communication misattributions and misunderstandings (see Giles and Bourhis 1976; Platt and Weber 1984).

In sum, then, we do not just passively listen to someone's voice; we actively construct and perhaps reconstruct our impressions of it according to incoming contextual data (cf. Street and Hopper 1982; Roloff and Berger 1982) and in ways that have implications for our own linguistic forms. Yet who is _not_ there can be just as, if not more, important a vocal and linguistic determinant of one's self-presentations as those physically present. On occasions, many more significant others get to hear about a message's meaning and form than ever heard the message at the time of delivery. Hence, speakers can accommodate their speech styles strategically to absent influential people who are known to pluck the grapevine of highly active social networks.

Group identities. Given our disciplinary backgrounds, we have been fascinated, as the foregoing attests, by the cognitive mechanisms that mediate language attitudes and linguistic forms. For instance, we have long recognized the linguistic implications of there being no necessary overlap between investigators' allocations of respondents to ethnic group X and the latter's feelings of group belongingness on that occasion, nor any inevitable direct correspondence between assigning speakers to context Y and the informants' subjective assessment of that situation. Hence, taping a very elderly person's linguistic forms in a supposedly formal context can be less predictive of his or her language behaviors if this person feels middle aged and construes the social atmosphere as very relaxed and informal. Obviously, sociolinguists such as Fishman (1966), Hymes (1967), Labov (1966), and Gumperz (1982) have articulated this actor's-eye-view for some time, particularly as it can relate to social identity. Yet, such a cognitive stance has not been realized in any really extensive and sophisticated manner in either methodologies or theories. Whilst recognizing the potential, conceptual sterility of artificially dichotomizing language and context, we attempted recently to fill these voids by proposing models of how linguistic forms can be mediated by participants' cognitive representations of the social situations they are in and their group identities at that time. We also discussed some of the ways in which language behaviors in social interaction can also, reciprocally, mould interlocutors' cognitive representations of the context and their group identities (Giles and Hewstone 1982). This was achieved by recourse to work in the social psychologies of social situations on the one hand (Wish 1978; Forgas 1983) and intergroup relations on the other (Tajfel and Turner 1979). Space precludes any real discussion of these models, but we would like to highlight one of these mediating cognitive constructs, viz. the interindividual----intergroup continuum.

Tajfel and Turner (1979) argued that whilst on many occasions our interactions are fully determined by our personal attributes (the so-called 'interindividual' pole), on other occasions social interaction can be almost exclusively dependent on our social group memberships, be they academic discipline, gender, age, class, etc.; this is the 'intergroup' pole. Studies referred to in the previous section can be typified at the interindividual pole where personal identities were our focus. Let us now expend some time talking about language forms at the intergroup pole where our group identities assume contextual salience and de-individuation can occur (Turner 1982). Precisely how much of our everyday social behavior is located near this extreme pole is, of course, an empirical question (see Stephenson 1981). Nevertheless, perhaps much of what is included under the generic rubric of 'interpersonal communication' (e.g. male-female interactions, young-old encounters) could arguably and profitably be reinterpreted in intergroup terms.

'Ethnolinguistic identity theory' is our current theoretical approach for studying language behaviors at the intergroup pole (Giles and Johnson 1981), the core of which depends heavily on Tajfelian principles of social identity (Tajfel 1978, 1982). One important proposition of our perspective is that if a speaker experiences a strong sense of group belongingness whilst subjectively defining an interaction as an 'intergroup' one, he or she will wish to achieve a positive group identity in that very context. The realization of the positive-negative affect associated with group identity comes through making 'intergroup' comparisons between the position of your own group and that represented by an outgroup speaker on valued dimensions such as relative power, resources, capabilities, etc. Much of ethnolinguistic identity theory and the empirical research attending it has been concerned with articulating the conditions necessary, and strategies used, for achieving a positive identity. Given that language forms can be important dimensions of social group memberships, particularly class and ethnic ones (Giles 1977; Giles and Saint-Jacques 1979), one strategy for achieving such a positive group identity would involve linguistic differentiation from outgroup speakers. This process of so-called 'psycholinguistic distinctiveness' (Giles, Bourhis, and Taylor 1977) can be manifest by language code-switching, emphasizing an ingroup dialect, slang, or argot; diverging phonological, grammatical, and discourse structures, etc. We have argued that the extent of this ethnolinguistic differentiation, either in the long term of community-wide sociolinguistic change or in the shorter term cases of interpersonal divergences, is dependent on a variety of intergroup, contextual variables (Giles and Johnson 1981). Two of these are now mentioned briefly.

The first is the status relations existing between in- and outgroup as perceived by the individuals themselves, as well as the nature of the social comparisons made by them. Put more concretely, we argue, and we have data to support this (Johnson 1984), that the more individuals identify strongly with their ethnic group and the more they perceive any status differences existing between them as illegitimate and potentially changeable (see Turner and Brown 1978), the more likely it is that forms of ethnolinguistic differentiation will occur. A second set of variables we deem important are referred to collectively as 'vitality' factors (Giles et al. 1977) and were formulated out of a dire need to place social psychological processes in language studies in their proper macrosociostructural contexts (see also Ryan, Giles, and Sebastian 1982). Vitality factors were envisaged as forming three independent clusters of variables: the relative sociohistoricolinguistic status of groups in contact; their demographic profiles in terms of birth rates, proportions, emigration patterns; and the institutional support their cultures and languages enjoy. We have argued that members of ethnic groups cognitively represent such societal forces (e.g. Bourhis, Giles, and Rosenthal 1981; Johnson, Giles, and Bourhis 1983). Yet, not only do we have evidence that they actually can do this, but that in- and outgroups construe these forces differently, and attach different cognitive weights to them (Bourhis and Sachdev 1984; Giles, Rosenthal, and Young in press). Furthermore, we argue that the more of these vitality factors individuals construe in their group's favor, the more likely their perception of societal forces can bolster their sense of ethnic identification, and consequently, the more likely ethnolinguistic differentiation will ensue in a wide array of intergroup contexts (Johnson 1984).

Recently, we have begun to explore how the areas of ethnic language attitudes, on the one hand, and second language acquisition, on the other, can be theoretically enriched by recourse to these mediating cognitive contextual variables. Despite the fact that both domains pay lip service to them, we nonetheless believe that they are operating in 'intergroup vacua'. Space again precludes a development of these ideas but, suffice it to say, we can proffer concrete propositions, based on an analysis of individuals' intergroup belief structures, concerning what language attitude profiles certain listener-judges will emit and why (Ryan, Hewstone, and Giles 1984), and what levels of proficiency minority group members will exude in the dominant group's language, and why (Giles and Byrne 1982; Ball, Giles, and Hewstone 1984).

Couple identities. The discussion so far has provided a flavor of how contextual factors, often cognitively mediated at the individual and intergroup levels by personal and group identity processes, can influence linguistic forms and attitudes. Interestingly, we have, as has mainstream literature in the language sciences, passed by a crucial level of analysis, viz. that involving contexts where relational identities are paramount. It is our view that cognitive processes attending 'couple identities' (intimate heterosexual, as well as others) can mediate the social meanings of linguistic forms; our methods and theories seem to have bypassed such a relational context analysis. Indeed, Bolton (1961) has shown how psychologically meaningful it is for partners in a heterosexual relationship to arrive at a consensus of their being a 'couple'. Spiegelberg (1973) provides an interesting analysis of how this is manifest linguistically, for instance, by statements such as <u>we feel..., we did...</u> (see also Rausch, Barry, Hertel, and Swain 1974), while Hopper, Knapp, and Scott (1981) have explored the fascinating world of intracouple talk through pet names, abbreviations, and neologisms. Whilst again our field is hardly devoid of dyadic and relationship constructs and measures (see, for example, Berger and Kellner 1975; Bochner and Krueger 1979; Brown and Levinson 1979; Krueger 1982), it is nevertheless the case that the predominant unit of analysis is the individual. It may well be that we are missing important social meanings in our studies of language behaviors if we neglect to probe how a sense of couple identity defines what we listen to and how we speak (see Bradac 1983). Relatedly, Wiemann and Kelly (1981) argued that interpersonal competence and empathy are not skills inherent in individuals' communicative behaviors as much as in their jointly negotiated relationship performance.

As an initial exploration into the empirical world of couple identity and language attitudes, we designed and conducted an experiment to be discussed in due course. It was our belief that just as people have speech stereotypes of competent individuals as fast talking, standard-accented speakers, so too, people may have speech stereotypes of how different couple types sound. Moreover, and as we demonstrated earlier, stereotyped beliefs may color listeners' rememberings of such talk. In this vein, and building upon various assumptions of labeling theorists (e.g. Garfinkel 1956; Kitsuse 1962; Lofland 1966), Snyder (1981:184), from a 'cognitive bolstering' perspective, stated:

> An individual having adopted stereotyped beliefs about a target will: (1) remember and reinterpret past events in the target's life history in ways that bolster and support these current stereotyped beliefs; and (2) will act upon these current stereotyped beliefs in ways that cause the actual behavior of the target to confirm and validate the individual's stereotyped beliefs about the target.

Hence, the prime aim of our admittedly embryonic investigation was to determine whether the 'retrospective speech halo effect' found operating at the individual level in the first section of this paper could also function relationally. More specifically, would providing listener-judges with contextual information about a couple's state of marital adjustment, on the one hand, or their relational identity, on the other, evoke sufficient stereotyped communication beliefs about them that would influence perceptions of their talk as a couple? The empirical enterprise of eliciting linguistic judgments of couples as relational units seems an important innovation in the language attitudes domain, conceptually and methodologically, as it has archetypally adopted the individual as its unit of analysis (see reviews in Ryan and Giles 1982). Before proceeding to a description of our study, let us survey briefly the research traditions which led to the formulation of specific hypotheses concerning the content of these relational speech stereotypes which might color linguistic reconstructions of couple talk.

Scholars in a variety of disciplines, including historians, sociologists, psychologists, and clinicians, have pursued the search for the causes of the success or failure of a marriage, each offering a variety of explanations for marital satisfaction and stability. Nevertheless, there emerges a surprisingly consistent viewpoint: that is, in our culture, subjectively experienced contentment in a marriage is the primary determinant of whether it will remain stable or intact (Lewis and Spanier 1979). Furthermore, the communication that takes place between a husband and wife leads to this contentment or satisfaction. Thus, a whole tradition of research has sprung up, investigating the linguistic/communicational correlates of marital disturbance. Dozens of studies now attest (be it in self-report, informal observation by case studies, laboratory role-playing, etc.) that maritally nonadjusted couples exude more negative affect, verbally, vocally, and visually, as well as portray inconsistencies between these channels. Less information (particularly personal) is exchanged, fewer problem-solving acts are attempted, and their interpersonal conflicts are dealt with in a mutually less accommodating manner (e.g. Lederer and Jackson 1968; Mishler and Waxler 1968; Altman and Taylor 1973; Gottman 1982; Krueger and Smith 1982; Noller 1982). Figure 1 displays some of these differentiating items. It was our hypothesis that laypeople may well possess cognitive representations of marital communication in accord with at least some of the findings, such that these stereotyped beliefs could potentially bias listeners' linguistic judgments of an unfamiliar couple's talk in the direction of their known marital adjustment-nonadjustment. Hence, items appearing in Figure 1 were included as dependent measures in our study to follow.

Another approach to this research area has been that of Fitzpatrick and her associates (Fitzpatrick 1977, in press; Fitzpatrick and Best 1979), which empirically types marital relationships in terms of their levels of interdependence, their ideologies of relationships, and their communication patterns. More specifically, this typology emerged after a series of large-scale pilot tests and finally after an analysis of over 1,000 married partners' responses to a questionnaire (the 'Relational Dimensions Instrument': RDI) which includes such items as: 'We tell each other how much we love or care about each other' (agree---disagree) and 'The ideal relationship is one which is marked by novelty, humor and spontaneity'. Three ways of defining a relationship arose (seemingly independent of demographic correlates), viz. 'traditional', 'separate', and 'independent'. About 60% of couple partners agree on the basic dimensions of their marriage in terms of interdependence, ideology, and communication (i.e. the 'pure' types), while the other 40% comprise the 'mixed' varieties (e.g. 'traditional-separate').

Figure 1. Some communicational correlates of marital adjustment-nonadjustment also serving as predictions for the present investigation.

Items		Couple type:	
		Adjusted	Nonadjusted
Marital adjustment	1a	+	−
Self-disclosed	2a	+	−
Talked frequently	2a	+	−
Stopped communication less often	2a	+	−
Accurate interpretations of spouse meaning	3a	+	−
Generally positive	4b	+	−
Generally negative	4b	−	+
Cross-complaining sequences	4b	−	+
First reciprocated positive remarks, then stopped	4b	−	+
Interaction patterned	4b	−	+
Discussing a problem, wife uses a negative tone	5b	−	+

Key. The letter a refers to findings from self-report studies, while b indicates behavioral observation studies. Numbers refer to the study in question, viz. 1, Spanier (1976); 2, Kahn (1970); 3 Bienvenu (1970); 4, Gottman (1979); 5, Noller (1980). Plus sign (+) indicates this item is evoked by the couple type. Minus sign (−) indicates that item is not clearly apparent.

Very briefly, let us outline the attributes of these couples. Traditionals hold conventional ideological values in relationships, favor a high degree of interdependence between marital partners, and report that they are expressive with their mates. Independents hold fairly nonconventional values about relational and family life, favor interdependence yet push for autonomy, and report that they are extremely expressive with their mates. Separates vacillate between conventional and nonconventional ideologies of family life, are not companionate with their mates, and report a distinct lack of expressiveness in their relationships. Importantly, research by Fitzpatrick and others suggests that not only do self-reports of couples' communicative behaviors differentiate meaningfully between the types, but that their actual exchange of messages can be observed objectively as predictive of the typology in both casual and conflict resolution situations (see Fitzpatrick in press; Fitzpatrick, Vance, and Witteman 1984). Figure 2 displays a fair number of these differentiating behaviors. Therefore, as earlier, it was our further hypothesis that laypeople may well hold cognitive representations of marital communication in accord with at least some of the findings relating to Fitzpatrick's typology, such that these stereotyped beliefs could feasibly bias listeners' linguistic judgments of an unfamiliar couple's talk in some settings in the directions of their relational identities (cf. Wilmot and Baxter 1983). Hence, items appearing in Figure 2 were also included as dependent measures in the study to follow.

Figure 2. Some communicational correlates of Fitzpatrick's typology also serving as predictions for the present investigation.

Items		Couple types:		
		Traditional	Independent	Separate
Showed affection	1a	++	+	+
Marital adjustment	2a	++	+	+
Agreed with each other	2a	++	–	+
Took partner into account	3a	++	+	–
Self-disclosed	3a	++	+	–
Husband (sounded) masculine	4a	+	+	++
Husband (sounded) feminine	4a	–	+	–
Wife (sounded) feminine	4a	+	+	–
Wife (sounded) masculine	4a	–	+	–
Talked frequently	5b	+	+	–
Cooperated in conflicts	5b	+	–	–
Negotiated verbally	6b	+	–	–
Flexible communication	7b	+	–	–
Vocal emotional tones negative	8b	–	+	–
Each partner tried to control the conversation	9b	–	++	– –
Complementary in communication style	10b	–	– –	+

Key. The letter <u>a</u> refers to findings from self-report studies, while <u>b</u> indicates behavioral observation studies. Numbers refer to the study in question, viz. 1, Fitzpatrick (1976); 2, Fitzpatrick and Best (1979); 3, Fitzpatrick (1977); 4, Fitzpatrick and Indvik (1982); 5, Fitzpatrick, Fallis, and Vance (1982); 6, Fitzpatrick, Tenney, and Witteman (1983); 7, Fitzpatrick (1983); 8, Sillars, Pike, Redman, and Jones (1983); 9, Williamson (1983); 10, Fitzpatrick (in press b). Plus sign (+) indicates that this item is evoked by the couple type, and double plus sign (++) indicates this is extremely so. Minus sign (–) indicates this item is not clearly apparent, and double minus sign (– –) suggests it is definitely not evoked.

To reiterate, the research questions prompting this exploratory research were: (1) would contextual information pertaining to marital adjustment-nonadjustment and Fitzpatrick's three 'pure' couple types have enough psycholinguistic reality to bias retrospectively listeners' judgments of a couple they had just heard talking on audiotape? and (2) would these reconstructions be in the direction of the linguistic and communicational profiles displayed in Figures 1 and 2?

Participants in our investigation were 244 undergraduates enrolled in an introductory communication class at a midwestern university. They were assigned randomly to one or other of our ministudies, viz. the marital adjustment, or the typology experiments. All participants listened to the same 90-second conversation between a young married couple concerning the purchase of a used automobile. The speaking roles of husband and wife were equalized to the extent that they engaged in the same number of floor switches and used the same number of words. In addition, the number of agreements and disagreements used by each spouse was not signifcantly different.

This conversation was pretested to determine whether the conversation itself revealed any information about the type of marriage of the conversants. Thirty-seven individuals, drawn from a pool of subjects similar to those who would be participants in the experiment proper, listened to the tape and completed 17 questions drawn from the RDI. On 14 of these, the pretesters saw the couple as not significantly different from the mid-points on these scales. In other words, we were satisfied that this conversation was emotionally neutral, although the remaining three items suggested listeners viewed the couple as nonconflict-ridden and traditional.

All participants in the main study listened to the stimulus tape in the knowledge that they would be required to answer questions about it subsequently. Immediately after having listened to the taped couple, and just prior to making a series of ratings along 9-point scales, listeners were provided with typewritten information about the couple (cf. Ball et al. 1982). In the marital adjustment ministudy, participants received descriptions of the couple as being either very satisfied or very dissatisfied with their marriage (see Spanier 1976), viz.:

> John and Susan want to stay together very much and have few intense or serious conflicts. They have never discussed separation or divorce. They are very satisfied with their marriage and tend to kiss one another every day.

> John and Susan do not want to stay together very much and have frequently discussed separation or divorce. They are very dissatisfied with their marriage and tend not to kiss one another every day.

In the typology ministudy, participants were provided with one or other of the following three paragraphs representing the basic marriage types (viz. traditional, independent, and separate, respectively).[1]

> John and Susan have very strong traditional values on marriage and family life. They share almost all aspects of their lives with one another. They have very regular daily time schedules and do not feel the need for private space in their home away from one another.

> John and Susan have very strong nontraditional values on marriage and family life. They share many, but not all, aspects of their lives with one another. They have irregular daily time schedules and feel the need for private space in their home away from one another.

> John and Susan outwardly have very traditional values about marriage and family life but often doubt these values. They share few aspects of their lives with one another. They have very regular daily time schedules and feel the need for private space in their home away from one another.

Recall now that all listener-judges had listened to exactly the same tape-recording of this couple talking. The only difference between the five subgroups of listeners was in the contextual information provided them concerning John and Susan. As can be seen from the foregoing, arguably few explicit details were provided raters about the couple's linguistic and communicational habits when talking together; this was particularly so for the typology ministudy. Having read this brief information, all participants were instructed to rate the language and communicational behaviors of the couple specifically as they had just heard them talk on tape on that particular occasion. These ratings were evinced by means of a 40-item questionnaire derived from Figures 1 and 2, and also included a large number of items relating to social evaluation (see Table 1 for a synopsis of most of these scales).

Let us now survey the results. A correlation matrix for the 40 dependent measures for all participants was submitted to a Principal Components Analysis to determine the number of factors utilized by raters. Cattell's Scree test suggested that five factors appeared to define this data set, accounting for 51% of the variance. The relatively small amount of variance accounted for here may well have been due to the very heavy cognitive demands placed on our respondents; that is, assessing a more or less bland conversation by means of 40 nine-point rating scales. Obviously, future work would profit from invoking an evaluatively less arduous judgmental task. A subsequent factor analysis using squared multiple correlations in the diagonals of the matrix, followed by a varimax rotation, yielded five interpretable factors which could serve as dependent measures, in addition to the individual item data, in further analyses (see Table 1).

The first factor was labelled 'social evaluation', and defined by such terms as: 'Would you like this couple as close friends?', 'Would you go to them for advice?', etc. The second factor was labelled 'negative communication style', and included items which viewed the couple as using negative voice tones with one another, engaging in cross-complaining sequences, etc. The third factor was labelled 'open communication style' and included such items as sharing thoughts and feelings, showing affection, and taking one another into account. The fourth factor was labelled 'cooperative communication style', and included items suggesting that the couple generally agreed with, and were positive about, each other. The fifth factor was labelled 'sex stereotyped voices' (see Smith 1980) and included items asking for evaluations of the masculine or feminine nature of the voices of the husband and wife on tape. (In subsequent data analyses, this factor was split into a masculine and feminine vocal judgment factor in order not to sum evaluations of the husbands and wives into one index.) Thus, the first factor that emerged was an overall evaluation of the dyadic identity presented by our couples while the other four factors dealt with the make-up of that identity. Respondents appeared to have little trouble in evaluating these couple identities or in seeing relationships among the component parts of these identities.

Table 1. Factors and item loadings.

Factor	Loading
(1) Social evaluation (eigenvalue = 6.79; 48.2% variance)	
Would you like to have a marriage like theirs?	.79
Would you like them as close friends?	.76
Would you go to them for advice?	.73
Would you discuss issues as they do?	.69
Do you think they are really compatible?	.57
Do you respect this couple?	.56
Do they seem a typical married couple to you?	.52
It is clear that this couple does not talk much together.	-.50
Do you think their marriage will last?	.47
(2) Negative communication style (eigenvalue = 2.68; 19% variance)	
This couple was generally negative toward one another.	.61
When she was discussing a problem with her husband, the wife had a negative tone.	.58
Each member of this couple tried to control the conversation.	.57
This couple engaged in 'cross-complaining sequences'.	.55
This couple was quick to reciprocate a negative remark of the spouse.	.53
This couple initially reciprocated positive remarks of the spouse, but later in conversation stopped doing so.	.46
The vocal emotional undertones of this couple were negative.	.45
This couple interrupted one another fairly frequently.	.37
(3) Open communication style (eigenvalue = 1.97; 14% variance)	
This couple took into account each other's feelings.	.65
This couple shared their thoughts and feelings with one another.	.63
Overall, this couple shows a high degree of marital adjustment.	.57
This couple showed their affection for one another.	.51
This couple verbally negotiated with one another.	.48
(4) Cooperative communication style (eigenvalue = 1.54; 10.9% variance)	
This couple was generally positive toward one another.	.43
This couple agreed with one another on most matters.	.41
This couple used a neutral tone of voice.	.40
Overall, this couple used far more agreement than disagreement statements.	.38
The interaction between this couple was extremely 'patterned' in that one remark can easily be predicted from another.	.38
This couple gave in to one another.	.33

Table 1 (continued).

Factor	Loading
(5) Sex stereotyped voices (eigenvalue = 1.12; 7.9% variance)	
Husband type:	
The husband in this marriage sounded masculine.	.56
The husband in this marriage sounded feminine.	-.57
Wife type:	
The wife in this marriage sounded feminine.	.63
The wife in this marriage sounded masculine.	-.57

Let us now examine the findings relating to the marital adjustment ministudy. Given that Hotelling's T^2 on this particular data set differentiated ratings of listeners in the adjusted and nonadjusted conditions ($p < .01$), one-way ANOVAs were computed for each of the six factors as well as for the individual items.[2] As can be seen from Table 2, a significant difference emerged on the social evaluation factor (i.e. factor 1), showing that listeners were more favorably disposed toward the adjusted couple. Table 2 also pinpoints the individual items of social evaluation which were also significantly disposed in this direction.

Table 2. Mean ratings and F values for listeners' judgments in the marital adjustment ministudy.

Dependent measures	Mean ratings*		F_s	P_s
	Adjusted couple	Nonadjusted couple	(df=1,108)	
Social evaluation	3.65	3.33	4.22	.04
Open communication	5.46	5.04	2.19	.14
Showed affection	3.18	2.18	6.38	.01
Marital adjustment	5.63	4.62	6.29	.01
Generally positive	6.12	4.93	8.70	.003
Generally negative	2.45	3.27	4.04	.04
Cooperated in conflict	7.16	6.40	4.84	.03
Made each other laugh	1.16	0.53	5.92	.01
Agreed with other	6.59	5.82	4.83	.03
Talked to frequently	4.98	3.85	4.41	.04
Went to for advice	2.98	2.03	4.90	.03
Really compatible	4.49	3.62	3.79	.05
Marriage will last	5.29	3.33	20.71	.0001

*The higher the mean rating, the more listeners perceived the dependent measures in question.

Although the overall mean values for open communication (factor 3) in Table 2 were not significantly different statistically, an examination of the means on the individual items indicates that listeners viewed the maritally adjusted as having a more 'open' (as well as 'cooperative') communication style (cf. Table 1).

Moving along to the typology ministudy, where an overall MANOVA on this particular data set differentiated ratings for the three couple types ($p < .01$), similar ANOVAs provided somewhat more extensive differences than the foregoing. As Table 3 indicates, both the factors of 'social evaluation' and 'open communication' were significantly different for the couple types. An examination of the individual items specifies this trend. Here, the traditionals were perceived to have shown more affection, were seen to be more adjusted, were generally more positive and hence less negative, cooperated in conflict, self-disclosed more, and were less likely to stop positive reciprocity cycles in their communication than the independents, who in turn were more 'open' and 'cooperative' (cf. Table 1) than were the separates. In addition, our respondents evaluated the traditionals significantly more favorably than the independents, who were in turn judged more positively than the separates.

Table 3. Meaning ratings and F values for listeners' judgments in the marital adjustment ministudy.

Dependent measures	Mean ratings*, couple type			F	P
	Traditional	Independent	Separate	(df=2,131)	
Social evaluation	4.13	3.14	2.71	3.06	.05
Open communication	6.21	5.66	4.89	14.35	.00
Showed affection	3.68	3.45	2.06	9.95	.0001
Marital adjustment	6.45	5.50	5.09	6.60	.002
Generally positive	6.30	6.13	5.40	3.59	.03
Generally negative	2.06	2.05	2.81	3.06	.05
Cooperated in conflict	7.58	6.87	6.75	3.54	.03
Took partner into account	6.58	6.00	5.62	3.31	.04
Self-disclosed	6.34	5.95	4.28	11.45	.0001
Stopped positive reciprocation	3.19	3.45	4.19	3.36	.04
Flexible communication	3.64	4.66	2.85	5.36	.005
Patterned communication	6.53	5.68	7.00	5.10	.007
Respected this couple	5.11	4.53	4.00	2.92	.05

*The higher the mean rating, the more listeners perceived the dependent measure in question.

In general, the differences emerging as statistically significant across both ministudies, although not numerous, are nonetheless striking and in line with our predictions. Interestingly, items not formally predicted on the basis of Figure 1 to differentiate adjusted and nonadjusted perceptions did emerge in Table 2 (e.g. 'made each other laugh'). Similarly, items not formally predicted to differentiate between the three couple types from Figure 2 also appeared in the perceptual profile of Table 3 (e.g. 'stopped positive reciprocation'). It appears therefore that speech stereotypes associated with different relational types may be conceptually distinct from the objective (and self-report) communication measures which differentiate them (see Moscovici and Hewstone 1983). Nevertheless, there is a good degree of isomorphism between the two. An exception emerged with respect to findings on the measures of flexibility and patterning of communication styles in Table 3. In line with previous observational research on the couple types (see Figure 2), the separates were viewed as the most rigid in their communication with the spouse. The predicted differences for the traditionals and the independents, however, did not occur. Indeed, the traditionals were viewed by our respondents as more rigid and patterned in their communication than were independents. In the couple realm, this may be akin to the phenomenon of 'psychological convergence but linguistic divergence' introduced in the first section of this paper (see Thakerar et al. 1982). The patterns which emerge in the stereotype of the various relationships do not reflect what occurs linguistically when the interaction of actual couples is analyzed. Although psychologically our respondents link the conservative ideological orientation in marriage and family life of the traditionals to a rigid communication style, linguistically such rigidity does not occur in traditional dialogues with a spouse. Similarly, the independents are not as flexible as they seem to our respondents.

Respondents did converge, however, on questions concerning the frequency of certain communicative behaviors (e.g. self-disclosures, generally positive). Only on questions concerning interaction did reactions shift away from our predictions. Our respondents, and perhaps couples themselves, may not notice and store interaction patterns but rather respond to the frequency of occurrence of specific communicative behaviors. When respondents, and again couples themselves, evaluate dyadic encounters, they may remember only first-order acts (he said/she said) and not the complex strings of interaction favored by observational researchers. The relationships between self-reports, behavioral frequencies, and interaction patterns in the minds of those evaluating couple identities may differ from actual relationships among these factors in couple communication. Such questions will be of obvious import for future work in this realm.

It is our belief that if the taped conversation had been less 'bland', with the couple evincing a little more interpersonal conflict and tension, retrospective speech halo effects may well have permeated other judgmental dimensions as well (e.g. the negative communication factor). We also think that, had the contextual information regarding couple types been introduced prospectively rather than retrospectively, similar findings would have emerged (see Snyder 1981). Indeed, our previous research on this phenomenon at the individual level (Thakerar and Giles 1981; Ball et al. 1982) supports such a contention. Therein, listeners had an opportunity of hearing the stimulus tape a second time, with the chance to modify their ratings in an additional phase of these experiments. On both occasions, respondents re-rated in a manner identical to their original, and biased, linguistic judgments. Obviously, future work should orient itself to discover the communicational and social environments which attenuate and accentuate the relational retrospective speech halo effects found herein. Moreover, it would be interesting to determine whether superimposing linguistic and communication behaviors in Figure 2 onto an emotionally neutral conversation between spouses would induce raters to see them along the lines of Fitzpatrick's typology (see Bradac 1983); our guess is that they would.

Two important findings emerge from this study for our present purposes. First, listener-judges appear able to form linguistic judgments along an interesting set of constructs (see Table 1) of a couple as a relational unit. This is a far cry from the individual speaker/monologue paradigm of language attitudes with which this paper started. Indeed, it is our contention that very often we do not listen to the linguistic forms and meanings of partners of a cohesive dyad as separate individuals; we process their message 'as a couple' (cf. Pearce and Conklin 1979). Second, what we think we know about couples can lead us sometimes to hear them as such. Or rather, this contextual information can evoke relational speech stereotypes which admittedly, within certain limits, may form a template for constructing and reconstructing our linguistic impressions of them (cf. Snyder 1981).

The foregoing study was presented as a mere illustration of the type of research that is needed if we are to explore the social meanings of linguistic forms in a relational context. Obviously, we have just scratched the surface empirically, and a whole plethora of more consequential studies loom on the horizon, enabling us to tap the complexity and richness of a couple identity approach to language behaviors. Yet, our findings on how couple identity can cognitively mediate our relational language attitudes allow us the luxury of speculating briefly about how language forms and other social behaviors are likewise affected. When few objective standards are available for comparison, individuals compare themselves to similar others to see how they are faring (Festinger 1954; Suls and Miller 1977). Tajfel (1974) has extended such interpersonal comparisons to the intergroup level. We hereby suggest that intercouple comparisons are also prevalent and psychologically informative. Hence, we track the linguistic and nonlinguistic behavior of other couples to help us to define the state of our own relationship, or even relationships. Our data seem to indicate, furthermore, that individuals eschew as standards of evaluation or comparison any couple judged to be having any type of relational difficulty. At the same time, however, such a comparison may cognitively bolster our own relationship's sense of worth and vitality. Yet, it may be that once a couple is judged by members of a social network as experiencing relational stress, they are cut off from social contact. When the public couple identity is damaged, internal relational difficulties may be further exacerbated, because the couple is cut off from their external social support networks.

There are good reasons for believing that such a postulated couple comparison process is utilized extensively to help us define the oft-quoted 'meaningfulness' of our relationships, and 'where we are at'. As Berger and Bradac (1982) point out, while there are literally hundreds of terms for describing individuals—and we would add for describing groups—there are few for couples. This lack of categorical language for describing relationships may only add to the problems we have in decreasing cognitive uncertainty about our relationships. Numerous researchers (e.g. Duck and Sants 1982) remind us that such uncertainty is high not only at the beginning of a relationship but at many phases throughout the development and dissolution of a relationship. Ragan and Hopper (1984) proffer the intriguing suggestion that certain fiction provides us with the fodder for our supposed idiosyncratic 'love talk'; after all, who drills us into our 'sweet nuthins'? Feminists and others interested in the construction of social reality through talk often warn of the difficulty of not having terms to describe interpersonal experiences. Consider the ontological dilemma of an unhappily married individual who has only exceedingly happy TV and real life couples against whom to compare his or her own relationship. We can only speculate that the ramifications of these comparisons for the satisfaction and stability of his or her own evaluated relationship are negative ones.

In our thinking about couple identities, we have been influenced by two major theoretical perspectives: the Meadian (1934) perspective which holds that other individuals' reactions to us can in time determine our own view of our personal identities; and self-presentational theory (Goffman 1959; Tedeschi 1981) which sees people actively attempting to manage and influence others' impressions of them. Obviously, an important means of achieving such ends is via verbal strategies (Tedeschi and Reiss 1981), vocal patterns (Giles and Street in press), and communicator styles (Norton 1983). We would desire explicitly to extend these analyses also from their personal bases into the couple identity arena. In other words, in parallel with couple comparison processes, we feel that others' reactions to our own relationships can in time determine our views of them (see Milardo, Johnson, and Huston 1983). But we can be highly active in determining the nature of this process by presenting what 'we', at least, regard as a valued couple identity through language behaviors. Such dyadic presentations can be fundamental to our couple identity in many social networks. This 'couple talk', as implied earlier, will be a function of the type of relational identity the partners wish to espouse. For instance, managing a couple image of 'still being madly in love after all these years' could be effected through expressed egalitarian roles, shared involvements, and joint achievements; mutual expressions of trust and integrity, use of private codes and taken-for-granteds, overt nonverbal indices of affection, an attentive, empathic communication style, politeness and conversational synchrony, etc., etc. Needless to say, effecting a couple presentation of marital distress, or of 'independence', would be differently managed, linguistically.

Such impression management occurs in good times and also in bad ones. Duck (1982) implicitly discusses couple presentation, albeit of a grossly different ilk, at the end of a relationship. His so-called 'grave dressing phase' allows couples to effect a public, socially appropriate scenario where often mutual blame for the relationship is accorded. This allows both partners to disengage from the couple identity to a personal identity as well. Negotiating the change from a couple identity to a personal one may present difficulties for both relational outsiders and for insiders. Often, we see and know others only as members of a couple. When we meet them unexpectedly in another context, we find it difficult sometimes to operate communicatively at a personal identity level (Wiemann, personal communication). Communication therefore might be awkward at times until interactants have negotiated which identity is to predominate in a given interaction. Furthermore, interacting without one's spouse or partner physically present does not necessarily imply that the relationship is not paramount when one is talking to a third party. In the same way as a cognitive definition of group membership allows one to act in accord with it thousands of miles away from other group members (Giles and Johnson 1981; Turner 1982), so, too, we can effect couple talk when separated from our partner. In such instances, couple identity could mediate individual linguistic choices through 'we...'-related topics, references to 'our' activities, and an 'us' focus manifest in expressedly shared attitudes and couple- (rather than self-) disclosures.

Finally, the importance of recognizing the powerful mediating influence of couple identity is also evident in its capacity to induce different dimensions of contextual construing. And on this note, we have returned full circle near to where we started at the outset of this paper. For example, the situational parameters defining a supposedly formal interaction between unknown, different individuals will of necessity be quite different if these strangers define the context as an intergroup one, and different again if they negotiate a romantic or even sexual relationship (Rands and Levinger 1979; Forgas and Dobosz 1980).

Conclusion. Our message has been this. It is true that context affects language attitudes and linguistic forms, and examples were drawn from our work in this respect. However, we advocate expending more research effort on exploring the ways in which personal attitudes and perceptions of others' speech and the situation we are in (not to mention a host of other construals, such as subjective norms; see McKirnan and Hamayan 1984; Giles and Street in press) cognitively mediate the social meanings of language behaviors. Yet, an important development beyond this approach is to extend our understanding of the linguistic implications of the contextually based notion of group identity. We have argued that cognitive mediators of ingroup identification, as well as intergroup belief structures, have important linguistic correlates and consequences. Finally, we envisaged a 'relational vacuum' in current language research and have begun flushing this out empirically in a judgmental vein whilst speculating about its significance in production processes. Exciting prospects are therefore ahead, not least of which will ultimately be mapping out how people shift linguistically back and forth between their personal, group, and couple identities sequentially, and conceivably, how they maintain these different identities simultaneously by means of different linguistic features and communicational devices. As we have emphasized elsewhere on a number of occasions, a social psychological approach to the study of meaning, form, and context is but one cog in the language and society wheel. There are many others. Sometimes, like a figure ground illusion, a social psychological analysis comes to the fore; at other times (and often), it is in the faded background of explanatory power. As you may have surmised from this paper, or from a general reading of the social psychology of language and communication science more generally, we are desperately in need of linguistic input and sophistication in our analyses of language data and in our theoretical models. But we do believe that through its methodologies, techniques, instruments, and theories, a social psychological complement has the potential for linguistic applications too. The time is ripe for us to move beyond routinized multidisciplinarian service to a truly interdisciplinary context for language study, not only in form, but also in our shared meanings.

Notes

Further information on all aspects of this study, including more detailed statistical data, can be obtained from the second author. We are grateful to Diane Badzinski, Scott Broetman, Jane Byrne, and Hal Witteman for their invaluable assistance in material preparations, recordings, data collection, and analyses. This investigation was designed and the data collected when the first author was Brittingham Visiting Professor in Communication Arts, University of Wisconsin-Madison. We are also grateful to James Bradac, Jane Byrne, Dorothy Krueger, Tony Mulac, and John Wiemann for their helpful and constructive comments on an earlier draft of this paper.

1. Since this was our initial exploration into this particular domain, only the 'pure' types were examined. Future research will consider 'mixed' (stimulus) types as well as explore the implications of varying listener-judges' own relational identity types and marital experiences.

2. In order to determine which ratings were meaningfully and significantly different from each other within each of the two ministudies, appropriate statistical tests were applied to the raw data. These were Hotelling's T^2, analysis of variance (ANOVA), and multivariate analysis of variance (MANOVA).

References

Altman, I., and D. Taylor. 1973. Social penetration: The development of interpersonal relationships. New York: Holt, Rinehart, and Winston.

Ball, P., J. Byrne, H. Giles, P. Berechree, J. Griffiths, H. Macdonald, and I. McKendrick. 1982. The retrospective speech halo effect: Some Australian data. Language and Communication 2.277-84.

Ball, P., H. Giles, and M. Hewstone. 1984. The intergroup theory of second language acquisition with catastrophic dimensions. In: The social dimension: European developments in social psychology. Edited by H. Tajfel. Cambridge: Cambridge University Press.

Beebe, L. M. 1981. Social and situational factors affecting the communicative strategy of dialect code-switching. International Journal of the Sociology of Language 32.139-49.

Bell, A. 1982. Radio: The style of news language. Journal of Communication 32.1:150-64.

Berger, C. R., and J. J. Bradac. 1982. Language and social knowledge. Baltimore: Edward Arnold.

Berger, P., and H. Kellner. 1975. Marriage and the construction of reality. In: Life as theater: A dramaturgical handbook. Edited by D. Brisset and C. Edgley. Chicago: Aldine.

Bienvenu, M. 1970. The measurement of marital communication. Family Coordinator 19.26-31.

Bochner, A. P., and D. L. Krueger. 1979. Interpersonal communication theory and research: An overview of some inscrutable epistemologies and muddled concepts. In: Communication Yearbook 3. Edited by D. Nimmo. New Brunswick, N.J.: Transaction.

Bolton, C. D. 1961. Mate selection as the development of a relationship. Marriage and Family Life 23.234-40.

Bourhis, R. Y., H. Giles, and D. Rosenthal. 1981. Notes on the 'Subjective Vitality Questionnaire'. Journal of Multilingual and Multicultural Development 2.145-55.
Bourhis, R. Y., and I. Sachdev. (1984) Subjective vitality perceptions and language attitudes in Hamilton. Journal of Language and Social Psychology 3.97-126.
Bradac, J. J. 1983. The language of lovers, flovers, and friends: Communicating in social and personal relationships. Journal of Language and Social Psychology 2.141-62.
Brown, B. L. 1980. Effects of speech rate on personality attributions and competency evaluations. In: Language: Social psychological perspectives. Edited by H. Giles, W. P. Robinson, and P. M. Smith. Oxford: Pergamon.
Brown, B. L., H. Giles, and J. N. Thakerar. 1983. The effects of accent, speech rate and context on the attributions of a speaker's personality characteristics. Mimeo. Psychology Department, Brigham Young University, Provo, Utah.
Brown, P., and S. Levinson. 1979. Social structure, groups and interaction. In: Social markers in speech. Edited by K. R. Scherer and H. Giles. Cambridge: Cambridge University Press.
Caporael, L. 1981. The paralanguage of caregiving: Baby talk to the institutionalized aged. Journal of Personality and Social Psychology 40.876-84.
Creber, C., and H. Giles. 1983. Social context and language attitudes: The role of formality-informality of the setting. Language Sciences 5.155-61.
Duck, S. 1982. A topography of relationship disengagement and dissolution. Personal relationships 4. In: Dissolving personal relationships, vol. 2. Edited by S. Duck. London: Academic Press. 141-62.
Duck, S., and H. Sants. 1982. On the origin of the specious: Are personal relationships really interpersonal states? Journal of Social and Clinical Psychology 1.27-41.
Festinger, L. 1954. A theory of social comparison processes. Human Relations 7.117-40.
Fishman, J. A. 1966. Language loyalty in the United States: The maintenance and perpetuation of non-English mother tongues by American groups. The Hague: Mouton.
Fitzpatrick, M. A. 1976. A typological approach to communication in relationships. Unpublished Ph.D. dissertation, Temple University, Philadelphia.
Fitzpatrick, M. A. 1977. A typological approach to communication in relationships. In: Communication Yearbook 1. Edited by B. Rubin. New Brunswick, N.J.: Transaction.
Fitzpatrick, M. A. 1983. Predicting couple's communication from couple's self-reports. In: Communication Yearbook 7. Edited by R. Bostrom. Beverly Hills, Calif.: Sage.
Fitzpatrick, M. A. (in press a) A typological approach to marital interaction: Recent theory and research. Advances in Experimental Social Psychology.
Fitzpatrick, M. A. (in press b) A typology of relationships. Journal of Communication.

Fitzpatrick, M. A., and P. Best. 1979. Dyadic adjustment in traditional, independent, and separate relationships: A validation study. Communication Monographs 46.167-78.
Fitzpatrick, M. A., S. Fallis, and L. Vance. 1982. Multifunctional coding of conflict resolution strategies in marital dyads. Family Relations 31.61-70.
Fitzpatrick, M. A., and J. Indvik. 1982. The instrumental and expressive domains of marital communication. Human Communication Research 8.195-213.
Fitzpatrick, M. A., B. Tenney, and H. Witteman. 1983. Compliance-gaining in marital interaction. Paper presented at the International Communication Association Conference, Dallas.
Fitzpatrick, M. A., L. Vance, and H. Witteman. (1984) Interpersonal communication in the casual interaction of marital partners. Journal of Language and Social Psychology 3.81-96.
Forgas, J. 1983. Language, goals and situations. Journal of Language and Social Psychology 2.267-93.
Forgas, J., and B. Dobosz. 1980. Dimensions of romantic involvement: Towards a taxonomy of heterosexual relationships. Social Psychology Quarterly 43.290-300.
Garfinkel, H. 1956. Conditions of successful degradation ceremonies. American Journal of Psychology 61.420-24.
Giles, H., ed. 1977. Language, ethnicity and intergroup relations. London: Academic Press.
Giles, H., ed. 1984. The dynamics of speech accommodation. International Journal of the Sociology of Language 46.
Giles, H., and R. Y. Bourhis. 1976. Black speakers with white speech--a real problem? In: Proceedings of the 4th International Congress of Applied Linguistics, vol. 1. Edited by G. Nickel. Stuttgart: Hochschul Verlag.
Giles, H., R. Y. Bourhis, and D. M. Taylor. 1977. Towards a theory of language in ethnic group relations. In: Language, ethnicity and intergroup relations. Edited by H. Giles. London: Academic Press.
Giles, H., and J. L. Byrne. 1982. An intergroup model of second language acquisition. Journal of Multilingual and Multicultural Development 3.17-40.
Giles, H., and J. R. Edwards, eds. 1983. Language attitudes in multilingual settings. Journal of Multilingual and Multicultural Development 4 (2 and 3).
Giles, H., C. Harrison, C. Creber, P. M. Smith, and N. H. Freeman. 1983. Developmental and contextual aspects of British children's language attitudes. Language and Communication 3.141-46.
Giles, H., and M. Hewstone. 1982. Cognitive structures, speech and social situations: Two integrative models. Language Sciences 4.187-219.
Giles, H., and P. Johnson. 1981. The role of language in ethnic group relations. In: Intergroup behavior. Edited by J. C. Turner and H. Giles. Chicago: University of Chicago Press.
Giles, H., D. Rosenthal, and L. Young. (in press) Perceived ethnolinguistic vitality: An Anglo/Greek-Australian setting. Journal of Multilingual and Multicultural Development.

Giles, H., and B. Saint-Jacques, eds. 1979. Language and ethnic relations. Oxford: Pergamon.
Giles, H., and R. L. Street, Jr. (in press) Communicator characteristics and behavior: A review, generalizations, and model. In: Handbook of interpersonal communication. Edited by M. Knapp and G. R. Miller. Beverly Hills, Calif.: Sage.
Goffman, E. 1959. The presentation of self in everyday life. Garden City, N.Y.: Doubleday.
Gottman, J. 1979. Marital interaction. New York: Academic Press.
Gottman, J. 1982. Emotional responsiveness in marital conversation. Journal of Communication 32.108-20.
Gumperz, J. J. 1982. Language and social identity. Cambridge: Cambridge University Press.
Hopper, R., M. Knapp, and L. Scott. 1981. Couple's personal idioms: Exploring intimate talk. Journal of Communication 31.23-33.
Hymes, D. 1967. Models of the interaction of language and social setting. Journal of Social Issues 23.8-28.
Johnson, P. 1984. Language and ethnicity: Welsh/English context. Ph.D. thesis, Bristol University.
Johnson, P., H. Giles, and R. Y. Bourhis. 1983. The viability of ethnolinguistic vitality: A reply to Khan and Husband. Journal of Multilingual and Multicultural Development 4.255-69.
Kahn, M. 1970. Nonverbal communication and marital satisfaction. Family Process 9.449-56.
Kitsuse, J. I. 1962. Societal reactions to deviant behavior: Problems of theory and method. Social Problems 9.247-56.
Krueger, D. L. 1982. Marital decision-making: A language-action analysis. Quarterly Journal of Speech 68.273-87.
Krueger, D. L., and P. Smith. 1982. Decison-making patterns of couples: A sequential analysis. Journal of Communication 32.121-34.
Labov, W. 1966. The effect of social mobility on linguistic behavior. Social Inquiry 36.186-203.
Lederer, W. J., and D. D. Jackson. 1968. The mirages of marriage. New York: Norton.
Lewis, R. A., and G. Spanier. 1979. Theorizing about the quality and the stability of marriage. In: Contemporary theories about the family: Research-based theories, vol. 1. Edited by W. Burr, R. Hill, F. I. Nye, and I. R. Reiss. New York: Free Press.
Lofland, J. 1966. Deviance and identity. Englewood Cliffs, N.J.: Prentice-Hall.
McKirnan, D. J., and E. J. Hamayan. (1984) Speech norms and attitudes toward outgroup members: A test of a model in a bicultural context. Journal of Language and Social Psychology 3.21-38.
Mead, G. H. 1934. Mind, self and society. Chicago: Chicago University Press.
Milardo, R. M., M. P. Johnson, and T. L. Houston. 1983. Developing close relationships: Changing patterns of interaction between pair mates and social networks. Journal of Personality and Social Psychology 44.964-76.
Mishler, E., and N. Waxler. 1968. Interaction in families. New York: Wiley.

Moscovici, S., and M. Hewstone. 1983. Social representations and social explanations: From the 'naive' to the 'amateur' scientist. In: Attribution theory: Social and functional extensions. Edited by M. Hewstone. Oxford: Blackwell.
Myers, D. G., and H. Lamm. 1976. The group polarization phenomenon. Psychological Bulletin 83.606-27.
Noller, P. 1980. Misunderstandings in marital communication: A study of couples' nonverbal communication. Journal of Personality and Social Psychology 39.1135-48.
Noller, P. 1982. Channel consistency and inconsistency in the communications of married couples. Journal of Personality and Social Psychology 43.732-41.
Norton, R. 1983. Communicator styles: Theory, applications, and measures. Beverly Hills, Calif.: Sage.
Pearce, W. B., and F. Conklin. 1979. A model of hierarchical meanings in 'indirect responses'. Communication Monographs 46.75-87.
Platt, J., and H. Weber. 1984. Speech convergence miscarried: An investigation into inappropriate accommodation strategies. International Journal of the Sociology of Language 46.131-46.
Price, S., M. Fluck, and H. Giles. 1983. The effects of language testing on bilingual preadolescents' attitudes towards Welsh and varieties of English. Journal of Multilingual and Multicultural Development 4.149-61.
Ragan, S. L., and R. Hopper. (1984) Ways to leave your lover: A conversational analysis of literature. Communication Quarterly.32.
Rands, M., and G. Levinger. 1979. Implicit theories of relationship: An intergenerational study. Journal of Personality and Social Psychology 37.645-61.
Rausch, H., W. Barry, R. Hertel, and M. Swain. 1974. Communication conflict and marriage. San Francisco: Jossey-Bass.
Roloff, M., and C. R. Berger. 1982. Social cognition and communication. Beverly Hills, Calif.: Sage.
Romaine, S. 1980. Stylistic variation and evaluative reactions to speech: Problems in the investigation of linguistic attitudes in Scotland. Language and Speech 23.213-32.
Ryan, E. B., and C. M. Bulik. 1982. Evaluations of middle-class speakers of standard American and German-accented English. Journal of Language and Social Psychology 1.51-61.
Ryan, E. B., and H. Giles, eds. 1982. Attitudes toward language variation: Social and applied contexts. Baltimore: Edward Arnold.
Ryan, E. B., H. Giles, and M. Hewstone. 1984. Language and intergroup attitudes. In: Attitudinal judgment. Edited by J. R. Eiser. New York: Springer Verlag.
Ryan, E. B., H. Giles, and R. J. Sebastian. 1982. An integrative perspective for the study of attitudes toward language variation. In: Attitudes toward language variation: Social and applied contexts. Edited by E. B. Ryan and H. Giles. Baltimore: Edward Arnold.
Sillars, A. L., G. R. Pike, K. Redman, and T. S. Jones. 1983. Communication and conflict and marriage: One style is not satisfying at all. In: Communication Yearbook 7. Edited by R. Bostrom. Beverly Hills, Calif.: Sage.

Smith, P. M. 1980. Judging masculine and feminine social identities from content-controlled speech. In: Language: Social psychological perspectives. Edited by H. Giles, W. P. Robinson, and P. M. Smith. Oxford: Pergamon.

Snyder, M. 1981. On the self-perpetuating nature of social stereotypes. In: Cognitive processes in stereotyping and intergroup behavior. Edited by D. L. Hamilton. Hillsdale, N.J.: Lawrence Erlbaum Associates.

Spanier, G. B. 1976. Measuring dyadic adjustment: New scales for assessing the quality of marriage and other dyads. Journal of Marriage and the Family 38.15-28.

Spiegelberg, H. 1973. On the right say 'we': A linguistic and phenomenological analysis. In: Phenomenological society. Edited by G. Psathas. New York: Wiley.

Stephenson, G. M. 1981. Intergroup bargaining and negotiation. In: Intergroup behavior. Edited by J. C. Turner and H. Giles. Chicago: University of Chicago Press.

Stewart, M. A., and E. B. Ryan. 1982. Attitudes toward younger and older adult speakers: Effects of varying speech rates. Journal of Language and Social Psychology 1.91-109.

Street, R. L., Jr., R. M. Brady, and W. B. Putman. 1983. The influence of speech rate stereotypes and rate similarity on listeners' evaluations of speakers. Journal of Language and Social Psychology 2.37-56.

Street, R. L., Jr., and H. Giles. 1982. Speech accommodation theory: A social cognitive model of speech behavior. In: Social cognition and communication. Edited by M. Roloff and C. R. Berger. Beverly Hills, Calif.: Sage.

Street, R. L., Jr., and R. Hopper. 1982. A model of speech style evaluation. In: Attitudes towards language variation: Social and applied contexts. Edited by E. B. Ryan and H. Giles. Baltimore: Edward Arnold.

Suls, J. M., and R. L. Miller. 1977. Social comparison processes. New York: Wiley.

Tajfel, H. 1974. Social identity and intergroup behavior. Social Science Information 13.65-93.

Tajfel, H., ed. 1978. Differentiation between social groups. London: Academic Press.

Tajfel, H., ed. 1982. Social identity and intergroup relations. Cambridge: Cambridge University Press.

Tajfel, H., and J. C. Turner. 1979. An integrative theory of intergroup conflict. In: The social psychology of intergroup relations. Edited by W. C. Austin and S. Worchel. Monterey, Calif.: Brooks Cole.

Taylor, D. M., and L. Royer. 1980. Group processes affecting anticipated language choice in intergroup relations. In: Language: Social psychological perspectives. Edited by H. Giles, W. P. Robinson, and P. M. Smith. Oxford: Pergamon.

Tedeschi, J. T., ed. 1981. Impression management theory and social psychological research. New York: Academic Press.

Tedeschi, J. T., and M. Reiss. 1981. Verbal tactics of impression management. In: Ordinary language explanations of social behavior. Edited by C. Antaki. London: Academic Press.

Thakerar, J. N., and H. Giles. 1981. They are--so they spoke: Noncontent speech stereotypes. Language and Communication 1.255-61.
Thakerar, J. N., H. Giles, and J. Cheshire. 1982. Psychological and linguistic parameters of speech accommodation theory. Advances in the social psychology of language. Cambridge: Cambridge University Press.
Turner, J. C. 1982. Towards a cognitive redefinition of the social group. In: Social identity and intergroup relations. Edited by H. Tajfel. Cambridge: Cambridge University Press.
Turner, J. C., and R. J. Brown. 1978. Social status, cognitive alternatives and intergroup behavior. In: Differentiation between social groups. Edited by H. Tajfel. London: Academic Press.
Wiemann, J. M., and C. W. Kelly. 1981. Pragmatics of interpersonal competence. In: Rigor and imagination: Essays from the legacy of Gregory Bateson. Edited by C. Wilder-Mott and J. H. Weakland. New York: Praeger.
Williamson, R. 1983. Relational control and communication in marital types. Ph.D. thesis, University of Wisconsin-Madison.
Wilmot, W. W., and L. A. Baxter. 1983. Reciprocal framing of relationship definitions and episodic interaction. Western Journal of Communication 47.205-17.
Wish, M. 1978. Dimensions of dyadic communication. In: Nonverbal communication. Edited by S. Weitz. New York: Oxford University Press.

COMMUNICATIVE COMPETENCE REVISITED

John J. Gumperz
University of California, Berkeley

In this paper I seek to develop arguments first made in 'The linguistic bases of communicative competence', presented at the 1981 Georgetown University Round Table on Languages and Linguistics (Gumperz 1981). The earlier paper made an initial attempt to explore some of the theoretical consequences that arise when we analyze discourse coherence from a speaker-listener oriented interactive perspective. The question can be put as follows: what does an interactive approach to communication, in which problems of understanding are studied not in terms of meanings inhering in a given text or stretch of discourse, but rather as outcomes of inferential judgments made in the course of situated processes of conversational exchange, imply for our theories of communication and language use?

Conversing, as we all know, is a cooperative activity that involves active participation and coordination of moves by two or more participants in the joint production of talk. There are good reasons to believe that such coordination presupposes verbal abilities and types of knowledge that are not as yet fully understood. Neither the theoretical linguists' grammatical analyses, nor the commonly accepted sociolinguistic studies that seek to formulate rules of language usage covering what can be said when and under what circumstances, can account for this knowledge. Nor do notions of schema or script defined in static terms as extralinguistic knowledge of the world explain how such information enters into discourse understanding.

When we look at problems of understanding from a participant's perspective, we see that what we must explain are on-line processing strategies. Conversationalists employ strategies in inferring the contextual presuppositions about what is expected in an encounter. Related strategies are also used in segmenting the stream of talk into information or idea units, in determining the transition-relevant points for turn taking, and in integrating what is said at various points in time into coherent themes. Empirical investigations of conversational exchanges have led to the discovery that in making the judgments relevant to these tasks, participants depend on their own perception of stylistic and prosodic signalling cues that have hitherto not been seen as having semantic import, and that are, thus, not ordinarily covered in sentence-level linguistic analysis. These features of speech performance are processed in accordance with contextualization conventions that retrieve schematic information and make it available as an input into the interpretive process.

My claim is that the capacity to contextualize, and thus make sense of what is heard in terms of what is already known, is governed by cognitive abilities that share many of the characteristics of grammatical competence. They are conventional in nature, learned as part of the everyday language socialization processes, and once internalized, they are usually employed automatically without conscious reflection. In principle, therefore, these processing abilities should be analyzable by in-depth qualitative methods similar to those employed in grammatical analysis. But conversational processes also have special characteristics of their own that derive from the very nature of conversations as multiparty interactive performances. These properties require us to look at the multiplicity of linguistic signs involved in conversing from a different perspective.

To begin with, although it is true that all conversations are governed by general and in large part universal organizing principles, these principles operate in a manner that is quite different from the operation of all-or-none categorical grammatical rules. Conversational principles, as Levinson (1983) has argued, are defeasible; that is, they do not determine what counts as an utterance in a language, or what can, or cannot, be said or understood. On the contrary, they act as guidelines or standards of evaluations that give rise to expectations which, when violated, generate the implicatures on which rests interpretation of so much of what a speaker intends to convey.

Second, the phonetic, prosodic, and stylistic cues that participants in face-to-face encounters rely on in contextualizing their performances, are typically quite fleeting or transitory in nature. Since the relevant information is not coded in lexical form, it becomes hard to retrieve after the event. It cannot easily be communicated in contexts other than those in which it originally occurs, so that recalling what was actually perceived at any one time for the purpose of later analysis and preservation of information in the form of adequate transcripts, presents a major problem. In fact, until about ten years ago, when unobtrusive means for recording everyday talk first became available, we simply did not have the data necessary for systematic investigation.

Thus, while theory suggests good reasons to believe that in-depth methods of analysis patterned on those employed in the study of spoken language can yield insights into conversational processes not otherwise obtainable through quantitative correlational techniques, the phenomena to be studied also present by their very nature serious empirical and analytical problems. It seems clear that although conversationalists build on phonological, syntactic, and semantic knowledge in contextualizing what they hear, contextualization conventions are as distinct from sentence-level linguistic rules as phonology is from syntax, and syntax from semantics. They must therefore be analyzed on their own terms.

What, then, does a qualitative, participant-centered approach to the study of conversational phenomena entail? In arguing for methods of analysis patterned on those employed in linguistics, I mean to suggest that the analytical goals must parallel the linguist's concern with structural determinants of grammaticality. In other words, conversational analysis should focus on the conditions that make possible shared interpretation, rather than seeking to predict correct or appropriate usage. For this reason, I proposed that the notion of communicative competence be redefined as: 'The knowledge of discourse processing conventions and related communicative norms that participants must control as a precondition to being able to enlist and sustain conversational cooperation.' In what follows I would like to discuss what this approach to communicative competence implies for the study of the issues of meaning, form, and use in context that form the subject of this Round Table, and for enabling us to integrate into the study of discourse processing and discourse understanding the ethnographer's insights into culture and cultural variability and context.

Let me begin with some background. The notion of communicative competence was first proposed by Hymes in the context of the 1960s debate on the limits of formalization in linguistics. In order to highlight the role that cultural and linguistic variability play in speaking, Hymes argued that communication in the sense of engaging in meaningful interaction with others is a function of membership in a speech community, and not simply a matter of grammatical competence. Speech communities are human collectivities held together by shared history and long-term participation in networks of relationship. Ethnographic evidence shows that such communities are frequently not identical with collectivities defined by control of grammatical rules (Gumperz 1972). We cannot therefore assume that our studies become more socially relevant by correlating sentence-level linguistic categories with independently determined social variables. The extent to which culture is shared in relation to speaking must be empirically determined by examining the norms, values, and ecological constraints on behavior as they function in human groups.

Yet no matter how we select the population units to be studied, patterns of language usage are never quite uniform. Apart from individual performance factors, language usage varies with boundaries of class, gender, ethnic allegiance, power relationships, and education. All these are factors which, in the rapidly changing societies of today, are often quite resistant to measurement. Even in small communities that appear as relatively homogeneous, economically and socioculturally uniform entities to the outsider, detailed ethnographic studies tend to reveal sharp divisions among members who do, and members who do not, share a sense of local identity. Thus, models of analysis that assume the existence of clear, stable social boundaries will necessarily have difficulty in specifying the social motivations of language behavior.

There are at least two interrelated and partially independent dimensions of variabilities that we must account for in the study of cultural sharing: the societal and the contextual. A major concern of ethnography of communication has been to clarify the relationship between linguistic and sociocultural categories through comparative studies along both of these dimensions. Given the facts of variability, a human community defined in purely geographical terms cannot be the unit of analysis for this comparative endeavor. Ethnographers of communication therefore chose to focus on speech events, culturally defined units of interaction bounded in time and space, such as ritual performances, ceremonies, public meetings. Such culturally sanctioned units of social interaction stand apart from everyday talk, and thus form a convenient starting-point for studying the interplay of social and linguistic aspects of communicative behavior. To account for the role of culture and social norms in speaking, it seemed useful to treat events as if they were miniature social systems, that is, as if one could speak of norms of conduct, constraints on choice of communicative content and on roles that participants can play, which function like the norms of human communities. The goal of speech event analysis was to formulate rules of appropriateness showing how speaker's choice from a range of stylistically alternate expressions relates to the norms governing behavior in such events.

The data obtained in this type of study have been important in providing basic background information on hitherto little understood sources of variability in speech form, as well as in speech function, and in demonstrating that the analysis of linguistic form cannot ultimately be abstracted from cultural considerations. But the information we have so far tells about the role of cultural factors in what Hymes calls the communicative economy of human groups. It specifies the knowledge that is potentially available, but does not tell us what aspects of this knowledge are actually used in communicative situations, and how they are brought into the communicative process to affect the interpretation of what transpires. If the claim that cultural knowledge forms part of communicative competence is to have anything more than metaphorical significance, we have to find ways of looking at verbal data that enable us to work out empirical procedures for testing hypotheses about how our understanding of what is said at any one point is affected by culture. For this reason we need more detailed insights into how verbal encounters actually work.

By far the largest and most exhaustively described body of information on conversation comes from the work of sociologists working in the ethnomethodological tradition. Ethnomethodologists were the first to look at conversation as social action. Their studies provide empirical evidence to show how the sequential organization of turns at speaking can serve to constrain conversationalists' ability to make themselves understood, to introduce, establish, and change topics, and otherwise to affect the course of a conversation. But their goals were quite different from the ethnographer's concern with showing that sociocultural factors are important in communication. Their work must be understood within the context of the internal sociological debate over the empirical validity of commonly accepted social science generalizations. Symbolic interactionists, for example, tended to limit their analysis of human encounters to categories of roles, statuses, and motives, derived from theory alone, without raising the question of the relationship of theory to practice. To bring out the limitations of this type of a priori theorizing, verbal data were collected to provide empirical evidence of how social control was exerted in everyday interaction.

Since speech act analysis could be seen as an instance of such a priori theorizing, its social premises were clearly unacceptable. Instead, ethnomethodologists focused on everyday talk which lacked the formal constraints that characterized the ritual and ceremonial occasions that speech act analysts tended to study. As Schegloff (1981) puts it:

> Quite aside from whatever individual cognitive or processing achievements might be involved, the production of a spate of talk by one speaker is something which involves collaboration with the other parties present and that collaboration is interactive in character and interlaced throughout the discourse. That is, it is an ongoing accomplishment rather than a pact signed at the beginning after which discourse is produced entirely as a matter of individual achievement. The character of this interactional accomplishment is at least in part shaped by the sociosequential organization of participation in conversation, for example, by its turn taking organization...

I want to argue here that while the sociosequential organization of speakers' moves is as basic to conversational analysis as clause boundaries are to syntax, conversational analysts have gone only part way to giving us an understanding of conversational processes. What they have done is to give us some of the basic constraints that affect the working of conversational processes in societies of all kinds. But these constraints, like the linguist's grammatical rules, are in large part universal and thus abstracted from actual situations of usage. To see how communication works on the ground, we cannot look at organizational features of communication alone, but we must look in detail at the actual processes of conversational inference, that is, the situated interpretations that participants make of each other's moves at any one point in time. Let me illustrate with an example of the type commonly analyzed by conversational analysts.

(1) Making arrangements for lunch (Levinson 1983:316-17).

1. R: Why don't we all have lunch
2. C: Okay so that would be in St Jude's would it?
3. R: Yes (0.7)
4. C: Okay so:::
5. R: One o'clock in the bar
6. C: Okay
7. R: Okay?
8. C: Okay then thanks very much indeed George ===
9. R: ===All right
10. C: //See you there
11. R: See you there
12. C: Okay
13. R: Okay // bye
14. C: Bye

This exchange constitutes the concluding portion of an encounter, the rest of which is not reproduced here. R proposes a luncheon meeting and C accepts. They agree on a time and place and then say good-bye. What readers of the transcripts are likely to find odd is the form of the leave-taking and the amount of time it takes. The substantive portion of the event is completed in six turns while the departing formalities extend over eight turns, more than half of the total sequence. C's Okay in turn 6 is followed by R's Okay, pronounced with question intonation. This evokes a formulaic expression of gratitude on C's part, presumably an allusion to some favor obtained. R's acknowledgment in 9 is followed by a simultaneous exchange of see you there, followed by another set of Okay and a set of bye.

Levinson (1983:316-17), in discussing this example, suggests that it might reflect a common general schema for closing sections, consisting of four basic stages: (1) a closing down of some topic, such as the making of arrangements in turns 1-5; (2) one or more passing turns (turns 6 and 7); (3) a typing of a call followed by a further exchange of pre-closing items; (4) a final exchange of terminal elements. Yet neither Levinson in his discussion of ethnomethodological approaches to conversations, nor Schegloff and others who have done the primary research, deal with the theoretical status of such notions as schema and negotiation. Nor do they raise the question of how findings from the empirical study of situated conversational exchanges can be integrated into what we know about discourse understanding.

Most reports of conversational analysts' findings take the form of empirical statements about patterned features of language usage occurring in a variety of conversational texts that can be shown to have a significant effect on the course of an interaction. The most frequently cited examples of such regularities are the so-called adjacency pairs: question-answer, greeting-acknowledgment, offer-acceptance, and the like. In characterizing the regularities which underlie the occurrence of such pairs, Sacks and Schegloff (1973) suggest that they reflect conversational rules such as the following: having produced the first part of some pair, the current speaker must stop speaking and the second speaker must at that point come up with a second part. Yet the status of such rules is not made clear. Does the schema of example (1) reflect such a rule? Given Schegloff's view of conversation as an 'ongoing accomplishment', which in large part is created by the local sequences of moves and countermoves, we would not want to say that we are dealing with a fixed script that applies to sequences of all kinds. Such a script would hardly require negotiation of transitions. Moreover, sequences such as conversational closings, extending as they do over a number of moves, are context- and to some extent culture-specific; thus they contrast with adjacency pairs, which occur in conversations of all types.

A more reasonable position, and one that does not inherently conflict with the conversational analysts' basic arguments, would be to assume that schemata such as the one Levinson suggests specify knowledge acquired through previous communicative experience of what could potentially happen in situations like the one at hand. The actual on-line processing and production strategies through which the closing sequence is produced could then be regarded as the outcome of local inferential processes to which schematic knowledge is one of several inputs. A closer examination of both the form and the content of the moves and countermoves that make up the exchange provides some insights into the workings of this inferential process.

After R's confirmation of the meeting in turn 3, the encounter is interrupted by a pause. C then continues the interaction with <u>Okay so:::</u> R's answer in 5 indicates that he interprets this as a request for more information. C's <u>Okay</u> confirms this interpretation. When R follows with a questioning <u>Okay?</u>, C counters with his formulaic expression of gratitude, which is then confirmed by R's <u>all right</u>. What do R and C have to know in order to respond in such a way as to have their moves understood? Seen in purely referential perspective, turns like <u>Okay so:::</u> and <u>Okay</u> can perhaps be regarded as contentless. But the form in which they are spoken--that is, both the elongated vowel and the question intonation used--does have communicative import. They can be paraphrased as queries like: is there anything else to be said? In turn 5 the answer is affirmative, whereas in turn 8 it is negative.

In arguing that message form communicates, I do not mean to say that features such as prosodic contours have meanings. As Bolinger (1972) points out, intonation contours are not meaningful elements in the linguist's sense of the word. What we are talking about here are context-bound judgments; such judgments build on schematic knowledge generated through previous talk, as well as knowledge of contextualization conventions, grammatical and semantic knowledge, and participants' understanding of the sociosequential positioning of the utterance at hand. These are matters of discourse-level interpretations, not matters of meaning as such.

Examples (2) and (3) provide some further insights into the linguistic and interactional nature of these interpretive processes.

(2) Secretary (B) talking to recently appointed research assistant (A), who has just entered the building.

1. A: Good morning.
2. B: Hi John.
3. A: Howdi.
4. B: How're ya doin'.
5. A: Fine... ah... do you know... did you get anything back on those forms ah... you had me fill out?
6. B: Hm... like what?
7. A: I wondered if they sent you a receipt or anything or a copy of
8. B: ⌞You mean your employment forms?
9. A: Yea.
10. B: Yea, I kept a copy. Why is there a question?
11. A: 'Cause I just left it with the Anthropology Department.
12. B: Oh, that's O.K., they'll just send them over to L and S and they'll send them on.
13. A: O.K., because the chairman wasn't there and...
14. B: Oh, she called me later... I guess it was you. She said that a student had been over and that she was just going to hold on to the forms and then send them. And she sent you on, you know... She told you to go ahead and leave them and not wait around.
15. A: I just wanted to make sure they're O.K.
16. B: Oh yea. Don't worry about it.

The opening of this encounter is an example of what ethnomethodologists have called a presequence. The second of the two greeting exchanges is treated as a bid for further talk. The remainder of the interaction is typical of informal office enquiry or information sequences. A wants to know if his employment forms have been processed and B answers by telling him something about what the procedures are. Yet, even though the exchange, when seen in its entirety, seems familiar, the way in which the two participants go about carrying out the activity makes it seem highly unlikely that either of them has approached the encounter with a predetermined plan or script. On the contrary, the interaction moves forward step by step. Each move is replied to and evaluated before the next one is initiated.

The initial exchange through which entry into the encounter is negotiated also sets the tone for what follows. When B counters A's rather formal <u>good morning</u> with an informal <u>hi</u>, A follows suit and B continues in the same informal mode. It appears that they have agreed upon a tone of informality which is then maintained throughout the encounter. Note that while sequential organization is crucial in the negotiation process, this informality and the indirectness it entails also make demands on the participants' ability to infer information not directly reflected in the lexical content of what is said. After A's somewhat vague enquiry in line 5, B asks for more clarification. When A's reply is similarly vague, she guesses that he is referring to his employment forms. Her guess is confirmed and she assumes he wants to know if she kept a copy of the forms in her office. Her misunderstanding is cleared up through further indirect inferences without overt reference to the need for repair. A's statement that the chairman was absent then evokes a narrative description of what happened with the form. Throughout the interaction, A has pursued a strategy of not providing detailed information and relying on A's ability to guess. Why he should do this is outside the scope of this analysis. Yet what is important is that speaker and listener are able to make these indirect inferences and have them understood, and that they do this by appealing to shared knowledge of previous interactions and to organizational knowledge of the workings of the university administration.

(3) An excursion (Falk 1979).

1. P: Yeah ⌈where'd you go, where'd you all go.
2. J: Well, y'wanna tèll em, where we wént?
3. R: We went uh... almost éverywhere, except that it was fòggy, for half the time we were over thẹre
4. M: Yeah, you don't sẹem too enthusiàstic about it.
5. R: ⌈Oh it was a good trìp, yeạh, it wạs, yẹah.
6. J: Well, ⌈it was a gréat trìp. except that it was a fòggy day. and we started out by going to Twin Pèaks,.. at 9:30

```
                in the mǒrning. ..on a fǫggy day. you know what we sáw,
                we saw fŏg, ͺup to here.
 7.   R:                       ⌞We saw a fi̋re down the hill.
 8.   J:                                          ⌞A fire
                down the hill, that's right.
 9.   R:                    ⌞There was a (f  ) was on fi̩re.
10.   P:   That was good (    ).
11.   J:                      ⌜And then after the fŏg, and it was wi̩ndy,
                we.. decided to go to the bęach. we went to the beạch
                and it was, we saw some sea lions, though,
12.   R:                                     ⌞There were=
13.   J:                                        Then we had=
      R:   =about thrę̧e.
      J:   =ho.. hǫt dogs on a stick.
14.   M:                          ⌞uh-huh.
15.   R:   Sǒme of them. sǒme of them, had hǫt dogs on a sti̋ck.
16.   M:   (            ) Hi G. (G. enters)
17.   J:   Hi G.. . and uh, we uh.. , talked (    ) about the tǒurists
                there.  and we lęft, and went to the Pạlace,.. of the
                Legion of Honǒr. ri̋ght?
18.   R:                       ⌞Again, for a view of the Golden
                Gạte.
19.   J:           ⌞For a view, of the Gǒlden Gate Bridge.  and there=
20.   G:                                  ⌜Aaaaah.
      J:   =was no vi̋ew.
```

The following transcription conventions are used in this example:
    ˵ low falling contour   ˋhigh falling contour
    ˏ low rising contour   ˊhigh rising contour
(The preceding accent marks are doubled for extra loudness.)
    ⌜register shift upward   ⌞register shift downward
    acc accelerated tempo   ⌉latching
    ( ) unintelligible speech

The content of this exchange readily identifies it as an informal narrative. Two ESL instructors, J and R, have taken a group of students on an excursion to San Francisco to see the sights and are telling their colleagues about the trip. Yet the structural characteristics we normally associate with narrative are nowhere overtly marked. There is, for example, no overt introduction, no initial summary statement of what the trip was about. In response to the question as to where they went, R answers we went almost everywhere, and then goes on to say that while it was foggy it was a good trip. J then makes the transition into the substantive part of the narrative by first repeating R's statement, and then shifting to slow rhythm and starting to list the things they did. The exchange has some of the characteristics of a picaresque narrative, inasmuch as the action moves forward by the way things are said, rather than by what is said. The trip is described in a manner that seems unusually vague and lacking in detail. Mention is made of some of the sites visited (such as Twin Peaks, the beach, and the Palace of the Legion of Honor), of what they saw (a fire, fog, sea lions) and of what they ate (hot dogs on a stick). There is no attempt to explain what is interesting about all this. Considering the fact that speakers and audience are all local residents, the list sounds strangely uninformative. Yet no one queries the account or asks for more detail. On the contrary, in line 10, after the third mention of the fire, P remarks that was good.

All this seems at first to be a violation of Gricean principles of relevance. It is only in lines 13-17, where we in J's statement we had hot dogs on a stick is corrected by R to some of them, that we begin to see the significance of this apparent violation of Gricean principles of relevance: even though J and R speak in the first person plural, the story is not being told from the narrators' perspective, but from the students' perspective. There is nothing in the surface form of the description to indicate this.

Note, also, that the narrative is not one person's performance: it is jointly produced by J and R. The transcript reveals many instances of what Falk (1979) has called duetting, where two speakers complete each other's thoughts so that their utterances together make up a single turn at speaking. For example, R's we saw a fire... in line 7 is latched to J's ...up to here in 6. That is, the two follow each other without the rhythmic interval that normally marks transitions between turns. The same is true for J's line 8 and R's lines 9 and 12. Lines 17-19 are similarly cooperative, although there is no latching. Furthermore, J and R regularly employ parallel syntactic constructions: their lexical choices are stylistically congruent, with one person often anticipating what the other has to say. It would be difficult to imagine that two individuals could be as successful at managing this type of cooperation, and entering into the spirit of what the other intends to convey, without shared frames of reference and some level of shared culture.

The three examples illustrate the role that turn-taking and negotiation of situated interpretations play in everyday encounters. But they also show that conversing involves more than context-free principles of sequentiality that can be applied by anyone who knows the language. Participants do not enter into the negotiation process relying only on their command of grammar and lexicon. The ability to enter into conversations, that is, to fit one's contributions into locally established themes and lines of argumentation, depends on largely indirect inferential processes which draw on knowledge of the world to make sense of what is said.

Culture enters into this process in two ways. It is an integral component of what discourse analysts call schematic knowledge. Although we customarily think of schemata as ways of organizing factual information in terms of basic conceptual structures, conversational analysis shows that assumptions about norms, interpersonal relationships, and interactive or communicative goals are also involved. When seen in this perspective, schemata come to take on forms that bear great similarity to the ethnographer of communication's speech events, in that they reflect values and experiences acquired through participation in culturally bounded networks of social relationships. The difference is that they do not predict action or determine judgments of what is appropriate. They must be seen as cognitive constructs that give rise to expectations about what is to be looked for in an encounter, which in turn enter into our interpretations of what transpires.

Cultural background and culturally channeled interactive experience also determine the acquisition of the contextualization conventions by virtue of which the choice among various performance features acquires situated significance, for example, the choice between <u>hi</u> and <u>good morning</u> in example (2), the prosodic contour of <u>okay</u> in (2), the pausing, utterance latching, and pitch register and tempo alternations that mark all three conversations.

It must be emphasized that what we are talking about here are not context-free meanings. Interpretations can be seen as the outputs of inferential processes, which have as their input knowledge of lexicon, schemata, and control of contextualization conventions. Note that while grammatical knowledge and control of the basic lexicon is shared, other conventions entering into conversational inference are differentially distributed in accordance with social and occupational boundaries, and communicative experience. It is the interplay or tension between context-free, clause-level linguistic competence, on the one hand, and situation and subculturally specific knowledge of the discourse level conventions that enter into communicative competence, on the other hand, and the implication of this interplay for learning and understanding in everyday communicative situations, that promise to become one of the most fruitful areas for future sociolinguistic research.

References

Bolinger, D.L., ed. 1972. Intonation. Harmondsworth, England: Penguin.
Falk, J. 1979. The duet as a conversational process. Ph.D. dissertation, Princeton University.
Gumperz, J.J. 1981. The linguistic bases of communicative competence. In: Georgetown University Round Table on Languages and Linguistics 1981. Edited by Deborah Tannen. Washington, D.C.: Georgetown University Press. 323-34.
Gumperz, J.J., and D. Hymes, eds. 1972. Directions in sociolinguistics. New York: Holt, Rinehart and Winston.
Levinson, S. 1983. Pragmatics. Cambridge: Cambridge University Press.
Sacks, H., and E. Schegloff. 1973. Opening up closings. Semiotica 7.4:289-327.

Schegloff, E. 1981. Discourse as an interactional achievement: Some uses of 'uh-huh-' and other things that come between sentences. In: Georgetown University Round Table on Languages and Linguistics 1981. Edited by Deborah Tannen. Washington, D.C.: Georgetown University Press. 71-93.

PHONOLOGICAL STYLE IN BILINGUALISM: THE INTERACTION OF STRUCTURE AND USE

Susan Gal
Rutgers University

1. Various types of massive language change, such as pidginization, creolization, language acquisition, and language death have become particularly interesting for recent linguistic theories, not only because of what they promise to reveal about human cognitive processes, but also because they occur as responses to equally great changes in the social use of linguistic varieties (Halliday 1973, Hymes 1971, Slobin 1977). My aim in this paper is to clarify the complex relationship between linguistic structures and social uses by looking at how one of these factors changes in relation to changes in the other. In a bilingual community undergoing language shift, as one of the languages expands in use, the other language is utilized for ever fewer communicative tasks in an ever narrower range of social contexts and in ever fewer role relationships. Such a community, therefore, provides a partially controlled situation in which to examine how speakers' knowledge of a linguistic variety is affected by limitations on the opportunities and motivations for its use. Thus this study differs from most of the research on the effects of bilingualism on linguistic structure because it does not investigate the influence of the two linguistic systems on each other (interference), but explores instead the effects on linguistic structure of different patterns and contexts of use.

I propose to show that, in the first-learned but less used language, stylistic variation in phonology is often substantially simplified during language shift. However, in studying the interdependence of use and structure it is just as important to outline the social and communicative constraints as to describe the formal linguistic consequences or correlates. Therefore, I look to speakers' patterns of language use and of social interaction, as well as the social meanings of their linguistic choices, in order to understand why for some bilinguals phonological style is narrowed in their first-learned language while for other bilinguals it is not.

Emphasizing differences between bilinguals within a single community allows me the opportunity to point out yet another way in which the quasi-theoretical notion of the 'native speaker' is problematical. The 'native speaker' has long been a useful theoretical idealization which fuses the idea of exposure to a language from birth with the quite different concept of a natural or complete command of a language. No matter how common the cooccurrence of these two phenomena actually is, it is important to emphasize that conceptually they are distinct and not inseparably mated. The language one acquires in early childhood is not necessarily the same as the language one later learns to speak with facility and expressive power. The two are united or divorced by historical contingencies. It is these, and not any linguistic factors, which determine whether or not speakers have access to the social contexts and institutions in which phonological styles gain their rhetorical effectiveness. Fusing the two allows us to see language largely as a cognitive phenomenon and thus slight the role of history and social structure in the formation and loss of linguistic skills by individuals and communities. Another aim of this paper, then, is to highlight the disjunction veiled by the 'native speaker' concept by showing stylistic reduction in a language that is learned first, used daily, but is limited in its social functions.

'Stylistic reduction' implies a definition of style. This is a thorny issue, even in the relatively straightforward and narrow case of phonological variants (see Romaine and Traugott 1981, Irvine 1979). Here I have taken a strategic approach which implies that in attempting to gauge a speaker's stylistic repertoire the analyst is required to understand the meanings, intents, and effects of choices between referentially equivalent phonological variants. It is not enough to note the components (e.g. setting, participants, topic) of the situations in which variants occur.

While many broadly stylistic strategies which are well documented for bilinguals, such as code-switching, will not be considered directly in this paper, the phonological styles which are the focus here have an importance of their own. It should be remembered that a reduction in phonological styles is not simply dispensable icing missing from the language cake. From the point of view of linguistic structure, studies by Labov (1972a) and others on sound change show that stylistically significant variation is centrally involved in the structural rearrangement of phonological systems. From the point of view of the speaker, such variation, while referentially neutral, is necessary in conveying essential social meanings about the identity of the speaker and the nature of the social situation. Further, Gumperz's work (1982; Blom and Gumperz 1972) indicates that such variation can also be used to express momentary communicative intent, so that in a community that uses them, speakers without phonological styles may, in some circumstances, sound less subtle verbally and risk social misunderstanding.

Recent studies of language death, working within a broadly functionalist framework, have adopted a form of the research strategy I have outlined here. They have selected and compared speakers within a single bilingual community who know the nearly obsolescent language to different degrees. The works of Dorian (1981) on East Sutherland Gaelic, Hill and Hill (1977) on Nahuatl, and Dressler (1972, Dressler and Wodak-Leodolter 1977) on Breton have been exemplary in examining the grammatical and lexical structures used by speakers of such languages. But, although Hill and Hill (1978) have explored changes in honorifics, there has been little attention paid to the possibility of changes in the variable, stylistic part of the phonological system.[1]

The few studies which have addressed this issue are variationist analyses of bilingual repertoires.[2] The most relevant work is Lavandera's (1978) paper showing that in their second language, Spanish, a community of Italian migrants in Buenos Aires fails to exploit one of the most salient phonological variables. These fluent bilinguals use only one variant of a phonological variable which, in its several realizations, marks socioeconomic status and formality of the speech event in the speech of Spanish monolinguals. Lavandera argues convincingly that since these bilinguals have available the strategy of switching between languages to express nonreferential meanings that monolinguals must express through phonological styles, their phonological styles remain undeveloped in their second language. However, it is important not to assume from this that we are dealing with a structural complementarity between two kinds of stylistic expression, such that where one exists the other will not survive. Rather, I suggest that such complementarity is but one of several sociohistorical possibilities. The differentiation of phonological styles is absent in some cases of bilingualism, even in a <u>first</u> language, as I will show. And language-switching is used by such bilinguals to express social meanings. However, my evidence suggests that the simple availability of language-switching as a stylistic device does not in itself entail lack of phonological range. In fact, some bilinguals exploit both language-switching and phonological variation for stylistic effects. The difference between those who do and those who do not is their location in the community's social structure and the consequent role and meaning of each language in their daily communication.

2. The Hungarian-German bilingual neighborhood in which this study was done is located in a town within Austria very near the border of Hungary. For about 400 years it has been one of three Hungarian-speaking enclaves completely surrounded by German-speaking villages. But only in 1921 did the area actually become part of a German-speaking polity. At that time the territory, which had previously been part of Hungary, was attached to Austria. Today, although the town itself is largely German-speaking, the neighborhood of about 2,000 people is bilingual, in a variety of ways. Both German and Hungarian are in daily use within the Hungarian section of town. All bilinguals have Hungarian as a home language; most read German newspapers. Hungarian reading material is extremely scarce. All listen to German radio and TV. Many older people also listen to Hungarian radio, but although Hungarian TV is available at a slight expense only some musical and sports events attract large numbers of bilingual viewers.

Importantly, speakers are divided by education: those over about 35 have Hungarian, those under 35 German elementary schooling. From 1921 until 1955 the local elementary schooling was conducted in Hungarian but with German lessons. By the early 1950s some bilingual parents were sending their children to a German-language school. After 1956 all schooling was conducted in German and optional weekly Hungarian lessons were not instituted until the late 1960s. Another political note of lingustic importance is that the Hungarian border was virtually closed to traffic in labor, goods, and tourists from the end of World War II until the late 1960s. Only in the last decade has the crossing into Hungary been relatively free of red tape.

The material discussed in what follows is part of a larger participant-observation study that also included systematic collection of information about the language usage patterns and social networks of a sample of speakers chosen to represent a range of age, occupation, and network type within the bilingual neighborhood.[3] The phonological styles of 20 of these speakers will serve to illustrate some of the patterns found in the community. The usage of these speakers does not exhaust the variation in phonological styles in the bilingual neighborhood, but it does represent two major patterns. Since it is the social experiences of speakers that are to be related to their linguistic strategies and abilities, it will be essential here to outline the social histories of these speakers. I will concentrate on two factors: (1) their social identities as indexed by age, occupation, and some aspects of their social networks; and (2) their patterns of choice between German and Hungarian.

The 20 speakers can be divided into two age groups, with men and women represented in each. The 10 older speakers range in age from 69 to 84 years. The younger speakers range from 23 to 40 years. This age difference provides an accurate indication of acquisition history and occupation. All speakers learned Hungarian first at home. The younger group started learning German by the age of five, either in nursery or from parents and siblings. The older group started to learn German by about the age of 12 or 15, usually by being sent to a nearby German village to serve as farmhand or domestic servant. The older people are farmers, now mostly retired, and each has been or still is active in some way in the local church or government. Those in the younger group all come from farming families, but have a range of occupations: farmer, housewife, several waitresses, several salespeople, a hairdresser, chauffeur, bookkeeper, postal worker. The important thing about these mostly service occupations is that they do not differ enough in income, conditions of work, or prestige to create barriers of status or social network among the young people. Many of the occupations require exclusive use of German on the job. These young people also take a relatively active role in public life, mostly in church activities or in clubs and volunteer rescue squads.

What separates the younger group from the older most decisively is their pattern of language use. Those in the younger group use Hungarian only to their parents (and this not always) and to those in their grandparents' generation. With their siblings, age-mates, work-mates, spouses, and children they use German, even if these people are themselves bilinguals. In sharp contrast, those in the older group use Hungarian to everyone except, of course, monolingual German speakers with whom they must interact in service encounters or in the state bureaucracy, and sometimes with their own grandchildren.

All speakers sometimes engage in conversational language-switching, using German remarks in an otherwise Hungarian interaction for communicative effect. All the cases of such language-switching which I have analyzed in this community can be interpreted as the juxtaposition of 'low, in-group' and 'high, out-group' codes, to allow inferences of, for instance, interpersonal authority or expertise, or to deliver the final winning retort in a hostile exchange. These interpretations depend on the fact that within the bilingual neighborhood Hungarian now tends to carry connotations of peasant agriculture and the past, while German is decidedly the more prestigious language related to mobility out of agriculture into wage labor and education (see Gal 1979).

The present source of prestige for German is both economic and political. Although older people remember a time when Hungarian was the langauge of the cultural and political elite and was used in schools and offices, the language of the town's well-to-do business and professional stratum is now German, and German is also the language now supported by virtually all educational and other state institutions.[4] The current difference in prestige between the two languages is reinforced by a widespread fear of Hungarian communism and by the substantial difference in standard of living between Austria and Hungary which occasional tourist trips to Hungary make evident to everyone. In addition, there is the often hostile reaction of German monolinguals to the use of Hungarian in their presence and even to Hungarian accents. For the younger group, which has moved out of agriculture and which has no experience of Hungarian as a prestige language, the use of Hungarian is much more limited, and more limited in value, than for the older group. In sum, the two age groups contrast in their history with the languages and in the range of social relationships in which they now use Hungarian. They could as well be labeled the broad users and the narrow users.

3. Before the speakers can be compared, it is necessary to describe their linguistic varieties and the methods used in this study to assess speakers' stylistic ranges. Although interviews in German were also conducted, I restrict the analysis here to the Hungarian portion of the repertoire.

The local forms of Hungarian constitute a relatively divergent dialect of Hungarian which nevertheless shares many features with other western Hungarian dialects, but also shows the centuries-long influence of German. A likely example of the latter is the frequent loss of the voiced/voiceless distinction in final stops, matching the lack of this distinction in the surrounding German dialects (Keller 1961). An example of the former is the virtually universal use of a long high front vowel [i] where standard Hungarian has a long mid front vowel [e] (Imre 1971). Many of the differences between standard Hungarian and the local forms show no variation between speakers and between situations. They are easy to spot on a single visit, sound regional to the urban Hungarian, and identify the speaker as provincial.

More important for my purposes, however, were those features of the local Hungarian dialect which seemed to carry social meaning for the speakers themselves: what Labov (1972a) has called 'markers'. The candidates were those local forms which had been mentioned in earlier descriptions of the dialect but which I did not hear in my first weeks of field work, when my initial contacts were limited to church-related public events and interviews with older speakers. This indicated that some local forms are not ordinarily used by older speakers in speech to outsiders such as myself or to occasional visitors who speak Hungarian. I

Phonological style in bilingualism / 295

first noticed the local forms of these variables in conversations I overheard between family members and neighbors. This is, of course, the classic situation in many European dialects where the more standard forms take on, by association with their urban users and their contexts of use, connotations of publicness, outsideness, and the particular kind of prestige associated with education and social mobility (Trudgill and Chambers 1980). Notice that there is a parallel here with some of the contrasting connotations of German and Hungarian.

In attempting to record systematically, I first wanted to create a situation in which the seriousness, publicness, and on-recordness or outsideness of the circumstances would give speakers the motivation--indeed, the interactional responsibility--to present themselves as people aware of the wider world.[5] The interviews were arranged well ahead, the microphone was placed in front of the speaker, who was asked to use Hungarian. The speaker and I were usually alone. The topics included opinions and information about current public issues and policies, the high divorce rate, child-rearing ideals, the significance of ethnicity, the consolidation of land, the mechanization of farming, as well as life histories. But what distinguished these events from other interactions more than anything else was the distribution of rights and duties among participants. I asked all the questions and selected topics; interruptions and overlaps were extremely rare, as were disagreements. I had the powerful role of generally defining the situation. They, on their part, had consented to the interview and, thus, to consciously presenting themselves convincingly as spokespersons, even authorities about public or historical affairs, to a foreigner. I dwell on these fairly obvious aspects of the interview situation in order to convince you that these sessions were, indeed, occasions on which speakers would have several overlapping strategic reasons to use standard forms.

There are indications that speakers did respond in this way to the constraints of the occasion. As one might expect, metalinguistic awareness was high during interviews for young as well as old speakers. People corrected themselves if they started to use dialect words which are widely known to be restricted in distribution, or recent German loans that are otherwise in common use. People sometimes declined to answer some questions and jokingly or irritatedly rebuffed some inquiries, but no one overturned the structure of the situation itself--for instance, by taking over the questioner's role, or changing the topic. Sensitivity to the overlapping constraints was also apparent in a negative way when one speaker, an elderly woman, announced at the start of the interview that although other people would probably talk szíp 'pretty' to me under these circumstances, she was not about to try. She did not, and thus was an exception among older speakers, while at the same time explicitly affirming the general social expectation.

To tap the use of local forms was more difficult for me, largely because of my identity as an outsider and my standard speech. All of these barriers were lifted somewhat on my third and fourth visits. But from the first, I tried a variety of tactics which would neutralize my presence: leaving the tape recorder on a kitchen table or sideboard and walking out; asking young people to take my tape recorder when visiting their relatives and friends; and mostly, of course, hanging around so that conversations which developed around me did not always include or focus on me. Needless to say, these tapes show very different interactional rights and obligations among participants. Quite other identities than local authority were linguistically claimed and defended. There are the interruptions, overlaps, arguments, laughing, and desultory talk common among people who have known each other for their entire lives and meet frequently.

Many situations I was able to tape were neither interviews nor such family-centered conversations. But I am isolating these two types of events because they are circumstances in which, for strategic as well as normative reasons, different linguistic forms would seem to be appropriate. Although subtler uses of style shifting also occurred within situations, the global contrast between these two kinds of interaction was particularly strong and therefore revealing for my purposes.

4. I compared older and younger speakers by examining their use of three phonological variables. In Figure 1, a line indicates a single speaker, connecting his/her percentage of local forms in the interview with his/her percentage of local forms in the conversation. 'I' indicates interview and 'C' refers to a tape of several family members and/or neighbors in their kitchens or porches, in which I was either not present at all or was barely spoken to. None of these tapes have the question/answer structure and role distribution which characterize the interviews.

Variable 1 in Figure 1 is (gy/dzs) and its voiceless counterpart (ty/cs), written here in standard Hungarian orthography. In each pair the first is the standard value, a palatal stop [ɟ, c], and can occur in initial, intervocalic, and final positions. The local forms are more affricates than stops and are strongly fronted to alveolar position [dʒ, tʃ]. Because in final position standard [ɟ] is sometimes softened to a glide by urban standard speakers of Hungarian as well as bilinguals, this was also counted as a standard form. In addition, when in final position and followed across the word boundary by the palatoalveolar fricatives [ʃ],[ʒ], or affricates, the palatal stops regularly assimilate to the fricative's place of articulation for all speakers. These environments were therefore omitted from the count, as was the indefinite article which ends with a palatal stop (egy) but has its own particular alternations. No further linguistic constraints were evident.

Notice that on Variable 1, the older speakers go from 30-50% local forms in the interviews to more than double that in the conversations, while the younger people show virtually no increase. What is more, the percentage of local forms the young people use in the interviews is often as high as the percentage that the older people use in conversations.[6]

Variable 2 is the separable verbal prefix el in its two realizations. The prefix means 'away' or 'off' and is also a marker of completed action. The local form includes an initial glide with systematic dropping of [l] before consonants: standard [εl] or [ɛ], local [jε] or [jæ]. The older people show a clear situational difference, often going from virtually no dialect forms in the interview to 50-90% local forms in the conversations. The young people make no systematic contrast between situations. For some young people the percentage of local forms in the interviews is as high as the percent used by many older people in conversations.

Figure 1. The percent of local forms for three phonological variables in the Hungarian of bilinguals.

1.1 Variable 1. gy/dys, ty/cs

1.2 Variable 2. Separable verbal prefix el/je

1.3 Variable 3. The definite article a/e

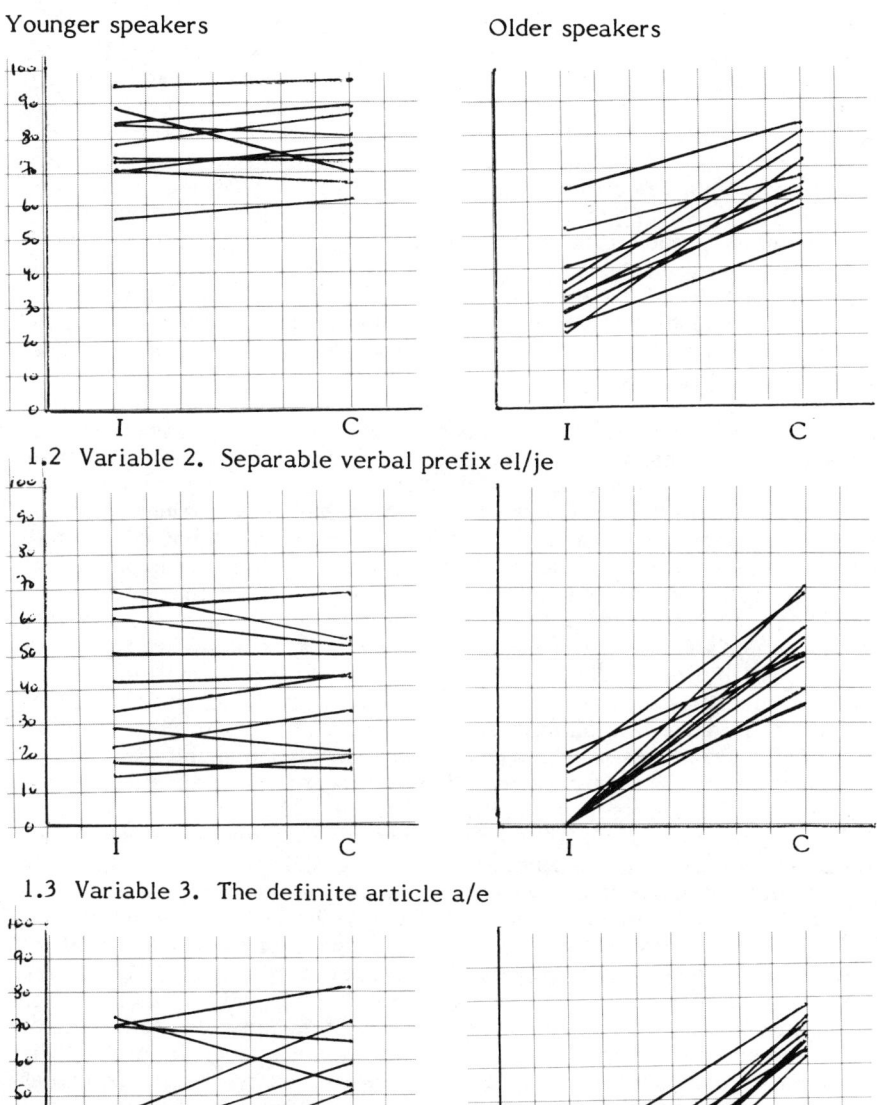

Variable 3 is the definite article (a/e) which is realized as the low back vowel [ɒ] or [ɒz] before vowels in the standard form, and is raised and fronted to [ɛ] locally. The situational pattern of the older people is clear. Among the young people, none makes a marked distinction between situations and some use as high a percentage of dialect forms in the interview as the older speakers use in conversations.

Another way to look at the quantitative distinctions between the two groups of speakers is to compare the amount of difference between interview and conversation for each group for each variable. If the old people distinguish the situations in their phonological styles and the young people do not, then the difference between the scores for the two situations should be considerably greater for the old than the young. For variable 1, the young group's range of difference between situations is 1-7%, the older group's 13-48%. For variable 2, the young group's range of difference between situations is 1-14%, the older people's 28-78%; for variable 3 it is 1-28% for the young people and 39-66% for the older speakers. In none of the three variables do the ranges of the two groups overlap. These differences are strong enough to make statistical tests of significance unnecessary.

Several other variables show the same pattern: the stylistic differences in phonology which are clear among the older speakers do not appear systematically for the younger speakers. We can see from their variable use of both local and standard forms that the young people know the forms themselves. Contrary to my earlier expectations, and the results reported by Lavandera (1978), their usage does not completely eliminate one stylistic variant. Rather, what they lack is the pattern of shifting styles which conveys both the tone of the situation and the presentation of self. If there is a regularity and significance to these young people's choice among Hungarian variants, it is difficult to track down. No interactions that I taped showed systematically higher or lower frequencies of one of the variants, and thus far, closer analysis of particular interviews and conversations has failed to yield specific topics or discourse contexts in which even a briefly sustained shift to local or standard forms is clearly evident and interpretable. Rather, it seems that the distinction itself has lost significance.

To understand this, it is important to recall that the young people are speakers who do not use Hungarian with age-mates at all. Since the social network of peers is a powerful force in the maintenance of phonological norms (Labov 1972b, Milroy 1980), it is particularly significant that for these speakers there is no social network of Hungarian-speaking peers which could maintain separate stylistic norms within Hungarian. Furthermore, there is, for them, no social institution (such as school or state bureaucracy) which would demand that they actively use a distinction between the social significance of standard and local forms. The symbolic contrasts most salient to them, reinforced by school as much as by their own work lives, are contrasts among variants of German and those between the two languages. The latter they exploit frequently in conversational code-switching. Judging by a certain reluctance and the complaints expressed in some interviews that 'I can't bring it out' properly in Hungarian (nem tudom rendesen ki hozni magyarul), I suspect that these young speakers feel frustrated having to use Hungarian alone.

The speech of the older generation remains as a possible source for learning the meanings of the Hungarian variants. However, as I have argued elsewhere (1979), the moral and economic power of the older generations to enforce their own norms of language use has been seriously deteriorated by the postwar decline in the value of land and agriculture (as, indeed, has their power in other social domains). The younger generation does not look to the older bilinguals but, rather, to the industrial-bureaucratic and German monolingual world for its models. Thus, not only is the young people's access to the use of standard forms in Hungarian limited by the narrow range of contexts in which they hear and actively use Hungarian, but their motivation to learn the social meanings of the variants is attenuated by widespread social changes.

5. With these contrasting patterns I have suggested, on the one hand, some of the systematic relations between language usage patterns and communicative motivations of speakers, and, on the other hand, the stylistic range in phonology which speakers exploit for communicative effect. Clearly, the patterns cannot be explained by interference between the two languages. Rather, what I have indicated is the kind of constraint or limit on phonological style that operates on a language even when it is learned first, remains in daily use, is spoken frequently, but is severely limited in its social functions.

Under normal circumstances, when speaking with other bilinguals in their accustomed manner, young people who do not use a stylistic range in Hungarian do not experience embarrassment or communicative difficulty. Their repertoire and that of their listeners includes German, and switching to German is available to them as a meaningful way of indicating authority, publicness, and other social meanings. However, I suggest that the flattening or simplification of phonological style is linked not simply to their bilingualism and the availability of language-switching for stylistic effect, but rather, to the lack of social contexts, networks, and institutions which would support stylistic norms and meanings in Hungarian. It is the political and economic developments of the postwar years that have deprived many young speakers of the social contexts in which the phonological variants of Hungarian are meaningfully distinguished and in which those variants are rhetorically significant. The contrasting case of the older speakers highlights this. They are also bilinguals and make use of conversational language-switching in some communicative contexts. Yet, they systematically and meaningfully use phonological style as well. The juxtaposition of these cases, found within a single community, suggests the way in which linguistic skills are dependent on specific historically located social contexts. Speakers' knowledge of a linguistic variety is affected by the socially constructed limitations on the opportunities and motivations for its use.

Notes

My thanks to Susan Dannenbaum, Dee Garrison, Judith Gerson, and Carol Nackenoff for their suggestions and to James Boster, John Gumperz, Jane Hill, and especially Kit Woolard for their criticism of an earlier version of this paper. The research was funded by the National Science Foundation (BNS 80-05889), whose support is gratefully acknowledged. This paper is drawn from a longer report dealing with some of the same issues (Gal 1984).

1. Dressler noted briefly that 'stylistic shrinkage' is a phenomenon of decaying language (1972:454) and Dressler and Wodak-Leodolter (1977) mention 'monostylism' as characteristic of some Breton speakers, but do not go on to explore or document these changes. See also Lambert and Freed (1982) for related research on language loss.

2. Segalowitz and Gatbonton (1977) discuss the stylistic range in the second language of adults first learning that second language. Their work is thus about nonfluent speakers, while the research reported here concerns fluent speakers using their first language. Ma and Herasimchuk's (1971) careful work is not comparable for another reason. They contrast reading and speaking as their measure of style, a strategy I decided not to use (see note 4). Nevertheless, Ma and Herasimchuk's study lends some indirect support to the viewpoint presented in this paper since they found limitations in stylistic range in some, but not all, of their demographically defined bilingual groups.

3. The study is based on a total of 20 months of field work: 11 months in 1974, the rest in 1979, 1981, and 1982.

4. The recent introduction of Hungarian instruction in the early grades is the exception. The Reformed Church also continues use of Hungarian.

5. Following Labov's (1972a) early work, reading passages and word lists are often used to tap speakers' phonological styles, especially in urban dialect surveys, on the assumption that reading evokes the high-prestige standard forms. I decided against this method in the present study for a number of reasons. Recent work on literacy indicates that reading, if it is done at all, is a speech event with a particular place in the communicative economy of a community. Thus, the evaluation of reading and the kind of pronunciation deemed appropriate to it may well vary crossculturally, as with any speech event. One cannot assume that reading of word lists, for instance, will contrast maximally with pronunciation in 'casual' speech events in all communities. Milroy (1980:99-105) showed convincingly that in working-class Belfast, word lists were read with more vernacular pronunciation than that used in interviews. She suggests that there are norms for reading pronunciation in Belfast which have little to do with pronunciation norms in nonreading speech events. Similarly, when I asked speakers to read a folk tale collected in the community, spelling pronunciation swamped all differences on most variables. What is more, for the agricultural segment of the neighborhood I am describing here, and for those young people who did not attend Hungarian-language schools, reading in Hungarian, in most cases, is a problematic activity done rarely and haltingly, if at all. It may not reflect these speakers' nonreading repertoires.

6. Approximately 40 minutes of tape were examined for each speaker, about 20 minutes in each of the two situations. The average number of tokens per person per variable was: 305 for variable 1 (range 96-651), 36 for variable 2 (range 9-62), 233 for variable 3 (range 84-446). There was a reliability of 90% on the coding judgments for these and several other variables in a 30-minute sample of tape coded twice, about a month

apart. Two further checks of different 30-minute samples showed 81% and 92% reliability.

References

Blom, Jan-Peter, and J. J. Gumperz. 1972. Social meaning in linguistic structures: Code-switching in Norway. In: Directions in sociolinguistics. Edited by J. Gumperz and D. Hymes. New York: Holt, Rinehart and Winston. 407-34.

Dorian, Nancy. 1981. Language death: The life cycle of a Scottish Gaelic dialect. Philadelphia: University of Pennsylvania Press.

Dressler, Wolfgang. 1972. On the phonology of language death. Chicago Linguistic Society Papers 8. 448-57.

Dressler, Wolfgang, and Ruth Wodak-Leodolter. 1977. Language preservation and language death in Brittany. International Journal of the Sociology of Language 12.33-44.

Gal, Susan. 1979. Language shift: Social determinants of linguistic change in bilingual Austria. New York: Academic Press.

Gal, Susan. 1984. Contraction and expansion of phonological styles. MS.

Gumperz, J. J. 1982. Conversational code-switching. In: Discourse strategies. Edited by J. Gumperz. London: Cambridge University Press. 59-99.

Halliday, Michael. 1973. Explorations in the functions of language. New York: Elsevier.

Hill, Jane, and Kenneth Hill. 1977. Language death and relexification in Tlaxcalan Nahuatl. International Journal of the Sociology of Language 12.55-69.

Hill, Jane, and Kenneth Hill. 1978. Honorific usage in modern Nahuatl. Lg. 54.1:123-55.

Hymes, Dell. 1971. Introduction, Part III. In: Pidginization and creolization of languages. Edited by D. Hymes. London: Cambridge University Press. 65-90.

Imre, Samu. 1971. A felsőőri, nyelvjárás The Felsőőr dialect. Nyelvtudományi Értekezések 72. Budapest: Akadémiai Kiadó.

Irvine, Judith. 1979. Formality and informality in communicative events. American Anthropologist 81.4:773-90.

Keller, R. E. 1961. Upper Austrian. In: German dialects: Phonology and morphology. By R. E. Keller. Manchester: Manchester University Press. 200-47.

Labov, William. 1972a. On the mechanism of linguistic change. In: Sociolinguistic patterns. By William Labov. Philadelphia: University of Pennsylvania Press. 160-82.

Labov, William. 1972b. The linguistic consequences of being a lame. In: Language in the inner city. By W. Labov. Philadelphia: University of Pennsylvania Press. 255-96.

Lambert, Richard D., and Barbara F. Freed, eds. 1982. The loss of language skills. Rowley, Mass.: Newbury House.

Lavandera, Beatriz. 1978. The variable component in bilingual performance. In: Georgetown University Round Table on Languages and Linguistics 1978. Washington, D.C.: Georgetown University Press. 391-409.

Ma, Roxana, and Eleanor Herasimchuk. 1971. The lingusitic dimensions of a bilingual neighborhood. In: Bilingualism in the barrio. Edited by J. Fishman et al. Bloomington: Indiana University Press. 347-464.
Milroy, Lesley. 1980. Language and social networks. Baltimore: University Park Press.
Romaine, S., and E. Traugott. 1981. The problem of style in socilinguistics. Paper presented at the Winter Meeting of the Linguistic Society of America, New York.
Segalowitz, Norman, and Elizabeth Gatbonton. 1977. Studies of the non-fluent bilingual. In: Bilingualism: Psychological, social and educational implications. Edited by P. Hornby. New York: Academic Press. 77-90.
Slobin, Dan I. 1977. Language change in childhood and in history. In: Language learning and thought. Edited by J. Macnamara. New York: Academic Press. 185-214.
Trudgill, Peter, and J. K. Chambers. 1980. Dialectology. Cambridge: Cambridge University Press.

SOME COMMENTS ON THE SUBJECTIVE LEXICON

George A. Miller
Princeton University

When you learn a language, several kinds of learning occur: pronunciation, vocabulary, grammar, usage, each characterized in a separate body of linguistic theory. All of these--phonology, syntax, semantics, pragmatics--describe things that a language user has to learn, and that a skillful speaker knows.

Now, what people know and how they learn it are basic questions for cognitive psychology; when those questions concern what people learn and know about languages, we call it psycholinguistics. In principle, a psycholinguist should be interested in all these kinds of learning. In fact, however, lexical learning is generally considered uninteresting. That evaluation is a mistake. There are as many fascinating puzzles in the lexical as in any other aspect of language.

To know the vocabulary of a language is to know the sounds and meanings of the basic words in the language. I acknowledge the technical difficulties with this formulation--the problems of determining what a word is, what a meaning is, and what makes a word important--but they are not my present concern. However those problems are solved, what it means to know a lexical unit eventually comes down to one or both of two criteria:

(1) The 'receptive criterion': knowing what the word means when you hear it used;
(2) The 'productive criterion': using the word naturally and appropriately in sentences that express your own thoughts.

The receptive criterion. The receptive criterion involves recognizing the word and retrieving its meaning from lexical memory. Since the operational test is to give (or at least recognize) the word's definition, retrieval from lexical memory is usually likened to looking up the word in a dictionary. Therefore I shall focus my comments about the receptive criterion for word knowledge on the implicit assumption:

(3) The 'receptive assumption': A language user's lexical knowledge is organized into independent lexical entries, the way a printed dictionary is.

Of course, with a printed dictionary you have to use alphabetical retrieval, whereas you can get access to your own lexical entries either by way of their pronunciation or by way of the ideas they express. Except for that, however, a printed dictionary is generally viewed as an explicit theory of lexical knowledge.

Not until I had thought about (3) for some time did I realize how improbable it is. Lexicographers who compile dictionaries are not thinking about psychology--how wonderful that they should manage to produce psychological theories! The way you go about writing a dictionary is not at all the way you would go about constructing a psychological theory. And it is certainly not the way a child goes about learning a vocabulary.

I want to consider some differences between objective and subjective dictionaries; I introduce my comments by considering briefly the growth of vocabulary in children.

The growth of vocabulary. Recent studies of cognitive development have not totally ignored vocabulary, but I think it is fair to say that the principal interest in it has been as a convenient window on conceptual development. Interest in the words themselves has been secondary.

It was not always so. During the 1930s and 1940s, no doubt stimulated by the observation that vocabulary is the most dependable part of any intelligence test, psychologists devoted considerable attention to the growth of vocabulary in children. It was found that the first word appears between 12 and 18 months of age, then new words begin to appear more and more rapidly until by the age of three a parent can no longer tell whether the child knows a particular word. Thereafter, vocabulary grows so rapidly that dictionary-sampling techniques are required to track it.

Several careful, cross-sectional studies of vocabulary growth were conducted back in the days before transformational generative grammar was invented. The results that I have most faith in were collected by Mildred Templin and published in 1957. Accoding to Templin, a six-year-old child of average intelligence knows 13,000 words and the average eight-year-old child knows 28,300.

In order to appreciate these numbers, it helps to convert them into words learned per day. Between the ages of six and eight years, an average child learns 21 words per day. Children of superior intelligence probably learn words at twice that rate.

This estimate may seem high, but all the other studies of vocabulary growth that I have seen give even higher rates. Apparently, a broad and rapid learning process goes on during childhood and psychologists know very little about it. At least two things do seem clear, however: first, young children are very good at acquiring vocabulary; second, since nobody teaches children 21 words every day, they must be very good at educing meanings from context.

In 1974, Susan Carey and Elsa Bartlett invented a way to observe this rapid learning in more detail (Bartlett 1977; Carey 1978; Carey and

Bartlett 1978; Miller 1977). They used color names. First, they established that a group of three-year-old children did not know the color olive; most called it green, some called it brown. Carey and Bartlett decided to teach the children a nonsense name for olive, a name that they would not have heard anywhere but in our nursery school. So they painted one tray olive and another tray blue and asked each child casually, 'Hand me the chromium tray. Not the blue one, the chromium one.' The child would pause, perhaps point to the olive tray and ask, 'This one?' A week later, with no further guidance the children were again asked to name the colors. This time, when olive was presented, they paused. They couldn't remember the nonsense name for it, but now they knew it wasn't green or brown. A single exposure was enough to begin a reorganization of their color lexicon.

Carey thought she saw a two-step learning process. First, children notice a new word and assign it to an appropriate category. After hearing chromium just once, they had assigned it to the semantic field of color names. Children are good at keeping these fields separate, even when they don't really know what the words mean.

The second step is to work out the distinctions among words within a category; that may take a long time. When you calculate that an average child learns 21 words a day, it does not mean that the learning process is complete in one day. A child will be alert to and working out the relations among many words at the same time, but exactly how many are being learned at any one time is not known.

One thing is reasonably sure, however. Children could not memorize 21 arbitrary, unrelated facts every day. Words can be learned rapidly because they are not unrelated, because they form conceptually related patterns. A vocabulary is a coherent, integrated system of concepts. In other words, a feature that tends to be ignored in objective dictionaries--the organization of words into semantic fields--is what makes rapid vocabulary learning possible. If we hope to understand this process, we must have some reasonably definite characterization of lexical organization.

Lexical organization. Lexical memory must be organized in (at least) two ways, phonologically and semantically. A variety of common observations--that it is easy to think of words starting with the same sound or of words that rhyme, that confusions in memory and slips of the tongue often occur between words that sound alike, and so on--all support the assumption of a phonological organization. But an equal array of common observations--that people associate words with similar meanings, that similar meanings are used to define new words, that relations of entailment between words are easily recognized, and so on--all support the assumption of a conceptual organization, an organization into semantic fields. Children exploit both kinds of organization in their effort to learn words, but my present interest is primarily in the conceptual organization of the subjective lexicon.

Most printed dictionaries of English recognize specialized semantic fields, although the recognition is buried under the alphabetical ordering and very difficult to use. For example, technical senses of a word will be marked medicine or jurisprudence or physics or whatever. If you gathered together all those senses with a given marking, you would have a reasonably good glossary of technical terms in that specialty. Unfortunately, however, with a printed dictionary there is no easy way to retrieve all and only those senses bearing a particular meaning. And no English language dictionary that I know of uses markers in this way to distinguish among nontechnical semantic fields. What they do use, of course, are synonyms. If you trace out the network of cross-references provided by synonyms and antonyms, you can get an idea of the relevant semantic field. But this is tedious work with a printed dictionary, whereas it comes immediately with the subjective lexicon. That is to say, the subjective lexicon seems to be organized more like a collection of dictionaries on many different subjects.

Semantic fields are sometimes explained as a natural reflection of the semantic decomposability of lexical concepts. For example, I have argued (Miller 1972, Miller and Johnson-Laird 1976) that the semantic field of motion verbs can be defined as including all those verbs whose semantic decomposition includes the primitive (or atomic) concept of change-of-location-over-time. In addition to motion, however, some motion verbs indicate the method of moving--walk versus run, for example; some require knowledge of the speaker's location--come versus go; many indicate the direction of motion--rise, fall, approach--or the medium through which the motion occurs--swim versus fly. You can tease out about a dozen different components, so that each one of the verbs of motion looks like a particular package of semantic concepts, and the semantic field consists of many other related but slightly different packages of concepts.

Not every shared concept can serve as the nucleus of a semantic field, however (Miller and Johnson-Laird 1976). Although the set of verbs that share a concept of movement do form a semantic field, the set of verbs that share a concept of causation do not. Move, kill, give, and tell, for example, are all causative verbs, but they clearly do not form a semantic field. Johnson-Laird and I speculated that some concepts, like motion or possession, can provide a nucleus around which a semantic field can develop, whereas other concepts, like cause or instrument, are used to elaborate concepts within many different semantic fields.

Learning words from context. Sometimes you can satisfy the receptive criterion when you do not really know a word, because the context makes the meaning apparent. Indeed, context is a major source of the information used in learning the meanings of many new words. In 1950, Werner and Kaplan reported an experiment designed to reveal how well children could guess the meaning of a new word after hearing it used in a succession of sentences. After hearing A corplum may be used for support, Corplums may be used to close off an open space, A wet corplum does not burn, and so on, the children offered their opinions of what a corplum was. Children eight years old seemed to have difficulty disentangling the new word from the context in which it occurred, but 13-year-old children could usually solve the problems.

The question raised by Werner and Kaplan was ignored until 1981 when two workers in Amsterdam, M. M. van Daalen-Kaptjens and M. Elshout-Mohr, reopened it. What they contributed was an insightful analysis of protocols that they collected from college students who were asked to think out loud while they solved such problems.

The process of transforming several contexts of use into an acceptable definition was called 'decontextualization' by Daalen-Kaptjens and Elshout-Mohr. They claimed that it requires at least two steps: first, a reformulation of the context into a sentence about the unknown word, e.g. to reformulate <u>The painter used a corplum to stir his paints,</u> which is about a painter, into a sentence like <u>Corplums can be used to stir paints,</u> which is a sentence about corplums; second, the transformation of this reformulated information into an aspect of the meaning, e.g. <u>Corplums can be implements.</u>

Subjects who could perform both steps generally succeeded in formulating an acceptable definition; subjects who performed only the first step were not as successful. Daalen-Kaptjens and Elshout-Mohr speculated that their successful subjects used the first context, plus their general knowledge, to select a schematic model, then used successive contexts to narrow down the exact properties of the model. Less successful subjects seemed to have difficulty because they did not carry out the second step, the translation of contextual information into further aspects of the model.

The preferred way to write a definition is to give the name of the superordinate class to which the concept belongs, and to follow that with a relative clause that differentiates this particular instance of the class from all other instances. This strategy is not always available but when it is, it seems to lead to clear, simple definitions. The general format is as follows.

(4) Definitional format: 'An X is a Y that . . .,' where the phrases following <u>that</u> provide distinguishers.

College students have far more world knowledge to draw upon than do young children, but it seems to me that the Carey and Bartlett three-year-olds and the Daalen-Kaptjens and Elshout-Mohr college students were both trying to impose format (4) on the meanings of new words via a two-step path: first identify a general category, later work out the distinguishing particulars. No doubt there are exceptions to this rule, but a substantial fraction of word learning probably does follow some such pattern.

A more psychometric approach has been adopted by Sternberg and Powell (1983), who found that high school students' scores on a learning-from-context task correlated about 0.6 with IQ, vocabulary, and reading comprehension scores. They suggest that context is valuable insofar as it provides information about certain general aspects of the target word's meaning. Indeed, the aspects that they list resemble the kind of meaning components that Johnson-Laird and I used to characterize motion verbs, and that others have developed for other kinds of semantic decomposition. I take it, therefore, that Sternberg and Powell share my own intuition:

(5) The 'contextual learning assumption': An ability to perform conceptual decompositions is valuable for learning word meanings from context.

If assumption (5) is correct, it suggests how semantic fields and learning-from-context might work together in some eventual theory of vocabulary growth.

These comments indicate some of the differences between objective and subjective lexicons: differences in organization, use, and method of construction. In view of these differences, I think it is important to reconsider the all too pervasive assumption (3) that lexical retrieval from a dictionary is a good model for lexical retrieval from personal memory.

The productive criterion. The productive criterion for knowing a word is less easily applied than is the receptive criterion, because the investigator must wait for the speaker to introduce the word--which may entail a very long wait indeed. However, school teachers have the authority to reduce this wait by assigning pupils the task of using particular words in sentences. Indeed, this assignment is frequently used as part of the students' training in 'dictionary skills'.

Polysemy. As dictionaries are written, many different senses are distinguished and a reader is expected to be able to tell which one is appropriate in any given context. Most intelligent adults are able to solve this problem, but it is easy to show that children have great difficulty with it. For example, Deese (1967) reported on one teacher of seventh grade English who gave her pupils the assignment of looking up certain words in the Webster's Collegiate Dictionary and using them in a sentence. Here is a slightly simplified summary of the definitions that the children found when they looked up the word chaste:

> chaste: 1: innocent of unlawful sexual intercourse. 2: celibate. 3: pure in thought and act, modest. 4: severely simple in design or execution, austere.

With that lexical entry in mind, let me read you Deese's report (1967) of what some children did with it:

> Here are some sentences written by these youngsters after they had looked up the word chaste. You will have to admit that they are all consistent with at least one of the senses supplied by the dictionary.
>
> 1. 'The amoeba is a chaste animal.' Evidently, the youngster who wrote this sentence is following that part of the entry that says chaste means simple in design. . .
>
> 2. 'The plates were still chaste after much use.' Here the notion of being unstained seems to be critical.
>
> 3. 'The milk was chaste.' Evidently, the sense of pure is meant here.

Such examples demonstrate that dictionaries are reference books, not teaching instruments. If you already know something about the word, a dictionary will remind you of it. But if you are totally innocent, you cannot trust a dictionary as your sole source of lexical information. Not only do dictionaries make too many distinctions among meanings--they often do not make the right ones.

At Princeton, Patricia Gildea and I are following up on Deese's project and trying to extend it. We have made contact with local school teachers who are interested in teaching dictionary skills and have found them most cooperative. They have allowed us to see their students' worksheets, and we are beginning to build up an inventory of mistakes that children make when they use a dictionary. We have not gotten far enough with this project to draw any generalizations. At the moment we are puzzling over why a child might think that two boxers <u>engaged</u> in fisticuffs were <u>betrothed,</u> or why the person who stuck his <u>digit</u> in his ear put a <u>number</u> in his ear, and similar confusions. As yet, however, we have not collected enough examples to make any guess about the sources of the children's difficulties.

Along similar lines, Julia Jorgensen and I tried to analyze what you do when you look up an unfamiliar word in the dictionary (Jorgensen 1984). It is an intellectually challenging task. The continuity of your reading is interrupted, but the context in which the word occurred must be kept in mind. Once the word is found in the dictionary, you may need to choose among alternative lexical entries on the basis of part of speech; then, within the right entry, you may have to choose among several alternative senses on the basis of context. That is to say, the context of the original passage must be compared with a succession of contexts suggested in the dictionary until a best guess can be made as to the intended sense.

In order to study this process in a simplified form, Jorgensen (1984) developed a questionnaire based on 40 words (20 frequent words and 20 relatively rare ones). For each word, phrases defining two different senses, with a sentence illustrating each sense, were taken from a children's dictionary. The words were then replaced in the illustrative sentences by nonsense syllables, and subjects were asked which definition of the nonsense syllable was most appropriate in the context provided by the sentence.

For example, one item presented the sentence:

The snow is hattay with the windows.

Then two senses for <u>hattay</u> were given: (1) 'level, flat, smooth'; (2) 'at the same level'. Subjects were asked to choose the better of the two senses of the word as it is used in the illustrative sentence.

The questionnaire was given to 20 Princeton undergraduates and to 20 fourth grade children. College students identified the correct sense on 83% of the items, fourth graders on 63%: chance, of course, was 50%. The fact that adult performance was not perfect suggests that the illustrative sentences found in dictionaries leave something to be desired. That the children made even lower scores confirms the difficulty they have with such context-matching tasks.

After going through the questionnaire, the subjects then went through it a second time, but this time trying to guess what the real words were for which nonsense syllables had been substituted. (For the example just given, the original word was <u>even</u>.) College students guessed right 59% of the time for high frequency words, but only 24% of the time for low frequency words; the comparable figures for children were 18% and 5%. Moreover, the ones they guessed correctly were not always the same ones that they had gotten right in the context matching task--so their success could not be attributed to seeing through the nonsense substitutions.

What interested us most, however, was the consistent and reliable difference between high and low frequency words. Since we had substituted nonsense syllables, we expected that they would all be treated like very low frequency words. The most likely explanation of the difference is that dictionaries do not define high and low frequency words the same way. Definitions for the high frequency words seemed better, at least in this particular sample.

Which raises the interesting question of how to evaluate the quality of a proposed definition.

The quality of a definition. The problem of definitional quality arises repeatedly in attempts to experiment with lexical materials. Do children have difficulty using dictionaries because the definitions are poor? Do lexicographers write better definitions for senses that are represented by a greater number of instances of use? If you wanted to improve the quality of dictionary definitions, how would you evaluate your work? And so on. Obviously, it would be very useful to have some convenient way to assess the quality of definitions.

One possible solution is the subjective rating scale. Sternberg and Powell (1983) found that judges could agree in rating the quality of definitions written by high school students. But such ratings are hardly sensitive enough to evaluate the work of professional lexicographers, and, lacking further specification, critical questions about the rater's criterion are left open: what is a good definition supposed to be good for?

Jorgensen (1984) proposed the following method for evaluating definitional quality. First, a nonsense syllable was inserted into a definition and subjects were requested to write sentences using the nonsense syllable in the intended sense. Then the original word was restored in these sentences and the resulting sentences were submitted to a second group of subjects for evaluation. A good definition was taken to be one that enabled a person to write an acceptable sentence using the word in the intended sense. Otherwise said:

(6) The 'productive criterion of definitional quality': A good definition is one that provides the information required to satisfy the productive criterion for knowing the word.

Note that (6) is a much more modest requirement than the traditional criterion of synonymity:

(7) The 'synonymity criterion of definitional quality': A good definition is one that is substitutable for the word it defines in all contexts without altering truth values.

An operational test for (7) might challenge subjects to pair words with their definitions--a task that should be easy if the words and their definitions were synonymous. Experience suggests that this challenge becomes very difficult to meet when the words involved are at all similar in meaning.

A still different criterion might require that the definition be useful for helping someone--a child, perhaps--learn the meaning of an unfamiliar word:

(8) The 'pedagogical criterion of definitional quality': A good definition is one that provides the information required to add the word to one's vocabulary.

This criterion would impose different requirements on definitions intended for learners of different sophistication. For a given learner, however, a definition satisfying (8) should also satisfy (6), although the reverse would not necessarily hold.

I have no firm favoritism for any one of these alternatives, but I do feel a need to reserve the possibility that the quality of a definition might depend on the use you plan to make of it, and that definitions good for one purpose might not be optimal for some other.

In the time available I have been able to do little more than hint at the variety and complexity of lexical problems worthy of theoretical and experimental investigation. I hope, however, that this small sample will be enough to revive your interest in this often neglected suburb of linguistic studies.

Note

This talk was prepared with the help of grants to Princeton University from the Alfred P. Sloan Foundation and the Spencer Foundation.

References

Bartlett, E. J. 1977. The acquisition of the meaning of color terms: A study of lexical development. In: Proceedings of the Stirling Conference on the Psychology of Language. Edited by P. Smith and R. Campbell. New York: Plenum.

Carey, S. 1978. The child as word learner. In: Linguistic theory and psychological reality. Edited by M. Halle, J. Bresnan, and G. A. Miller. Cambridge, Mass.: MIT Press.

Carey, S., and E. J. Bartlett. 1978. Acquiring a single word. Papers and Reports on Child Language Development 15.17-29. Department of Linguistics, Stanford University.

Daalen-Kaptjens, M. M. van, and M. Elshout-Mohr. 1981. The acquisition of word meanings as a cognitive learning process. Journal of Verbal Learning and Verbal Behavior 20.386-99.

Deese, J. 1967. Meaning and change of meaning. American Psychologist 22.641-51.

Jorgensen, J. 1984. Polysemy and psycholexicology. Ph.D. thesis, Princeton University.

Miller, G. A. 1972. English verbs of motion: A case study in semantics and lexical memory. In: Coding processes in human memory. Edited by A. W. Melton and E. Martin. Washington, D.C.: Winston.

Miller, G. A. 1977. Spontaneous apprentices: Children and language. New York: Seabury Press.

Miller, G. A., and P. N. Johnson-Laird. 1976. Language and perception. Cambridge, Mass.: Harvard University Press.

Sternberg, R. J., and J. S. Powell. 1983. Comprehending verbal comprehension. American Psychologist 38.878-93.

Templin, M. C. 1957. Certain language skills in children: Their development and interrelationships. Minneapolis: University of Minnesota Press.

Werner, H., and E. Kaplan. 1950. Development of word meaning through verbal context: An experimental study. Journal of Psychology 29.251-57.

A SONG WITHOUT MUSIC AND OTHER STORIES: HOW COGNITIVE PROCESS CONSTRAINTS INFLUENCE CHILDREN'S ORAL AND WRITTEN NARRATIVES

Marilyn Shatz
University of Michigan

Narratives as a kind of language use exhibit a remarkable range of length, complexity, style, and content. The minimal unit of a narrative is the relation of two events or actions, as illustrated in (1), a story by a three-year-old (reported in Sacks 1972).

(1) The baby cried. The mommy picked it up.

More elaborated instances can have introductory segments, evaluative and resolving statements, and recapitulations or specific ending statements (see Labov 1972). Narratives can be about personal experiences, reported events, or fantasy.

Children's ability to deal with narrative language in comprehension and production tasks has recently received much attention from cognitive and developmental psychologists. Researchers have investigated children's understanding of story structure (e.g. Brown 1975, Stein and Glenn 1979), their story retellings (McNamee 1979), and their story creations (Pitcher and Prelinger 1963). Findings from these and other efforts show that even quite young children have some understanding of story structure (see Mandler 1983 for a review). Moreover, they use some of the formal devices characteristic of narrative segments. For example, four-year-olds studied in my laboratory produced introductory statements in their narratives. They used phrases like <u>one time, one day, once upon a time</u>, and my favorite--<u>once of a little time.</u> Applebee (1978) reports that children as young as two years of age recognize such phrases as appropriate to the narrative register.

Yet, young children's narrative skills are far from mature. The fact that many children are reluctant even to attempt the narrative task when requested to do so suggests that narration is a difficult mode for them. One researcher has reported only a 50% success rate in story elicitation with two-and-one-half-year-olds (Ames 1966). In my data with four-year-olds, about the same success rate was achieved. My elicitation situation was quite informal and unconstrained, with children often encouraged to elaborate on topics they themselves had introduced into a casual conversation with a parent or an experimenter they knew well. Nonetheless, the task regularly proved to be more than the children wanted to handle. When encouraged to elaborate, children would typically respond, 'I forgot' or 'I don't know'. However, it is unlikely that memory was the real problem, since some children on occasion overcame their hesitations and actually went on to narrate an experience, or they did so after a more explicit question from the listener. Examples (2) and (3) illustrate this hesitant behavior in a four-year-old girl.

(2) Experimenter: And what did you do in the sand?
Child: I forgot. Dig. You dig fishes and stones.
(3) Child: He (Uncle Timmy) plays it (music) from a guitar.
Experimenter: Tell me about Uncle Timmy's guitar playing.
Child: No.
Experimenter: Why not?
Child: 'Cause it's a secret.

What, then, makes narration a difficult task? A hint comes from Scollon and Scollon's (1983) discussion of the oral tradition of the Athabascans living in Alaska and Canada. Scollon and Scollon report that Athabascan stories, although preserved from generation to generation, are rarely told the same way twice. Instead, any particular telling of a story is modified to take into account the characteristics of the audience. The Scollons' claim, then, is that oral narratives are no less a communicative task than is conversation. They require perspective-taking and adjustment skills just as other forms of talk do. If we accept this claim, then we can see that narrative production is not merely a problem of memory or imagination or knowledge of narrative structure. It involves these but it also involves the ability to create a sequence of utterances that provides an appropriate format for a specific listener. Of course, just as with rules of conversation, the rules governing narrative performances are to some extent culture-dependent. Not all of the constraints governing Athabascan story-telling pertain in other cultures. Nonetheless, the general principle does hold: narration is a complex communicative skill requiring attention to listener characteristics.

Accommodating to heavy cognitive workloads. If children were egocentric, that is, unaware of differences in perspective among listeners, then one might expect them to plunge into the narrative task without concern for the communicative aspects of it. This is not the case. We know from my work, and others' as well, that children do take account of the age or knowledge level of their listeners and adjust their speech accordingly in a variety of explanation and description tasks (see Shatz and Gelman 1973; Shatz 1983, for a review). As is shown later in this paper, children know that narratives too require some tailoring to the level of the listener. Now, the point to be stressed is that the knowledge that a narrative requires adjustment is one of the complicating factors making the narration task so difficult for young children.

It is one thing to know something about the formal devices and topics that are appropriate to narrative. It is another to know which ones are appropriate to which listeners. Part of the reluctance of preschoolers to narrate, I would argue, is a result of the cognitive overload they experience when they are asked to communicate in a register that makes all of the communicative demands on them that other modes do and that has, in addition, its own set of structural characteristics that are not yet well controlled.

The argument that I am making is consonant with the cognitive process theory I advanced several years ago to account for children's variable performance on other sorts of communication tasks, for example, those involving referential and explanatory skills (Shatz 1978). The essentials of the argument are that a child has limited resources to carry out any task. A complex task can be divided into component skills necessary for adequate performance on the task. Each skill can be controlled by information-handling techniques--devices for spreading resources farther than they would otherwise go. For example, knowledge of social conversational conventions can be considered such a technique. One can initiate and carry on a conversation for several minutes with little effort if one knows the conventional forms for doing so. Much more effort would be involved if one had to search out and create new openings each time an interaction was attempted. Nonetheless, some degree of cognitive work is involved in the accessing and use of any skill or technique. The better learned and more practiced the technique, the lower the workload value it has; that is, the fewer resources it takes to execute.

Moreover, there is additional work involved in a complex task, which requires identifying the subskills, selecting the information-handling techniques, and integrating their outputs. Subskills are not independent of one another in that they draw from the same resource pool in order to be accessed and executed. Thus, in one context, a given component skill may be displayed with ease because the other components required in that context are well learned. However, the same skill may not be well executed or even displayed at all in a context where the resources are absorbed by other more central and high-cost skills. The potential for exhibiting any particular ability, then, must be considered with regard to the context of its display.

Figure 1 is not a process model of complex task execution, but instead graphically illustrates the central constructs of the theory and their relations. Especially noteworthy is the variation in the amount of resources different information-handling techniques (IHT) draw from the central resource pool, and the assumption that selection and integration functions also draw resources from the same pool. Not clearly apparent in Figure 1 is the system's potential to select one of several possible information-handling techniques to control a subskill with relative success, depending on the resources available. For example, one technique may do the job passably but not superbly, but use fewer resources than the technique of choice in less resource-demanding circumstances. Thus, the theory allows trade-offs between the elegance, precision, or appropriateness with which a particular subskill is carried out and the amount of resources devoted to its execution.

Figure 1. Constructs of limited resource-cognitive process theory.

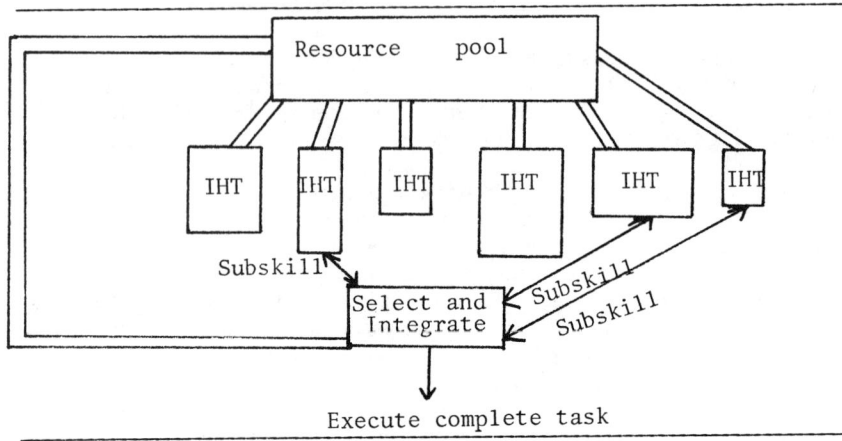

How can the cognitive process theory be used to understand better children's early narrative performances? Several aspects of my data on children's narratives are especially compatible with the limited resources view. First, an examination of some early narratives shows that children recruit a variety of information-handling techniques from other kinds of language use to assist in the successful execution of their narratives. While these techniques may not be strictly appropriate to a narrative style, they are well learned, and hence cheap in terms of resources. Thus, they can be executed even in a fairly difficult context. Moreover, narratives can be quite variable with regard to style, and children may be encouraged by this flexibility to borrow devices from other sources.

Second, I noted that children do adjust their narratives according to their listeners, although sometimes they cannot meet the various demands that both listener adjustment and narrative style exact. Third, it is also noted that when first using a narrative style, children are reluctant to stray far from what they know best--their own personal experiences. It seems that a well-known topic is less costly to express in a novel format than venturing far into fantasy is. Finally, an examination of early written attempts at narration by one child shows that working in a new mode is resource-costly, requiring other concomitant component skills to operate at a high level of efficiency. That is, the transition from oral to written narrative is a drain on resources; the nascent skills of spelling and writing encourage a return to well-learned forms and topics of narratives common in younger children's oral productions. This return to earlier, easier forms is an example of the selective trade-offs the limited resource system can make when confronted with novel complex tasks taxing its capacity.

In sum, I will show that children do have considerable knowledge of what constitutes an appropriate narrative. However, integrating all the components of that knowledge into a smooth, mature performance on any given occasion is a difficult task for the novice. Instead, the child's solutions often combine more and less appropriate topics and devices in order to express their fragile narrative ability.

Oral narratives. I turn now to some examples of narratives to illustrate the points I have just made. My first examples are oral narratives, each told by four-year-olds to a familiar listener in the casual conversational context of looking at magazine pictures. Before the story illustrated in (4), the female narrator and an adult experimenter had been discussing the ocean and beach depicted in a picture.

(4) Child: <u>Guess what</u>. Once we went--The last time we went down there (to the beach)--over the weekend, <u>guess what</u> happened to us.
Experimenter: What?
Child: We had a hurricane. It was in the evening and--and the house was shaking...'cause it was really old. <u>Guess what</u>. The next day when we went to the beach, the--the water was only half way up the beach.

Of note is the child's use of the conversational attention-getter <u>guess what?</u>, not only to begin her narrative, but also as a marker of each segment of the story. Uses of phrases such as <u>guess what</u> or <u>know what</u> are common in children's conversations. The use of <u>guess what</u> makes very clear that there are three segments to the story. <u>Guess what</u> operates much like the phrase <u>and then</u> in the narratives of slightly older children. Of the seven four-year-olds who produced narratives for me, only one used <u>and</u> or <u>and then</u> to mark the segments of his stories, four used <u>guess what</u> or <u>you know what,</u> and one child produced both kinds of markers.

The child who produced the more conventional narrative markers, <u>and</u> and <u>and then,</u> seemed more sophisticated on several counts than most of the other children. He seemed to have an easier time with the storytelling mode generally, telling more stories to all varieties of listeners than 12 of the 14 children in my sample. He also was the only child to produce a reasonably coherent--and quite extended--retelling of a story, as illustrated in (5).

(5) I went on the subway to the movies to watch Pinocchio on the movies. <u>And</u> his father been eaten up by a whale but he was still alive.***[1] Well, he was in a boat <u>and then</u> the whale dived out of the water <u>and then</u> dived and caught the boat because it was in the sky and it was straight going to the boat. <u>And</u> Pinocchio went diving down and he used a rock. ***They jumped on a raft and the raft broke apart and they swimmed on the shore. <u>And</u> Pinocchio's father named Gepetto laid on the sand. <u>And</u> Pinocchio was laying on the water. <u>And</u> the whale died because he bumped hisself on the rocks.

I suggest, then, that conversational devices customarily used to gain attention in an interaction get recruited to a different function in narratives. The children seem to know that marking the segments of a narrative is reasonable. In lieu of control of the appropriate markers, they borrow forms from another aspect of language use they know well.

The result is a narrative with the outline of well-marked structure, but a deceptively conversational style.

It might be argued that perhaps children using such forms are not really producing narratives, but rather protonarratives--the relation of two or more experienced events in sequence without the structure or marking of narrative. I would argue this is not the case for several reasons. The first is that phrases such as <u>once,</u> <u>one day,</u> and <u>one time</u> appear right along with the conversational devices, but such time adverbials occur only in narrative contexts and nowhere else in the children's speech. Another argument concerns the content of the narratives in which the conversational phrases occur. <u>You know what</u> and the like are not limited to the recounting of personal experiences. Examples (6) and (7) illustrate that such devices occur in third person fantasy and in first person fantasy as well. In both of these stories, the placement of the marker is crucial: it sets off the resolution statement for the whole narrative. Yet another indication that these devices are more a part of the child's attempt at structuring his or her story and less an attentional device is the fact that the devices occurred in stories directed to highly attentive adults as well as to peers and older two-year olds. Thus, attentiveness of the listener did not seem to be a criterion for their use.

(6) One day when the bear saw something in Tuney and Looney, went downstairs and they saw their rhinosores. And one time the rhinosore ate them, and they-- *** Tuney is three and a half and Snoofy is three and a half, and Goody is four and a half. <u>Ya know how they got away from him?</u> They holded hands and they runded downstairs all the way to their house, and the rhinosore didn't get them.

(7) There was a big sea monster comin' onto the land. The sea monster was getting all the--he was getting all the dead fish for--to eat the crabs. *** I was way down there with my father. My sister Annie and my mother were down there. I was taking a walk. Soon I saw a sea monster get close to get the crab in their teeth. <u>You know what he did?</u> The crab did pinch me. We brought rubber bandaids, so I got a bandaid on my feet.

However, this is not to say that listener characteristics have no influence on the choice of devices. The four-year-old who produced the sea monster story was later encouraged to repeat the story to one of our least mature two-year-old listeners, who was barely verbal. As can be seen by a comparison of (7) and (8), the story--and its structure--change quite radically. Not only does the marker of the resolution disappear, so does the resolution.

(8) I saw a sea monster. Wynne, there was a sea monster. But Wynne, a crab (unintelligible) in the water, in and out. He ate fish also. He was green all over. He really was green. See big, big waves. Big rocks.

Interestingly, there are several other phrases in this retelling that seem to function as attention-getters and are age-appropriate: the use of the child's name and the directive see. It might appear that the narrator was switching to a strategy of simply describing the picture he had been shown. Unfortunately, in our picture, there weren't any big, big waves or big rocks to be seen. Apparently, the task of creating a coherent narrative for such a limited listener with the devices at his disposal was a bit more than this four-year-old could manage.

Nonetheless, that the child was adjusting for his listener is confirmed by a quantitative comparison of the two versions of the story. In Table 1, the child who told the sea monster story is Subject 1. It can be seen that the mean length of utterances (MLU) in the story directed to the adult was considerably longer than that directed to the two-year-old. Moreover, even though each utterance in the story was more elaborated, there were also more utterances directed to the adult. There were only three children who were willing to tell the same story to both an adult and a younger child, and each of the subjects shows pretty much the same pattern of adjustment: more sentences and longer sentences to adults. These are the same kinds of adjustments found in the conversational speech of these children (Shatz and Gelman 1973).

Table 1.   Number of utterances and mean length of utterances for stories told to both adult and two-year-old listeners.

	Type of listener		No. utterances in story	MLU in words
Subject 1	Adult		9	9.22
	Two-year-old		8	5.00
Subject 2	Adult		5	8.6
	Two-year-old		3	6.3
Subject 3	(a)	Adult	10	7.3
(2 stories)		Two-year-old	6	7.3
	(b)	Adult	8	14.5
		Two-year-old	9	10.1

It should be noted, however, that narrative language in all our subjects generally involved longer MLUs that did spontaneous conversation about toys, regardless of listener. Again, this suggests that children's narratives did differ somewhat from their more conversational styles. It also suggests that the narrative task places more of a burden on the child's sentence-making ability than does conversational speech. Thus, yet a third factor, in addition to unfamiliar structural demands and perspective-taking, adds to the difficulty of the narrative task--namely, the increased use in narrative of more complex sentence structure. Indeed, the use in narrative style of sequences of long, nonelliptical sentences seems to be at odds with the directive style children typically address to younger children--full of short, elliptical utterances, such as see? or don't. Little wonder, then, that the task of telling stories to two-year-olds proved difficult for the children.

One way that some children had of handling the demands of the narrative task was to stay in familiar territory so far as content was concerned. Four-year-olds' narrations were more often about personal experiences than about fantasy. Example (4) about the hurricane is a typical example. Narrations of personal experience conform well to a conversational interaction style. Moreover, the multiple memory cues the child has for the order of events must make sequencing the story relatively easy in comparison to retelling a nonexperienced story or creating a sequence from scratch. Stories that are partly fantasy but set in the context of real-world personal experience and told from a first-person perspective are the second most frequent kind of story. Again, the first person style should be the most familiar to the child, and keeping either events, locations, or the cast of characters firmly grounded in the familiar should ease the burden of production. The sea monster tale (7) is an example of first person fantasy.

In my sample of four-year-olds' stories, there were no stories that were completely original third-person creations. The only examples of third person fantasy were the retelling of the Pinocchio movie (5) and several more original efforts by the child who told the story of the rhinoceros (6). Even she, however, relied on conventional characters from television or story books to create her list of characters. As can be seen in example (9), she also borrowed bits of well-known stories and tucked them in among her original events. Thus, the danger of being eaten and going to grandmother's house is more reminiscent of Little Red Riding Hood than of Goldilocks' adventures.

(9) Once of a little time Goldilocks and hims friends went out on a story show. They had a picnic on the story show. And then the story--and then it went talkervingle *** Whaley get-there were two whaleys. One was a bad one and one was a good one. And the bad one wanted to eat Snoofy, and Tuney and Rooney and Goldilocks. And then they all run in the water to their Grandmother's house. And then the shark whale can't get her. The whale holded the door so he--and he gotted back and he was holding it with hims little shark pointey.

This example confirms that the use of familiar devices, characters, and events functions like a prosthetic device, allowing children to stretch their limited narrative abilities into sequences of discourse that are clearly recognizable as narrative--chaotic though they may be.

Written narratives. As we turn to written narratives, it is worth noting that children just a few years older than those I have been reporting on are considerably more willing and able to tell stories. They use more standard narrative devices and they regularly tell and retell fantasies. What about their first written stories? The data to be considered come from only one child, but a particularly interesting one, since she taught herself to read when she was five, before any formal training. Having mastered reading, she set about writing, painstakingly practicing letters and words and inventing nonstandard spellings as do many self-taught preschoolers who read (Read 1975). Then, shortly before formal schooling began, she started writing stories. Often these first attempts were no more than two or three sentences long. Many were merely descriptions of her daily life, and in that sense questionably narratives.

Yet, they were undeniably sequences of connected propositions, if not actions or events. She called them stories, and she meticulously marked most with the words <u>The End</u> in the appropriate place. Examples (10), (11), and (12) illustrate some of these early efforts. Spelling has been corrected, but grammar and punctuation are intact. Example (12) is particularly interesting because it is in the first person, but obviously is a fantasy of sorts.

(10) I like to be inside in my house when it is cold out there. My house is hot and sometimes it is cold in my house.

(11) I love mommy. I love dad. My mom and dad love me so we can have fun.
 The end.

(12) I am a snowflake floating down onto the ground. I can be a snowman.
 The end.

As the year progressed, the stories became longer and more elaborate. Some began to get titled. Interestingly, however, these stories show the same reliance on external supports that the younger children's oral stories did. One of the most creative uses of external supports was a story that recruited a nursery rhyme. It was titled 'A Song without Music' and is reproduced as example (13).

(13) A SONG WITHOUT MUSIC
 A tisket a tasket a green and yellow basket. I wrote a letter to my love and on the way I drop it. A boy picked it up and put it in his pocket he took it home and drop on the way and I picked it up. I took it to my love and went back to see my ma. A tisket a tasket a green and yellow basket I write a letter to my love and on the way I lost it. I went to my loves and I made another note and went back home to see my mommy working. My mommy said lets try to play the song on the piano.

Another interesting aspect of these more elaborate stories is that they contain more errors of grammar and punctuation than the shorter ones. Typically, the shorter stories were in the present tense. The later, longer stories start out in the past tense and then often fluctuate back and forth between present and past. Apparently, the child knew that stories were told in the past, but it was difficult to maintain that aspect of narrative style while doing all the other work required for a longer story. This is aptly illustrated in the child's attempt to express in narrative style a common experience in her family--the removal of ticks from the adventuresome family dog (see example (14)). Similar switchings of tense occurred in the longer oral narratives by four-year-olds (see example (9)). Whereas the use of present tense can be a highlighting device in narrative, it is questionable whether young children intend it as such. Its rather arbitrary sprinkling among verbs marked for past in example (14) and the increased frequency of present tense in longer over shorter stories suggests instead that the mixing of tenses may be a consequence of cognitive overload, not intentional highlighting.

(14) THE FAMILY
Once upon a time there were two children one was a boy and one was a girl. The boys name was George, and the girls name was Ann, and they <u>live</u> together of course. They lived with their mother and father. And they even <u>live</u> with their dog, which name <u>is</u> Toto. My mother and father <u>have</u> to take his ticks out because he always <u>gets</u> ticks in his skin. One night when my brother and my father and I were playing Sorry, my dog came over to my father and my dog said I have two ticks. And my father said tick-Toto and he did have two ticks. And my brother Geoffrey said thanks for telling us Toto that you had two ticks. Then we finished the game and we had supper. Then I went right to bed and fell asleep.
      The end.

Within a year's time, and after considerable practice at the art of story-writing, our young writer was indeed able to write a more coherent narrative. Example (15) is of a third-person fantasy, with a title, a proper beginning, a resolution, and a conclusion.

(15) WHY IT IS RAINING TODAY
One day the whole school had a big jar of water. They all drank it all up. Their cheeks were very fat. Someone said let's laugh. So they all laughed and the water went up in the air and came down and poured and poured til there were puddles everywhere.
      The end.

One might quibble that the context is still a familiar one, or that the referent for the school has not been properly established. Admittedly, there were still a few things left to improve on in second grade. Yet, the obvious progress in the child's written work over the course of the year suggests that the knowledge expressible in oral narratives only gradually transferred to the written mode. In the interval, some of the devices I had observed four-year-olds using to make oral narratives a manageable task again appeared as crutches in the written domain. As the mechanics of writing and punctuation became better learned and more practiced, much of what could be done orally began to show itself again in the newer mode. The written narrative is the oral task taken to a still higher level of complexity, requiring the intercoordination of the nascent skills of writing and spelling with much that was learned in the oral mode.

Summary. Both oral and written narration are complex tasks requiring a period of practice at integrating the component skills of the task before smooth performance can be achieved. Unfortunately, storytelling is not quite like tennis, where one can practice strokes independently from footwork or body stance, and after practicing all parts separately, can work at putting them together. It is not very easy to eliminate content and work on structure, or vice versa. Children make modest attempts to do something like that when they narrate personal experiences or when they borrow well-known devices from other registers to support their primitive narrative structures. Such strategies do ease the processing burden of having to produce a novel speech genre. Parents and teachers of young children apparently also help out by providing conversational structure to carry the children through a narrative. McNamee (1979) reports that listeners regularly ask questions like <u>What happened next?</u> or <u>And then what did he do?</u> to help the child structure and resolve narratives.

One implication of the arguments made here is that teachers of young children might assist them in learning how to produce written narratives by providing prosthetic devices for them. Especially for children in the early primary grades, teachers might provide the children with the written propositions of a story and let the children practice providing the narrative devices structuring them into a story. Alternatively, they could provide the structure and let the children produce the events.

My final point concerns future research on narrative development. I have presented only a small amount of data from a small number of children. Nevertheless, the data I have are quite consonant with other reports in the literature--for example, the emphasis in early narratives on personal experience. I have offered a cognitive process explanation to account for these common characteristics found in children's narratives. Yet, the universal processing constraints that all children--and adults, for that matter--labor under should not be allowed to obscure possible individual differences in the creative means developed to surmount those limitations. We need to know more about how these means develop and display themselves as the child overcomes processing limitations. Longitudinal studies of the development of narrative production in the same children as they transit from the oral to the written mode should be particularly revealing.

Note

1. Asterisks indicate interruptions by listener.

References

Applebee, A. N. 1978. The child's concept of story. Chicago: The University of Chicago Press.

Ames, L. B. 1966. Children's stories. Genetic Psychology Monographs 73.337-96.

Brown, A. L. 1975. Recognition, reconstruction, and recall of narrative sequences by preoperational children. Child Development 46.156-66.

Labov, W. 1972. Language in the inner city: Studies in the Black English vernacular. Philadelphia: University of Pennsylvania Press.

Mandler, J. 1983. Representation. In: Cognitive development, vol. III. Edited by J. H. Flavell and E. M. Markman. Handbook of child psychology, 4th ed. Edited by P. H. Mussen. New York: John Wiley.

McNamee, G. D. 1979. The social interaction origins of narrative skills. The Quarterly Newsletter of the Laboratory of Comparative Human Cognition 1.63-68.

Pitcher, E. G., and E. Prelinger. 1963. Children tell stories: An analysis of fantasy. New York: International Universities Press.

Read, C. N. 1975. Children's categorization of speech sounds in English. Research Report No. 17. Urbana, Ill.: National Council of Teachers of English.

Sacks, H. 1972. On the analyzability of stories by children. In: Directions in sociolinguistics. Edited by J. J. Gumperz and D. Hymes. New York: Holt, Rinehart and Winston.

Scollon, R., and S. B. K. Scollon. 1983. Cooking it up and boiling it down: Athabascan story retellings. In: Coherence in spoken and written discourse. Edited by D. Tannen. Norwood, N. J.: Ablex.

Shatz, M. 1983. Communication. In: Cognitive development, vol. III. Edited by J. H. Flavell and E. M. Markman. Handbook of child psychology, 4th ed. Edited by P. H. Mussen. New York: John Wiley.

Shatz, M., and R. Gelman. 1973. The development of communication skills: Modifications in the speech of young children as a function of listener. Monographs of the Society for Research in Child Development 38 (5, serial no. 152).

Stein, N. L., and C. G. Glenn. 1979. An analysis of story comprehension in elementary school children. In: New directions in discourse processing, vol. 2. Edited by R. Freedle. Norwood, N. J.: Ablex.

CLARIFICATION AND CULTURE

Elinor Ochs
University of Southern California

0. Introduction. For some time now, scholars from several fields have been grappling with the concept of the social event or social activity and its importance. A primary concern has been the ways in which the stream of behavior is divided and organized by members of a social group. This concern has been articulated by a long list of scholars, including Bateson (1972), Goffman (1974), and Minsky (1975), in their discussions of event frames; ethnosemanticists (cf. Frake 1961, 1969), in their discussions of event domains; Wittgenstein in his discussion of language games (1958); Prague school linguists (Jakobson 1960); and ethnographers of speaking (Hymes 1974, Bauman and Sherzer 1975, Gumperz 1983, Duranti in press), in their discussions of speech events; cognitive psychologists, in their discussions of event schemata (Piaget 1929, Flavell 1977), event scripts (Schank and Abelson 1975, Nelson 1981, Nelson and Greundel 1981), and the ecological validity of experimental tasks (Cole and Means 1981).

Certain discussions have been directed more specifically at the effects of mental representations of events (whether they be called frames, schemata, scripts, or domains) on the production and interpretation of behavior. Much of the work in artificial intelligence, for example, concerns the role of knowledge of event goals in the interpretations of particular behaviors (Grosz 1972). In another field, interpretive anthropologists such as Gumperz have indicated (Gumperz 1983) that interactions may break down when participants have vastly different conceptualizations of the event taking place. When speakers from different social groups interact, they may fail to understand how one another's actions relate to the overall goal of the interaction, creating what Gumperz has termed 'cross talk'. Phenomenologically oriented sociologists have been arguing for some time that even members of the same social group do not always concur on their understandings of what is going on between them. In the phenomenological perspective, participants of an interaction usually negotiate and cooperatively define and construct the events taking place.

Still another concern in the study of events has been the impact of participation in events on social, emotional, and cognitive development. We have learned from several decades of intense research that children bring biologically based capacities and dispositions to their interactions with the world. Most influential have been Freud's discussions of the role of instinct and impulse in emotional development (1960, 1965), and Piaget's argument that the child is an active agent in his intellectual development, constructing action schemata from reflexes and logic from action schemata. Of course, these same scholars have stressed the impact of experience. Freud emphasized that construction of one's ego and superego is influenced by life's experiences, and Piagetian research has emphasized that children construct knowledge through their interactions with objects and persons in their environment. Freud's concern with the impact of social experience on one's concept of self has been taken up by numerous social scientists, including George Herbert Mead (1956), who proposed that one's sense of self is influenced by the roles one habitually assumes in social interactions. That is, one's sense of self is to a large extent a social construction, constructed in and through participation in social activity. Currently, a number of developmental psychologists have combined Piagetian models of event schemata with cognitive science notions that knowledge is organized in terms of event representations (cf. Bretherton 1984, Nelson 1981). This work suggests that children's understanding of objects, persons, actions, states, and roles is a dimension of their understanding of events at any one point in developmental time. Children display their understanding of events through pretend activities, elicited retellings, and descriptions of events.

In addition to these approaches, the Vygotskian school of Soviet psychology, also called the sociohistorical or sociocultural approach, has developed the idea that intrapersonal psychological processes emerge not only in but through interpersonal ones, i.e. through social activities (Vygotsky 1978, Luria 1976, Leontyev 1981, Wertsch 1980, in press, LCHC 1981). In contrast to other approaches, this school has emphasized the role of knowledgeable persons in facilitating the acquisition of higher order cognitive functions. Leontyev wrote, for example, 'The individual, the child, is not simply thrown into the human world; it is introduced into this world by the people around it, and they guide it in that world' (1981:135). Further, the sociohistorical school has emphasized the role of society and culture in organizing activities. Vygotsky, Luria, and Leontyev have all stressed the point, first, that activities vary in content and structure across societies; and second, that this variation has impact on members' cognitive skills.

In Europe and the United States, the Soviet approach has influenced the work of scholars such as Bruner (1975), Cazden (1981), Cole (Cole and Griffin 1980, Scribner and Cole 1981), Goody (1977), Greenfield (Greenfield and Smith 1976), Griffin (Cole and Griffin 1980), Scribner (Scribner and Cole 1981), and Wertsch (1980). This orientation is evident in their research on the impact of literacy and schooling. The well-known research of Scribner and Cole (1981), for example, indicates that the development of cognitive skills within an individual is not so much the effect of literacy per se but rather the effect of participating in particular types of literacy activities. For example, participation in literacy activities characteristic of European schooling enhances the development of hypothetical reasoning, whereas participation in literacy activities characteristic of Koranic schooling does not. I have used the term 'enhances' rather than 'determines' in discussing the effects of participation, because we know that many factors influence participation in an activity. For example, individuals may involve themselves or direct their attention to the activity to varying extents (Wentworth 1980). Further, early life experiences in literacy events differ (Heath 1983, Scollon and Scollon 1981, Michaels 1981), and these differences affect children's participation in classroom literacy events at school. That is, primary socialization experiences influence secondary socialization experiences.

All of this research on activities and events has important consequences for understanding the relation between language, thought, and culture. The sociohistorical approach in particular implies that not only literacy activities but language activities in general have an impact on social, emotional, and cognitive development. Along with anthropological approaches (such as ethnography of communication, ethnosemantics, and interpretative sociolinguistics), the sociohistorical approach suggests that we need to examine closely the organization of language activities, including the verbal means used to achieve goals, the sequential organization of verbal means, and the contexts in which goals, means, and sequential orders are taken up by language users, and relate these organizational patterns to cognitive skills and to systems of belief and social order.

Further, this body of research calls for a reconsideration of the notion of linguistic relativity. Let us consider again Sapir's classic statement on this topic (quoted in Mandelbaum 1949:162).

> It is quite an illusion to imagine that one adjusts to reality essentially without the use of language and that language is merely an incidental means of solving specific problems of communication or reflection. The fact of the matter is that the 'real world' is to a large extent unconsciously built up on the language habits of the group...We see and hear and otherwise experience very largely as we do because the language habits of our community predispose certain choices of interpretation.

Sapir here speaks of language habits. Whorf spoke of fashions of speaking. What is needed is to strip the linguistic relativity hypothesis of its undesirable deterministic elements and preserve Sapir's notion that language habits predispose certain choices of interpretation. The notion of predisposition is akin to phenomenological views that experiential frames influence construction of interpretations. It is also akin to the sociohistorical view that habitual participation in language activities enhances the emergence of certain psychological skills. We want to make certain that we allow for creativity and individual difference in our reconsidered theory of linguistic relativity. We want to say that persons are oriented to ways of viewing the world through habitual participation in language activities, but this process is open-ended. World views developed through verbal interactions can be transformed through further participation in language activities. The extent to which such transformations occur depends on personal and social conditions, but for most, socialization is a lifespan process.

While many would accept this interpretation of linguistic relativity, opinions will vary concerning the scope of its application. Most accept the idea that there is variation in literacy and school language activities and that this variation has consequences for the acquisition of skills and conceptual orientations. But what about earlier verbal activities that infants and young children experience? What about just ordinary conversational activities in the child's social environment? Do these activities vary cross-culturally and does this variation have an impact on the child's understanding of the world?

These are important questions to pose. Everyday, nothing-special sort of conversational activity is the kind of social behavior that those in cognitive science would call unscripted. It is not represented in memory as a spatially or temporally bounded activity like going to the grocery store or eating out at a restaurant or going to the doctor. It is ubiquitous. Indeed, informal conversation is the most basic of verbal activities and as such, it is the critical sociolinguistic context for the socialization of knowledge and skills. If we want to know if language activities have an impact on psychological development, then a most reasonable place to look is the organization of everyday conversational discourse.

My own interest within this area is the relation between participating in routine everyday conversational activities and the acquisition of cultural knowledge. Over the past several years, Bambi Schieffelin and I have worked collaboratively and independently, comparing, across several societies, coversational interactions in which children participate. We have found that conversational activities involving small children vary in ways that systematically relate to beliefs, values, and social order (Ochs 1982, in press; Ochs and Schieffelin 1982, in press; Schieffelin and Ochs 1983; Schieffelin 1979, in press). We have suggested that children acquire sociocultural knowledge through exposure to and participation in everyday, run-of-the-mill verbal exchanges. As Bateson (1972) has noted, novices abstract from an event not only information specific to that event but more general information concerning roles, relationships, emotions, self, tasks, causality, temporal and spatial relationships, and other dimensions of the sociocultural environment. Our orientation is compatible with the sociohistorical approach and with phenomenological approaches to socialization such as those provided by Cicourel (1973), Giddens (1976), and Wentworth (1980).

1. Clarification

1.1 Clarification and epistemology. I would like now to turn to a type of conversational activity that is pervasive in the daily lives of all of us, namely, the activity of clarification. Making clear our own and others' behaviors is surely a universal endeavor, necessary for social order and survival. I would like to put forward several suggestions concerning the nature of clarification exchanges cross-culturally and their role in the socialization of world view.

First, I would like to suggest that while clarification is a universal activity, the manner in which clarification is accomplished varies cross-culturally. Preferences for accomplishing clarification are embedded in local principles of social order and local epistemologies. More specifically, I would like to suggest that both the conditions under which clarification takes place (what gets clarified, who participates in the activity of clarification, in which roles), and the discourse procedures speakers prefer to use, index members' views of knowledge, particularly members' views on the limits of knowledge (what can be known) and the paths to knowledge (how knowledge is acquired). Another way of looking at this is to say that when members engage in the activity of clarification, they display and construct tacit guidelines and principles for creating knowledge. These guidelines and principles in turn are tied as well to local theories of meaning, of learning, and of self. I am interested in those cases of clarification where the participants are caregivers and young children. As caregivers involve infants and small children in clarification exchanges, they are displaying and constructing with them more general, socially valued epistemologies. In Sapir's terms, the language habits of their communities predispose children to view knowledge in a certain light. In the following discussion, I examine patterns of clarification between children and caregivers and their relation to folk epistemologies in two societies: American White Middle Class (WMC) and Western Samoan.

1.2 Structure of clarification sequences. Let us now try to formulate a working definition of the activity of clarification. A clarification sequence contains a verbal or nonverbal behavior that is seen as unclear by at least one participant to an interaction. Unclarity may involve both surface expression and/or underlying meaning. An utterance, for example, may be unintelligible because it has been poorly articulated, because it has not been heard, and so on. On the other hand, even when the surface form of an utterance is intelligible, its meaning may not be clear.

Using the terminology of conversation analysis, we can say that the unclear behavior is a trouble source for some participant and that the clarification sequence attends to the work of repairing or attempting to resolve that trouble (Schegloff, Jefferson, and Sacks 1977). That is, clarification is a goal of at least one participant.

As a type of repair sequence, the clarification sequence has the structural options that have been noted for repair sequences generally. Clarification may be self-initiated (i.e. initiated by the party who produces the unclear behavior) or other-initiated. Attempts to clarify may also be carried out either by self or by other.

1.3 Other-initiated clarification in two societies. I would like now to turn to one of these structural varieties, namely, those clarification sequences in which clarification is other-initiated. This type of clarification sequence has received considerable attention in the language acquisition literature, because transcripts are laced with children's utterances and nonverbal behaviors that are followed by caregivers' initiations of clarification, as illustrated in examples (1) and (2).

(1)   Jordan is a 14-month-old male infant, being served his lunch.
       (From Golinkoff 1983:58-59.)
1.   Jordan: (Vocalizes repeatedly until his mother turns around.)
2.   Mother: (Turns around to look at him.)
3.   Jordan: (Points to one of the objects on the counter.)
4.→   Mother: Do you want this? (Holds up milk container.)
5.   Jordan: (Shakes his head 'no'.)
                  (Vocalizes, continues to point.)
6.→   Mother: Do you want this? (Holds up jelly jar.)
7.   Jordan: (Shakes head 'no'.)
                  (Continues to point.)
8, 9, 10, 11.   (2 more offer-rejection pairs.)
12.→   Mother: This? (Picks up sponge.)
13.   Jordan: (Leans back in highchair, puts arms down, tension leaves body.)
14.   Mother: (Hands Jordan sponge.)

(2)   Allison is 16 months, 3 weeks old. (From Bloom 1973:152-53.)
1.   Mother: What do you see?
2.   Allison: (A leans forward; looking in bag)
                  pig/
                  (A stands up)
3.→   Mother: What?
4.   Allison: pig/
5.→   Mother: Play? Is that what you're saying? Play?
6.   Allison: oh/ pig/ ---/

For some researchers, these caregiver responses have been taken as evidence that caregiver speech facilitates the acquisition of grammar (Cross 1977, 1981). For others, these responses have been treated as a means by which caregivers are able to sustain communication with a young baby or child (Brown 1977, Snow 1977).

Western Samoan and WMC caregivers both initiate clarification of children's verbal and nonverbal behavior. However, the set of procedures used by rural Western Samoan caregivers to initiate clarification is a subset of those used by WMC caregivers.

1.3.1 WMC clarification strategies. WMC caregivers rely heavily on two related strategies for initiating clarification. The first strategy is to exhibit minimal or no grasp of what the child has said or done and to rely primarily on the child to resay or redo the unintelligible utterance or gesture. Let us call this strategy the 'minimal grasp strategy'.[1] This may be accomplished indirectly by the caregiver expressing nonunderstanding through a quizzical expression or through a verbal statement such as <u>I don't understand, I can't understand what you are saying,</u> and the like. Or the caregiver may directly ask the child what he said or to supply a piece of what he said, using WH interrogatives such as <u>What? Who? He went where?</u>, and so on. This type of clarification request is illustrated in example (2), line 3. The caregiver may also request or order the child to resay or redo through utterances such as <u>Say it again sweetie, Show me another time, Could you say it once more?</u> and so on.

A second strategy of WMC caregivers is to articulate a guess at what the child's unclear utterance or gesture could be or could mean. Let us call this strategy the 'expressed guess strategy'.[2] In contrast to the minimal grasp strategy, here it is the caregiver who attempts a reformulation of the unclear act. The child is asked to validate or confirm the caregiver's guess. This strategy is illustrated in example (1), lines 4, 6, and 12, and in example (2), line 5. In the case of disconfirmation, the child may resay or redo his utterance or gesture and the caregiver may continue to supply alternate guesses, as illustrated in example (1).

The speech act of guessing covers a range of uncertain knowledge. A caregiver or any speaker may formulate a guess when she is not at all certain of her knowledge. In interactions with infants, this is often the case. Caregivers often find themselves articulating wild guesses at what the infant could be signalling. On the other end, caregivers and others may formulate guesses when they are fairly certain of what an infant is saying or doing. In these cases, the caregiver is using the guess to make sure of, or to double check, her understanding.

Not only WMC caregivers but WMC speakers generally prefer constructions that display the most of what they have understood of the problematic utterance. That is, speakers show a preference for using the strongest form they can in initiating repair of another's utterance (Schegloff, personal communication). For example, speakers prefer specific interrogative pronouns (Where? Who?, etc.) over the weaker construction Huh?, and prefer partial repetitions plus an interrogative pronoun (He went where?, etc.) over the interrogative pronoun on its own. Relevant to our concerns here, the preference of WMC speakers is for the expressed guess strategy over the minimal grasp strategy, where conditions of hearing and understanding permit.

1.3.2 Samoan clarification strategies

1.3.2.1 Caregiver strategies. In Western Samoan households, caregivers prefer strategy 1 (the minimal grasp strategy) but not strategy 2 (the expressed guess strategy) to initiate clarification. They use quizzical expressions, statements of nonunderstanding, WH questions, and other directives to elicit from the child a reformulation of all or part of the unclear utterance or gesture. An example of this strategy is provided in (3).

(3) Maselino (4 years) is with Sililo, (16 years), Olagi (5 years), and his mother's brother's wife, Atoa.

Mas (to Sil): Mai Liaga le kusia sou igoa le kegi
'Uliana said they are not going to write your name (on the list of workers) for the gang.'
Sil: E aa?
'What?'
Olagi: // ((laughs))
Mas: //mai Liaga le kusia e sau igoa le kegi e e.
'Uliana said that they are not going to write your name (on the list of workers) for the gang (warning particle).'

Atoa (to Sil): Mai e aa? ( )
'She said what?'
Sil: Mai le kusia so'u igoa le kegi.
'She said they are not going to write my name (on the list of workers) for the gang.'

In the corpus of interactions that we recorded, we did not find cases in which caregivers (either sib caregivers or adult caregivers) formulated an explicit guess at what an unclear utterance or gesture of the child may be. This dispreference was also manifest when members of the family or others would listen with me to recordings of children's unclear utterances. Almost everyone found my own enterprise of explicitly guessing at a garbled or telegraphic utterance of a child puzzling and not worth the time.

This does not mean that these caregivers and others listening to and watching children do not guess silently. However, silent guesses differ from expressed guesses. First, expressed guesses make explicit a possible proposition. Expressed hypotheses, conjectures, and speculations all commit their makers tentatively to the possibility that some state of affairs may hold. Second, expressed guesses elicit the involvement of the original speakers who produce the enigmatic utterances in the process of understanding, whereas the silent guess does not. In the case of caregiver-child interaction, the expressed guess of the caregiver gives the child a role in the assignment of meaning; the child is given veto power, so to speak, over the caregiver's understanding. In the expressed guess, then, meaning is negotiated before it is assigned. In the silent guess, any negotiation of meaning that may occur takes place after the caregiver's initial assignment of meaning.

The Samoan preference for repetition is manifested more generally in situations in which instruction is taking place. As in many societies, Samoans rely heavily on repeated, often passive, observation of behaviors as a means of transmitting and acquiring knowledge and skills. Dance practice, for example, consists of one person modelling entire dances over and over in front of novices, who imitate the dance movements or watch to one side. As Samoan caregivers engage young children in clarification sequences, they are then socializing them into broader, socially valued methods of education, namely, that the path to knowledge is through repeated exposure--through listening and watching over and over.

In WMC society, repetition of information is also an important strategy in the transmission and acquisition of new information. However, the tradition of clarifying thought through Socratic, dialogic methods is also strong in this society. In the Socratic method, knowledge is pursued through formulating and pursuing initial hypotheses, that is, through laying out for others explicit guesses. WMC caregivers who initiate clarification of children's utterances or gestures through yes-no interrogatives or other forms of guessing are socializing children into this socially valued procedure for gaining knowledge, just as when they elicit resayings or redoings, they are socializing them into the alternative procedure whereby knowledge is enhanced through repeated observations.

2. **Social rank.** Goody (1978) has noted that among the Gonja of Northern Ghana, the use of questions is socially constrained. In adult-child interactions, questions are appropriate speech acts of adults but not of young children. In Samoan society, the speech act of guessing is also affected by social status.

Samoan society is highly stratified. Rank is assessed in terms of political title (e.g. chief, orator, and positions within each of these statuses), church title (pastor, deacon, etc.), age, and generation, among other variables. Titled persons have higher rank than untitled persons and older, higher generation persons have higher rank than younger persons (Mead 1930, Shore 1982). Among the demeanors associated with distinctions in social rank is that of perspective-taking. Lower ranking persons are expected to assume the perspective of higher ranking persons more than higher ranking vis-à-vis lower ranking parties in a social situation. Lower ranking persons are expected to notice and anticipate the wishes of higher ranking persons. They stand in a service relation to those of higher status. As I have noted elsewhere (Ochs 1982), young Samoan children are socialized early in their lives to a sociocentric perspective. As infants, they are often held and fed facing outward toward others in a group. When they begin to speak, much time and effort is devoted to instructing the young child to notice others and to repeat their personal names. In Samoan society, sib and parental caregivers work hard to get children, even before the age of two years, to take the perspective of others. This demeanor is a fundamental component of showing respect, a most necessary competence in Samoan daily life.

The process of communication is affected by these social expectations concerning perspective-taking. It is obvious that communication requires degrees of perspective-taking by all participating parties, i.e. degrees of what has been called 'intersubjectivity' (Trevarthen 1979).

In Samoan interactions the extent to which parties are expected to assume the perpective of another in assigning a meaning to an utterance of another varies with social rank. In speaking to those of lower rank, higher ranking persons are not expected to do a great deal of perspective-taking to make sense out of their own utterances or to make sense of the utterance of a lower ranking interlocutor. Higher ranking persons, then, are not expected to clarify and simplify for lower ranking persons. For example, caregivers are not expected to simplify their speech in talking to young children (Ochs 1982). And exactly the reverse is expected of lower ranking persons. Lower ranking persons take on more of the burden of clarifying their own utterances and the utterances of higher ranking interlocutors.

Of the two clarification strategies discussed earlier, the 'expressed guess' strategy involves more perspective-taking than the 'minimal grasp' strategy. One reason why we do not see caregivers making explicit guesses at what their charges are saying is that such a response demands an orientation that is generally inappropriate to the social role of caregiver. Only in situations in which a small child is speaking on behalf of someone of high status (e.g. when the child is a messenger) is this degree of perspective-taking expected. Typically, when very small Samoan children produce unintelligible utterances, they are disregarded or addressed with a construction indicating noncomprehension and directed to redesign their utterances to meet the communicative needs of others. Through such procedures, children develop early in life a sensitivity to the demands of their social environment and communicative skills to meet them.

Looking at transcripts of interactions across many contexts (adult-adult, adult-child, child-child), I have found few instances of explicit guessing. Of those instances located, most occur in interactions among peers and a few occur in interactions in which a higher ranking person has produced an unclear utterance. While guessing appears across several speech activities in peer interaction, when a lower ranking person directs a guess at a higher ranking person it is situationally constrained. As audience to personal narratives, gossip, or speeches of higher ranking persons, lower ranking persons do not typically guess explicitly at the meaning of their utterances. However, when a higher ranking person directs the lower ranking person to do something, then he may clarify by directing a guess to the speaker. I emphasize that this strategy is not very frequent. It is generally dispreferred for lower ranking persons to guess at the utterances of higher ranking persons. The expectation is that the lower ranking person should be attending (and therefore not need to clarify on grounds of not having heard the utterance) and should understand. In multiparty situations, lower ranking persons may get out of this bind by directing to a co-present peer a guess as to part or all of the utterance of the higher ranking person. This strategy is illustrated in example (4), in which a group of boys of differing ages are playing on the beach, pretending to be preparing a meal. In their play, the older boys direct the preparation and the younger boys carry out the directives (just as in daily life). The oldest boy (Boy 1) directs a younger one (Sesi, Boy 3) to make <u>saka</u> 'boiled taro'. The younger boy then turns to a boy close to his age and requests confirmation of his understanding of what was said.

(4) Boys Playing on Beach
Boy 1: Sole, alu Sesi fai saka ee!
'Mate, go Sesi to make saka (emph. particle)!'
Ke iloa fai--
'You know how (to make it)'
Boy 2: ((hums))...eli ma'a
((hums))...'dig stones.'
Boy 3: Fai mai 'Fai saka'?
'He said 'Make saka'?
Boy 1: Sole, alu oe e e (pause) koli mai ulu.
'Mate, you go to twist off and fetch down breadfruit.'

3. The trouble. In addition to social rank, the nature of the trouble or the object of clarification is an important variable constraining the use of explicit guessing in Samoan interactions. In the WMC caregiver-child interactions observed, the clarification sequences pursue at least two major goals. One is to clarify what the child has just said or done, that is, to obtain an output that is intelligible. A second goal is to assign a reading to that output that is compatible with the child's intended meaning. In all speech, but particularly in children's speech, utterances may have several meanings. In WMC caregiver-child interactions, a major problem is to sort out which meaning is the 'correct' one, where correctness is based on the caregiver's assessment of the child's intentions (what Grice 1968 calls 'utterer's meaning'). So important is the understanding of the child's intentions that caregivers will check with the child if their understanding of the child's intended meaning is correct or not. This job is accomplished through the expressed guess. In guessing, the caregiver displays a tentative reading before a final interpretation. The child has an option, indeed is directed, to influence the caregiver's understanding of some particular utterance or action before a meaning is assigned.

In so doing, WMC caregivers are conforming to a cultural theory of communication in which speakers' personal intentions are critical to the interpretation of an utterance or action. Certain philosophical theories of meaning, such as that of Searle (1969) and Grice (1968) articulate the system of knowledge that underlies this folk theory. In the work of both Searle (following Austin 1962) and Grice, the issues taken up focus on the relation between convention and intention, locutionary and illocutionary meaning, sentence and utterer's meaning, evaluating the relative importance of each in a theory of meaning and language use.

Recently, several sociolinguists and anthropologists have discussed this orientation to meaning in relation to cultural beliefs and orientations (Duranti 1984, Kochman 1983, Ochs 1982, Rosaldo 1982, Shore 1977, 1982). All of these discussions have focused on the concept of person that emerges from language behavior and from folk and academic theories of meaning. The emphasis on personal intentions in Anglo society and scholarship is tied to a cultural ideology in which persons are viewed as individuals, i.e. coherent personalities, who have control over and are responsible for their utterances and actions.

Personal intentions are important in a vast range of situations. Members of Anglo WMC society seek to clarify an individual's personal intentions for a range of purposes. For example, members of this society usually base their assignments of responsibility and sanctions on the speaker/actor's particular intentions behind an utterance or action. This society distinguishes, for example, between inadvertent and planned behaviors, and between accidental and purposeful behaviors. In legal and other contexts, if it is established that a negatively valued behavior was consciously intended, then sanctions are usually more severe than if the speaker/actor 'didn't mean to do it' or could not help doing it or otherwise was not in control. Note that establishing intentionality is not always critical to sanctioning. In many situations, members of this society say 'It doesn't matter whether you meant it or not.' The important point is that in Anglo-American WMC society, what a person means or meant to do or say is an important cultural variable. For this social group, what a person means to do is distinguished from what he does. This orientation leads members to take seriously, and to pursue the establishing of, individual's motivations and psychological states.

This concern with and emphasis on personal intentions is not matched in other societies. In societies such as American Black working class (Kochman 1983), Ilongot (Rosaldo 1982), Ifaluk (Lutz 1982), and Samoan (Duranti 1984, Ochs 1982), the consequences of an utterance or action play an important role in assigning meaning.

In certain accounts, the emphasis on consequences takes the form of focusing on the social ramifications of a behavior (rather than on speaker/actor's intentions). Lutz (1982), for example, notes that the Ifaluk focus on the 'wake' of an action. In Ochs (1982), I have discussed the primacy of consequences of an action in Samoan evaluations of actions. In Samoan households, children will be sanctioned according to the negative effects of their behaviors. This is also the case in the legal arena, where actions are assessed almost exclusively in terms of social and economic losses and disturbances. In the context of assessing misdeeds, in Samoan society, the focus is much less on personal intentions behind an utterance/action. In this context, it is not terribly important if the wrongdoer did something by accident, inadvertently, or on purpose. Indeed, Samoans see persons as not in control of their misdeeds (Shore 1977, 1982). Samoan children may try to get out of punishment by denying that they did that culpable act, but they do not try to worm out by saying <u>I didn't mean it</u>, <u>It was just an accident</u>, <u>I did it by mistake</u>, <u>I couldn't help it</u>, <u>I didn't do it on purpose</u>, as do WMC children almost by routine.

Other accounts, following a more phenomenological approach to communication, have focused on the importance of the hearer's role in the assignment of meaning. Kochman (1983), for example, has commented that for this community of Black speakers, very often the perlocutionary effect on the hearer takes precedence over speaker's intended meaning. Indeed, here as in other societies such as Samoan society, speakers often leave ambiguous what is meant, waiting to see how a hearer will take it up. In this sense, meaning is in the hands of the audience more than in those of the speaker; the audience has the final word.

Taking these accounts altogether, we might propose that we have found a variable in terms of which societies contrast. There are societies like the WMC in the United States that focus primarily on the personal sources of utterances/actions and other societies--such as the Ilongot of the Philippines, the Ifaluk of the Caroline Islands, the Samoans, and the working-class Blacks in the United States--that focus primarily on the social consequences of utterances/actions.

This distinction, however, is too simplistic. For example, there are theories supported by scholars within the WMC society in the United States that argue against the primacy of personal intentions in establishing meaning. Sociohistorical theories of meaning such as that held by Bakhtin (Volosinov 1973), deconstructionist theories within literary criticism, and hermeneutic perspectives (e.g. Gadamer 1976) are alive and popular within this country. (Notice, however, that these traditions stem from scholarly lines outside the United States.) This observation and ethnographic observations of Samoan interaction suggest that within each society, both orientations persist. The difference between societies lies in the contexts in which these two orientations prevail, the relative importance given to each of them, and the frequency with which these orientations mark social interaction.

In Samoan society, personal intentions are a focus of concern in a restricted set of contexts, primarily when the speaker/actor is of high social status and/or of higher social rank relative to the hearer/audience. For example, Shore (1977, 1982) and Duranti (1981) have noted that in the context of political meetings of titled persons, only high chiefs and high status orators are entitled to voice personal opinions. In this sense, high status speakers in this context are treated more as individuals than are others present, and their personal intentions are attended to. In addition, when a higher ranking person orders a lower ranking person to carry out some action, personal intentions of the speaker are also of primary importance. The lower ranking party cannot assign his own interpretation but rather must grasp that intended by the higher ranking speaker.

Where the speaker is of low status and/or of lower rank than the hearer, then his or her personal intentions tend to assume low priority in assigning meaning and the interpretation of the higher ranking hearer takes precedence. Notice that whether the higher ranking party is speaker or hearer, that high party controls meaning.

Given that explicit guessing is tied to the pursuit of speaker's intentions, it is somewhat understandable, in light of the foregoing comments, that we would observe very little explicit guessing directed to lower ranking speakers. The personal intentions of lower ranking speakers, such as children talking to caregivers, do not 'count' in the same way as do those of higher ranking speakers. It would be particularly improbable for caregivers to direct guesses at infants, since at this early point in life, infants are seen neither as personalities nor as conversational partners (Ochs 1982).

While the two perspectives on meaning are variable within WMC and Samoan society, the two have different contextual distributions and salience in each of the two societies. That theory of meaning which Holquist (1983) calls the 'personalist' view of meaning (the view that 'I (the speaker) own meaning') is far more salient in WMC society than in traditional rural Western Samoan communities. When WMC caregivers attend very carefully to the unclear gestures and utterances of their infants and young children, when they explicitly guess at what the child means, they are socializing children into this prevailing view of meaning in which personal intentions are of primary importance. The absence of explicit guessing by Western Samoan caregivers is tied to the restricted relevance of this theory of meaning to Samoan social life, in particular to its inappropriateness in a wide range of contexts, including those in which children communicate with caregivers. Samoans generally display a strong dispreference for guessing at what is going on in another person's mind. This dispreference has reflexes in a range of verbal activities and accounts for the rarity of activities such as test questions, riddles, and guessing games of the 'Twenty Questions' and 'I Spy' variety. These activities are not part of traditional instruction settings nor are they common in informal adult-child, adult-adult, or child-child interactions. (They appear mainly in the context of formal classroom instruction in Christian churches and Western-oriented public schools.) Western Samoan caregivers' behaviors, then, are congruent with traditional Samoan theories of knowledge, including their theories of learning and their theories of meaning.

Notes

I am grateful for the helpful comments of Elaine Andersen, Yigal Arens, Niko Besnier, Alessandro Duranti, and Edward Finegan, and for

the long discussions with Emanuel Schegloff on earlier drafts of this research paper.
1. I am indebted to E. Schegloff for providing this term.
2. This strategy is roughly comparable to the notion of 'candidate understanding' within the paradigm of conversation analysis (Schegloff, personal communication).

References

Austin, J. L. 1962. How to do things with words. Oxford: Oxford University Press.
Bateson, G. 1972. Steps to an ecology of mind. New York: Ballantine.
Bauman, R., and J. Sherzer. 1975. Explorations in the ethnography of speaking. Cambridge: Cambridge University Press.
Bloom, L. 1973. One word at a time. The Hague: Mouton.
Bretherton, I. 1984. Symbolic play. New York: Academic Press.
Brown, R. 1977. Introduction. In: Talking to children: Language input and acquisition. Edited by C. E. Snow and C. Ferguson. Cambridge: Cambridge University Press. 1-27.
Bruner, J. 1975. The ontogenesis of speech acts. Journal of Child Language 2:1-19.
Cazden, C. 1981. Performance before competence: Assistance to child discourse in the zone of proximal development. Quarterly Newsletter of the Laboratory of Comparative Human Cognition 3.5-8.
Cicourel, A. 1973. Cognitive sociology. London: Macmillan.
Cole, M., and M. Griffin. 1980. Cultural amplifiers reconsidered. In: Social foundations of language and thought. Edited by D. Olson. New York: W. W. Norton and Co.
Cole, M., and B. Means. 1981. Comparative studies of how people think. Cambridge, Mass.: Harvard University Press.
Cross, T. 1977. Mothers' speech adjustments: The contribution of selected child-listener variables. In: Talking to children: Language input and acquisition. Edited by C. E. Snow and C. Ferguson. Cambridge: Cambridge University Press. 151-88.
Cross, T. 1981. The linguistic experience of slow language learners. In: Advances in child development. Edited by Nesdale et al. University of Western Australia.
Duranti, A. 1981. The Samoan fono: A sociolinguistic study. Pacific Linguistics, series B, vol. 80. Canberra: The Australian National University, Department of Linguistics, R.S. Pac.S.
Duranti, A. 1984. Intentions, self, and local theories of meaning: Words and social action in a Samoan context. MS. Laboratory of Comparative Human Cognition. University of California, San Diego.
Duranti, A. (in press) Sociocultural dimensions of discourse. In: Handbook of discourse analysis. Edited by T. van Dijk. London: Academic Press.
Duranti, A., and E. Ochs. 1982. The social organization of other-correction in Samoan verbal interaction. Paper presented at the American Anthropological Association Annual Meetings, Washington, D.C.
Flavell, J. 1977. Cognitive development. Englewood Cliffs, N.J.: Prentice-Hall.

Frake, C. 1961. The diagnosis of disease among the Subanun of Mindanao. American Anthropologist 63.1:113-32.
Frake, C. 1969. A structural description of Subanun religious behavior. In: Cognitive anthropology. Edited by S. Tyler. New York: Holt, Rinehart and Winston.
Freud, S. 1960. The ego and the id. New York: Norton.
Freud, S. 1965. New introductory lectures on psychoanalysis. New York: Norton.
Gadamer, H-G. 1976. Philosophical hermeneutics. Translated and edited by D. E. Linge. Berkeley: University of California Press.
Giddens, A. 1976. New rules of sociological method. New York: Basic Books.
Goffman, E. 1974. Frame analysis. New York: Harper and Row.
Golinkoff, R. 1983. The pre-verbal negotiation of failed messages: Insights into the transition period. In: The transition from prelinguistic to linguistic communication. Edited by R. Golinkoff. Hillsdale, N.J.: Lawrence Erlbaum. 57-78.
Goody, E. 1978. Towards a theory of questions. In: Questions and politeness. Edited by Esther Goody. Cambridge: Cambridge University Press. 17-43.
Goody, J. 1977. The domestication of the savage mind. Cambridge: Cambridge University Press.
Greenfield, P., and J. H. Smith. 1976. The structure of communication in early language development. New York: Academic Press.
Grice, H. P. 1968. Utterer's meaning, sentence-meaning, and word-meaning. Foundations of Language 4.1-18.
Grosz, B. 1977. The representation and use of focus in dialogue understanding. SRI International Technical Note 151. Menlo Park, Calif.: Stanford Research Institute.
Gumperz, J. 1983. Discourse strategies. Cambridge: Cambridge University Press.
Heath, S. 1983. Ways with words: Language, life, and work in communities and classrooms. Cambridge: Cambridge University Press.
Holquist, M. 1983. The politics of representation. Quarterly Newsletter of the Laboratory of Comparative Human Cognition 5.I:2-9.
Hymes, D. 1974. Foundations in sociolinguistics: An ethnographic approach. Philadelphia: University of Pennsylvania Press.
Jakobson, R. 1960. Linguistics and poetics. In: Style in language. Edited by T. Sebeok. Cambridge, Mass.: The MIT Press. 350-77.
Kochman, T. 1983. The boundary between play and nonplay in black verbal dueling. Language in Society 12.3:329-38.
LCHC [Laboratory of Comparative Human Cognition, University of California, San Diego]. 1981. Culture and cognitive development. To appear in: L. Carmichael's manual of child psychology: History, theories, and methods. Edited by W. Kessen. New York: John Wiley.
Leontyev, A. N. 1981. Problems of the development of mind. Moscow: Progress Publishers.
Luria, A. R. 1976. Cognitive development: Its cultural and social foundations. Cambridge, Mass.: Harvard University Press.
Lutz, C. 1982. The domain of emotion words on Ifaluk. American Ethnologist 9.1:113-28.

Mandelbaum, D. G., ed. 1949. Selected writings of Edward Sapir. Berkeley/Los Angeles: University of California.
Mead, G. H. 1956. On social psychology. Chicago: University of Chicago Press.
Mead, M. 1930. The social organization of Manu'a. Honolulu: B. P. Bishop Museum.
Michaels, S. 1981. Sharing time: Children's narrative styles and differential access to literacy. Language in Society 10.3:423-42.
Minsky, M. 1975. A framework for representing knowledge. In: The psychology of computer vision. Edited by P. Winston. New York: McGraw-Hill.
Nelson, K. 1981. Social cognition in a script framework. In: Social cognitive development. Edited by J. Flavell and L. Ross. New York: Cambridge University Press.
Nelson, K., and J. Gruendel. Generalized event representations: Basic building blocks of cognitive development. In: Advances in developmental psychology, vol 1. Edited by M. Lamb and A. Brown. Hillsdale, N.J.: Lawrence Erlbaum.
Ochs, E. 1982. Talking to children in Western Samoa. Language in Society 11:77-104.
Ochs, E. (in press) Culture and language acquisition: Acquisition of communicative competence in a Western Samoan village. New York: Cambridge University Press.
Ochs, E., and B. Schieffelin. 1982. Language acquisition and socialization: Three developmental stories. In: Working Papers in Sociolinguistics. Edited by R. Bauman and J. Sherzer. Austin, Texas: Southwest Educational Laboratory. To appear also in: Culture theory. Edited by R. Schweder and R. Levine. New York: Cambridge University Press.
Piaget, J. 1929. The child's conception of the world. London: Routledge and Kegan Paul.
Rosaldo, M. 1982. The things we do with words. Ilongot speech acts and speech act theory in philosophy. Language in Society 11:203-37.
Schank, R.C., and R.P. Abelson. Scripts, plans, goals and understanding. Hillsdale, N.J.: Lawrence Erlbaum.
Schegloff, E., G. Jefferson, and H. Sacks. 1977. The preference for self-correction in the organization of repair in conversation. Lg. 53.361-82.
Schieffelin, B. (in press) How Kaluli children learn what to say, what to do, and how to feel. New York: Cambridge University Press.
Schieffelin, B., and E. Ochs. 1983. Cultural perspectives on the transition from prelinguistc to linguistic communication. In: The transition from prelinguistic to linguistic communication. Edited by R. Golinkoff. Hillsdale, N.J.: Lawrence Erlbaum.
Scollon, R., and S. Scollon. 1981. Narrative, literacy, and face in interethnic communication. Norwood, N.J.: Ablex.
Scribner, S., and M. Cole. 1981. The psychology of literacy. Cambridge, Mass.: Harvard University Press.
Searle, J. 1969. Speech acts. Cambridge: Cambridge University Press.
Shore, B. 1977. A Samoan theory of action. Doctoral dissertation. University of Chicago.

Shore, B. 1982. Sala'ilua: A Samoan mystery. New York: Columbia University Press.
Snow, C. E. 1977. The development of conversations between mothers and babies. Journal of Child Language 4.1-22.
Trevarthen, C. 1979. Communication and co-operation in early infancy: A description of primary intersubjectivity. In: Before speech: The beginnings of interpersonal communication. Edited by M. Bullowa. Cambridge: Cambridge University Press. 321-47.
Volosinov, V. N. 1973. Marxism and the philosophy of language. New York: Academic Press.
Vygotsky, L. 1978. Mind in society. Cambridge, Mass.: Harvard University Press.
Wentworth, W. 1980. Context and understanding: An inquiry into socialization theory. New York: Elsevier.
Wertsch, J. 1980. The significance of dialogue in Vygotsky's account of social, egocentric and inner speech. Contemporary Educational Psychology 5.150-62.
Wertsch, J. (in press) Cognitive development theory: A Vygotskian perspective. Cambridge, Mass.: Harvard University Press.
Wittgenstein, L. 1958a. Philosophical investigations. Oxford: Blackwell.
Wittgenstein, L. 1958b. The blue and brown books. Oxford: Blackwell.

Contents

Ruth M. Kempson. Pragmatics, anaphora, and logical form
Laurence R. Horn. Toward a new taxonomy for pragmatic inference
William Labov. Intensity
Michael L. Geis. On semantic and pragmatic competence
Sandra A. Thompson. 'Subordination' in formal and informal discourse
Wallace Chafe. Speaking, writing, and prescriptivism
Gillian Sankoff. Substrate and universals in the Tok Pisin verb phrase
Talmy Givón. The pragmatics of referentiality
Jerrold M. Sadock. Whither radical pragmatics?
Richard Hudson. A psychologically and socially plausible theory of language structure
Richard Bauman. The making and breaking of context in West Texas oral anecdotes
Thomas A. Sebeok. Enter textuality: Echoes from the extraterrestrial
Michael Silverstein. On the pragmatic 'poetry' of prose
Thomas Kochman. The politics of politeness
Don H. Zimmerman. Talk and its occasion: The case of calling the police
Alan Davies. Idealization in sociolinguistics
Ellen F. Prince. Language and the law: Reference, stress, and context
Howard Giles and Mary Anne Fitzpatrick. Personal, group, and couple identities
John J. Gumperz. Communicative competence revisited
Susan Gal. Phonological style in bilingualism
George A. Miller. Some comments on the subjective lexicon
Marilyn Shatz. A song without music and other stories
Elinor Ochs. Clarification and culture

Georgetown University Press

ISBN: 0-87840-119-9

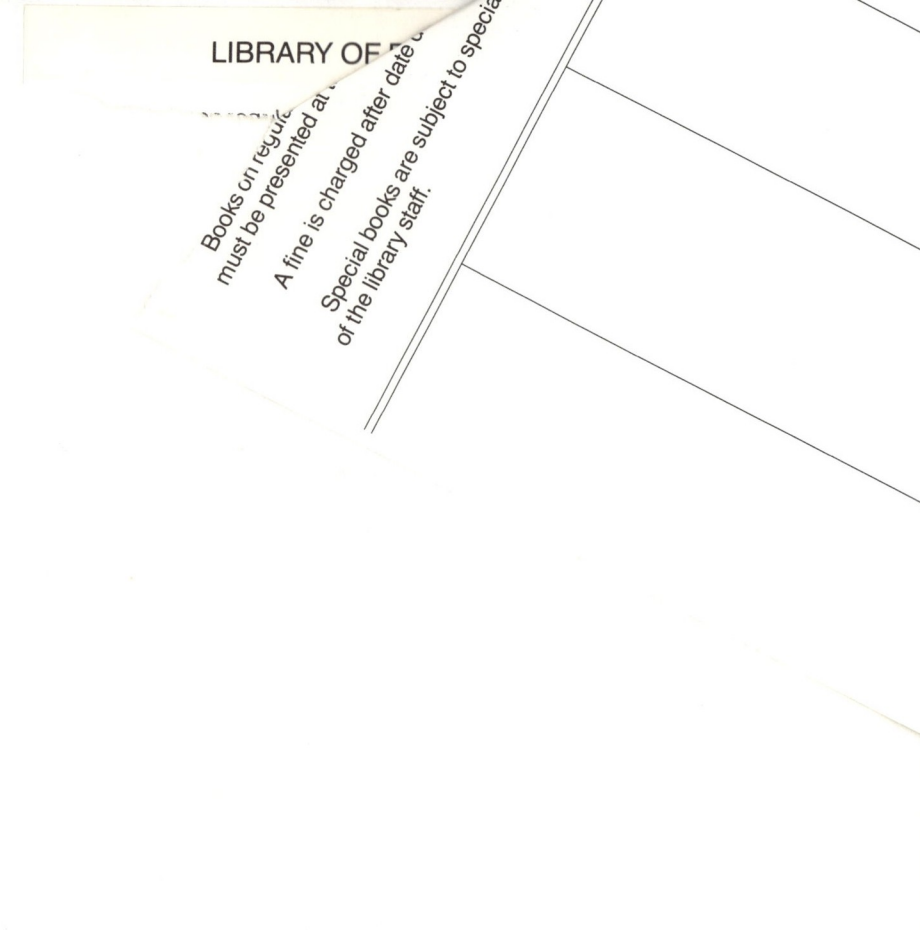